Global Political Marketing

There is increasing awareness of growing similarities in political marketing practices around the world. *Global Political Marketing* is a comprehensive analysis of why, how and with what effect parties use political marketing in a range of political systems – presidential, parliamentary, two- and multi-party, and established and emerging democracies.

Written by a team of 25 international expert authors, the volume explores the impact of systemic features such as the party and electoral system, analyzing how parties use marketing through 14 detailed country studies. The book explores the notions that political marketing is used by parties to both sell and design political products, that it is by no means confined to the opposition, and that many opinions besides those of the voters are considered in product design, including ideological anchors, expert opinion and party members' input.

The authors also explore how other factors impact on political marketing effectiveness, such as the ability of governments to communicate delivery and stay in touch, the role of the media, and party unity and culture. Finally the work discusses the democratic implications of market-oriented parties, highlighting the need for debate about the relationship between citizens and governments and the prospects for democracy in the twenty-first century.

Including a practitioner perspective as well as rigorous academic analysis, this collection provides the first global comprehensive overview of how political parties market themselves and the extent to which they are sales- or market-oriented. It will be of great interest to all scholars of political marketing and communication, parties and elections and comparative politics.

Jennifer Lees-Marshment is Senior Lecturer at the University of Auckland, New Zealand.

Jesper Strömbäck is professor in Media and Communication and Lubbe Nordström Professor and Chair in Journalism at Mid Sweden University, where he is also research director at the Centre for Political Communication Research.

Chris Rudd is Senior Lecturer in the Department of Politics at the University of Otago, New Zealand.

Routledge Research in Political Communication

Global Political Marketing

Edited by Jennifer Lees-Marshment,
Jesper Strömbäck and Chris Rudd

Routledge
Taylor & Francis Group

LONDON AND NEW YORK

First published 2010
by Routledge
2 Park Square, Milton Park, Abingdon, Oxon, OX14 4RN

Simultaneously published in the USA and Canada
by Routledge
270 Madison Avenue, New York, NY 10016

Routledge is an imprint of the Taylor & Francis Group, an informa business

Typeset in Times New Roman
by Keystroke, Tettenhall, Wolverhampton
Printed and bound in Great Britain
by CPI Antony Rowe, Chippenham, Wiltshire

British Library Cataloguing in Publication Data
A catalogue record for this book is available
from the British Library

Library of Congress Cataloging in Publication Data
Global political marketing / edited by Jennifer Lees-Marshment,
Jesper Strömbäck & Chris Rudd.
    p. cm.
Includes index.
1. Public relations and politics. 2. Communication in politics.
3. Marketing–Political aspects. 4. Campaign management.
5. Political campaigns. I. Lees-Marshment, Jennifer.
II. Strömbäck, Jesper. III. Rudd, Chris.
JF2112.P8G56 2009
324.7′3–dc22
                                                    2009013443

ISBN 10: 0–415–42722–3 (hbk)
ISBN 10: 0–203–86933–8 (ebk)

ISBN 13: 978–0–415–42722–7 (hbk)
ISBN 13: 978–0–203–86933–8 (ebk)

Contents

Illustrations

Figures

Tables

Contributors

Masahiko Asano is Professor for Political Science at Takushoku University (Tokyo, Japan). His research focuses on the effects of institutional change (such as electoral systems) on the behaviour of parties and candidates in comparative politics. Email: asanom@d9.dion.ne.jp

Alexander Braun is Senior Director of Penn, Schoen & Berland Associates, specializes in international political campaigns and lived in several European countries before moving to the USA. He has worked on high-level international political campaigns including leading parties and candidates in Britain, Czech Republic, Slovakia, Slovenia, Estonia, Lithuania, Thailand, Indonesia and the Philippines. He has also advised large corporate clients such as Microsoft, Procter and Gamble, and MSNBC. He also worked as a TV news reporter and as a PR consultant. He is a featured commentator in several European media outlets and teaches a course about strategy in political campaigns at Charles University. Email: abraun@p-sb.com

Isabelle Cheng, PhD, Department of Political Studies of the School of Oriental and African Studies (SOAS) in London. She is working on the national identities of Chinese and South East Asian migrant brides in Taiwan. Email: isabelle.nt.cheng@googlemail.com

Stephen Dann is a Senior Lecturer in the School of Management, Marketing and International Business, College of Business and Economics at the Australian National University. His research spans numerous books, conference papers and journal articles in the fields of social, political and commercial marketing. Email: stephen.dann@anu.edu.au

Otto Eibl is a researcher of the Institute for Comparative Political Research at the Faculty of Social Studies of Masaryk University. He has a Master's Degree in Political Science from the Faculty of Social Studies of Masaryk University (Master Thesis: Pragmatic Shift in Political Communication: From Cleavages to Issues?). Currently he is a Ph.D. Candidate at the Political Science Department of Masaryk University. The field of his professional interest is political communication, rational choice theory and political marketing. He has contributed to various books and published several articles. In 2007 he took first place in the contest 'Brno 2020 – Think on Brno' (marketing and promotion section). Email: eibl@fss.muni.cz

Andrew Hughes is a Lecturer in the School of Management, Marketing and International Business, College of Business and Economics at the Australian National University. His research spans numerous books, conference papers and journal articles in the fields of social, political and commercial marketing. Email: andrew.hughes@anu.edu.au

Dafydd J. Fell is the Senior Lecturer in Taiwan Studies at the Department of Political Studies of the School of Oriental and African Studies (SOAS), University of London. He has published numerous articles on political parties and electioneering in Taiwan. His first book was *Party Politics in Taiwan* (Routledge, 2005). In 2006 he co-edited *What has Changed? Taiwan's KMT and DPP Eras in Comparative Perspective* (Harrassowitz). In 2008 he edited a four-volume reference collection titled *Politics of Modern Taiwan* (Routledge). He is also the editor for the new Routledge Research on Taiwan book series. Email: df2@soas.ac.uk

Derek S. Hutcheson is Head of Subject in European Studies in the UCD School of Politics and International Relations, University College Dublin, Ireland. His research focuses on electoral politics in the post-communist region. He would like to acknowledge the assistance of BA-SRG 40918 and UCD Seed Funding SF-149 grants with the research for the current chapter. Email: derek.hutcheson@ucd.ie

Mark Gill is a Director of Woodnewton Associates, a strategic research and communications consultancy. Mark was Head of Political Research at MORI between 2003 and 2007 and continues to work closely with Sir Robert Worcester (founder of MORI) on a number of political and social research assignments in the UK and internationally. Email: mark@woodnewton.eu

Balázs Kiss is the director of the Centre for Political Communications Research at the Institute for Political Sciences of the Hungarian Academy of Sciences. He also teaches political communications studies at the Eötvös Loránd University, Budapest, Hungary. Email: kiss@mtapti.hu

Iordanis Kotzaivazoglou is a visiting lecturer in Advertising and Communication at the Department of Advertising and Operations Management of the University of Macedonia, the Department of Marketing of the Technological Institutes of Thessaloniki and the Department of Business Administration of the Technological Institutes of Serres, Greece. His research interest focuses on professionalization of political communication, modern campaigning and social aspects of advertising dealing with stereotypes. Email: ikotza@jour.auth.gr

Jonathan Knuckey is Associate Professor of Political Science at the University of Central Florida. His research interests encompass voting behavior, elections and political parties, with a particular emphasis on partisan change in the American South. Email: jknuckey@mail.ucf.edu

Jennifer Lees-Marshment is senior lecturer at the University of Auckland and her research focuses on how parties use political marketing strategy. Her earlier work on UK politics broadened the concept of political marketing from selling to the design of political products, and more recent work is comparative. She is author or co-editor of seven books, including *Political Marketing and British Political Parties*, second edition (2008), *Political Marketing in Comparative Perspective* (2005), *Current Issues in Political Marketing* (2005), and the first political marketing textbook *Political Marketing: Principles and Applications* (2009). Email: j.lees-marshment@auckland.ac.nz

Kobby Mensah, PhD, Department of Journalism, University of Sheffield, United Kingdom. He is also an associate member of the Chartered Institute of Marketing, UK. Email: info@kobbymensah.com

Michaela Maier is Professor for Applied Communication Psychology at the University of Koblenz-Landau, Germany. Her research focuses on internal and external organizational communication and political communication with a specific interest in the reception and effects of campaign communication. Email: mmaier@uni-landau.de

Anna Matušková is currently a Visiting Researcher at the Institute for Social and Economic Research and Policy, Columbia University, USA. Her focus is on the influence of using political marketing in electoral campaigning and US influence in European campaigns. She is the holder of a Fulbright scholarship. She is a Ph.D. candidate at the Political Science Department of Masaryk University. She has contributed to various books, published many articles and participated in many conferences. She teaches Theory of Political Marketing. She used to work as a journalist and cooperated with various advertising agencies. Email: matuskov@fss.muni.cz

Zsuzsanna Mihályffy, PhD, is affiliated with the Hungarian Academy of Sciences, Institute for Political Science. Her fields of interest include campaigning, political parties and political marketing. Email: zsmihalyffy@mtapti.hu

Roger Mortimore is Director of Political Analysis at Ipsos MORI, the United Kingdom arm of the multi-national Ipsos research organization. Dr Mortimore was co-editor of the last two Political Communications studies of British general elections, and co-author of a number of other books on British elections. Email: roger.mortimore@ipsos-mori.com

Pedro Patrón Galindo, PhD, is Head of the Media Relations Department at Solsona Comunicación PR Agency in Barcelona, Spain. Email: pepatron@hotmail.com

Robin T. Pettitt is Lecturer in Comparative Politics at Kingston University, London. His research focuses on the role of party members and the impact of the political and media environment on the internal life of political parties. Email: r.pettitt@kingston.ac.uk

Chris Rudd is Senior Lecturer in the Department of Politics at the University of Otago, New Zealand. He is co-author of *The Politics and Government of New Zealand* (2004) and co-editor of *Sovereignty under Siege?* (2005), *Political Communications in New Zealand* (2004), *The Political Economy of New Zealand* (1997) and *State and Economy in New Zealand* (1993). Email: chris.rudd@stonebow.otago.ac.nz

Kirsten Schüller is a graduate student at the Department of Psychology at Radboud Universiteit Nijmegen, Netherlands. She is currently enrolled in the postgraduate programme in Communication Psychology and Media Pedagogics at the University of Koblenz-Landau, Germany. Her research interest is in the field of communication psychology. Email: kirsten.schueller@gmx.de

Jesper Strömbäck is professor in Media and Communication and Lubbe Nordström Professor and Chair in Journalism at Mid Sweden University, where he is also research director at the Centre for Political Communication Research. His most recent books are *Handbook of Election News Coverage Around the world* (2008), co-edited with Lynda Lee Kaid, and *Communicating Politics: Political Communication in the Nordic Countries* (2008), co-edited with Mark Ørsten and Toril Aalberg. Website: www.jesperstromback.com. Email: jesper.stromback@miun.se

Mick Temple is professor at Staffordshire University. Email: M.Temple@staffs.ac.uk

Jens Tenscher is Senior Post Doc at the Innsbruck School of Political Science and Sociology, Austria. Recently his research and academic interest have focused on the professionalization of political communication, modern campaigning and political orientations towards the European integration process. Email: Jens.Tenscher@uibk.ac.at

Bryce Wakefield is an associate in the Asia program at the Woodrow Wilson International Center for Scholars in Washington, DC. Before starting work at the Center, Bryce was a temporary lecturer in political studies at the University of Auckland, where he taught Comparative Politics. He has also taught classes on Japanese society and international relations theory. His interests include Japanese national identity, foreign policy and electoral politics. He holds a master's degree in international relations from Osaka University, and is currently completing a PhD at Auckland University. Email: bryce.wakefield @wilsoncenter.org

Yorgos Zotos is Professor of Marketing at the School of Economics, Department of Business Administration of Aristotle University of Thessaloniki, Greece. His research interests are focused on social aspects of advertising dealing with stereotypes, and cross-country comparisons on perception and attitude formation. He has published articles in the following journals, among others: *European Journal of Marketing, Journal of Business Ethics, Psychological Reports, Journal of Current Issues and Advertising Research*, and *Journal of Retail and Distribution Management*. Email: zotos@econ.auth.gr

Preface

Global Political Marketing is a result of growing political marketing networks facilitated by the UK Political Studies Association Political Marketing group; awareness not just of the utilization of political marketing in an increasingly broad range of countries but the sharing of techniques, product ideas and consultants across countries, and my move to Auckland University and diversification from UK politics to comparative political analysis. Since the publication of *British Political Parties and Political Marketing* in 2001, greater consideration has been paid to the use of strategy by political parties. *Political Marketing in Comparative Perspective* (2005), which I co-edited with Darren Lilleker, was the first attempt to explore the extent to which the market-oriented party was occurring in countries other than the UK. *Global Political Marketing* builds on this but adds many more countries of increasing diversification, as well as the application of a more systematic framework and consideration of causal factors of political marketing behaviour.

One of the wonderful developments of modern academia is the way your work can reach scholars across the world, and this new book comes out of discussions mostly with Jesper Strömbäck whom I first met when he invited me to be one of the guest speakers at a conference he organized in Sundsvall, Sweden in September 2004. Jesper was curious about political marketing strategy despite the lack of MOP type behaviour in Sweden then – a situation since changed during the production of this book. Further discussions, including one held over coffee in Covent Garden in London during the PSA Political Marketing Conference in February 2005 and then on email after I moved to New Zealand in November 2005, brought us to develop the proposal for this book, including another co-editor, Chris Rudd from Otago in New Zealand. I would like to thank the Political Marketing Group for facilitating the global networks this book drew on to complete, including the committee I chaired between 2002 and 2005, and in particular Dr David Dunn, my co-organizer of the 2005 PMG conference in London. I appreciate our publisher Routledge for being open to the proposal and the useful comments made by reviewers. I must thank my co-editors for their work during the past three years. The book would not exist without the work of the authors of each country chapter and I have enjoyed many conversations with them over the past two years, including one over dinner in New York with Anna

Matušková and Alex Braun about practice in the Czech Republic and also the use of marketing techniques around the world. The book is considerably enhanced by the practitioner perspectives provided by Roger Mortimore and Mark Gill, and the political science perspective of Mick Temple. *Global Political Marketing* provides a fresh, comprehensive and more rigorous analysis of the practice of political marketing and will foster continued debate on an exciting if controversial development in political party behaviour.

Dr Jennifer Lees-Marshment, lead editor
Auckland University, New Zealand
June 2008

Acknowledgements

Jennifer Lees-Marshment wishes to thank Auckland University for providing funding for interviews in the UK and New Zealand and research assistance for the formatting of the manuscript and her family for personal support.

Jesper Strömbäck wishes to thank Karl Staaffs fond för frisinnade ändamål, Mid Sweden University and the Sweden-American Foundation that provided funding for him to be a visiting professor at the University of Florida, where a major part of his work on this book was carried out.

1   Global political marketing

Jennifer Lees-Marshment

Political marketing – the utilization of commercial marketing techniques and concepts in politics – is being used to varying degrees around the world. Many political parties conduct market intelligence in the form of polls or focus groups and use it to inform the way they present their policies to the voting public. However, not only do parties use marketing techniques to sell themselves and their policies, they also use marketing to decide what to offer the public in the first place – what policies to adopt, which leaders to select to best present those policies, and how to best communicate policy delivery. Political marketing, then, is not just about 'spin' and public relations during the electoral campaign. It is much more than that. Parties can utilize a range of marketing tools including voter profiling, segmentation, micro-targeting and e-marketing to inform their communication. They can also respond to market intelligence in the way they design the political product they offer, becoming market-oriented rather than primarily sales-oriented.

Whilst the spread of professionalization and modernization in campaigning has been studied extensively (Holtz-Bacha, 2002; Kavanagh, 1995; Lilleker and Negrine, 2002; Plasser and Plasser, 2002) there has never been a systematic and scientific comparative analysis of political marketing behaviour in the sales- or market-oriented sense where the ways in which tools and concepts which are specifically from marketing are considered. Concerns about the effectiveness of political advertising are commonplace, but it is only recently with the proliferation of 'Global New Labour' that attention has turned to the influence of marketing on the political party product. Of course, politicians may utilize tools without embracing a comprehensive market-orientation, and this book seeks to explore variance as well as convergence in empirical behaviour. Indeed, the success of e-marketing or virtual networking in the 2008 US presidential election has led parties in other countries to want to copy the new initiative. But it is important to remember that behind the US innovation is market-oriented type thinking; the internet was used not just to sell to voters but to provide engagement mechanisms that are designed to meet volunteers' varied needs and enable them to participate in politics in the way that suits them rather than the candidate. Bryant (2008) notes how Obama's presidential nomination bid in 2007–8 offered potential volunteers a specific goal and date (e.g., '1.5 million calls by Tuesday') and made them actionable and realistic through easy-to-use online tools (e.g., 'click on this button and make 20 calls from this list'). Furthermore there are now a number of well-known world examples of marketing the product, with the most famous being the transfer and adaptation of the product used by Bill Clinton's New Democrats in 1992 to Tony Blair's New Labour in the UK in 1997, to the German SPD and Labour in New Zealand in 1999 with the use of targeting on new markets, and pledge cards to suggest delivery, representing a move away from selling ideologically driven policy to using a voter-responsive strategy. Cross-country similarities continue: in 2007 Australian Labour leader Kevin Rudd's successful campaign was likened to Tony Blair's (*New Zealand Herald*, 2007). In these cases, political marketing is employed *before* the electoral campaign: indeed the aim was to develop a product that people want so that, if successfully achieved, the campaign itself becomes a less important, if not a redundant, exercise.

This intrusion of marketing into the political sphere has stimulated debate about the consequences of voter-led or market-oriented politics for the democratic polity. Not everyone believes that using market intelligence before you decide on policy is desirable; there are concerns about whether the public should be so paramount in deciding how political parties formulate policy and how leaders lead (see Coleman, 2007) or that politicians should segment and target only those sections of society which are likely to influence a close election (see Savigny, 2007 and 2008 for example). A market-orientation is used by business the world over to attain and retain market share, and is the basis of capitalism; but in politics, to decisively shift responsibility to the voter for deciding policy preferences and the suitability of leaders, raises fears of populism and the abandonment of collectivist ideals informed by ideological world views. Abandoning the political direction of a country to the vagaries of the electoral marketplace has significant implications for the functioning of a representative democracy.

Given the potential consequences of Market-Oriented party (Lees-Marshment 2001a, b) behaviour, it becomes very important to understand what causes some political parties to become more market-oriented than others, and what impact this is having on the political system as a whole. The book explores the extent of political marketing, its nature, its utility, its variance across different political systems and its consequences for democracy. It will conduct academic analysis of systemic features that inhibit or facilitate the adoption of professional political marketing techniques and approaches within different nations. It will consider whether the rise of political marketing is related to the professionalization of parties, encouraging the international sharing of ideas and consultants; or to Americanization; or whether it is a natural response to the globalization of political culture and information (Blumler and Gurevitch, 1995; Bowler and Farrell, 1992; Plasser and Plasser, 2002). We also want to know more about the effectiveness of political marketing; to explore the limitations of consultants moving from one country to another without adapting their approach to suit the new environment; to discuss the problems that sales-marketing techniques can cause; and also to raise debate about whether or not the more voter-friendly, responsive market-oriented approach is good for democracy.

Alongside country studies, two chapters provide an academic and a practitioner overview of political marketing, considering not only the utility of academic frameworks and analysis but more normative issues such as whether governments around the world should be responding to public opinion when they decide how to govern, and voters should be treated like political consumers. Political marketing is influencing the way political parties behave, which could have both negative and positive consequences for the relationship between citizen and state, and may vary from one political culture to another. The closing chapter discusses issues such as the effect of political marketing on ideology and members; the problems of focusing on certain segments; and the range of sources politicians respond to, including public opinion, the mitigating effect of the media, difficulties with delivery, and whether political marketing really does make politicians responsive to the public.

In order to ensure this book explores the influence of political marketing on all aspects of the behaviour of parties rather than just short-term electoral campaigning, we will use a model that makes such a distinction and provides an overall framework for party behaviour from one election to the next. Whilst it used to be the case that the common misconception of political marketing was that it was all about spin doctors and sound bites and political advertisements, there is now an understanding that political marketing is more than that. The Lees-Marshment model of a product-, sales- and market-orientation provides both a 'way of thinking' and a stage-by-stage suggested development of party activity to reach that orientation. It looks at how parties create their political product – i.e. their behaviour – including leadership, staff, activities, symbols, candidates and MPs, constitution, policies and membership. Parties 'behave' or 'produce' all the time, not just in election campaigns; therefore, like commercial organizations, as Kotler and Levy (1969) said, 'everything about an organisation talks' – and it talks all the time. Behaviour is ongoing and developmental, both local and national, and includes prospective as well as existing policies, leaders, and MPs (see Lloyd, 2006 for further discussion and an alternative view of the political product). This can make it a complex and ever-evolving being, and perhaps hard to judge. Ultimately what characteristics are important depends on what voters judge to be an issue. For our purposes, we need to examine a wide range of characteristics in relation to voter demands, and therefore the market-oriented concept.

There is now a broad range of marketing theories and frameworks in political marketing (see Savigny, 2009 for a recent literature review and Lees-Marshment's 2009 textbook on political marketing for detailed overview), but this book focuses on orientation to ensure analysis of the extent to which parties respond to public opinion in how they behave as well as well as communicate. There are alternative theories of market-orientation; several scholars have utilized the marketing philosophy and other marketing strategy concepts in political analysis, using different terms (customer-centric, consumer-led, market-oriented, marketing-orientated, voter-responsive) and different models (e.g. Lees-Marshment, 2001a, b; Newman, 1994, 1999; O'Cass, 1996; and Ormrod's 2005 extended political market-orientation model), but the Lees-Marshment (2001a) POP–SOP–MOP framework enables a greater and richer variety of empirical analysis pertinent to the questions of this book in several ways:

- This framework takes a comprehensive view of political marketing that is broader in scope than previous conceptions.
- The three-orientation framework distinguishes between two very different approaches with divergent democratic implications: the sales- and the market-oriented form of political marketing. Both have potential positive and negative democratic consequences, but very different relationships with voters at their core – one being to persuade and change their minds, the other being to respond to, if not follow, voter views.
- Whilst the MOP concept shares the same historical roots as Ormrod and Newman (all are rooted in the traditions of two disciplines: in political science, the Downsian model of rational-choice (Downs, 1957); and in marketing, Kotler and Levy's initial statement that marketing can be broadened beyond commerce to all organizations), it is very much a party-based framework – it proposes a Market-Oriented Party in the same vein as the Catch-all or Mass Party type models.
- In terms of communication, the sales-oriented concept is broader than standard political communication works (see Strömbäck, 2007 for discussion of the difference).
- Both the SOP and MOP consider a range of behaviour, not just positioning like Butler and Collins (1996); or marketing applied to campaigning/advertising (see Robinson, 2005, 2007; Wring, 1997, 2002).
- The model considers strategy, not just techniques: a complex and subtle political behaviour but with significant implications for electoral outcomes.

The book does not seek to prove this particular model, and aims to avoid a focus on the model where possible, utilizing it more as a framework for empirical analysis than theoretical debate. Nor does the book argue for superiority to others; there is significant benefit in the diverse range of political marketing literature and theory now available, both in political marketing communications (especially Jackson, 2005, 2006; Robinson, 2005, 2007) or market-orientation (see Henneberg and O'Shaughnessy, 2007; Ormrod, 2006, 2007, for further discussion). It is simply that for our purposes the Lees-Marshment model remains the most appropriate. The next section will explore the Lees-Marshment concept of the Market-Oriented Party.

The Market-Oriented Party (MOP)

The basic essence of a Market-Oriented Party is one that will use various tools to understand and then respond to voter demands, but in a way that integrates the need to attend to members' needs, ideas from politicians and experts and the realities of governing (Lees-Marshment, 2001). A Market-Oriented Party uses party views and political judgement to design its behaviour to respond to and satisfy voter demands in a way that that meets their needs and wants, is supported and implemented by the internal organization, and is deliverable in government. Political marketing is used to understand the public, rather than manipulate it. Parties may use their ideology as a means to create effective solutions to public demands, but party elites try to respond to market demand, rather than trying to influence its opinion.

The market is complex and includes members, related think tanks, and politicians. Needs, not just wants, must be considered, in the long as well as the short term. A market-orientation is not about simply giving people what they want, because a party needs to ensure that it can deliver the product on offer. It also needs to ensure that the new product will be accepted within the party and so needs to adjust its product carefully to take account of this. Market-Oriented Parties will not all become the same, or assume the characteristics of catch-all parties, or simply move to the Downsian centre-ground. Political marketing in this form is not all about following focus groups: that is a parody of political marketing, or a misrepresentation of practice.

The political marketing process and checklist

If parties become Market-Oriented, we expect to see them go through and carry out a process of activities – known as the market-oriented party political marketing process. This was first detailed in Lees-Marshment 2001a, and then developed in Lilleker and Lees-Marshment (2005); Table 1.1 is a checklist for what observers would expect to see a party do if they went through this process:

Table 1.1 The market-oriented party process and checklist

Stage 1: Market intelligence

Theory:
The party should:
- use a variety of methods including polling, focus groups, segmentation, listening exercises and informal gut feel;
- ask what voters want the party to do, in the short- and long-term, not just whether they like the party as it is now;
- continue this from one election to the next;
- include segmentation of a party's market to identify target markets who do not already support the party but might in the future, and understand their demands;
- disseminate this information in the party as widely as is appropriate and interpret it carefully, preferably by objective professionals.

Checklist:
- Does the party conduct market intelligence?
- If so, what methods does it use? (e.g. focus groups, polling, listening exercises, membership consultation, consultation of think tanks)
- What does it conduct market intelligence on? (e.g. what voters would like to see changed, as well as what they think of the party as it currently stands)

(*continued*)

Table 1.1 Continued

Stage 1: Market intelligence

- When does it conduct market intelligence? (e.g. post-election, before new developments in policy and organization, before creating the campaign, or continually)
- How accurate/unbiased/representative is the market intelligence? (e.g. are there any weaknesses or strengths in its methods)
- How are the results disseminated? (e.g. to strategy groups, policy development committees, as well as leaders and campaign committee – or just the leader)
- Who conducts the intelligence?
- Does the party respond to this intelligence in campaign formation, or product design?

Stage 2: Product design

Theory:
The party then designs product according to the findings from its market intelligence; involving no, little or significant change as led by the results of market intelligence. This is then modified in Stage 2.

Checklist:
- Do the core product aspects relate to voter demand: e.g. does the party have popular policies; does its leader offer the leadership style voters want?
- Can you see whether the results of market intelligence have impacted on the product design – has anything changed after intelligence?
- Is there an awareness and desire amongst politicians and party staff to try to change the party in response to vote awareness? This is a market-orientation – difficult to measure – but interviews and/or surveys may suggest it.

Stage 3: Product adjustment

Theory:
The party then develops the product to consider:
- achievability: ensures promises are realistic and the party team can deliver them;
- internal reaction: it ensures changes will attract adequate support from MPs and members to ensure implementation, taking into account a party's ideology and history, retaining certain policies to suit the traditional supporter market and also to create a product distinct from that of the competition;
- competition: that it identifies the opposition's weaknesses and highlights own corresponding strengths; is distinctive; and in a multi-part system it will also seek co-operation with appropriate potential partners;
- support: develops targeted aspects of the product to suit target market segments.

Checklist:
- Has the party done anything to ensure its proposals and changes are achievable? E.g. pledge cards to make the product tangible; mechanisms for ensuring delivery in government; realistic economic pricing of policies; creation of a delivery unit to monitor delivery; discussion of the difficulties of governing.
- Do voters see the product as achievable and realistic?
- Has the party done anything to create and portray a team that is capable of delivering?
- Do voters think it is capable of delivering its promises? Do they see it as unified, trustworthy, a good leader, capable of economic management, and honest, for example?

- Does the final product design also meet internal markets to some degree; e.g. are there identifiable policies drawn from the party's ideological traditions or to meet a demand of the members?
- Is the party distinct in any way to its main competitors?
- Does the party have any advantages over its competitors; has it sought to increase its strengths against their weaknesses?
- If in a PR-multi party system, has the party conveyed an ability to co-operate with potential coalition partners?
- Is the party aware of who the party faithful are, and who its target market is, and is it gearing its product to gain the support of its target?

Stage 4: Implementation

Theory:
Changes are implemented throughout the party, needing careful party management and leadership over an appropriate timeframe to obtain adequate acceptance, to create party unity and enthusiasm for the new party design.

Checklist:
- Have members and MPs been consulted on any changes, or had the opportunity to be involved in the process of change and development?
- Are there any signs of significant internal disquiet?
- Do the majority of senior political figures seem on board with the new product design?
- Do candidates and members at local level accept and implement the new product design?

Stage 5: Communication

Theory:
Communication is carefully organized to convey the new product, so that voters are clear before the campaign begins; communication techniques are used to inform and to manipulate; media management is practiced where appropriate.

Checklist:
- Did the party formulate a communications strategy that began at least 12 months before the election?
- Was it informed by market intelligence?
- Was it targeted?
- Did it try to inform, or persuade?
- Did it include positive as well as negative communication?
- Did it highlight the party's main product changes?
- Do voters show awareness of the party's new product?

Stage 6: Campaign

Theory:
The party reminds voters of the key aspects and advantages of its product with effective organization and management, utilizing effective communication techniques and conveying a positive, effective product to voters.

Checklist:
- Does the party appear united and professional in the campaign to voters?
- Is the campaign informed by market intelligence and targeted?
- Is it a reminder of what the party has already communicated?
- If in a PR system, does the party deal with potential coalition partners effectively?

(*continued*)

8   *Jennifer Lees-Marshment*

Table 1.1 Continued

Stage 7: Election

Theory:
The party should win not just votes but attract positive perception from voters on all aspects of behaviour including policies, leaders, party unity and capability, as well as increased quality of its membership.

Checklist:
•   How did the party do in the election in terms of numbers of votes and seats?
•   Who did the party attract support from?
•   Did it attract its target market?
•   Did it retain its core vote?
•   How was its product evaluated as measured by polls and focus groups on any aspect of their product such as leadership, main policies, unity, economic management, and in relation to the competition?
•   Did it increase its membership?

Stage 8: Delivery

Theory:
The party then needs to deliver its product after the election. For major parties who win the election they must deliver on their promises and communicate progress or otherwise, involving careful media management. Smaller or opposition parties will be assessed in terms of their goals, such as their ability to put issues on the agenda, or, within a multi-party system, to work in a coalition, or to provide effective opposition and representation.

Checklist:
•   Has the party delivered in government?
•   If a party has gone into a coalition, are they still delivering the product they promised to their members and voters, or have they had to compromise?
•   Are all parties in the coalition receiving credit for delivering on their particular, distinct policies?
•   If in opposition, is the party fulfilling its role? Is it seen as a capable opposition?
•   If a party lost badly in the election, is it showing signs of realizing it needs to listen and learn from the electorate?

Stage 9: Maintaining a market-orientation – cyclical marketing

---

Theory:
To maintain a market-orientation, the party needs to engage in continual political marketing whether in opposition, the sole party of government or in coalition. In government it needs to ensure space and time to think about product design/development for the next election especially as public opinion or the economic situation changes given the realities of government and unexpected developments that occur. In all cases, it is essential that parties maintain the market-oriented concept and continue to conduct market intelligence to inform their future planning.

Checklist:
•   Has the party continued to conduct market intelligence?
•   Does it continue to be responsive to voters?
•   If in opposition, is it reflecting on losing the election and beginning to go through the process again?
•   If in government, is the party allowing time for discussion and debate about future developments?

The MOP process is a very complex one, difficult in practice, and arguably difficult to measure in analysis, but when parties do appear to follow it to a significant degree – as in the UK New Labour case – they enjoy long-term electoral success, which is why the interest in this particular approach to electioneering. However this may not prove to be the case in all circumstances, as this book will explore. Additionally, smaller parties with different goals may find it more rational, and/or ideologically appealing, to use marketing purely to present their product more effectively without changing their communication. The other main political marketing approach is that of a sales-orientation, which is perhaps easier for parties to adopt.

The Sales-Oriented Party (SOP)

Sales-oriented parties (Lees-Marshment, 2001a, b) aim to sell what they decide is best for the people, utilizing effective political marketing communication techniques. Market intelligence is used not to inform the product design, but to help the party persuade voters it is right. Below is a brief summary of the process SOPs might go through, again with a checklist.

In PR (proportional representation) electoral and multi-party political systems minor parties, with little chance of winning power, will predominantly want to influence the agenda and potential coalition partners, and therefore a sales-orientation can be a rational option to use marketing to present their argument most effectively to the segments most open to persuasion. Like any approach, the use and effectiveness of political marketing depends on the goals of the organization and the nature of the environment.

The Product-Oriented Party (POP)

A POP is the most traditional approach to party behaviour and as such attracts less attention. The main difference between a sales- and a product-oriented party is that it is devoid of awareness and utilization of communication techniques and market intelligence. A product-oriented party argues for what it stands for and believes in. It assumes that voters will realize that its ideas are the right ones and therefore vote for it. This type of party refuses to change its ideas or product even if it fails to gain electoral or membership support.

Few parties will fall into this model, but we may find some in our comparative analysis especially with new parties without much funding for campaigning and intelligence. Parties may also choose to opt for a more old-fashioned approach to maintain their elite-driven beliefs and policies because they believe so much in their argument they assume electors will see the merit of their argument without the need for modern communication methods. In some rare cases this may be effective for new, single-issue dominated, short-lived political movements that capture the public mood and respond to a concern other established parties are ignoring. However we think that the desire for long-term survival tends to encourage parties to be sales- or market-oriented, but comparative analysis in this book will show the extent to which this is true or not.

Table 1.2　The sales-oriented party political process and checklist

---

Stage 1: Product design

Theory:
The party designs its behaviour according to what it thinks best.

Checklist:
- Do party staff and politicians indicate that their approach to politics is that politicians know best?
- Do party staff and politicians indicate that their role is to represent party beliefs and ideology, and persuade voters, as opposed to following them?
- Does the product design have significant elements which do not follow the majority of public opinion?
- Does the policy-design process show it was designed to include party views rather than the results of market intelligence?
- Was the leader elected to suit the party rather than the public?

Stage 2: Market intelligence

Theory:
Market intelligence is used to ascertain voters' response to its behaviour, and identify which voter segments offer support, which do not, and which might be persuaded. Research can also explore how best to communicate with target markets.

Checklist:
- Does the party conduct market intelligence?
- Does it keep the results closely guarded, e.g. limited either to the leader or their inner circle?
- Is the intelligence focused on how the party is doing in the polls, and how it is perceived, rather than what voters would like to see changed?
- Has the party segmented the market to identify a target market of voters who might be persuaded to vote for them, as well as the core vote?
- Is market intelligence conducted to ascertain how best to communicate with the target market and core vote, what communication methods to use, and how to persuade – e.g. to sell the party, rather than change it?

Stage 3: Communication

Theory:
Communication is devised to suit each segment, targeting presentation on the most popular aspects of the product whilst downplaying any weaknesses. Communication uses modern but also traditional marketing communication techniques depending on what is perceived to be most effective.

Checklist:
- What communication techniques does the party use? Do they include the latest modern tools?
- Is the communication designed to persuade voters, rather than just inform them?
- Is communication designed in response to market intelligence?
- Do party staff focus on communication rather than policy and other behaviour?
- Has the party enlisted professionals to help with its communication?

Stage 4: Campaign

Theory:
The party continues to communicate effectively as in Stage 3, bringing communication to a crescendo as this is the final sales period, using whatever techniques help persuade undecided voters.

Checklist:
- How effective is the campaign?
- Does the party try to get its core vote out?
- Does it focus on its target market(s)?
- Does it produce any last-minute surprises or gimmicks?
- Does it engage in attacking and weakening its main opponent?
- Again, is it informed by market intelligence?
- Is it organized effectively?

Stage 5: Election

Theory:
The party should see an advance in terms of its votes, members, seats and opinion polls, depending on its goals.

Checklist:
- How does the party perform in the election?
- Do polls and other research suggest that the party is unpopular with voters in terms of some key aspects in its product?
- Is the party perceived to be ideological and to hold true to its convictions?
- Is the party perceived to be radical?
- After the election, does the party win any awards for running a good campaign?

Stage 6: Delivery

Theory:
The party will deliver its promised product in government or continue to offer effective opposition and put its issues on the agenda. This will obviously involve careful media management.

Checklist:
- Does the party, if it wins, deliver its product in government?
- Does it continue to communicate effectively?
- If it has different goals, does it hold true to its ideals and continue to campaign for those issues after the election?

POP checklist:

- Is the party's attitude more traditional?
- Does it firmly believe in its product and think the public will agree?
- Did the party emerge to represent a particular group in society or a particularly strong new issue?
- Does the party lack funds?
- Does the party tend to eschew or avoid full-scale communication?
- Does it neglect or ignore polls and other forms of market intelligence?

A word of caution: criticisms of the Lees-Marshment model

As with any models, it has naturally attracted its fair share of criticism. Ormrod (2006) provides a comprehensive summary of concerns (see also Coleman, 2007; Egan, 2004; Henneberg, 2004; Lilleker and Negrine, 2002; Lilleker, 2006; Moloney, 2004; Savigny, 2004; Strömbäck and Nord, 2005; Washbourne, 2005; and see Lees-Marshment, 2006a, b for response). Some of these points relate to comparative practice of political marketing, which we will address in this book by exploring the impact of systemic features on the use of marketing. Others relate to how to test for an orientation, and this is a very difficult process, but Chapter 2 will go some way towards this and guide a more scientific and systematic analysis in the country studies. Whilst there will however undoubtedly remain critics and sceptics of the Lees-Marshment model, this is not really the focus of this book. The model is purely a means to frame empirical research in a way that will help answer our questions as to the way political marketing is used, its effectiveness, its nature, its relation to systemic features, and the implications for democracy.

The structure of this book

The rest of this book therefore seeks to examine the use of political marketing by parties in the way they behave; to assess to what extent they become sales- or market-oriented; and to explore the issues arising from this in both practical and normative terms. In order to facilitate more objective and scientific analysis, Jesper Strömbäck will outline a comparative political marketing framework which the authors will use in their country studies. Then the book will examine marketing in the United States, United Kingdom, Australia, New Zealand, Sweden, Germany, Japan, Greece, Czech Republic, Russia, Hungary, Peru, Taiwan and Kenya. By exploring political marketing in established Anglo-Saxon countries, Europe, and emerging democracies, it will also discuss the implications of global political marketing practice for ideology, representative democracy, and citizenship. It will also include two overview chapters, one from an academic, Mick Temple, and another from practitioners Mark Gill and Roger Mortimore, on the implications of political marketing from a broad political science and prac- titioner perspective, before providing a comparative overview and conclusions about global political marketing.

References/further reading

Blumler, J. G. and Gurevitch, M. (1995) *The Crisis of Public Communication.* London: Routledge.
Bowler, S. and Farrell, D. M. (eds) (1992) *Electoral Strategies and Political Marketing.* London: Macmillan.
Butler, P. and Collins, N. (1996) 'Strategic Analysis in Political Markets', *European Journal of Marketing*, 30(10/11): 25–36.

Butler, P. and Collins, N. (1999) 'A Conceptual Framework for Political Marketing', in B. I. Newman (ed.) *Handbook of Political Marketing*, Thousand Oaks, CA: Sage Publications.

Bryant, I. (2008) 'An Inside Look at Obama's Grassroots Marketing', *Adweek*, 12 March 2008. Available at <http://www.adweek.com/aw/content_display/community/columns/other-columns/e3i714b5acb6525107fda1eb890ff94a48a> (accessed 1 June 2009).

Coleman, S. (2007) 'Review', *Parliamentary Affairs*, 60(1): 180–186.

Downs, A. (1957) *An Economic Theory of Democracy*, New York: Harper and Row.

Egan, J. (2004) 'Book Review of *Political Marketing and British Political Parties* by Lees-Marshment', *Journal of Political Marketing*, 3(1): 114–116.

Henneberg, S. C. M. (2004) 'The Views of an *Advocatus Dei*: Political Marketing and its Critics', *Journal of Public Affairs*, 4(3): 225–43.

Henneberg, S. C. and O'Shaughnessy, N. (2007) 'Theory and Concept Development in Political Marketing: Issues and an Agenda', *Journal of Political Marketing*, 6(2/3): 5–31.

Holtz-Bacha, C. (2002) 'Professionalization of Political Communication: The Case of the 1998 SPD Campaign,' *Journal of Political Marketing*, 1(4): 23–37.

Jackson, N. (2005) 'Vote Winner or a Nuisance: Email and Elected Politicians' Relationship with their Constituents', in W. Wymer and J. Lees-Marshment (eds) *Current Issues in Political Marketing*, Binghamton, NY: Haworth Press.

Jackson, N. (2006) 'Banking Online: The Use of the Internet by Political Parties to Build Relationships with Voters', in D. Lilleker, N. Jackson and R. Scullion (eds) *The Marketing of Political Parties*, Manchester: Manchester University Press.

Kavanagh, D. (1995) *Election Campaigning: The New Marketing of Politics*, Oxford: Blackwell.

Kotler, P. and Levy, S. (1969) 'Broadening the Concept of Marketing', *Journal of Marketing*, 33(1): 10–15.

Lees-Marshment, J. (2001a) *Political Marketing and British Political Parties*, Manchester: Manchester University Press.

Lees-Marshment, J. (2001b) 'The Marriage of Politics and Marketing', *Political Studies*, 49(4): 692–713.

Lees-Marshment, J. (2003) 'Political Marketing: How to Reach that Pot of Gold', *Journal of Political Marketing*, 2(1): 1–32.

Lees-Marshment, J. (2006a) 'Political Marketing Theory and Practice: A Reply to Ormrod's Critique of the Lees-Marshment Market-Oriented Party Model', *Politics*, 26(2): 119–125.

Lees-Marshment, J. (2006b) 'The Trial of the Market-Oriented Party Model: Comparing UK and New Zealand Political Marketing', paper presented at the UK Political Studies Association Conference, Reading, April 2006.

Lees-Marshment, J. (2009) *Political Marketing: Principles and Applications*, Abingdon, Oxon; New York: Routledge.

Lilleker, D. (2006) 'Political Marketing: The Cause of an Emerging Democratic Deficit in Britain?' in J. Lees-Marshment and W. Wymer (eds) *Current Issues in Political Marketing*, Binghamton, NY: Haworth Press.

Lilleker, D. and Lees-Marshment, J. (eds) (2005) *Political Marketing: A Comparative Perspective*, Manchester: Manchester University Press.

Lilleker, D. and Negrine, R. M. (2002) 'Marketing Techniques and Political Campaigns: The Limitations for the Marketing of British Political Parties', paper presented at the UK PSA conference.

Lloyd, J. (2006) 'Square Peg, Round Hole?: Can Marketing-Based Concepts such as the "Product" and the "Marketing Mix" have a Useful Role in the Political Arena?' in J. Lees-Marshment and W. Wymer (eds) *Current Issues in Political Marketing*, Binghamton, NY: Haworth Press.

Moloney, K. (2004) 'Is Political Marketing New Words or New Practice?', paper delivered at the UK PSA Conference, Lincoln, 6–8 April. Available at: <http://www.psa.ac.uk/journals/pdf/5/2004/Moloney.pdf> (accessed 9 June 2009).

Newman, B. (1994) *The Marketing of the President: Political Marketing as Campaign Strategy*, Beverley Hills, CA: Sage Publications.

Newman, B. (1999) *The Mass Marketing of Politics: Democracy in an Age of Manufactured Images*, Beverley Hills: Sage Publications.

New Zealand Herald (2007) 'Rudd Momentum Stirring Déjà Vu', Wednesday 7 November. Available at: <http://www.nzherald.co.nz/topic/story.cfm?c_id=467&objectid =1047 4421> (accessed 17 April 2008).

O'Cass, A. (1996) 'Political marketing and the marketing concept', *European Journal of Marketing*, 30(10/11): 45–61.

Ormrod, R. P. (2005) 'A Conceptual Model Of Political Market Orientation,' in J. Lees-Marshment and W. Wymer (eds) *Current Issues in Political Marketing*, Binghamton, NY: Haworth Press. [47–64]

Ormrod, R. P. (2006) 'A Critique of the Lees-Marshment Market-Oriented Party Model', *Politics*, 26(2): 110–118.

Ormrod, R. P. (2007) 'Political Market Orientation and its Commercial Cousin: Close Family or Distant Relatives?' *Journal of Political Marketing*, 6(2/3): 69–90.

Plasser, F. and Plasser, G. (2002) *Global Political Campaigning: A Worldwide Analysis of Campaign Professionals and Their Practices*, Westport, CT: Praeger.

Robinson, C. E. (2005) *Advertising and the Market Orientation of Political Parties Contesting the 1999 and 2002 New Zealand General Election Campaigns*, unpublished PhD thesis, Massey University, Palmerston North.

Robinson, C. E. (2007) 'Images of the 2005 campaign,' in S. Levine and N. S. Roberts (eds) *The Baubles of Office: The New Zealand General Election of 2005*, Wellington: Victoria University Press.

Savigny, H. (2004) 'Political Marketing: A Rational Choice?', *Journal of Political Marketing*, 3(1): 21–38.

Savigny, H. (2007) 'Focus Groups and Political Marketing: Science and Democracy as Axiomatic?', *British Journal of Politics and International Relations*, 9(1): 122–137.

Savigny, H. (2008) *The Problem of Political Marketing*, New York: Continuum International.

Savigny, H. (2009) 'Political Marketing', in C. Hay, M. Kenny, M. Flinders and A. Gamble (eds) *The Oxford Handbook of British Politics*, Oxford: Oxford University Press.

Strömbäck, J. (2007) 'Political Marketing and Professionalized Campaigning: A Conceptual Analysis', *Journal of Political Marketing*, 6(2/3): 49–67.

Strömbäck, J. and Nord, L. (2005) 'Political Marketing: The Road to Electoral Success or to Electoral Backlash?', paper presented at the Political Marketing Group Conference, London, February.

Washbourne, N. (2005) '(Comprehensive) Political Marketing, Expertise and the Conditions for Democracy', paper presented at the UK PSA Political Marketing Group Conference London, February.

Wring, D. (1997) 'Reconciling Marketing with Political Science: Theories of Political Marketing', in *Proceedings of the 1997 Academy of Marketing Conference*, Manchester: Manchester Metropolitan University.

Wring, D. (2002) 'Conceptualising Political Marketing: A Framework for Election-Campaign Analysis', in N. J. O'Shaughnessy and S. Henneberg (eds) *The Idea of Political Marketing*, New York: Praeger. [171–186]

2 A framework for comparing political market-orientation

Jesper Strömbäck

Introduction

The literature about political marketing and political market-orientation has expanded significantly during the last twenty years. However, it can be argued that the cumulativity of this research has been limited. One reason is that most studies are single-country studies. A second reason is that many studies focus on only a limited number of parties within the chosen country, typically the largest or the most successful parties. A third reason is that most studies are British or American in their origins, which limits the generalizability of the results. To this one should add the lack of consensus regarding the central concepts being used, which has characterized this field of research.

Perhaps this lack of cumulativity is not so surprising considering that 'attempts to merge two diverse research areas are replete with problems of context, understanding and approach' (Butler and Collins, 1996: 33). If political marketing as an academic field should be perceived as a 'marriage of politics and marketing' (Lees-Marshment, 2001a), then it is also a marriage that thus far has been marked by tensions and conflicts.

Hence, it appears obvious that more research needs to be done, and this is particularly true with regards to comparative and cross-cultural studies. This is why we started to think about editing a comparative volume on political marketing and political market-orientation. The purpose of this particular chapter is to suggest a framework for comparing political market-orientation across countries, in order to facilitate analyses and comparisons of the individual country studies in this book and beyond. First, however, I will briefly set out how the central concepts will be used in this text, in order not to add to any conceptual confusion.

On political marketing and market-orientation

The philosopher Karl Popper once remarked that there is no empirical way of defining a concept (1959/1992: 74). Concepts are tools, but they do not possess any inherent meanings. To argue over the 'essential' meaning of concepts is thus futile. What is important is that we strive for clarity while using different concepts so that everyone can understand what they signify in the context in which they are being used. Thus, the purpose of this conceptual discussion is not to define what the central concepts 'really' mean. Rather, it is to describe how they are being used in this chapter.

While political marketing and political communication are not synonymous, the terms have much in common and political marketing always involves communication (Lock and Harris, 1996). This communication might be aimed at or coming from different target groups located in different arenas or markets, such as party members in an internal arena, journalists and editors in a media arena, members of parliament in a parliamentary arena and voters in an electoral arena (Kotler and Kotler, 1999; Strömbäck, 2007b), to take just a few examples. Thus, in some respects, marketing has always been part of politics (Perloff, 1999). When marketing their products, political parties and other organizations make use of *marketing techniques*, such as polling (Rademacher and Tuchfarber, 1999), voter segmentation (Baines, 1999), television advertising (Kaid and Holtz-Bacha, 2006) and direct mail (Scherman, 1999). This brings the discussion on political marketing and the use of marketing techniques close to the discussion on political campaigning and the professionalization of political campaigning (Baines and Egan, 2001; Gibson and Römmele, 2001; Negrine, 2008; Plasser and Plasser, 2002).

However, political marketing in this broad sense and the usage of political marketing techniques is not synonymous with the *marketing concept* or with a party or campaign being *market-oriented* (Lees-Marshment, 2001b; Strömbäck, 2007a). Whereas all political actors make use of marketing techniques to some extent, only some can be considered to be market-oriented, that is guided by the marketing concept. Thus, I use the term market-orientation to mean essentially the implementation of the marketing concept (Kohli and Jaworski, 1990: 1).

The marketing concept has its origins in marketing research. As such, the marketing concept holds that 'an organization's purpose is to discover needs and wants in its target markets and to satisfy those needs and wants more effectively and efficiently than competitors' (Slater and Narver, 1998: 1001). As similarly noted by Gummesson (2002: 14), 'The essence of the marketing concept is understanding customer needs and wants'.

Being market-oriented can thus be contrasted to two other approaches: sales-orientation and product-orientation (Henneberg, 2002; Lees-Marshment, 2001b, 2004; Newman, 1994;). The defining characteristics of these orientations are summarized in Table 2.1 (see further Lees-Marshment, 2001b; Strömbäck, 2007a; see also Chapter 1).

The distinction between these three orientations is crucial, not least with regard to the conceptual relationship between political marketing and the use of marketing techniques on the one hand, and the marketing concept on the other. Simply put, whereas product- as well as sales- and market-oriented parties make use of marketing techniques, it is only market-oriented parties that follow the marketing concept. Making use of marketing techniques is not restricted to market-oriented parties, whereas following the marketing concept is what makes market-oriented parties unique.

From the perspective of relationship marketing, being market-oriented also means being continuously involved in exchange processes and having relationships

Table 2.1 Defining characteristics of product-, sales- and market-oriented parties
(adapted from Lees-Marshment 2001a, b)

	Product-oriented party	*Sales-oriented party*	*Market-oriented party*
Defining characteristic	Argues for its own ideas and policies; assumes that voters will realize that its ideas are the best and therefore vote for it.	Believes in its own ideas and policies, but realizes that they must be 'sold' to the public; does not change its behavior or policies to give people what they want, but tries to make people want what the party offers.	Uses market intelligence to identify voter needs and demands, and designs its policies, candidates and behavior to provide voter satisfaction; does not try to change what people want, but give people what they want.
If the party does not succeed in elections	Believes that the voters just do not realize that the party's policies are the best ones; refuses to change policies.	Tries to make better use of market intelligence and persuasion techniques, i.e., become more professionalized in its campaigning.	Uses market intelligence to re-design the product, so that it becomes better suited to the wants and needs of targeted people.

with selected target groups and stakeholders in different arenas or markets, as well as with competitors (Butler and Collins, 1996; Christopher, Payne and Ballantyne, 2002; Dean and Croft, 2001; Gummesson, 2002; Henneberg, 2002; Kohli and Jaworski, 1990; Lafferty and Hult, 2001). No party can be seen in isolation from its competitors (Butler and Collins, 1996; Collins and Butler, 2002; Ormrod, 2005), which means that market-oriented political organizations not only need to be voter-centred. They also need to be competitor-centred.

In the previous literature it has been discussed whether politics should be perceived mainly as service marketing or product marketing (Lloyd, 2005; Henneberg, 2002). There are obviously several differences between services and products, as well as important differences between politics and the commercial marketplace (Lock and Harris, 1996). In this context, and without investing too much meaning into the word 'product', it suffices to say that the political product consists of three core components (Wring, 2005: 4) – party image, leadership image and policy commitments – and a mindset of voter-centredness (O'Cass, 1996: 40. See also Lees-Marshment, 2001b, 2004).

To summarize, in this context *political marketing* refers to all activities involved in planning and managing the communication with different target groups in different arenas or markets. *Marketing techniques* refers to how parties go ahead when planning and conducting strategic communication with selected target groups. Product-oriented as well as sales-oriented and market-oriented parties all make use of marketing techniques. *Market-orientation* refers to a needs assessment approach and a relational exchange process where parties make use of market intelligence to identify the wants and needs of selected target groups in the electorate and to design a product to meet the expressed as well as latent wants and needs of these groups, while also taking the relationships with other important stakeholders within or outside the party into account in order to build strong long-term relationships. *The political product* refers to the party image, leadership image and policy commitments of the parties.

What, then, can explain the extent to which political parties are, attempt to be or are likely to become market-oriented in different countries around the world? What factors are likely to facilitate or hinder the process of political parties becoming market-oriented? To answer questions like these we need a framework for comparing political market-orientation.

To structure this discussion, I will take as a starting point the notion that the overall political system matters and that political parties are active in an electoral arena, a media arena, an internal arena and a parliamentary arena (Strömbäck, 2007b). Thus, I will firstly analyze the importance of different political and electoral systems, before turning to the parliamentary arena, the electoral arena, the internal arena and the media arena.

The political system matters

On a very general level the political system in a particular country shapes the whole working of the different parts of the political system. Of particular importance in this context might be whether the system is party-centred or candidate-centred, the electoral system, the number of political parties, and the political culture.

With regard to electoral systems it is common to make a distinction between majoritarian, proportional and combined types, each including a number of subcategories (Lijphart, 1999; Norris, 2004). For example, majoritarian systems can make use of a First-Past-the-Post system (FPTP) or a second-ballot system, whereas in proportional systems people can vote for party lists (closed or open) or rank their preferences among the candidates as in the Single-Transferable Vote (STV) system. On a global level, approximately half of the countries make use of a majoritarian system, whereas about one-third make use of a proportional system and the remainder combine these systems (Norris, 2004: 40). Generally speaking, there is a correlation between majoritarian systems and an emphasis on creating government accountability, whereas in proportional systems there is an emphasis on parliamentary inclusiveness. The aim of majoritarian systems is to create a parliamentary majority in order to produce an effective one-party government and thus government accountability. The aim of proportional systems is to include as many voices as possible, emphasizing the need for bargaining and compromise within parliament, government and the policymaking processes. Majoritarian systems are often called adversarial systems whereas proportional systems are called consensus systems (Lijphart, 1999; Norris, 2004).

One important aspect of the electoral system is that it shapes the party system in the sense that majoritarian systems foster a two- or few-party system, whereas proportional elections foster a multi-party system. The mean number of parliamentary parties in the former system is 5.22 and in the latter 9.52, whereas the mean number of relevant parliamentary parties (with more than 3 per cent of the seats) is 3.33 in majoritarian systems and 4.74 in proportional systems (Norris, 2004: 85). Thus, the electoral systems matter, creating different dynamics and a more crowded political landscape in proportional than in majoritarian systems. The more crowded a particular political landscape is within a country, the more difficult it is for the parties to differentiate themselves from the competitors, and the more difficult it might be for them to re-position themselves along the left–right ideological dimension as other positions are likely to already be occupied. It also becomes more difficult to choose a 'flight to the centre' as a strategy – a strategy that would otherwise be the likely result of parties becoming market-oriented (Downs, 1957; Wring, 2002).

This observation is supported by the notion that the influence of socio-demographic cleavages and ideology is stronger in proportional than majoritarian electoral systems, indicating that in the former, political parties function more as channels for particular groups in society than in the latter (Norris, 2004: 119–121). As a consequence, bonding appeals directed at particular groups in society are more likely in proportional systems, in contrast to majoritarian systems where catch-all and bridging appeals are more likely. This implies that it is also more important for parties in multi-party systems to rely on their ideological and historical policy positions and images than for parties in few-party systems. Taken together this suggests that parties are more likely to be or become market-oriented in a) majoritarian systems with b) few significant parties and c) a less crowded political landscape where d) social, political and ideological cleavages are not very pronounced. A higher number of parties also implies that strength in terms of sizes, power and resources is unevenly distributed across parties, restricting the choice of freedom for the smaller and mid-sized parties. Providing that it takes more resources to be market-oriented than sales- or product-oriented, this implies that smaller or mid-sized parties are less likely to be market-oriented than larger parties.

Another important difference relates to whether the political system is candidate- or party-centred. In candidate-centred countries and systems it is the individual candidates who decide which orientation to follow, in cooperation with their advisers and consultants. In party-centred systems the decision to be product, sales- or market-oriented involves the whole party organization, which arguably might make it more difficult to re-position and re-orient. The internal arena is composed of a number of different stakeholders, such as members, activists, internal officeholders and elected representatives for the party, and there might be several different factions fighting internally to take control over the party and its political product. Thus, it is likely that it is more difficult to change concept and become more market-oriented in party-centred than in candidate-centred systems. Such changes might need to be marketed internally before it is possible to change and implement the changes, and this is a process that might be replete with conflicts (Wring, 2005).

The political culture in a particular country might also be relevant in understanding the likelihood that political parties will be or become market-oriented. For one thing, the degree to which social, political and ideological cleavages structure politics is part of the political culture. Besides this, it might be argued that different perceptions of responsiveness and populism are predominant in different countries. Listening to and adapting to the wants and needs of people can be framed both as responsiveness and as populism, but it might be the case that it is more likely to be perceived as populism – and hence negative – in some countries than in others. If so, this would likely be the case in countries with a rather hierarchical and top-down tradition, in contrast to countries with an equalitarian and bottom-up tradition, or in parties with a similar kind of hierarchical and top-down tradition.

The parliamentary arena matters

The goal in the parliamentary arena is to maximize parliamentary influence, and the primary actors are the members of parliament from different parties (Sjöblom, 1968). In majoritarian systems, the government is usually supported by a majority of the members of parliament, and it has no urgent need to find support from the opposition parties. If government is divided between two chambers of parliament or there is a clear division of power between different branches of government, there might however be a need for bargaining and compromise between the different chambers or branches of government. This is often the case in majoritarian and presidential systems, whereas in parliamentary and proportional systems the processes of bargaining and compromising take place within parliament. Different systems create different dynamics and different needs to take the competitors into account between elections.

As the parliamentary strength of different parties is dependent upon the number of seats, on the surface it is perhaps somewhat less important with regards to the market-orientation of parties than are the other arenas. However, the members of parliament are very influential both within the parties and with regard to the image of the party. Thus, it would be very difficult for a party to be market-oriented if its members of parliament did not approve of such an orientation. The attitudes of individual members of parliament are crucial. A market-oriented party needs members of parliament with positive attitudes towards the market-orientation of the party, and no party can be market-oriented without at least a significant majority of the MPs having market-oriented attitudes. Furthermore, one of the crucial challenges for a market-oriented party is to deliver on its promises, staying market-oriented between elections (Lilleker and Lees-Marshment, 2005). Maintaining a market-orientation also requires the support of most although perhaps not all MPs.

What is also important here in studying variations across countries is the extent to which members of parliament act mainly on behalf of their local constituents or their own conscience, or whether there is a centralized control over the behaviour of the parliamentary body of a party. A reasonable assumption might be that it is more difficult for a party to be or become market-oriented if the party lacks control over its members of parliament, especially if the MPs have strong ties with different interest groups, as interest groups are usually the most strongly committed to promoting a certain policy agenda. What is also crucial here is the importance of the left–right dimension in structuring parliamentary decision-making, bargaining and procedures, as discussed above. The more important this dimension is, and the more crowded the political landscape, the more difficult it is for parties both within and outside the parliamentary arena to re-position and re-orient themselves.

Another important point with regard to the parliamentary arena is whether a particular party is in government or in opposition. A governing party has to face different issues; it has a responsibility to make tough decisions when called for, which makes it difficult to maintain a market-orientation. Although people have both expressed and latent wants and needs, some governmental decisions might have to be made that are in opposition to people's expressed wants and needs, creating dissent among the voters as well as among some MPs. A party in opposition has fewer responsibilities and more freedom to operate according to what market intelligence indicates are either the expressed or latent wants and needs, or both. On the other hand, a party in government also has a responsibility to represent the whole electorate, which might call for moderation and a market-orientation. It usually also has more resources available than its competitors.

There might also be differences depending on whether a country has a single-party government or a coalition government. As suggested by Lilleker and Lees-Marshment (2005: 225), 'the energy and time needed to maintain [a] coalition and consider the other party's (or parties') markets can reduce the energy and time available to consider and respond to the main market'. Smaller coalition parties can also be tempted to focus on smaller niches and target groups rather than larger target groups, making it difficult for the other parties to respond to their voters and target groups – providing the larger party or parties need the cooperation of the smaller parties to stay in government.

One further problem for parties in government might be that some sub-divisions within such parties might think that being market-oriented is only a campaign strategy. Thus, they might accept a market-orientation before Election Day, while thinking that once in government the party should pursue policies that are product-rather than market-oriented. Thus, the leadership of a party that recently won an election and governmental power might face dissent and challenges from back-benchers if or when it attempts to maintain a market-orientation. This could be expected to be particularly true if a party in government has to make tough decisions that are unpopular and that lead to the party losing ground in the polls. This also indicates that it clearly matters whether a party is in opposition or in government, and the degree to which the central leadership is in command of the party. Parties in government are also likely to face a tougher scrutiny by the media, which can create tensions within the parties – especially if such scrutiny affects public opinion.

The electoral arena matters

Within the electoral arena the most important decision makers are the voters, which decide which party or candidate to support. During the last decades, people's political behaviour has changed considerably in a number of countries across the world. To start with, electoral turnout has decreased in many, although not all, established democracies since the late 1970s (Dalton, 2002; Franklin, 2004). Party identification, which measures people's psychological attachment to political parties, has also decreased sharply in many countries. The United States constitute one important exception however, as party polarization has increased significantly there during the last couple of decades (Jacobson, 2007). Nevertheless, one study, covering 19 countries across the world and the trends during the last decades, showed that the percentage of voters identifying with any political party decreased in 17 countries, whereas the percentage of strong identifiers decreased in all countries (Dalton, 2000: 25). Thus, the trend of declining partisanship appears almost universal, making the 'voter market' less frozen and more open for competition than it used to be. When most people identify with a particular party there are few incentives for the parties to try to steal voters from other parties, as the likelihood of success is low and as they might lose their own voters if deviating from their expectations. This is particularly true in countries with a crowded political landscape. When fewer people identify with a party, the incentive to become market-oriented is much stronger, both because parties in such a situation cannot take their own voters for granted and because they might be able to win new voters.

Closely related to the trend towards decreasing party identification is the rising electoral volatility in many if not most established democracies since the 1980s. Across the world, more and more people tend to switch party either between elections or during the election campaigns, thereby also changing the dynamics of electoral competition. Split-ticket voting has also become increasingly common, and more and more voters wait until late during a campaign before deciding which party or parties to vote for (Dalton *et al.*, 2000).

Another clear trend is that political distrust has increased in many countries around the world, especially if operationalized as the level of trust in the national parliament (Klingemann, 1999) or as trust in politicians (Dalton, 1999). This is yet another indicator of a widening gap between the electorate on the one hand, and political parties and politicians on the other, a gap evident not only in a few but in many different countries across the world. This clearly indicates that there are more opportunities for parties nowadays than there used to be with regard to the prospects of winning new voters, but also more risks associated with each election. It thus also indicates a stronger need for present-day parties to listen to and adapt to the electorate, as they cannot count on the continued support from other than the most devoted activists and sympathizers. Moreover, this need is more urgent the more volatile and the more mistrustful the electorate in a particular country are and the less the voters in a particular country identify with the parties.

Another important aspect is related to the correlation between voter support for the parties and the voter's placement of the parties on the left–right scale. The stronger this correlation, the more important is the left–right scale, and the more difficult it might be for the parties to change positions along this scale. This correlation (eta) can vary between 0 and 1, and in some countries such as Sweden it is very strong (.77), whereas in others, such as the United States, it is significantly weaker (.31). The perceptual agreement (PA) regarding how the voters place the parties on this scale also varies between countries, as does the Wing Party Distance (WPD) (Holmberg and Oscarsson, 2004: 105–106). Thus, in some countries the voters tend to agree on the placement of the parties on the left–right scale while also tending to vote according to the left–right positioning of the parties, whereas in other countries these semi-structural factors are of less importance. The implication is that in some countries the parties are more restricted in their positioning, whereas there are more opportunities to re-position in other countries. These restrictions apply particularly in countries where cleavage and class voting is strong, but less in countries where voters are more value-oriented.

Thus, although there are some very general trends with regard to political behaviour worldwide, there are exceptions to the rule and important differences between countries and between parties within countries. These have implications for the likelihood that parties will be or become market-oriented – implications which I will return to. What is important here from a relationship marketing perspective is that the general trends clearly indicate that the relationships between the parties and their voters have become significantly weaker. Thus, these relationships are in need of improvements, and following the marketing concept might offer opportunities for such improvements.

These weakened relationships also have implications for the parties' internal arenas.

The internal arena matters

The primary actors in the internal arena are members, activists, officeholders and staff within the party and the representatives for the party. In some cases this arena is particularly important, if the party is based on mass membership and has the character of a grass-roots organization. In such cases the leadership acts on behalf of the larger number of members and activists, and is hence restricted to act within the mandate provided to it when elected by the members and activists. The leadership is perceived as an agent acting on behalf of and as representatives of the activists and members, which in turn are perceived as acting on behalf of and as representatives of the voters and sympathizers of the party. In such parties the members expect to have a decisive role in designing the political product, and significant changes need to be approved by the members gathered at party conventions.

This has of course not been the only party model. In some countries the parties do not even have a membership base to speak of, such as in the United States where the parties have been described as 'empty vessels' (Katz and Kolodny, 1994). Furthermore, the mass party model is just one among a number of other party models identified in the literature. Among these party models are elite and cadre parties, catch-all, electoralist parties and cartel parties (for an overview, see Krouwel, 2006). Some parties are also more policy-seeking, whereas other parties are more office- or vote-seeking (Strom, 1990; Wolinetz, 2002).

What seems clear, when looking at the broad picture, is that the number of members has declined in most parties around the world during the last decades (Mair, 1994; Scarrow, 2000; Webb, 2002). Generally speaking, parties have become less dependent upon members, but also more dependent upon the state for funding and subsidies, and the power within parties has shifted towards the central level where the number of staff employed by the parties has increased (Katz and Mair, 1994; Webb, Farrell and Holliday, 2002; Webb and Kolodny, 2006). The party 'on the ground' has become less important whereas the party 'in office' has become more important, to the extent that it has been suggested that '[t]he leaders become the party; the party becomes the leaders' (Katz and Mair, 2002: 126). Political parties have also become more professionally organized, not only with respect to election campaigning but also with respect to how the organization as such is structured.

This indicates that membership decline should not be equated with a decline of party organizational strength (Scarrow, 2000). Parties with fewer members can in fact be stronger as organizations and with respect to their campaigning capabilities. It might also be easier for such a party to implement a market-orientation (Lilleker and Lees-Marshment, 2005). At the same time, there is a tendency for parties to try to shift some power back to grass-roots, for example with regards to leadership or candidate selection, in order to legitimize the organization as a democratic one. However, this intra-party shift of power is usually not at the expense of the central leadership, but rather at the expense of the middle-level elite, where the most ideologically radical members and activists can usually be found (Mair, 1994; Scarrow, Webb and Farrell, 2000). Thus, by empowering ordinary members, who are often more docile than the activists, the party leadership can actually gain power and increase the possibility of re-positioning or re-orienting the party.

This development is however not uniform across parties or across countries, suggesting that some parties are more likely to be market-oriented than others. These are the parties which on an overall level are office- or vote-seeking rather than policy-seeking, where the intra-party power rests with the central leadership, the central staff and the ordinary members rather than the middle-level elite, where the 'party in office' is more important than the 'party on the ground', and which has an internal culture or tradition of granting the leadership a substantial autonomy. Parties that are policy-seeking and where the internal power rests with the middle-level elite and activists, or parties that can be characterized as mass parties, should be less likely to be market-oriented. In such parties the internal arena is often more important than the electoral arena, and the internal arena is also mainly dominated by the ideologically radical activists rather than the party leadership or the ordinary members, the latter resembling the larger group of voters more than the activists. However, if a party faces a major electoral defeat or successive electoral defeats, a re-orientation and re-positioning of the party might be acceptable even to the activists, indicating that successive or major electoral defeats increase the likelihood that a particular party becomes more market-oriented. The internal arena and the intra-party power distribution thus matter, although more so in some parties than in others.

The media arena matters

Modern politics is mainly mediated politics (Bennett and Entman, 2001), in the sense that the news media are the most important channel of communication between the parties and the voters. The increasing importance of the Internet notwithstanding, the mass media still constitute the most important source of information for most people on matters beyond their personal experiences, especially in countries where paid political advertising is banned or insignificant. Political opinions can thus never be understood without taking the media coverage of political issues, actors and organizations into account (Strömbäck and Kaid, 2008). It is also widely acknowledged that the news media can have considerable power with respect to what issues people think are the most important (McCombs, 2004; Wanta and Ghanem, 2007), both in general and when evaluating political actors (Iyengar and Kinder, 1987), and, through framing, how people perceive different issues, actors and organizations (Iyengar, 1991; Reese, Gandy and Grant, 2001).

The importance of the news media makes skill in news management and 'spinning' essential for the parties (Franklin, 2004; Stanyer, 2007). The more commercialized and competitive the media landscape is, the more important it is for the parties to manage and spin the news in a favourable way.

This might be particularly true in countries in which the news media is independent of political parties or other political organizations, rather than a part of the political system (Strömbäck, 2008). As shown by Hallin and Mancini (2004), this is the case in countries that belong to a liberal model of media and politics, such as the United States, but also in countries that belong to a democratic corporatist model, such as Sweden (see also Strömbäck and Dimitrova, 2006). However, it is not necessarily the case in countries that belong to a polarized pluralist model, such as Spain, where the news media in general and the newspapers in particular form part of the party-political system (Hallin and Mancini, 2004; Petersson *et al.*, 2006).

In countries where the news media is highly commercialized and independent they are likely to be more critical towards political parties in general. This is partly an effect of the media responding to their audience markets. They are also more likely to frame politics as a strategic game rather than as issues (Patterson, 2000), with the implicit or explicit aim of disclosing what the parties might not want to disclose. Thus, in such countries the news is often very adversarial towards the parties and candidates, although the news can be adversarial also in countries in which the news media form part of the party-political system. In the latter case, however, the news media are more likely to be adversarial only towards some parties, whereas in liberal models the news media tend to be approximately equally hostile towards all parties, in order to avoid accusations of partisan bias.

The journalistic culture also matters, in the sense that the understanding of journalistic objectivity is different across different countries (Patterson, 1998) and that interpretive and assertive journalism as well as journalistic interventionism is more common in some countries and some news outlets than others (Esser, 2008). The more interpretive news journalism and the more common journalistic interventionism, the more difficult it might be for the parties to manage and spin the news in a favourable way, especially if such a tendency co-exists with an adversarial stance towards the parties. This might make it very difficult for the parties to communicate with the electorate – especially if paid political advertising is banned or the parties have few resources available for controlled and direct communication.

This might, however, also make it more important for the parties to be market-oriented, as it might make it more difficult for the media to frame them as unresponsive and elitist. Stated differently, the more the news frames politics as a strategic game, interprets the words and actions of politicians, intervenes in the political communication processes and adopts an adversarial stance towards the parties, the more important it might be for the parties to be able to frame themselves as 'speaking for the citizens' (Strömbäck, 2007b). Market-oriented news media might thus create incentives for political parties to become market-oriented. If the parties successfully manage to frame themselves as 'speaking for the citizens' they might be able to make it more difficult for journalists working in market-oriented media to criticize them and to focus on issues other than those the parties feel are important. Hence, it might be the case that parties are more likely to be market-oriented in countries with a highly commercialized and competitive media system where the news coverage of politics tends to be adversarial. Hence, parties are also more likely to be market-oriented in countries that belong to the liberal model of media and politics than in countries that belong to the democratic corporatist or, in particular, the polarized pluralist model.

Towards a framework for comparing political market-orientation

The previous discussion is obviously not exhaustive. Nevertheless, it has suggested a number of implications with regard to the likelihood that parties will be or become market-oriented. By generalizing and systematizing the factors that have been discussed, they can be divided into differences *between countries* and *between parties within countries* and offered as research propositions. These propositions are summarized in Table 2.2.

The overall conclusion of this analysis is that the likelihood that parties are or attempt to be market-oriented depends on a number of structural and semi-structural factors which can be located in the context made up of the political system and the media system, as well as within the parliamentary arena, the internal arena and, obviously, the electoral arena. Many of the discussed factors are connected, and while some might pull the parties in opposite directions, others might combine to create stronger incentives for parties to become market-oriented.

Table 2.2 Research propositions regarding differences between countries and between parties within countries

Propositions regarding differences between countries	Propositions regarding differences between parties within countries
(1) Parties in candidate-centred political systems are more likely to be market-oriented than parties in party-centred political systems.	(1) Large parties in terms of voter support and resources are more likely to be market-oriented than small parties.
(2) Parties in countries with majoritarian electoral systems are more likely to be market-oriented than parties in countries with proportional electoral systems.	(2) Parties where activists and middle-level elite have a strong influence on the political product are less likely to be market-oriented than parties where they have a limited influence as compared with the central leadership and ordinary members.
(3) Parties in countries where the left–right ideological dimension is of less importance in the minds of voters are more likely to be market-oriented than parties in countries where it is of major importance.	(3) Parties where the members and activists are ideologically committed on the left–right ideological dimension are less likely to be market-oriented than parties where they have a more value-oriented outlook.
(4) Parties in countries with few competing parties are more likely to be market-oriented than parties in countries with many competing parties.	(4) Parties whose voters are strongly identified with the party are less likely to be market-oriented than parties whose voters are weakly identified with the party.
(5) Parties in countries with a low degree of party identification are more likely to be market-oriented than parties in countries with a high degree of party identification.	(5) Parties that are part of, or have a competitive chance of forming, the next government, are more likely to be market-oriented than parties which are not part of government or do not have a competitive chance of forming the next government.
(6) Parties in countries with high electoral volatility are more likely to be market-oriented than parties in countries with low electoral volatility.	(6) Parties that have been in government for a longer period of time are less likely to be market-oriented than parties that have not been in government but have a competitive chance of forming the next government.
(7) Parties in countries with a highly commercialized media system are more likely to be market-oriented than parties in countries with a less commercialized media system.	(7) Parties that are historically linked with certain policy positions regarding major issues are less likely to be market-oriented than parties that are historically not linked to certain policy positions in major issues.
(8) Parties in countries with an adversarial journalistic culture are more likely to be market-oriented than parties in countries with a less adversarial journalistic culture.	(8) Parties that have suffered successive or major electoral defeats are more likely to become market-oriented than parties which have not suffered such defeats.
(9) Parties in countries with deep social or political cleavages are less likely to be market-oriented than parties in countries without such deep cleavages.	(9) Parties with a hierarchical internal culture are more likely to be market-oriented than parties with an egalitarian internal culture.

Table 2.2 Research propositions regarding differences between countries and between parties within countries (continued)

Propositions regarding differences between countries	*Propositions regarding differences between parties within countries*
(10) Parties in countries with an egalitarian political culture are more likely to be market-oriented than parties in countries with a hierarchical political culture.	(10) Parties whose members of parliament mainly answer to the central leadership of the party are more likely to be market-oriented than parties without a strong parliamentary party discipline.
(11) Parties in countries with a high level of political distrust are more likely to be market-oriented than parties in countries with a lower level of political distrust.	(11) Office- and vote-seeking parties are more likely to be market-oriented than policy-seeking parties.
(12) Parties in countries with news media independent of the party-political system are more likely to be market-oriented than parties in countries where the news media form part of the party-political system.	(12) Parties with strong ties to particular social or political cleavages are less likely to be market-oriented than parties with weak ties to particular social or political cleavages.

Thus, structural and semi-structural differences between countries or between parties within countries might help to explain why some parties choose to be market-oriented, whereas other parties choose to be sales- or even product-oriented. By systematizing and generalizing the factors that have been discussed, the analysis offers 24 research propositions. Together they suggest a framework for comparing political market-orientation, to facilitate analyses and comparisons of the individual country studies in this book – and beyond.

References/further reading

Baines, P. R. (1999) 'Voter Segmentation and Candidate Positioning', in B. I. Newman (ed.) *Handbook of Political Marketing*, Thousand Oaks, CA: Sage. [403–420]

Baines, P. R. and Egan, J. (2001) 'Marketing and Political Campaigning: Mutually Exclusive or Exclusively Mutual?', *Qualitative Market Research: An International Journal*, 4(1): 25–33.

Bennett, W. L. and Entman, R. M. (eds) (2001) *Mediated Politics*. New York: Cambridge University Press.

Butler, P. and Collins, N. (1996) 'Strategic analysis in political markets', *European Journal of Marketing*, 30(10/11): 25–36.

Christopher, M., Payne, A. and Ballantyne, D. (2002) *Relationship Marketing: Creating Stakeholder Value*. London: Elsevier Butterworth-Heinemann.

Collins, N. and Butler, P. (2002) 'Considerations on Market Analysis for Political Parties', in N. J. O'Shaughnessy and S. C. M. Henneberg (eds) *The Idea of Political Marketing*, Westport, ct: Praeger. [1–18]

Dalton, R. J. (1999) 'Political Support in Advanced Industrial Democracies', in P. Norris (ed.), *Critical Citizens: Global Support for Democratic Governance*, New York: Oxford University Press. [57–77]

Dalton, R. J. (2000) 'The Decline of Party Identifications', in R. J. Dalton and M. P. Wattenberg (eds) *Parties without Partisans: Political Change in Advanced Industrial Democracies*, New York: Oxford University Press. [19–36]

Dalton, R. J. (2002) *Citizen Politics: Public Opinion and Political Parties in Advanced Industrial Democracies*. New York: Chatham House.

Dalton, R. J., McAllister, I. and Wattenberg, M. P. (2000) 'The Consequences of Partisan Dealignment', in R. J. Dalton and M. P. Wattenberg (eds) *Parties without Partisans: Political Change in Advanced Industrial Democracies*, New York: Oxford University Press. [37–63]

Dean, D. and Croft, R. (2001) 'Friends and Relations: Long-Term Approaches to Political Campaigning', *European Journal of Marketing*, 35(11/12): 1197–1216.

Downs, A. (1957) *An Economic Theory of Democracy*, New York: Harper and Row.

Esser, F. (2008) 'Dimensions of Political News Cultures: Sound Bite and Image Bite News in France, Germany, Great Britain, and the United States', *The International Journal of Press/Politics*, 13(4): 401–428.

Franklin, B. (2004) *Packaging Politics: Political Communications in Britain's Media Democracy*, 2nd edn, London: Arnold.

Franklin, M. N. (2004) *Voter Turnout and the Dynamics of Electoral Competition in Established Democracies since 1945*, New York: Cambridge University Press.

Gibson, R. and Römmele, A. (2001) 'Changing Campaign Communications: A Party-Centered Theory of Professionalized Campaigning', *Harvard International Journal of Press/Politics*, 6(4): 31–43.

Gummesson, E. (2002) *Total Relationship Marketing: Marketing Management, Relationship Strategy and CRM Apporaches for the Network Economy*, Oxford: Butterworth Heinemann.

Hallin, D. C. and Mancini, P. (2004) *Comparing Media Systems: Three Models of Media and Politics*, New York: Cambridge University Press.

Henneberg, S. C. M. (2002) 'Understanding Political Marketing', in N. J. O'Shaughnessy and S. C. M. Henneberg (eds) *The Idea of Political Marketing*, Westport, CT: Praeger. [93–170]

Holmberg, S. and Oscarsson, H. (2004) *Väljare. Svenskt Väljarbeteende under 50 år*, Stockholm: Norstedts Juridik.

Iyengar, S. (1991) *Is Anyone Responsible? How Television Frames Political Issues*, Chicago: University of Chicago Press.

Iyengar, S. and Kinder, D. R. (1987) *News that Matters: Television and American Opinion*, Chicago: University of Chicago Press.

Jacobson, G. C. (2007) *A Divider, Not a Uniter: George W. Bush and the American People*. New York: Longman.

Kaid, L. L. and Holtz-Bacha, C. (eds) (2006) *The Sage Handbook of Political Advertising*, London: Sage.

Katz, R. S. and Kolodny, R. (1994) 'Party Organization as an Empty Vessel: Parties in American Politics', in R. S. Katz and P. Mair (eds) *How Parties Organize: Change and Adaption in Party Organizations in Western Democracies*, London: Sage. [23–50]

Katz, R. S. and Mair, P. (eds) (1994) *How Parties Organize: Change and Adaptation in Party Organizations in Western Democracies*, London: Sage.

Katz, R. S. and Mair, P. (2002) 'The Ascendancy of the Party in Public Office: Party

Organizational Change in Twentieth-Century Democracies', in R. Gunther, J. R. Montero and J. J. Linz (eds), *Political Parties: Old Concepts and New Challenges*, New York: Oxford University Press. [113–135]

Klingemann, H.-D. (1999) 'Mapping Political Support in the 1990s: A Global Analysis', in P. Norris (ed.) *Critical Citizens: Global Support for Democratic Governance*, New York: Oxford University Press. [31–56]

Kohli, A. K. and Jaworski, B. J. (1990) 'Market Orientation: The Construct, Research Propositions, and Managerial Implications', *Journal of Marketing*, 54(2): 1–18.

Kotler, P. and Kotler, N. (1999) 'Political Marketing: Generating Effective Candidates, Campaigns, and Causes', in B. I. Newman (ed.) *Handbook of Political Marketing*, Thousand Oaks: Sage. [3–18]

Krouwel, A. (2006) 'Party Models', in R. S. Katz and W. Crotty (eds) *Handbook of Party Politics*, London: Sage. [249–269]

Lafferty, B. A. and Hult, G. T. (2001) 'A Synthesis of Contemporary Market Orientation Perspectives', *European Journal of Marketing*, 35(1/2): 92–109.

Lees-Marshment, J. (2001a) 'The Marriage of Politics and Marketing', *Political Studies*, 49(4): 692–713.

Lees-Marshment, J. (2001b) *Political Marketing and British Political Parties:. The Party's Just Begun*. Manchester: Manchester University Press.

Lees-Marshment, J. (2004) *Political Marketing: The Key to Electoral Success or the Cause of Democratic Turmoil?* Sundsvall, Sweden: Centre for Political Communication Research.

Lijphart, A. (1999) *Patterns of Democracy: Government Forms and Performance in Thirty-Six Countries*, New Haven, CT: Yale University Press.

Lilleker, D. G. and Lees-Marshment, J. (2005) 'Conclusion: Towards a Comparative Model of Party Marketing', in D. G. Lilleker and J. Lees-Marshment (eds) *Political Marketing: A Comparative Perspective*, Manchester: Manchester University Press. [205–228]

Lloyd, J. (2005) 'Square Peg, Round Hole? Can Marketing-Based Concepts such as the "Product" and the "Marketing Mix" Have a Useful Role in the Political Arena?', *Journal of Nonprofit and Public Sector Marketing*, 14(1/2): 27–46.

Lock, A. and Harris, P. (1996) 'Political Marketing: Vive la Différence', *European Journal of Marketing*, 30(10/11): 14–24.

Mair, P. (1994) 'Party Organizations: From Civil Society to the State', in R. S. Katz and P. Mair (eds) *How Parties Organize: Change and Adaption in Party Organizations in Western Democracies*, London: Sage. [1–22]

McCombs, M. (2004) *Setting the Agenda: The Mass Media and Public Opinion*, Cambridge: Polity Press.

McNair, B. (2000) *Journalism and Democracy: An Evaluation of the Political Public Sphere*, London: Routledge.

Negrine, R. (2008) *The Transformation of Political Communication: Continuities and Changes in Media and Politics*, Basingstoke: Palgrave Macmillan.

Newman, B. I. (1994) *The Marketing of the President: Political Marketing as Campaign Strategy*, Thousand Oaks, CA: Sage.

Norris, P. (2004) *Electoral Engineering: Voting Rules and Political Behavior*, New York: Cambridge University Press.

O'Cass, A. (1996) 'Political marketing and the marketing concept', *European Journal of Marketing*, 30(10/11): 37–53.

Ormrod, R. P. (2005) 'A Conceptual Model of Political Market Orientation', *Journal of Nonprofit and Public Sector Marketing*, 14(1/2): 47–64.

Patterson, T. E. (1998) 'Political Roles of the Journalist', in D. Graber, D. McQuail and P. Norris (eds) *The Politics of News, The News of Politics*, Washington, DC: CQ Press. [17–32]

Patterson, T. E. (2000) 'The United States: News in a Free-Market Society', in R. Gunther and A. Mughan (eds) *Democracy and the Media: A Comparative Perspective*, New York: Cambridge University Press. [241–265]

Perloff, R. M. (1999) 'Elite, Popular, and Merchandised Politics: Historical Origins of Presidential Campaign Marketing', in B. I. Newman (ed.) *Handbook of Political Marketing*, Thousand Oaks, CA: Sage. [19–40]

Petersson, O., Djerf-Pierre, M., Holmberg, S., Strömbäck J. and Weibull, L. (2006) *Media and Elections in Sweden*, Stockholm: SNS Förlag.

Plasser, F. and Plasser, G. (2002) *Global Political Campaigning: A Worldwide Analysis of Campaign Professionals and Their Practices*, Westport, CT: Praeger.

Popper, K. (1959/1992) *The Logic of Scientific Discovery*, London: Routledge.

Rademacher, E. W. and Tuchfarber, A. J. (1999) 'Preelection Polling and Political Campaigns', in B. I. Newman (ed.) *Handbook of Political Marketing*, Thousand Oaks, CA: Sage. [197–222]

Reese, S. D., Gandy Jr, O. H. and Grant, A. E. (eds) (2001) *Framing Public Life: Perspectives on Media and Our Understanding of the Social World*, Mahwah, NJ: Lawrence Erlbaum Associates.

Scarrow, S. E. (2000) 'Parties without Members? Party Organization in a Changing Electoral Environment', in R. J. Dalton and M. P. Wattenberg (eds) *Parties without Partisans: Political Change in Advanced Industrial Democracies*, New York: Oxford University Press. [79–101]

Scarrow, S. E., Webb, P. and Farrell, D. M. (2000) 'From Social Integration to Electoral Contestation: The Changing Distribution of Power within Political Parties', in R. J. Dalton and M. P. Wattenberg (eds) *Parties without Partisans: Political Change in Advanced Industrial Democracies*, New York: Oxford University Press. [129–153]

Scherman, E. (1999) 'Direct Marketing: How does it Work for Political Campaigns?', in B. I. Newman (ed.) *Handbook of Political Marketing*, Thousand Oaks, CA: Sage. [365–388]

Sjöblom, G. (1968) *Party Strategies in a Multiparty System*, Lund: Studentlitteratur.

Slater, S. F. and Narver, J. C. (1998) 'Customer-Led and Market-Oriented: Let's not Confuse the Two', *Strategic Management Journal*, 19(10): 1001–1006.

Stanyer, J. (2007) *Modern Political Communication*, Cambridge, UK: Polity.

Strom, K. (1990) 'A Behavioral Theory of Competitive Political Parties', *American Journal of Political Science*, 34(2): 565–598.

Strömbäck, J. (2007a) 'Political Marketing and Professionalized Campaigning: A Conceptual Analysis', *Journal of Political Marketing*, 6(2/3): 49–67.

Strömbäck, J. (2007b) 'Antecedents of Political Market Orientation in Britain and Sweden: Analysis and Future Research Propositions', *Journal of Public Affairs*, 7(1): 1–11.

Strömbäck, J. (2008) 'Four Phases of Mediatization: An Analysis of the Mediatization of Politics', *International Journal of Press/Politics*, 13(3): 228–246.

Strömbäck, J. and Dimitrova, D. V. (2006) 'Political and Media Systems Matter: A Comparison of Election News Coverage in Sweden and the United States', *Harvard International Journal of Press/Politics*, 11(4): 131–147.

Strömbäck, J. and Kaid, L. L. (eds) (2008) *The Handbook of Election News Coverage Around the World*, New York: Routledge.

Wanta, W. and Ghanem, S. (2007) 'Effects of Agenda Setting', in R. W. Preiss, B. M. Gayle, N. Burrell, M. Allen and J. Bryant (eds), *Mass Media Effects Research: Advances Through Meta-Analysis*, Mahwah, NJ: Lawrence Erlbaum Associates. [37–51]

Webb, P. (2002) 'Political Parties and Democratic Control in Advanced Industrial Societies', in P. Webb, D. Farrell and I. Holliday (eds) *Political Parties in Advanced Industrial Democracies*, Oxford: Oxford University Press. [438–460]

Webb, P. and Kolodny, R. (2006) 'Professional Staff in Political Parties', in R. S. Katz and W. J. Crotty (eds) *Handbook of Party Politics*, London: Sage. [337–347]

Webb, P., Farrell, D. and Holliday, I. (eds) (2002) *Political Parties in Advanced Industrial Democracies*, Oxford: Oxford University Press.

Wolinetz, S. B. (2002) 'Beyond the Catch-All Party: Approaches to the Study of Parties and Party Organizations in Contemporary Democracies', in R. Gunther, J. R. Montero and J. J. Linz (eds) *Political Parties. Old Concepts and New Challenges*, New York: Oxford University Press. [136–165]

Wring, D. (2002) 'Conceptualising Political Marketing: A Framework for Election-Campaign Analysis', in N. J. O'Shaughnessy and S. C. M. Henneberg (eds) *The Idea of Political Marketing*, Westport, CT: Praeger. [171–186]

Wring, D. (2005) *The Politics of Marketing the Labour Party*, Basingstoke, UK: Palgrave.

3 Political marketing in Germany

Michaela Maier, Jens Tenscher and Kirsten Schüller

This chapter will explore the ways in which German parties use marketing. Starting with a discussion of the nature of the political and media system in Germany, it will consider the use of marketing techniques and then the extent to which parties use sales or market orientations using data from a survey, before drawing conclusions about political marketing in Germany.

The German political marketplace

The political system in Germany

The German political system can be labeled as a democratic 'hybrid', incorporating structures and procedures typical for consensual as well as for competitive democracies. Due to its federal structure there are numerous political duties and responsibilities (e.g. education, culture, taxes and fiscal policies) that continually require joint decisions between 16 regional states and the nation-state (Schmidt, 2000). Albeit there is an obligation for consensual negotiations in most cases, diverging interests and competition among regional states as well as between the federal and the regional states on the other hand are widespread.

Its current party system is best characterized as 'divided' between Eastern and Western regional states and fluid (see Niedermayer, 2002). There are five key actors and six parties which are represented in the German Bundestag: the so-called Union of Christian Democrats (CDU) and Christian Social Democrats (CSU)[1] with 226 seats, the Social Democrats (SPD) with 222 seats, the Liberals (FDP) with 61 seats, the Leftist Party (Die Linke) with 53 seats and the Greens (Bündnis 90/Die Grünen) with 51 seats.

According to the German Federal Electoral Law the members of the Bundestag 'shall be elected in a general, direct, free, equal and secret ballot by the Germans eligible to vote, in accordance with the principles of proportional representation combined with uninominal voting' (§1.1). Because every voter has two votes in Germany, it is a combination between a proportional representation and a relative majority voting system. When casting his or her first vote, the so-called 'Personenstimme' (vote for a person), the voter decides on the candidate of the electoral district based on the relative majority voting system. The second vote stands for the distribution of mandates between the parties based on the proportional representation principle (Rudzio, 2006). For the first vote, parties nominate candidates for each electoral district. The candidate who gains most of the regional votes gets a direct mandate for the national Parliament. For the second vote, parties create regional lists of candidates. As second votes are the basis for the calculation of the number of seats in the Parliament, they are even more decisive for political parties than direct votes. A party only obtains seats in the Parliament if it gets more than 5 per cent of the second votes or three direct mandates.

Summarizing the characteristics of the German political system and taking into account the assumptions of the Lees-Marshment (2001) model, it is more likely that German parties are sales-oriented than market-oriented. This is due to the multi-party system, the fact that parties are not so much person- but more party-oriented, and that the voting system is mainly based on the proportional representation principle. In such an environment, it should be difficult for parties to act in a completely market-oriented way.

Parties' and campaigns' finances

In Germany, the 'Parteiengesetz' (party law; PartG) defines how political parties are financed and what kind of financial support they receive from the state (Naßmacher, 2004).[2] The criterion for the allocation of these allowances is the relevance of a political party for the society. That relevance is measured by the success of the party in the last European, national or regional state elections as well as by the fees of party members and members of the parliaments as well as by donations to the party: see Table 3.1.

Table 3.1 Financing of party political activities in 2006 in Germany

Party	Votes[a]	Fees and donations in €[b]	Public subsidies in €[c]	Split between the German counties and the federal state[d]	
				German counties	Federal state
CDU	35,462,480	75,224,305	44,591,403	6,456,372	38,135,031
SPD	32,382,894	75,517,487	42,903,568	5,320,129	37,583,439
Grüne	9,636,909	12,256,436	9,910,264	1,359,428	8,550,837
CSU	8,667,141	16,818,517	10,781,100	1,554,466	9,226,634
FDP	8,550,438	14,136,084	9,872,068	1,168,432	8,703,636
Die Linke	7,333,176	12,161,126	8,548,936	817,932	7,731,004

Source: Deutscher Bundestag (2007: A2); only the parties represented in the national Parliament are shown here.

Notes: [a] Votes in the last European, national and 16 state elections, according to § 19a Abs. 2 PartG.
    [b] § 24 Abs. 8 PartG.
    [c] €0.85 for each of the first 4 million votes, €0.70 for each additional vote; €0.38 for every Euro in donations; taking into account a maximum of €133,000,000, according to § 19a Abs. 5 PartG.
    [d] Contribution of the German countries: €0.50 per vote in state elections, according to § 19a Abs. 6 PartG.

According to the party law, the President of the German Bundestag announces in February of each year how much subsidies the parties receive. Table 3.1 provides an overview of the revenues of the German political parties in 2006. The CDU, for example, from donations and state subsidies alone had about €120,000,000 at its disposal in 2006. According to the jurisdiction of the Federal Constitutional Court (BVerfG, 09.04.1992) this money may be used to cover the costs for election campaigns, as these are seen as part of the parties' political function.

Nature of the political market

Changes within the party system are visible reflections of ongoing transformations of Germany's political culture in general and the relationships between the party and citizens in particular. Concerning this matter, there are some key aspects which have profoundly altered the nature of the German political market. First, electoral volatility has grown continuously and rapidly especially after German reunification in 1990. While the percentage of voters changing their vote from one party to another in two consecutive national elections had been around 15 per cent until 1987, this portion had risen to an all-time maximum of 34 per cent in 2005; Eastern German voters in particular were floating between 2002 and 2005. Including those voters who had not cast their ballot in 2002 but participated in the 2005 elections or vice versa almost every second German (47 per cent) was changing his or her electoral behaviour within just three years (Weßels, 2007).

Obviously, political parties in Germany are nowadays confronted with a highly volatile electorate which asks them to do the splits between diminishing but still relevant vote bases that have to be activated and re-mobilized on the one hand, and rising numbers of floating voters on the other hand. Confronted with such a context, political marketing techniques become more and more crucial not only for electoral success, but also for holding up and re-establishing party alignments. Such attachments, i.e. party identifications, have been declining slowly and fairly constantly in Germany from the end of the 1970s to the 1990s mainly as a result of weakening traditional social ties (Arzheimer, 2006). While at the beginning of the 1980s only roughly 20 per cent of West German citizens expressed no party affiliations at all and 40 per cent were strongly attached to a party, by the mid-1990s 33 per cent of the people were completely dealigned and just 25 per cent had strong party ties (Niedermayer, 2005). The two major parties, SPD and CDU, reflecting the two most important cleavages in German society, namely class and religion, were especially affected by this decline. But still, they make up roughly 90 per cent of all party-identifiers in Germany nowadays (Schmitt-Beck *et al.*, 2006).

Since the mid-1990s the proportion of party-dealigned citizens has stayed almost constant not only in West Germany but in the Eastern part, too (Mößner, 2007). Yet, percentages of non-aligned Eastern Germans have at all times been significantly higher (above 40 per cent) and numbers of citizens with strong party-bonds have always been beneath West German levels. That is not only a result of the lack of societal roots of political parties but also of pronounced skepticism against political elites and organizations which is traditionally more widespread among East than West Germans.

Differences in political orientations and party alignments between voters in East and West Germany have not only affected their voting behaviour but also their general willingness to cast their ballots: at all national elections since reunification more East Germans were absent than West Germans – differences between the two parts of the country have varied from 2.9 per cent (1998) to 7.8 per cent (2002) (Völkl, 2007). In total, roughly 80 per cent of Germans have participated in national elections from 1990 to 2005. While turnout has almost been stable during that period, it has significantly dropped since the early 1970s when more than 90 per cent of (West) Germany's electorate cast their ballot. This is also an apparent signal for loosening ties between political parties and citizens, but also a chance and a challenge for modern political marketing.

Media system

The German media system is mainly characterized by two features: (1) its decentralization and (2) the consequences of the reunification of the two German countries in 1990 (Kleinsteuber, 2004). Although the structural relationship between the media system and the party system is not as pronounced as in other countries, the political parties in Germany still have some influence – namely on the broadcast pillar of the media system. While the Federal Constitutional Court emphasized the independence of the public broadcasting system founded after World War II from the state, it also acknowledged the possibility of introducing private broadcasting in Germany – which was finally realized in 1984. Private broadcasters quickly managed to establish themselves on the market beside the two public stations ARD and ZDF. Nowadays there is keen competition between the five most important public and private television channels in Germany.[3]

Most of the private stations nowadays belong to one of two big TV groups, the RTL Group and ProSiebenSAT.1, which are controlled by the Bertelsmann media company – actually the largest media group in Europe, comprising six investors including the Springer publishing house. They operate as international enterprises according to their business missions and without specified alliance with any political party or party political goals. The private TV programmes are licensed by state media authorities, in which all 'socially relevant groups' (political parties, churches, labour unions, trade unions and many more interest groups) have a voice regarding admission and supervision. The public TV stations are controlled by a similar construction, the Broadcasting Council, in which 'socially relevant groups' are represented. Within this Council the major political parties usually play the dominant role and fight out staffing policies (Kleinsteuber, 2004). In sum, the political parties do have some influence on the supervision of private TV channels and more significantly on important personnel decisions within the public German TV stations. However the overall impact of politicians on actual German TV programming can be seen as very moderate.

Table 3.2 Information sources before the 2005 German national elections

Medium	Germany			Age		
	Nationwide	Western part	Eastern part	18–29	30–49	50 and older
TV	56	54	66	49	56	60
Newspaper	24	25	18	23	22	26
Radio	8	8	7	7	11	5
Internet	6	6	5	14	7	1
Magazines	3	4	1	4	3	4

Source: ARD/ZDF-Wahltrend 2005, n=1.201 adults aged 18 years and older in per cent, in Geese *et al.* (2005: 614); question wording: 'From which medium did you get information with regards to the election campaign?'

The German print market is characterized by a large number of newspapers with relatively weak party political bonds. In 2006 137 independent editorial units existed, mostly local subscription newspapers, with a total circulation of around 20 million papers (Media Perspektiven, 2006). Although many German newspapers are known to have certain political standpoints, journalists' self-perceptions definitively rank journalistic standards and ethics of the profession higher than party political attitudes. As a result the political standpoint of a paper as a rule can only be identified in the commentaries: among the leading national newspapers, the *Frankfurter Allgemeine Zeitung (FAZ)* and *Die Welt* take a rather conservative position, while the *Süddeutsche Zeitung (SZ)* and the *Frankfurter Rundschau (FR)* are known to be moderate leftist and social democrat respectively (Meyn, 2004). Alternative, leftist or 'green' party positions find their platform in the *Tageszeitung (taz)*, while the most important German tabloid paper *Bildzeitung* has traditionally positioned itself as conservative or 'right-wing' (Kleinsteuber, 2004: 80)[4]: see Table 3.2.

The decisive question is how the citizens make use of these media structures. According to a representative survey by Geese *et al.* (2005), television was by far the most important information source for German citizens eligible to vote before the 2005 German national election (see Table 3.2). 24 per cent of the participants of the 2005 study said that the newspaper was the most important source for them. Radio (8 per cent), internet (6 per cent) and magazines (3 per cent) were rated as much less relevant. Regarding the relative importance of TV and newspapers, differences between East and West German citizens become visible: television is more important as a source for campaign news in the East, while newspapers have a relatively higher popularity in the West. When differentiating between age-groups it is clear that TV is the most important political news medium for citizens of every age. However, the internet has gained significance as a source for citizens younger than 30.

Political marketing techniques in Germany

Confronted with these transformations within the socio-cultural and media environment, political parties in Germany have been forced to *professionalize* their internal and external communication activities both in a structural and a strategic sense (Tenscher, 2003; see also Donges, 2000, 2008; Niedermayer, 2000; Römmele, 2002). Such processes of professionalization have become most evident during recent election campaigns and it was SPD's 1998 national parliamentary campaign which helped to leverage a new era of campaign organization and communication in Germany. In fact, as longitudinal campaign analyses demonstrate, that campaign was actually not new but in fact a lot more *sophisticated* compared to earlier campaigns – seen structurally in terms of centralization and specialization and seen strategically in terms of personalization and entertainization (Holtz-Bacha, 2007). Its lasting myth of pushing German parties to a new era of political communication has actually not been backed up by an extraordinary use of market intelligence or segmentation but has reflected primarily the *communicative* dimensions of the campaign in which chancellor candidate Gerhard Schröder, his 'war room' and 'spin doctor' became campaign issues on their own within a multi-channel campaign.

Such communicative features – the symbolic function of an external campaign headquarter and a prominent campaign manager, the personalization and entertainment value of the campaign, but also a strategic mix of intensive use of free media (particularly television) platforms and paid media channels – were adopted by other parties in consecutive elections on national and regional level too: in 2000 the FDP successfully ran the first clear market-oriented campaign at the North Rhine-Westphalia state elections. However it failed with a copy of such a campaign at the 2002 national elections.

In that year all major parties had learned their lessons from SPD's campaign victory in 1998 with respect to parties' campaign organization: all campaign headquarters were set up outside permanent party structures, most of them led by party-bound or candidate-affiliated consultants; campaign budgets were heightened significantly, campaign teams were ramped up allowing functional differentiation of campaign activities, the outsourcing of specific campaign tasks (especially online-communication and paid media activities) and different ways of market intelligence became widespread before and during that campaign (Tenscher, 2005). In the end, it was the two major parties, SPD and CDU, in particular which could profit from their financial resources and their manpower. They were perfectly equipped to conduct 'modern' campaigns. However, due to their ideological immobility their campaigns were rather sales-oriented than market-oriented. In addition, frictions between tempory campaign teams and parties' permanent personnel became apparent during the 2002 campaign – explicitly in the case of the Social Democrats, the Christian Democrats, the FDP and the PDS – forestalling clear-cut market-orientations and electoral success.

Such tensions were also manifestations of ongoing processes of professionalization in day-to-day political communications which are reflected in expanding resources and structures for in-house expertise as well as permanent collaborations with a handful of party-specific agencies doing market intelligence. Up to now such transformations with respect to routine political communications have been pushed forward in particular by the *better equipped* parties on the one hand, i.e. SPD and CDU, and the *most innovative* one, i.e. FDP, on the other hand (Tenscher, 2002). On the contrary, the Green Party has long been laggardly concerning this matter not only for financial reasons but also as a consequence of its party base's unwillingness for far-reaching marketing innovations. Still, it also conducted a centralized, candidate-driven, multi-media electoral campaign in 2002.

The most recent national campaign put political marketing in Germany to a remarkable test: elections took place on 18 September 2005 after one of the most intensive, confrontational and highly politicized campaigns post-World-War-II Germany has ever witnessed. Due to the fact that then-chancellor Gerhard Schröder surprisingly proclaimed early elections on 22 May a *high-density campaign* developed, predominantly limited to a crunch time of six weeks. Political parties were urged to condense their campaign efforts to a short period, sometimes conducting marketing activities simultaneously instead of stepwise. Time for extensive measures of market intelligence, product design and implementation as well as for the development of communicative strategies was restricted to a minimum. Consequently, those parties with the most sophisticated day-to-day structures for political marketing and largest budgets started with a competitive edge in the campaign (Tenscher, 2007). Those were namely the Social Democrats and the Christian Democrats which spent €7.2 million and €8.0 million respec - tively for their campaigns – significantly more than their smaller competitors CSU (€4.9 million), FDP (€3.5 million), the Greens (€3.8 million) and the Leftist Party (€4.3 million). All parties set up temporary campaign headquarters which were mostly managed by in-house experts, i.e. permanent and high-ranked party secretaries, and experienced campaign managers. All parties' campaign organizations were centralized, encompassing teams of up to 240 people (as in the case of SPD) and showed (with the exception of the Greens) medium to high levels of externalization and commercialization. FDP's collaboration with a team of about 40 consultants and agencies was unprecedented (Tenscher, 2007).

With respect to market intelligence, SPD's and CDU's campaigns were backed by own pre- and on-campaign polls as well as focus groups. On the contrary, all smaller parliamentary parties – with the exception of the regionally restricted CSU – abandoned focus group analyses in 2005 (as in earlier elections) which reduced their chances to identify relevant target groups and develop adequate communicative strategies. Thus, voter segmentation was mostly relevant for Christian Democrats and Social Democrats which contacted their prospective voters by different direct communicative means of narrowcasting (Gibson and Römmele, 2006). Strategically seen, those were also the two parties which conducted the most professional campaigns including various event and news activities, high degrees of personalization and negative campaigning – which holds particularly true for the Social Democrats.

Albeit their financial, personnel and structural handicaps smaller parties' campaign strategies were almost as professional as those of their major competitors in 2005. This became most obvious in their communicative strategies which included to a large extent free media platforms, namely television talk show performances of their candidates, to compensate for smaller budgets preventing extensive paid media activities. However, if asked for the relevance of different paid media and free media channels *all* campaign managers gave higher priority to gratuitous means of mass communication to reach voters (Tenscher, 2007: 80). Such a focus might impede the dissemination of political marketing in Germany – but it is foremost a reflection of relatively small campaign budgets and, not least, an extremely condensed campaign period in 2005. Consequently, sales-orientation predominated at that campaign; only SPD and CDU, backed by their comparatively sophisticated day-to-day communication structures and increased resources, showed significant, but temporary features of market-orientation.

Political marketing strategy in Germany: evaluations of parties' marketing experts

In order to provide an up-to-date picture on the attitudes of the German political parties – outside heated campaign periods – as well towards political marketing in general as on some specific features of the models proposed by Lees-Marshment, a postal survey was conducted among the marketing experts of the five major parties – CDU, SPD, FDP, Greens, and the Leftist party. The survey was conducted in October/November 2007,[5] and the results will be presented in the following. For reasons of a better clearness and understanding of our results we concentrate on comparing the two major parties, SPD and CDU, seemingly the most professionalized and best equipped parties, on the one hand, and the smaller opposition parties of the national parliament, FDP, Greens and Leftist Party, on the other hand.

Relevance of market intelligence

As reported above, on the occasion of the 2005 German national elections, a clear difference became visible between the two major and the three smaller parties with regard to the application of market intelligence during their campaigns: while all German parties nowadays make use of regular opinion polls (at least during campaign times) only the big parties invested money in focus groups. Such different evaluations regarding the relevance of market intelligence also became visible, two years later, in the results of our survey among the marketing experts of the parties (see Figure 3.1).

Big as well as small parties rated the importance of opinion polls similarly moderate with mean values of 2.5, respectively 2.3 on a scale from one ('very important') to five ('not important at all'). However, focus groups ranked significantly higher in the eyes of the big parties (mean=2.0) than in the evaluation of the small parties (mean=3.3). Taking into account the previous depiction it is not astonishing either that the marketing experts of the smaller German parties rated the relevance of the identification of target groups a little lower than representatives of the two big parties who granted that task highest priority. Although all experts found it important to find out about the needs and wishes of their voters

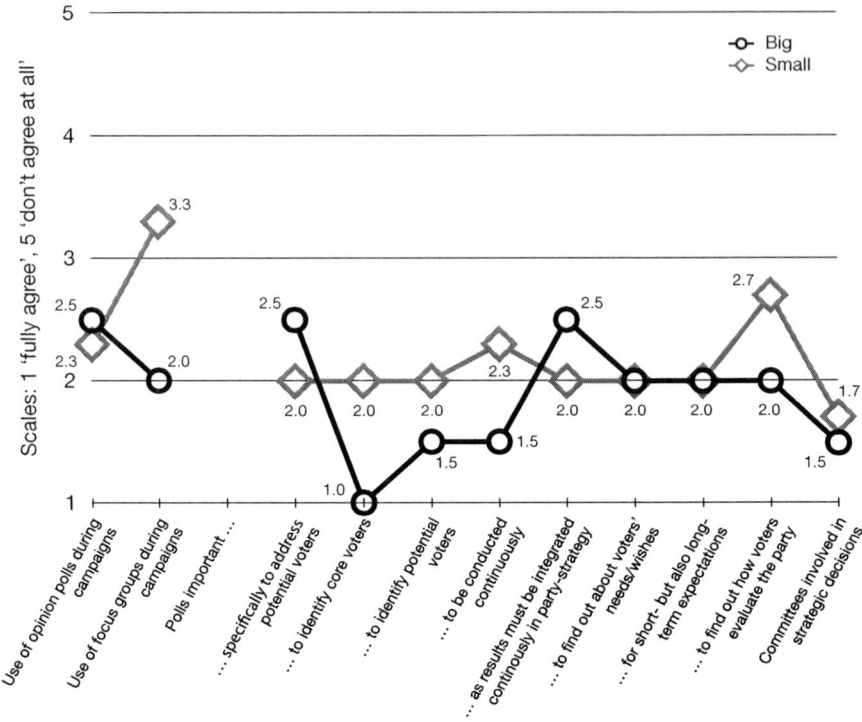

Figure 3.1 Relevance of market intelligence in Germany

and to take into consideration their short- and long-term expectations (all means 2.0), especially the big parties were a little sceptical whether the results from opinion polls had to be integrated continuously in the strategy of the party. That tackles the question how (in)flexible major parties with relatively strong societal roots and party bases might be with regards to political repositioning – especially when they are bound as grand coalitional partners (Strömbäck, Chapter 2 this volume). At the same time all parties' managers stressed the importance of getting the parties' committees involved in strategic decisions.

Influence of party and voters on the political programme

When it comes to the question as to whether party members or voters should have a stronger influence on the development of the party programme, the marketing experts of the two big parties especially come to a balanced or even reluctant estimation, rating all items in the middle of the scale (see Figure 3.2). It is interesting to see that they do not consider it so far-out to change the party's policies in order to gain votes. The smaller parties make much clearer that political programmes will always have to be a compromise between the interests of the voters and the

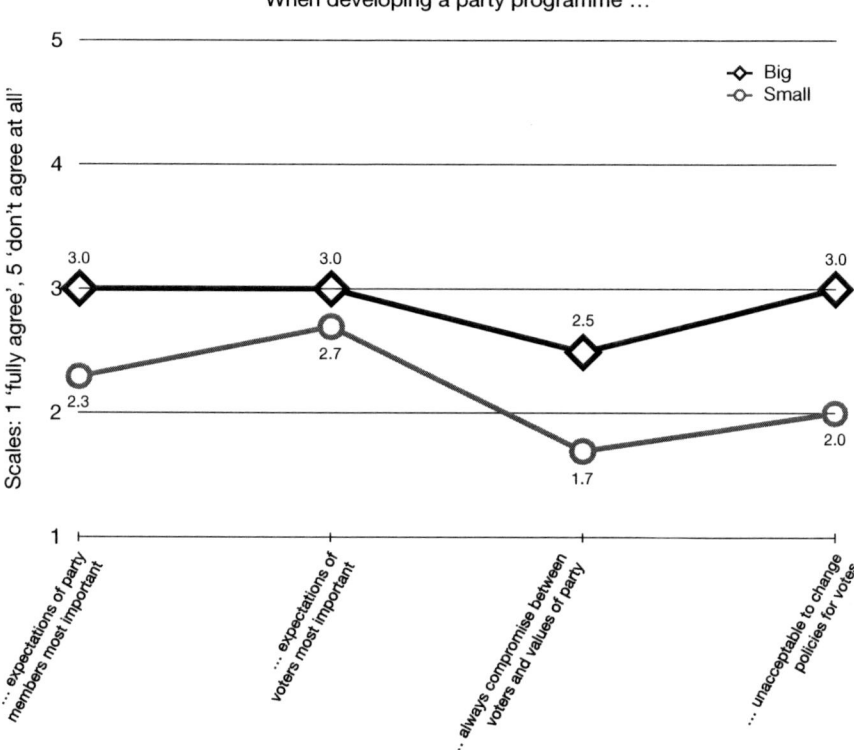

'When developing a party programme ...'

Figure 3.2 Influence of parties' and voters' interests on product design in Germany

values of the party, but that it would be unacceptable to change policies just to satisfy potential voters. Once again, this gives support to the assumption of politically – and thus strategically – rather inflexible 'catch-all' parties and rather elastic oppositional parties in Germany.[6] However, among the latter there are the Greens and the Leftist Party, who rely on relatively small and clear-cut voter groups and party bases which would not accept essential changes in policies.

Important features of the election campaign

According to the marketing experts the most important aspect during an electoral campaign in order to be successful is that the party has the appropriate policies to address important social problems (means 1.0; 1.3) and communicates these effectively enough (means 1.5; 1.3) (see Figure 3.3). However, the high ratings on the item asking for the relevance of running a professional campaign (means 1.5; 1.7) underpin our argument that the sensibility and awareness of the political parties in Germany for such a process of professionalization have considerably increased.

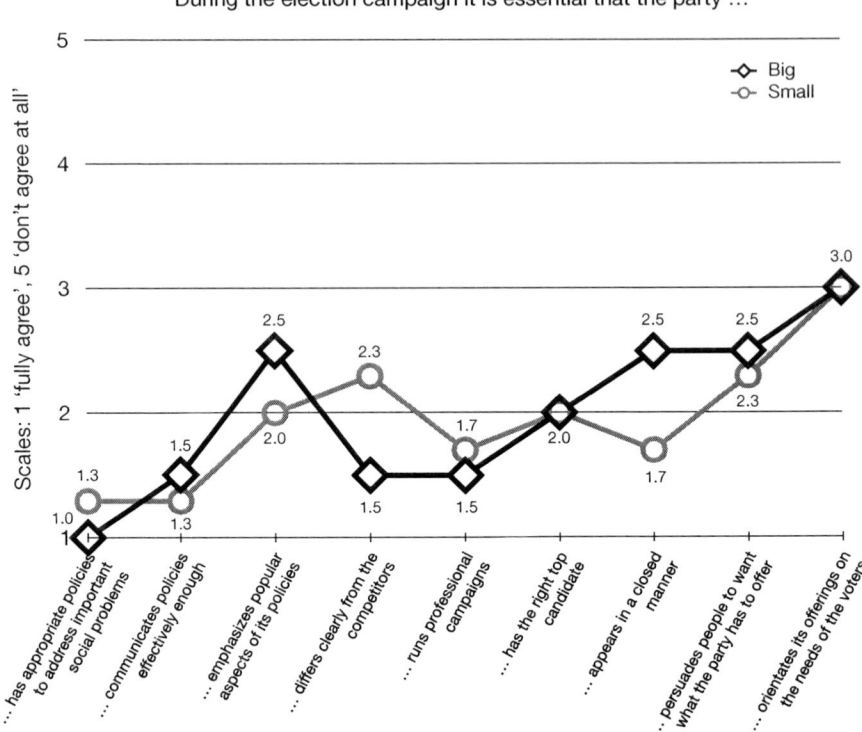

Figure 3.3 Important features of the election campaign in Germany

While the question whether a party has to persuade people of what it has to offer receives at least some approval (means 2.5; 2.3), neither the experts from the big nor from the small parties really agree that the party should orient its offerings on the needs of the voters (both means 3.0). This result is absolutely in line with the results presented above and points in the direction that even if German parties know about the importance of professional campaigns and at least partly use modern market intelligence, they are not willing to orient themselves too much towards the voters-market either. They would rather remain sales-oriented than become market-oriented.

Communication

Regarding the relevance of communication instruments and outlets during the campaign many similarities and a few characteristic differences exist between the evaluations of bigger and smaller political parties (see Figure 3.4). The election coverage by news media is regarded to be an important to very important factor by all German parties. That experts of smaller parties rank that item a little lower than bigger parties, might be due to the perception that bigger parties can draw more

'How important is/are ...'

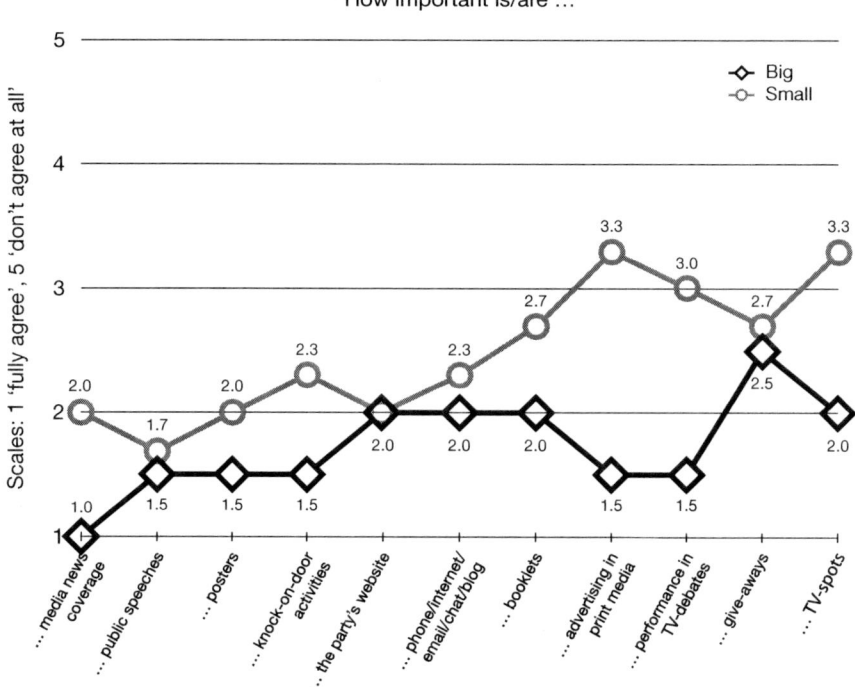

Figure 3.4 Communication instruments and outlets in Germany

media attention during a campaign. More astonishingly, good old-fashioned public speeches as significant campaign events are given very high priority. The same holds true for the use of 'traditional' posters. But immediately in the next positions are listed more 'modern' forms of campaign communication, i.e. canvassing activities on the one hand – emphasizing the increasing importance of individual campaign communication – and internet activities and interactive communication on the other.

While these forms are evaluated somehow similarly by the marketing experts of bigger as well as smaller German parties (deviation between means values maximum 1.0 scale-points), further down the list, one can find a couple of items where the size and therewith the financial potential of the parties obviously have a significant influence on the ratings: advertising in the print media as well as the performance of the top-candidates in televised debates are evaluated as very important by the big parties SPD and CDU, while smaller parties have a reluctant attitude towards these forms of communication and events.[7] There can be no doubt that the far lower financial resources of the small parties reflect in their judgement as to the importance of ads in print media. A similar argument holds true for the placement of televised ads: on German public TV all parties admitted to the election receive free airtime proportional to their influence in the national parliament. As a consequence, SPD and CDU get twice as much free advertising time as the smaller parliamentary parties. Airtime on private TV has to be bought to regular market-prices which also provides the financially better equipped parties with the opportunity to make use of this media outlet (see, e.g. Maier and Maier, 2008).

Regarding the effectiveness of different communication strategies, SPD and CDU seem to focus primarily on the demonstration of their own success and merits in the past, as one would expect from parties currently involved in the governing coalition (see Figure 3.5). At the same time they seem to feel regularly confronted with attacks from their respective political competitor and to be aware of the need to defend themselves. The relatively low ratings from all parties regarding the relevance of attack strategies are in line with other findings of current research indicating that negative campaigning is not a significant campaign strategy in Germany (Strömbäck, Maier and Maier, 2009; Tenscher, 2007).

Finally, the answers of the participants in our survey regarding the relevance of organizational aspects of the campaign again strengthen our argument regarding the increasing professionalization of electoral campaigns in Germany. All items in this section are rated as equally important: the organization of the campaign

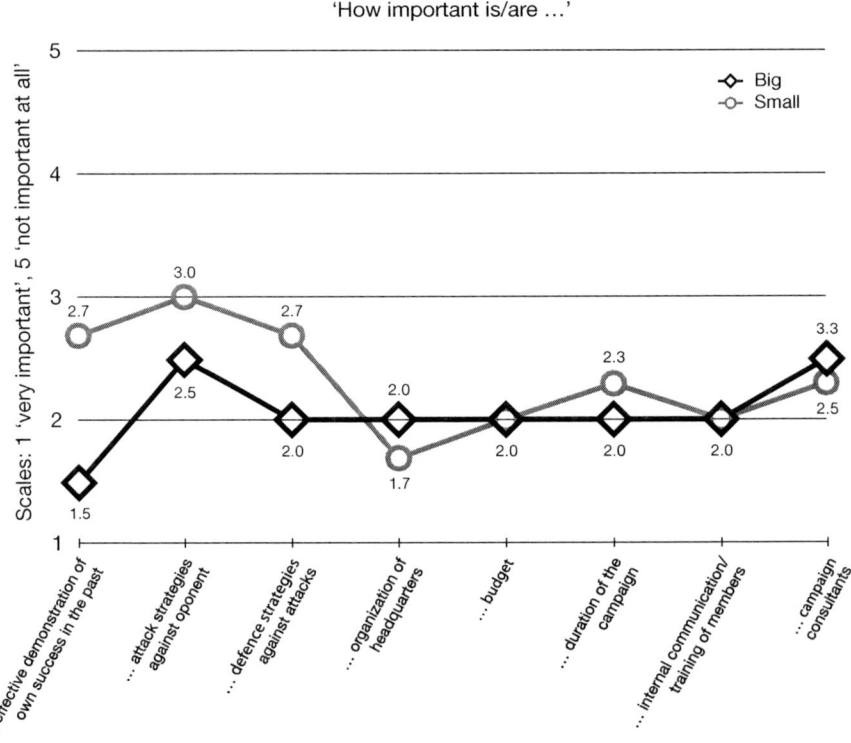

Figure 3.5 Communication strategy and organization in Germany

headquarter, the budget, the duration of the campaign as well as internal communication and training of team members – the only exemption being the use of campaign consultants which is ranked a little lower.

Political marketing trends and conclusion: status quo and trends of political marketing in Germany

As shown above, there have been some fundamental changes within the socio-cultural and media environment of German politics, especially since the 1980s, which have been altering the political market radically. On the one hand due to societal shifts and German reunification political parties have been urged to reposition themselves smoothly with respect to their ideological and political profiles. As just one example, in November 2007 SPD and CDU passed completely revised party manifestos for the first time after German reunification. On the other hand all German parties have accelerated their activities in professionalizing political communications since the late 1990s (Tenscher, 2003). Respective structural and strategic changes in political marketing have become most apparent during electoral campaigns so far, with a kick-off at the national elections in 1998, but the process of professionalization has been restrained where routine political communication is concerned (Holtz-Bacha, 2007).

Nowadays, German parties routinely use market intelligence and various 'modern' communication techniques. But they concentrate most of their efforts on electoral campaign periods. Thus, they have to be classified as *sales-oriented* (Lees-Marshment, 2001). None of the German parties has been showing *continuous* signs of marketing-orientation so far: there have been no permanent campaigns, no differentiated, ongoing efforts of marketing intelligence, no strictly voter-oriented 'product development' or nonstop efforts which could be interpreted as cyclical marketing (Lilleker and Lees-Marshment, 2005).

There are several reasons why German parties have not turned to radical market-orientation organizations yet, as we hypothesized in the introduction: first, although party attachments have been significantly declining in Germany since the 1970s, political parties still represent widely accepted ideologies and positions on the left–right continuum. As a consequence, parties are to a great extent immobile and inflexible in changing their political programmes – not least as a result of six nationally competing parties which minimize the potential for 'free' ideological repositioning. Second, with the exception of the Greens all parties are witnessing shrinking numbers of party members. Nevertheless, German parties' bases are still decisive for developing political programmes, for conducting electoral campaigns and for implementing 'modern' political marketing techniques (Donges, 2008; Wiesendahl, 2006). And there has been a widespread reluctance from parties' amateurs – not only among Greens party-members, traditionally rather base-oriented – against far-reaching, top-down structures and activities which are typical for market-oriented parties. Thus, a high degree of base-orientation has exacerbated the radical marketing orientations of German political parties. Third, as a consequence of comparatively strict rules on party financing, the predominant role of political parties and rare elections on the national and state level, the market of party-unbound political consultants, marketing and communication experts has been rather clearly arranged. Political marketing is primarily pushed forward from within the parties itself – including all restrictions mentioned.

In the end, such structural features of Germany's party and electoral system, of inter- and intra-party competition and of financial regulations will not change in the short-term. Therefore, we assume that in the long-run marketing orientations will continue to be primarily restricted to campaign periods – which rules out the idea of clear-cut market-oriented parties in Germany. In addition to that, our results suggest that the acceptance and use of political marketing techniques is – on the meso-level of the parties involved – to a negligible extent a matter of the parliamentary or government role of a party (Strömbäck, Chapter 2 this volume). In fact, party-driven political marketing seems to be foremost a consequence of financial and personnel resources, as the Social and Christian Democrats demonstrate, and the ability for top-down innovations in political communications – even against intra-party resistances. Consequently, the implementation of political marketing in Germany has been pushed forward from parties with 'strong leaders', well-equipped party structures and innovative communication managers – a process which we assume to go on with the two bigger parties leading, followed by the Liberals, and Greens and Leftist Party straggling behind.

Notes

1   CSU is running only in the state of Bavaria, and has been forming a permanent election alliance with the Christian Democrats (CDU). As a consequence, their electoral campaigns and to a lesser extent their day-to-day communications have routinely been coordinated – which has not been frictionless at all times (see Tenscher, 2005). Due to the fact that CSU is a regionally restricted party it will not be discussed in further detail.

2   Only parties which received at least 0.5 per cent of the votes in the last European or national election, or 1 per cent of the votes in one of the last state elections qualify for public subsidies.

3   In 2006 the market leader ARD with a market share of 14.3 per cent was ahead of ZDF with 13.6 per cent and the largest private TV channel RTL with 12.8 per cent. SAT.1 followed with a market share of 9.9 per cent and ProSieben with 6.6, while all other broadcasters had a market share of under 5.0 per cent (Media Perspektiven, 2006).

4   The average circulation numbers of these six papers in 2006 were: FAZ: 370,800 copies; Welt: 251,700 copies; SZ: 445,500 copies; FR: 161,300 copies; taz: 56,400 copies; BILD: 3,545,200 copies (Röper, 2006: 289).

5   The written questionnaire was developed on the basis of the survey devised by Jesper Strömbäck, discussed in Chapter 2, and adapted to the characteristics of the German political and media system. The questionnaire was sent to the marketing experts of the parties (one person per party), and it is available on request from the authors.

6   Generally speaking, the term 'catch-all parties' accentuates political parties' ambitions to reach as many voters as possible, and not only to target clear-cut, socially defined voter groups. However, such a positioning for broad voter basis implies ideological and policy-related ambiguities. As a consequence, catch-all parties seem to be strategically rather limited and inflexible when it comes to changes in their programmatic standpoints as such changes might attract some voters, but repel others.

7   With regard to the perceived importance of televised debates it has to be noted that on the occasion of the last two German national elections only the top candidates of SPD and CDU were invited to participate in these discussions (see Maurer *et al.*, 2007).

References/further reading

Arzheimer, K. (2006) 'Dead Men Walking: Party Identification in Germany, 1977–2002', *Electoral Studies*, 25: 791–807.

Deutscher Bundestag (2007) *Festsetzung der staatlichen Mittel für das Jahr 2006.* [Assessment of federal funds for the year 2006.] Stand: 26.01.2007. Verwaltung, Referat PM 3 (Parteienfinanzierung, Landesparlamente).

Donges, P. (2000) 'Amerikanisierung, Professionalisierung, Modernisierung? Anmerkungen zu einigen amorphen Begriffen', [Americanization, Professionalization, Modernization? Comments on some Amorphous Terms] in K. Kamps (ed.) *Trans-Atlantik-Trans-Portabel? Die Amerikanisierungsthese in der politischen Kommunikation* [Trans-Atlantic-Trans-Portable? The Americanization Thesis in Political Communication], Wiesbaden: VS. [27–42]

Donges, P. (2008) *Medialisierung politischer Organisationen. Parteien in der Mediengesellschaft* [Mediatization of Political Organizations: Parties in the Media Society], Wiesbaden: VS.

Geese, S., Zubayr, C. and Gerhard, H. (2005) 'Berichterstattung zur Bundestagswahl 2005 aus Sicht der Zuschauer' [News Coverage of the 2005 Parliamentary Elections from the Audience Perspective], *Media Perspektiven*, 12: 613–626.

Gibson, R. and Römmele, A. (2006) 'Measuring the Professionalization of Political Campaigning', paper presented at the 3rd International Conference on Political Marketing, Nikosia, 6–8 April.

Holtz-Bacha, C. (2007) 'Professionalisation of Politics in Germany', in R. Negrine, P. Mancini, C. Holtz-Bacha, and S. Papathanassopoulus (eds) *The Professionalisation of Political Communication*, Bristol, UK/Chicago, IL: intellect. [63–79]

Kleinsteuber, H. J. (2004) 'Germany', in M. Kelly, G. Mazzoleni, and D. McQuail (eds) *The Media in Europe: The Euromedia Handbook*, 3rd edn, London: Sage. [78–90]

Lees-Marshment, J. (2001) 'The Product-, Sales- and Market-Oriented Party: How Labour Learnt to Market the Product, Not Just the Presentation', *European Journal of Marketing*, 35(9/10): 1074–1084.

Lilleker, D. G. and Lees-Marshment, J. (eds) (2005) *Political Marketing: A Comparative Perspective*. Manchester: Manchester University Press.

Maier, M. and Maier, J. (2008) 'The Reception of European Election Campaigns and Political Involvement', in L. L. Kaid (ed.) *The EU Expansion: Communicating Shared Sovereignty in the Parliamentary Elections*, New York: Lang. [85–100]

Maurer, M., Reinemann, C., Maier, J. and Maier, M. (2007) *Schröder gegen Merkel. Wahrnehmung und Wirkung des TV-Duells 2005 im Ost-West-Vergleich* [Schröder vs. Merkel: An East–West Comparison of the Perceptions and Effects of the 2005 TV-Duel], Wiesbaden: VS.

Media Perspektiven (2006) *Basisdaten. Daten zur Mediensituation in Deutschland 2006* [Basis facts: Facts on the Media Situation in Germany in 2006], Frankfurt: Media Perspektiven.

Meyn, H. (2004) *Massenmedien in Deutschland* [Mass Media in Germany], Neuauflage 2004, Konstanz: UVK.

Mößner, A. (2007) 'Wie wahl- und wechselfreudig sind Parteianhänger? Parteiidentifikation, Nichtwahl und Wechselwahl' [How Eager are Partisans to Vote and to Change? Party Identification, Non-Voting and Volatility of Votes], in H. Rattinger, O. W. Gabriel and J. W. Falter (eds) *Der gesamtdeutsche Wähler. Stabilität und Wandel des Wählerverhaltens im wiedervereinigten Deutschland* [The German Voter: Stability and Change in Election Behaviour in Reunited Germany], Baden-Baden: Nomos. [253–275]

Naßmacher, H. (2004) 'Parteiensysteme und Parteifinanzen in West-Europa' [Party Systems and Party Finances in Western Europe], *Zeitschrift für Politik*, 1: 29–51.

Niedermayer, O. (2000) 'Modernisierung von Wahlkämpfen als Funktionsentleerung der Parteibasis' [Modernization of Election Campaigns as the Functional Depletion of the Party Basis], in O. Niedermayer and B. Westle (eds) *Demokratie und Partizipation. Festschrift für Max Kaase* [Democracy and Participation: Commemorative publication for Max Kaase], Opladen: Westdeutscher Verlag. [192–210]

Niedermayer, O. (2002) 'Nach der Vereinigung. Der Trend zum fluiden Fünfparteiensystem' [After Reunification: A Trend toward a Fluid Five-Party System], in O. W. Gabriel, O. Niedermayer, and R. Stöss (eds) *Parteiendemokratie in Deutschland* [Party Democracy in Germany], Bonn: Bundeszentrale für politische Bildung. [107–127]

Niedermayer, O. (2005) *Bürger und Politik. Politische Orientierungen und Verhaltensweisen der Deutschen* [Citizens and Politics: Political Orientations and Behaviour of the Germans], Wiesbaden: VS.

Römmele, A. (2002) 'Politische Parteien und professionalisierte Wahlkämpfe' [Political Parties and Professionalized Election Campaigns], in D. Fuchs (ed.) *Bürger und Demokratie in Ost und West. Studien zur politischen Kultur und zum politischen Prozess* [Citizens and Democracy in East and West: Studies of Political Culture and the Political Process], Wiesbaden: Westdeutscher Verlag. [448–461]

Röper, H. (2006) 'Probleme und Perspektiven des Zeitungsmarktes' [Problems and Perspectives of the Print Market], *Media Perspektiven*, 5: 283–297.

Rudzio, W. (2006) *Das politische System der Bundesrepublik Deutschland* [The Political System of Germany], Wiesbaden: VS.

Schmidt, M. G. (2000) *Demokratietheorien, eine Einführung* [An Introduction to Theories of Democracy], Opladen: Leske + Budrich.

Schmitt-Beck, R., Weick, S. and Christoph, B. (2006) 'Shaky Attachments. Individual-level Stability and Change of Partisanship among West German Voters, 1984–2001', *European Journal of Political Research*, 45: 581–608.

Strömbäck, J., Maier, M. and Maier, J. (2009) 'The Use and Effects of Negativity in Televised Debates: A Comparative Study of Germany and Sweden', paper presented at the 2009 *International Communication Association* Annual Conference, Chicago, USA.

Tenscher, J. (2002) 'Partei- und Fraktionssprecher. Annäherungen an Zentralakteure medienorientierter Parteienkommunikation', [Party- and Fraction Spokesmen: An Approach to Central Actors of Media-Oriented Party Communication], in U. von Alemann and S. Marschall (eds) *Parteien in der Mediendemokratie* [Parties in a Media Democracy], Wiesbaden: Westdeutscher Verlag. [116–146]

Tenscher, J. (2003) *Professionalisierung der Politikvermittlung? Politikvermittlungsexperten im Spannungsfeld von Politik und Massenmedien* [Professionalization of Political Communication? Political Communication Experts in the Conflicting arenas of Politics and Mass Media], Wiesbaden: Westdeutscher Verlag.

Tenscher, J. (2005) 'Bundestagswahlkampf 2002. Zwischen strategischem Kalkül und der Inszenierung des Zufalls' [The 2002 German National Election Campaign: Between

Strategic Calculation and the Staging of Coincidence], in J. Falter, O. Gabriel, and B. Weßels (eds) *Wahlen und Wähler. Analysen aus Anlass der Bundestagswahl 2002* [Elections and Voters: Cause Analyses of the 2002 Bundestag Parliamentary Election], Wiesbaden: VS. [102–133]

Tenscher, J. (2007) 'Professionalisierung nach Wahl. Ein Vergleich der Parteien-kampagnen im Rahmen der jüngsten Bundestags- und Europawahlkämpfe in Deutschland' [Professionalization to Preferencee: A Comparison of the Campaigns in the Recent National and European Election campaigns in Germany], in F. Brettschneider, O. Niedermayer and B. Weßels (eds) *Die Bundestagswahl 2005. Analysen des Wahlkampfes und der Wahlergebnisse.* [The 2005 Bundestag Parliamentary Elections: Analyses of the Election Campaign and the Election Results], Wiesbaden: VS. [65–95]

Völkl, K. (2007) 'Nichtwahl – die Alternative für parteilich Ungebundene am Wahltag?' [Non-voting: An Alternative for Voters with Party-Affiliation on Election Day?], in H. Rattinger, O. W. Gabriel and J.W. Falter (eds) *Der gesamtdeutsche Wähler. Stabilität und Wandel des Wählerverhaltens im wiedervereinigten Deutschland* [The German Voter: Stability and Change of Election Behaviour in Reunited Germany], Baden-Baden: Nomos. [15–35]

Weßels, B. (2007) 'Re-Mobilisierung, "Floating" oder Abwanderung? Wechselwähler 2002 und 2005 im Vergleich' [Re-Mobilization, "Floating" or Exit? Swing Voters 2002 and 2005 Compared], in F. Brettschneider, O. Niedermayer and B. Weßels (eds) *Die Bundestagswahl 2005. Analysen des Wahlkampfes und der Wahlergebnisse [The 2005 Bundestag Parliamentary Elections: Analyses of the Election Campaign and the Election Results]*, Wiesbaden: VS. [395–417]

Wiesendahl, E. (2006) *Mitgliederparteien am Ende? Eine Kritik der Niedergangsdiskussion* [An End to Membership-Parties? A Criticism of the Discussion of Decline], Wiesbaden: VS.

4 Political market-orientation in a multi-party system

The Swedish case

Jesper Strömbäck

The Swedish national election in 2006 was in many respects historic. Not only was it the first time that the centre- and right-wing parties formed an 'Alliance for Sweden', it was also the first time that the Social Democrats lost governing power while the economy was strong, and that the centre- and right-wing parties managed not only to win but also to form a majority coalition government. In addition, it was the first time that the largest right-wing party – the Moderate party – campaigned as 'the new Moderates' and as 'the new labour party'. On Election Day, 'the new Moderates' was the clear winner, increasing its share of voters from 15.2 per cent to 26.2 per cent.

Against this backdrop, the purpose of this chapter is to analyze the Swedish political scene, the use of political marketing techniques, and whether Swedish political parties should be characterized as product-, sales- or market-oriented.

The Swedish political marketplace

The political system

Sweden is a parliamentary monarchy where the parliament has one chamber with 349 seats. Elections are held in September every fourth year, and this includes national as well as regional and local elections. The electoral system is proportional, although there is a 4 per cent threshold that must be passed to gain parliamentary representation. There is no official campaign period, but normally the intensive phase of campaigning starts about four weeks prior to Election Day.

People primarily vote for party lists set up by the parties in the different constituencies. Since 1998 it is possible to express preference for a preferred candidate, but only 23 per cent did so in 2006. One reason for this is that a candidate, to be elected by means of preference voting, must receive at least 8 per cent of the votes cast for the party in the constituency. This works as a disincentive for preference voting. In essence, people thus vote for parties rather than for candidates, and candidates who wish to win a seat in parliament are dependent upon their parties rather than upon the electorate. This illustrates that the Swedish electoral system and democracy is very party-centred (Petersson *et al.*, 2000). Further contributing to this is that party discipline in the Swedish parliament is strong (Barrling Hermansson, 2004).

Table 4.1 Swedish elections and governments 1994–2006

	1994	1998	2002	2006
The Left party (V)	6.2%	12.0%	8.3%	5.8%
The Social Democrats (S)	45.3%	36.4%	39.8%	35.0%
The Green party (MP)	5.0%	4.5%	4.6%	5.2%
The Centre party (C)	7.7%	5.1%	6.%	7.9%
The Liberal party (FP)	7.2%	4.7%	13.3%	7.5%
The Christian Democrats (KD)	4.1%	11.8%	9.1%	6.6%
The Moderate party (M)	22.4%	22.9%	15.2%	26.2%
Turnout	**88.1%**	**81.4%**	**80.1%**	**82.0%**
Parties in government	**(S)**	**(S)**	**(S)**	**(M)+(FP)+(C)+(KD)**

Source: http://www.val.se; http://www.scb.se

Since 1994 there are seven parties represented in parliament. The Left party, the Social Democrats and the Green party belong to the left bloc, whereas the Centre party, the Liberal party, the Christian Democrats, and the Moderate party belong to the right bloc. Table 4.1 shows the election results in the last four elections, in addition to turnout and governments formed after each of the elections.

As can be seen, the Social Democrats are the largest party, and this has been the case since the 1930s. If any Swedish party can be characterized as a 'catch-all' party (Kirchheimer, 1966) it is the Social Democrats. With the exception of 1976–1982, 1991–1994 and after the 2006 election, the Social Democrats have been the governing party. Most of the time the Social Democrats formed single-party minority governments, and when the rightist parties were in government before 2006, they formed minority coalition governments.

Majority governments are thus exceptions in Sweden, and this has contributed to a political culture characterized by consensus seeking and corporatism (SOU, 1990: 44), and in comparative analyses of the political communication system, Sweden is characterized as a democratic corporatist country (Hallin and Mancini, 2004).

Table 4.1 also reveals that the election fortunes have varied significantly for different parties in the last elections. Particularly important in this context are the election results for the Moderates, that received one of their worst results in modern times in 2002 but rebounded and got their best result ever in 2006. It was in the period between these elections that the Moderates, traditionally a conservative party, elected Fredrik Reinfeldt as new party leader and re-branded itself as the 'new' Moderates and the 'new labour party'.

The major swings in the last elections are an effect of increasing electoral volatility in Sweden. The share of voters switching parties *between* two elections has increased from 11.4 per cent in 1960 to 37.1 per cent in the 2006 election. The share of voters switching parties *during* election campaigns has increased from 5.1 per cent to 20.1 per cent during the same period. Although most party-switchers change parties within the left and the right bloc, respectively, 11.8 per cent crossed the bloc line in 2006 (Oscarsson and Holmberg, 2008). Party identification has also decreased: in 1968, 65 per cent said that they identified with a particular party, and

39 per cent that they identified strongly with a particular party. In 2006, the corresponding shares were 31 and 15 per cent (Oscarsson and Holmberg, 2008). The share of late deciders – people who make their final vote choice during an election campaign – has also increased, from 18 per cent in 1964 to 57 per cent in 2006.

These trends suggest that the parties have a lot more to win, but also to lose, in each election, and that the parties have lost much of their former anchorage among the voters. Further evidence for this is that the parties, taken together, lost about half of their members between 1991 and 2004 (Petersson, 2005). This is a significant change, particularly because Swedish parties have a tradition, and a self-image, of being grassroots-movements and mass-parties rather than cadre parties (Pierre and Widfeldt, 1994). In combination with a strong egalitarian ethos in Swedish society, this can partly explain why there is skepticism towards the professionalization of politics in Sweden (Nord and Strömbäck, 2003).

The declining number of party members has however not had as severe consequences for the parties as might be expected, as the significance of party membership has also declined. One major reason for this is the introduction of state subventions to the parties in the 1960s that 'have developed into huge transfers of financial resources from the state to the parties' (Pierre and Widfeldt, 1994: 346). Today state subventions – and similar systems on the regional and the local levels – constitute the parties' main income source. The parties also seek to increase their financial resources through lotteries and fundraising, but it is mainly the Social Democrats that receive substantial sums of money through donations, primarily from the labour unions. In essence, then, the parties rely on the state for financial resources. In this, the Swedish parties are examples of the 'cartel' party-type (Katz and Mair, 2002; Krouwel, 2006). The end result is that the parties are weaker 'on the ground', but stronger as organizations and 'in office' (Nord and Strömbäck, 2003; Petersson *et al.*, 2000).

These trends notwithstanding, the left–right ideological continuum continues to be important in Swedish politics. For example, the correlation (eta) between party choice and voters' self-placement on the left-right ideological continuum was .77 in 1998, as compared with .52 in Britain (1997) and .31 (1996) in the United States (Holmberg and Oscarsson, 2004). Thus, the left–right ideological continuum continues to structure Swedish politics, while the fact that the political landscape is so crowded makes it relatively easy for a voter to switch between parties that are close to each other along this ideological continuum.

The Swedish media system

With respect to the Swedish media system, it has changed considerably during the last decades. One important change is related to the broadcasting media in general and TV in particular. Until the late 1980s, a public service monopoly was in place and there were only two TV channels and four national public service radio channels (Djerf-Pierre and Weibull, 2001). However, in the early 1990s the first commercial terrestrial TV channel was allowed, and today there are numerous TV channels to choose between. The most important channels with respect to news and public affairs are SVT1 and SVT2, both public service, and TV4, a commercial channel, but operating under a charter rather similar to the public service TV charters (Petersson *et al.*, 2006).

The broadcasting media system has thus become increasingly commercialized and competitive. This change has had consequences for the processes and the content of news journalism as well as other media genres. For example, evidence suggests an increase in soft news and in the framing of politics as a strategic game (Johansson, 2008; Strömbäck, 2008).

Another important change is related to the print media, where Sweden used to have a strong party press. Until the 1960s, people tended to read newspapers that reflected their own political views and that in terms of ownership had direct or indirect links to the parties (Nord, 2001). Nowadays all daily newspapers are politically independent, and news journalism no longer reflects party-political viewpoints (Asp, 2006). The norm of journalistic objectivity is strong (Petersson *et al.*, 2006) and mainly interpreted as 'going beyond the statements of the contending sides of a political dispute' (Patterson, 1998).

An additional change is that news journalism has increased its power vis-à-vis politicians (Esaiasson and Håkansson, 2002). If it once was the case that journalism adapted to and followed political leads, it is now rather politicians that have to adapt to the predominant media logic (Altheide and Snow, 1979; Petersson *et al.*, 2006; Strömbäck, 2008). If the relationship between journalists and their political sources is described as a continuous 'negotiation of newsworthiness' (Cook, 2005), it appears to be the case that journalists rather than politicians have the upper hand in the Swedish case (Strömbäck and Nord, 2006).

One reason for this state of affairs is that paid political advertising on TV is not allowed and the parties are not allowed any free airtime. When this book was going to print this situation changed, so now the parties are allowed to buy airtime on some of the national TV channels. The first national election where the parties can make use of paid political advertising on TV will be held in 2010. Thus, Swedish parties that want to communicate with the electorate need to do it through the news media, as news journalism constitutes the most important source of political information for most people (Petersson *et al.*, 2006). Swedish politics is thus not only mediated in the sense that it is mainly experienced through the news media but also in the sense that it has become increasingly adapted to the media logic and predominant news values employed by the media (Strömbäck, 2008). Further contributing to this situation is that few Swedes participate actively in politics or in trying to convince people to vote for a particular party (Petersson *et al.*, 2006), and that most parties are rather small and thus lack the resources needed to communicate directly and effectively with the electorate through press advertising or direct mail.

New challenges – and a conceptual clarification

The Swedish parties undoubtedly face numerous challenges. The news media they once could rely upon to transmit and support their messages have become independent; instead of the news media adapting to the parties, the parties have to adapt to the news media and their logic, and this logic often includes a critical stance towards politics. The number of members and faithful voters has declined, whereas the number of floating voters has increased. The parties have adapted to this situation by co-opting the state and through that securing their financial base, but also by strengthening the party organizations and increasing the number of employed (Petersson *et al.*, 2000; Pierre and Widfeldt, 1994; Sundberg, 2002). The question is whether they have also adapted to the changing circumstances by professionalizing their campaigning and by going from a product-orientation to a sales- or market-orientation.

In this context, the term 'professionalization of political campaigning' refers to a process characterized by increasing use of various marketing techniques, of expertise in fields such as news management, public relations and marketing, a focus on long-term or permanent campaigning, and in a centralization of power to the central campaign headquarters (Farrell and Webb, 2000; Gibson and Römmele, 2001; Strömbäck, 2007). Following the discussion in Chapters 1 and 2, a market-orientation refers to a needs assessment approach where parties make use of market intelligence to identify the wants and needs of selected groups in the electorate, and to design a political offering to meet the wants and needs of these groups. Following a market-orientation does thus not equal the use of various marketing techniques or attempts to professionalize the campaigning. Both sales- and market-oriented parties collect market intelligence and make use of marketing techniques, but only market-oriented parties do this to find out about the wants and needs of selected groups in order to meet and satisfy these.

The purpose of the rest of this chapter is to analyze the Swedish parties and their use of various marketing techniques, and whether they should be characterized as product-, sales- or market-oriented. The data comes primarily from two rounds of interviews with the party secretaries of the parties in parliament. The first round of interviews was done after the 2002 election and the second after the 2006 election. Aside from these interviews, the analysis rests upon accounts in the news media, informal discussions with party activists, and an analysis of others' research.

Political marketing techniques in Sweden

In the interviews, the party secretaries were asked whether, and to what extent, they made use of a number of specific marketing techniques. On the face of it, these questions were simple to answer, but on many occasions the interviewees were somewhat reluctant to reveal how they worked. Nevertheless, it is clear that some marketing techniques are used by all parties, if not to the same extent. All parties thus made use of direct mail and opinion polling, most parties made use of focus groups, and several parties made use of some kind of computerized databases. Several parties also did some opposition research, whereas no party did systematic research on their own strengths and weaknesses. Telemarketing was used by some parties, although not very extensively, whereas the use of public relations or media consultants external to the parties was very limited. Table 4.2 shows the marketing techniques used by the parties in the 2006 election.

Table 4.2 The use of marketing techniques in the 2006 Swedish election

	Left party	Green party	Social Democrats	Centre party	Liberal party	Christian Democrats	Moderate party
Telemarketing	No	No	Yes	No	No	Yes	Yes
Direct mail	Yes	Yes	Yes	Yes	Yes	Yes	Yes
PR/media consultants	No	No	Yes	Yes	Yes	Yes	Yes
Voter databases	No	No	Yes	Yes	Yes	Yes	No
Opinion polling	Yes	Yes	Yes	Yes	Yes	Yes	Yes
Focus groups	No	Yes	Yes	Yes	Yes	Yes	Yes
Opposition research	No	No	Yes	Yes	Yes	No	Yes
Research on own party	No	No	No	No	No	No	No
E-newsletter	No	Yes	Yes	No	Yes	Yes	Yes
External HQ	Partly	Partly	Partly	Partly	Partly	Partly	Partly

Using a particular marketing technique does not, however, equal an extensive use of it, and in fact, most parties only use the various marketing techniques to a rather limited extent. One study thus showed that on a four-point scale, where 3 represents extensive use and 0 no use at all, most parties that used a particular marketing technique only scored 1 or 2 (Strömbäck, 2009). For example, although most parties made some use of external public relations or media consultants, in general they only used their advertising agencies to stimulate thinking about messages and message strategies. Their function was only advisory. In essence, this means that the use of external campaign consultants was almost non-existent. Instead, the main strategy has been for the parties to expand their in-house expertise in campaigning. Consequently, the number of employees mainly occupied with media, public relations and marketing activities has increased by 27 between 1993 and 2003, while the total number of party employees has decreased by 168 over the same time period (Nord, 2007). As noted by Nord (2007: 88): 'there are more party people than ever engaged in modern communication practices', but 'the majority of party officials still work within traditional areas such as recruiting and training party members and articulating and consolidating political interests of the party supporters'.

While this conclusion appears to hold for all Swedish parties, there are still differences between them. The study that measured the usage of various marketing techniques (Table 4.2) thus found that in 2006, the Social Democrats ran the most professionalized campaign, while the Left party ran the least professionalized campaign (Strömbäck, 2009). A maximum use of all marketing techniques would yield a total score of 33. The Social Democrats scored 20, followed by the Moderate party (16), the Centre party, the Liberal party and the Christian Democrats (all 13), the Green party (9), and finally the Left party (6). The factors that were found to prime the parties to professionalize their campaigning were right-wing ideology, status as a catch-all party, a centralized organization, level of resources, size of the vote loss in the previous election, number of employees, and change of party leader since the previous election.

The overall conclusion that can be drawn is thus that Swedish parties do make use of marketing techniques, but the extent to which they do so varies significantly, and it is mainly the larger parties that make extensive use of various marketing techniques. Equally important is that not even the Social Democrats are close to receiving the highest score. Thus, the Swedish parties have become more heavily involved in the usage of marketing techniques, but they are far from making full use of them. Swedish parties should hence be characterized as running semi-professionalized rather than fully professionalized election campaigns.

One reason for this is that the parties are restrained by lack of resources, but other, and equally important, reasons include that most Swedish parties are rather small and that Swedish politics is still very issue-oriented. In fact, research suggests that most people vote for the party that they perceive to be closest to them on the left–right ideological continuum and with respect the issues that are considered as most important in a particular election (Holmberg and Oscarsson, 2004; Oscarsson and Holmberg, 2008). The crowded political landscape makes it relatively easy for a voter to switch from one party to another within the same bloc – thus partly explaining the high electoral volatility – but the importance of the ideological continuum shapes people's political behaviour so that they mostly switch between parties that are close to each other on the left–right ideological scale and with respect to the most important issues – thus partly explaining the electoral stability in terms of vote shares for the left and the right bloc, respectively. Election campaigns certainly matter, but a party that aims to change the basic dynamics of Swedish politics has to employ long-term strategies. In such a context, using marketing techniques might be a necessary, but certainly not sufficient, means. From this perspective, it is rather telling that all parties that increased their vote share significantly in any of the last four elections also lost ground in the following election.

Political marketing strategy in Sweden

Admittedly, investigating whether Swedish parties should be characterized as product-, sales- or market-oriented is somewhat complicated, because the terminology is rather alien in Swedish politics and no party is likely to accept any of these characterizations. Whether this is because they do not think that it is possible to apply such a framework to politics, or because it contradicts how the parties want to be perceived, is unclear. More certain, however, is that Swedish politics operates under some presumptions that might have effects on the parties' choices of orientation.

One such presumption is that party members matter and that internal party democracy is important (Petersson *et al.*, 2000; SOU, 2000:1). Another presumption follows from a mixture of two different, and partly opposing, ideals. On the one hand, there is a widespread skepticism towards elitism and professionalism in Swedish politics. Ideally, politicians should be socially representative (Petersson *et al.*, 1996; SOU 1990:44). They should also listen to people and their opinions. On the other hand, there is a widespread skepticism towards populism. To the extent that the word 'populism' is used in Swedish political discourse, it is commonly used as a word of abuse. Politicians are thus supposed both to listen to people and provide responsible leadership, and managing to listen to people without being perceived as populist is hence a tough balancing act. Yet another presumption is that the histories and the traditional policy positions of the parties are important, to the extent that major policy shifts might be taken as a betrayal of what the parties are supposed to stand for.

Thus, no party approaches a forthcoming election as a *tabula rasa*. No matter what public opinion might favour, a party cannot adopt that position if it deviates too much from that party's policy history, as interpreted by members and activists, and too radical changes might create a backlash even if the new policy position as such would be favoured by many.

Another way of putting this is to say that all parties started out as product- , that is, policy- , oriented, and this is still influencing how people, both within and outside the parties, tend to think about political parties and their rationale.

Having said this, the increasing use of political marketing techniques clearly suggests a move over time towards increasing sales-orientation. The first Swedish study guided by the Lees-Marshment framework (2001) also came to the conclusion that most parties should be characterized as sales-oriented, that no party should be characterized as market-oriented, and that some parties – the Left party, the Green party, and the Moderate party – even tended towards a product-orientation (Nord and Strömbäck, 2003). All parties emphasized their histories, their ideologies and the importance of putting out a message that was congruent with the expectations of members and activists, although all parties also acknowledged the importance of running campaigns that could reach uncertain and new voters. Thus, the main strategy was not to run campaigns based on solid market intelligence with respect to the wants and needs of selected target groups outside the parties, but to communicate a message defined through internal deliberations as effectively as possible.

Since then things might have changed, however, as suggested by the re-branding of the Moderate party as the 'new Moderates'. The question thus is: Did the 2006 election signal a market-orientation of Swedish politics in general and of the Moderate party in particular?

From the 'old' to the 'new' Moderates: A case study

In 2002, the Moderate party faced its worst election result since 1973. This happened after running a campaign with a strong emphasis on the need for lower taxes, despite polls showing that lower taxes was not high on the voters' agenda. After that election, the former leadership was heavily criticized and then-party leader Bo Lundgren had to resign. The new party leader, Fredrik Reinfeldt, was elected in October 2003, and already from the beginning it was clear that the new party leadership intended to initiate some changes in the party.

If the election of Reinfeldt as the new party leader was one starting point for the subsequent changes, an article by Reinfeldt and two of his close associates in

Dagens Nyheter, the main national newspaper, on April 4, 2004, was another. The headline was 'We are changing our economic policies'. In the article the authors explained that the party's former economic policies were unfair, in the sense that they would mostly benefit people with higher incomes, and that they in addition would result in weaker state finances. Therefore, the party leadership had decided to change economic policies, in essence moving the party more towards the centre of the Swedish political spectrum.

Never before had a party criticized itself so hard and so publicly, and never before had a party announced such a dramatic policy shift. Yet this was just the first policy shift, and in the following years, the party changed its policies with respect to many other policy areas. Already in July 2004, journalists wrote about the changes as 'a total renovation' of the party (Eriksson, 2004). This was also when the party started to talk about 'the new Moderates'. Later on, Reinfeldt started to talk about the Moderate party as the new 'labour' party.

Most of these policy shifts could be described as shifts towards the centre of Swedish politics, although people on the left insisted that the changes were only rhetorical. Internal criticism from people who defended the politics of the 'old' Moderates suggests, however, that the policy shifts were real and substantial, although the new leadership managed to get the new policies accepted at party congresses.

The motive for these changes was the conclusion that the Moderate party, in order to increase its share of voters and oust the Social Democrats from power, simply had to change and be perceived as less right-wing. The catastrophic election result in 2002 was interpreted as a clear signal that the 'old' Moderates could not continue as if nothing had happened, and it also gave the new leadership a mandate for change. Further contributing to this mandate was that the Moderate party is characterized by a rather hierarchical political culture (Barrling Hermansson, 2004).

To sum up, there is no question that the Moderate party changed a number of highly important policy stances, and that they have moved towards the middle. This move also made possible a formal 'Alliance for Sweden', made up of the centre- and right-wing parties and launched in August 2004.

One major change, underlying many of the more concrete policy changes, is that the 'new Moderates' seek to take the voters, and their understanding of everyday reality and what constitutes problems, as their starting point. As expressed by Gunilla Sjöberg, director at the Moderates' communications unit:

> To reach success it is imperative that we start from the voters' own realities. We need to talk about reality in a way that the voters understand and recognize in terms of word choice, tone and all such things, and we also need to talk about the issues, the policy issues, that voters think are the major and important issues. (Quoted in Caresten, 2006)

Per Schlingmann, the party secretary, similarly states that: 'it is the voters' everyday experiences that guide the policy formation and how we express ourselves'.

This whole change from the 'old' to the 'new' Moderates clearly suggests that the party has become more market-oriented. At the same time, in this interview Schlingmann denounces the notion that the party is market-oriented. According to him, there is a crucial difference between taking the voters' experiences and perceptions as a starting point and to seek to redress the problems that ordinary voters experience in their everyday lives, and simply following the results from various opinion polls and focus groups. Thus, according to him it is less important to use or to follow the results from polls and focus groups, and more important to do a thorough analysis of how people experience and perceive everyday life and the problems connected to that, and then formulate the policy solutions. He also says that it is important to challenge people, and that the branding of the party as the 'new labour party' was not the result of polls or focus groups.

Thus, according to the Moderates, it is not market-oriented. At the same time, it is clear that the party continuously attempts to calibrate its policies and messages so that they are in accordance with the wants and needs of selected target groups. Hence, if political market-orientation is characterized by a needs assessment approach where a party attempts to identify and then design a political offering to meet and satisfy expressed as well as latent wants and needs of selected target groups, then the Moderates should be characterized as highly market-oriented. In this context, the means used are less important than the overriding philosophy that a party should take the experiences and perceptions of ordinary people as the starting point for both policy formation and communication.

Political marketing trends and conclusion

The change of the Moderate party from the 'old' to the 'new' Moderates signals a fundamental shift in Swedish politics. It could be described as a shift from a sales- to a market-orientation, but it could also be described as a shift from the traditional concept of a political party as driven by ideology and history as interpreted by members and activists, to a new kind of pragmatism that starts from the experiences and perceptions of ordinary people. In this context it is noteworthy that the Social Democrats, after the 2006 election and under its new party leader Mona Sahlin, have signaled that they are rethinking their policies in areas where evidence suggests that the voters do not give the party high ratings. However, Sahlin has also said that the new policies must be in accordance with the party's values: 'We have to renew and modernize ourselves, but without losing the values that are ours' (TT, 2007).

Thus, there are reasons to be cautious when drawing conclusions. With respect to the Moderates, it is yet unclear how deep-rooted and lasting the changes are. As long as the 'new' Moderates are successful, members and activists that are dissatisfied with the changes will remain rather silent, but the question is what will happen when the 'new Moderates' face continuously low poll numbers or, in particular, an election defeat. Becoming *more* market-oriented does furthermore not equal *being* market-oriented. In addition, becoming more market-oriented is one thing; maintaining a market-orientation is another, and the latter can be just as difficult as the former (Lilleker and Lees-Marshment, 2005). This is particularly true when a party has governing power; sooner or later it has to make unpopular decisions. Hence, it remains to be seen how deep-rooted the changes of the Moderate party are. With respect to other parties, most notably the Social Democrats, the major question is if, or to what extent, its members and activists will accept a more than minor rethinking and renewal of the party's policies.

The conclusion with respect to Swedish political parties is otherwise that the dominant orientation is a sales-orientation, with some smaller parties, most notably the Left party and the Green party, tending towards a product-orientation. In this context it is significant that no party admits to using focus groups or polls *when developing policies*. To the extent that focus groups and polls are used, they are used to test already decided upon messages or marketing materials, or to create news that can be used to attract the media's attention.

For most parties, the members and activists – and their understanding of the parties' histories and ideologies – are crucial and decisive, and this will likely continue to be the case as long as the parties as organizations are strong and have institutional settings that allow members and activists a decisive say over policy. The 'new' Moderates notwithstanding, in the Swedish context there is a clear difference between political parties and businesses, and so far not much tolerance for a party that through its behaviour deviates too much from a traditional understanding of what political parties are and how they should act. This works as a disincentive for the market-orientation of political parties, as does the fact that Sweden has so many parties. In fact, the crowded political landscape in itself makes it difficult for more than a few parties to become market-oriented, because any significant policy shift would open up a policy space that can be occupied by another party. From this perspective it is not surprising that the first party to become more market-oriented is the Moderates: it does not have a competitor on its right flank. Thus, people on the right might continue voting for the 'new Moderates', not because they like the changes but because there is no alternative party to vote for.

To sum up, the major conclusion is that all Swedish parties make efforts to professionalize their campaigning and increase their skills and usage of marketing techniques, but at the present stage they should be characterized as running semi-professionalized rather than fully professionalized campaigns, and so far the majority of the Swedish parties should be characterized as sales- rather than as product- or market-oriented. Although it is highly likely that the Swedish parties will continue to professionalize their campaigning and expand their usage of marketing techniques, it is less likely that they – taken as a whole – will become significantly more market-oriented. As long as Sweden has a multi-party system and such a crowded political landscape, and as the cultures and institutional structures of the parties give the members and activists a decisive say over policies, a political sales-orientation will likely be the rule, and political market-orientation an exception.

References/further reading

Altheide, D. L. and Snow, R. P. (1979) *Media Logic*, Beverly Hills, CA: Sage.

Asp, K. (2006) *Rättvisa nyhetsmedier. Partiskheten under 2006 års medievalrörelse*, Göteborg: JMG/Göteborgs Universitet.

Barrling Hermansson, K. (2004) *Partikulturer*, Uppsala: Statsvetenskapliga institutionen, Uppsala Universitet.

Caresten, P. (2006) *Från gammalt högerspöke till nytt arbetarparti. De nya moderaternas politiska kommunikation under valrörelsen 2006*, unpublished BA-thesis, Uppsala: MKV/Uppsala Universitet.

Cook, T. E. (2005) *Governing with the News: The News Media as a Political Institution*, 2nd edn, Chicago: University of Chicago Press.

Djerf-Pierre, M. and Weibull, L. (2001) *Spegla, granska, tolka. Aktualitetsjournalistik i svensk radio och TV under 1900-talet*, Stockholm: Prisma.

Eriksson, G. (2004) 'M helrenoverar partiet', *Dagens Nyheter*, 7 July.

Esaiasson, P. and Håkansson, N. (2002) *Besked ikväll! Valprogrammen i svensk radio och TV*, Stockholm: Stiftelsen Etermedierna i Sverige.

Farrell, D. M. andWebb, P. (2000) 'Political Parties as Campaign Organisations', in R. J. Dalton and M. P. Wattenberg (eds) *Parties without Partisans: Political Change in Advanced Industrial Democracies*, New York: Oxford University Press. [102–128]

Gibson, R. and Römmele, A. (2001) 'Changing Campaign Communications: A Party-Centered Theory of Professionalized Campaigning. *The Harvard International Journal of Press/Politics*, 6(4): 31–43.

Hallin, D. C. and Mancini, P. (2004) *Comparing Media Systems: Three Models of Media and Politics*, New York: Cambridge University Press.

Holmberg, S. and Oscarsson, H. (2004) *Väljare. Svenskt väljarbeteende under 50 år*, Stockholm: Norstedts Juridik.

Johansson, B. (2008) 'Popularized Election Coverage? News Coverage of Swedish Parliamentary Election Campaigns 1979–2006', in J. Strömbäck, M. Ørsten and T. Aalberg (eds) *Communicating Politics: Political Communication in the Nordic Countries*, Göteborg: Nordicom. [181–193]

Katz, R. S. and Mair, P. (2002) 'The Ascendency of the Party in Public Office: Party Organizational Change in Twentieth-Century Democracies', in R. Gunther, J. R. Montero and J. J. Linz (eds) *Political Parties: Old Concepts and New Challenges*, Oxford: Oxford University Press. [113–135]

Kirchheimer, O. (1966) 'The Transformation of Western European Party Systems', in J. LaPalombara and M. Weiner (eds) *Political Parties and Political Development*, New Haven, CT: Princeton University Press. [177–200]

Krouwel, A. (2006) 'Party Models', in R. S. Katz and W. Crotty (eds) *Handbook of Party Politics*, London: Sage. [249–270]

Lees-Marshment, J. (2001) *Political Marketing and British Political Parties: The Party's Just Begun*, Manchester: Manchester University Press.

Lilleker, D. G. and Lees-Marshment, J. (2005) 'Conclusion: Towards a Comparative Model of Party Marketing', in D. G. Lilleker and J. Lees-Marshment (eds) *Political Marketing: A Comparative Perspective*, Manchester: Manchester University Press. [205–228]

Nord, L. W. (2001) *Vår tids ledare. En studie av pressens politiska opinionsbildning*, Stockholm: Carlssons.

Nord, L. W. (2007) 'The Swedish Model Becomes Less Swedish', in R. Negrine, P. Mancini, C. Holtz-Bacha and S. Papathanassopoulos (eds) *The Professionalisation of Political Communication*, Bristol: Intellect Books. [81–96]

Nord, L. W. and Strömbäck, J. (2003) *Valfeber och nyhetsfrossa. Politisk kommunikation i valrörelsen 2002*, Stockholm: Sellin & Partner.

Oscarsson, H. and Holmberg, S. (2008) *Regeringsskifte. Väljarna och valet 2006*, Stockholm: Norstedts juridik.

Patterson, T. E. (1998) 'Political Roles of the Journalist', in D. Graber, D. McQuail and P. Norris (eds) *The Politics of News – The News of Politics*, Washington, DC: CQ Press. [17–32]

Petersson, O. (2005) *De politiska partiernas medlemsutveckling*, Stockholm: SNS Förlag.

Petersson, O., Djerf-Pierre, M., Holmberg, S., Strömbäck, J., and Weibull, L. (2006) *Media and Elections in Sweden*, Stockholm: SNS Förlag.

Petersson, O., Hermansson, J., Micheletti, M., and Westholm, A. (1996) *Demokrati och Ledarskap*, Stockholm: SNS Förlag.

Petersson, O., Hernes, G., Holmberg, S., Togeby, L., and Wängnerud, L. (2000) *Demokrati utan partier?* Stockholm: SNS Förlag.

Pierre, J. and Widfeldt, A. (1994) 'Party Organizations in Sweden: Colossuses with Feet of Clay or Flexible Pillars of Government?' In R. S. Katz and P. Mair (eds) *How Parties Organize. Change and Adaption in Party Organizations in Western Democracies*, London: Sage. [332–356]

SOU (1990) 'Demokrati och makt i Sverige', Stockholm: Fritzes.

SOU (2000) *En uthållig demokrati. Politik för folkstyrelse på 2000-talet*, Stockholm: Fakta Info Direkt.

Strömbäck, J. (2007) 'Political Marketing and Professionalized Campaigning: A Conceptual Analysis', *Journal of Political Marketing*, 6(2/3): 49–67.

Strömbäck, J. (2008) 'The Swedish Election News Coverage: Towards Increasing Mediatization', in J. Strömbäck and L. L. Kaid (eds) *Handbook of Election News Coverage Around the World*, Mahwah, NJ: Lawrence Erlbaum Associates. [160–174]

Strömbäck, J. (2009) 'Selective Professionalization of Political Campaigning: A Test of the Party-Centered Theory of Professionalized Campaigning in the Context of the 2006 Swedish Election', *Political Studies*, 57(1): 95–116.

Strömbäck, J. and Nord, L. W. (2006) 'Do Politicians Lead the Tango? A Study of the Relationship between Swedish Journalists and their Political Sources in the Context of Election Campaigns', *European Journal of Communication*, 21(2): 147–164.

Sundberg, J. (2002) 'The Scandinavian Party Model at the Crossroads', in P. Webb, D. Farrell and I. Holliday (eds) *Political Parties in Advanced Industrial Democracies*, Oxford: Oxford University Press. [181–216]

Tidningarnas Telegrambyrå (TT) (2007) 'Självkritisk Sahlin lovade förnyelse', 1 May.

5 New Zealand political marketing

Marketing communication rather than the product?

Jennifer Lees-Marshment[1]

New Zealand is a small country, with only just over four million people, but its' politicians, journalists and advisors are internationally connected and Helen Clark, the Labour Prime Minister from 1999 to 2008, adopted many ideas from Tony Blair's UK New Labour. Although two main parties, Labour and National, dominate, proportional representation has fostered a multi-party system and coalition governments. This chapter will focus on Labour and National and consider the potential as well as limitations for political marketing. Like other chapters I will explore the nature of the political system, the use of political marketing techniques, overall strategy and orientation of parties, and current trends and issues.

The New Zealand political marketplace

The party and electoral system

New Zealand's voting system was previously first-past-the-post but changed to a MMP (mixed member proportional representation) system for the 1996 election. As this chapter focuses on party behaviour since 1996, all analysis comes under the PR system. MMP allocates seats according to the party's share of the total party votes cast, and to date governments have been made up of coalitions or support agreements between a major party and one or more of the minor parties. However, although the MMP system fosters smaller parties, the system remains dominated by the two main parties, Labour and National, in terms of seats and votes (see Table 5.1).

New Zealand's parliament is unitary, with just one chamber; furthermore it has short parliamentary cycles with elections having to be called within three years of each other. On one hand the three-year cycle might enhance permanent campaigning. However in government, this undoubtedly affects the ability of a party to deliver – but gives it greater justification to ask for re-election for the time to deliver so parties expect to be in power for at least two terms. The three-year electoral cycle also affects the potential for a party to change and adopt a market-orientation – three years is not long to have a post-election analysis, elect a new leader, do market intelligence, develop a new product design, adjust it, implement it, and communicate it to the public. This creates forces against the development

Table 5.1 Parties, election results and government formation in New Zealand: the 1999, 2002 and 2005 elections

Party	1999 *Seats won*	2002 *Seats won*	2005 *Seats won*	2008
Labour	49	52	50	43
National	39	27	48	58
Alliance	10	0	0	0
Act	9	9	2	5
Greens	7	9	6	9
New Zealand First	5	13	7	0
United Future	1	8	3	1
Progressive coalition	–	2	–	0
Maori Party	–	–	4	5
Jim Anderton's Progressive	–	–	1	1
Progressive Party	–	–	1	–
Government formed	Labour, in coalition with the Alliance, with support from the Greens	Labour in coalition with the Progressives, and with a supply-and-confidence agreement with United Future	Labour, in coalition with Jim Anderton and via a supply-and-confidence agreement with New Zealand First and United Future	National, in coalition (confidence and supply agreements) with Act, Maori and United Future

Source: New Zealand election study; see www.nzes.co.nz and New Zealand Electoral Commission, www.elections.org.nz/elections/article_126.html

of a market-orientation by the opposition party, and maintenance of responsiveness by the government in power. The system in New Zealand therefore both fosters and inhibits the development of market-oriented parties, and as analysis will show, there is every likelihood of more sales-oriented forms and focus on sales techniques to win elections rather than changing the product.

Party distribution and ideology

The two major parties generally occupy left- and right-wing positions on the ideological spectrum, but as with most political systems they compete in the middle ground. Debates about the free market occurred in the 1980s and changes were introduced by the Labour Party itself whilst in government, and National being pro-market supported this; since 1996 Labour has practiced effective internal management under Helen Clark and National's supporters remain deferent to the leadership. Whilst smaller parties are free to pursue particular views, they relate more to their particular controversial and well-known leaders than traditional ideological positions and increasingly practice pragmatism in relation to the major parties, remaining open to coalition with either Labour or National. There remains competition between some minor parties and the major ones: Act, which is traditionally focused on liberal economics, competes with National for the right-wing economic vote; whilst the Greens seek the same environmentally friendly voters and Maori non-white voters that Labour does (see Miller 2005 for further detail).

The political consumer

Whilst it could be argued that New Zealand has also seen a rise in the political consumer, available data fails to provide clear trends, with indicators such as party identification, satisfaction, and timing of vote showing variation from one election to the next. Satisfaction with democracy as measured by the New Zealand election study is fairly positive but up and down from one election to another, ranging from near 80 per cent in 1996 (the earliest election for which such data is available), to 57 per cent in 1999, to 75 per cent in 2002, and then 65 per cent in 2005. The variation in practice from one election to another creates a degree of uncertainty and unpredictability, rather than clear trends arguing for the wholesale rise of the political consumer. Data on when people decide to vote also indicates a mixed picture when considering when people decide to vote (see Table 5.2). This means parties have to consider all aspects of their behaviour at all times.

Election analysts suggest voters are volatile (see Vowles 2002: 17–18), but on the other hand party identification results suggest quite positive results, with between 38 and 47 per cent in the 1999/2002/2005 elections identifying strongly or very strongly with a party. However, this is arguably affected by significant missing data from the New Zealand Election Study of between 35 and 42 per cent.[2]

More qualitative discussion suggests more evidence in support for the political consumer. In terms of linkage between income and vote, both major parties have to compete for floating voters in the middle segment: the Labour Party's traditional supporters from low-income workers will not provide sufficient votes to maintain major party status or win power; and National does not have a large enough secure base from more affluent voters. It is difficult for both parties to respond to this middle ground whilst retaining a distinctive product offering which also draws on elements of their ideological history. Party strategists and politicians are aware of

Table 5.2 When decided to vote (party vote) in New Zealand, 1999, 2002 and 2005 (%)

	Long ago	Year of election but before campaign	Campaign, before last week	Last week	Election day
1992	25	20.3	20.5	13.3	12.2
2002	29.1	9.6	28.0	20.2	13.1
2005	31.7	20	19.1	11.7	10.2

Source: New Zealand election study; see nzes.co.nz

this but do not find easy solutions, as Murray McCully, National MP and strategist said when interviewed:

> In 2002 we fundamentally failed to secure our base, and just went fishing in the centre and that looked real bad, and was real bad. And the public rewarded us for it. If you look at the difficulties Mr Cameron is experiencing in the UK at the moment in that sort of territory. Don Brash reasserted the core beliefs of the National Party and re-established our core base. Now what John Key has been able to do is capitalize on that and start to build on it. (McCully 2007, interviewed by author)

Declining turnout is an issue of concern for the New Zealand Electoral Commission as in other countries. However, although data from the Electoral Commission shows a decline in turnout since 1984 where it reached 93.7 per cent, on average it has remained above the 80 per cent mark. What parties care more about is getting their *own* supporters out to vote. The Labour Party has worked hard to understand who is enrolled and who might not vote, and target them with an issue that gives them a reason to vote in order to increase turnout. In the 2005 election Labour mailshot to state house tenants in South Auckland increased voter turnout amongst their traditional supporters and thus significantly increased their overall support.

Political communication and political advertising

Political communication trends in New Zealand mirror those of other liberal democracies. Although the media market is much smaller, a reflection of the relatively small population, parties have no control over the media and need to engage in the usual media management (Atkinson 2006). Each region (the main centres being Auckland, Christchurch, Wellington and Dunedin) has its own distinct newspapers which remain in circulation although with falling numbers (see Hayward and Rudd 2004). The main source remains evening television news, either on commercial TV3 or the government regulated TVNZ. TVNZ is not a typical public service broadcaster and is run on commercial lines with advertising (Comrie and Fontaine 2006; see also Cocker 2006). In a smaller country where everyone knows each other there is not an endless supply of journalists, so relationships of trust between government and the media are even more important. The former Prime Minister Helen Clark (1999–2008), spent significant time courting and talking to journalists directly. Parties cannot purchase paid political advertising; it is only allowed during election campaigns and time is allocated by the Electoral Commission. Whilst the main parties are allowed to present relatively long, 12-minute campaign openings on television at the start of a campaign, all party election broadcasts after that are short – less than 30 seconds – and consequently parties rarely present detailed policy.

A further restriction came into place in 2008 after the government passed a new Electoral Finance Act at the end of 2007, which restricted the amount of money parties could spend in the campaign from the beginning of 2008. Strategists suggested the effect of this would be to encourage parties to put more emphasis on PR stunts to get free media attention and viral emails which did not cost. This was repealed after the 2008 election, but for that election it restricted spending and also added a further layer of uncertainty to election planning.

Effect on political marketing

Altogether, whilst New Zealand shares some of the same trends towards a volatile and consumerist- and media-dominated political market with other Western liberal democracies, the pattern is not one of a clear trend, resulting in varying market conditions at each election since 1996. As Levine and Roberts (2007: 359) noted in their post-2005 election study, polls in 2005 showed 'volatility rather than consistency, leaving commentators grasping for meaning in figures that left many gaping in disbelief'. New Zealand also presents some other distinctions: the three-year cycle discourages opposition parties from communicating their distinctive product a year in advance of the election as happens in the UK or in the USA during the primaries and long-campaign. Not only does the multi-party system discourage smaller parties from adopting market-oriented positions, as we would expect, but the overall nature of the whole system enables both major parties to adopt both market- and sales-oriented positions. Whilst parties may move closer towards a market orientation after losing successive elections, as Labour did in 1999, and National for 2008, in government they may revert to a sales-oriented approach, whilst minor parties in opposition tend to adopt product or sales approaches suitable to smaller, more defined markets. It is difficult for parties to follow the market-oriented framework in full, the overall system and market are more variable, and parties are as likely to be sales-oriented both in opposition as well as government.

Political marketing techniques in New Zealand

New Zealand party staff and politicians also convey a growing appreciation of the importance and value of sharing political marketing techniques and ideas on a global scale such as targeted, market-oriented communication. They often visit their counterpart's conference in Australia and the UK to share ideas. As James (2008) noted 'both major parties draw on United States, British and Australian innovations'. National employed the same expert in 2005, Mark Textor from the firm Crosby-Textor, as the Australian Liberal Party. UMR is the polling firm for Labour. John Key, who became leader of National from 2006, visited the UK Conservative Conference in 2006 and has emulated David Cameron in many ways. In 2007 National were using David Farrar with the company Colenso (first used by the Party in 1975 and 1978) for focus groups. Kiwi international links can work the other way: National gave John Ansell's billboards to the Australian Liberal Party who then gave them to the Canadian Liberal Party who used them in 2006.

The New Zealand Labour party's campaign in 2008 was influenced by the Australian Labor Party's 'Kevin07' campaign, while ideas drawn from their UK counterpart included the 'credit card of commitments' and the listing of party achievements in each electorate or on individual MP websites.[3] However the use of the internet and in particular more two-way communication involved in e-marketing and online networking utilized in the USA had not permeated New Zealand politics by the 2008 election, perhaps due to what it would cost parties both financially and in terms of time, lack of universal broadband internet usage and the relatively small size of the country. Whether the marketing expertise being used is imported or indigenous, the important point is that, in a multi-party market such as exists in New Zealand, marketing sales techniques in a close election can make a difference to the overall result.

Political marketing strategy in New Zealand

New Zealand political leaders and strategists are always looking to the rest of the world for ideas on how to win elections, creating forces for the development of market-oriented behaviour. Helen Clark came to power in 1999 after adopting a similar strategy to Tony Blair, using a Labour Listens exercise, pledge cards and a focus on key achievable issues to suit the middle ground, as well as strategic plans (Rudd 2005). Clark was successful in managing her party effectively and integrated leadership-/party-led policies into an overall responsive product, achieving a more balanced and comprehensive market-orientation (see Lees-Marshment 2006). Labour went on to win again in 2002 and 2005.

From this, we might expect this chapter to provide further evidence of the dominance of a market-oriented approach. However this is not the case. Analysis will focus on major party behaviour in the last two electoral periods, the 2005 election, and behaviour up to 2008, utilizing secondary sources, official primary interviews with key advertisers, party staff and strategists, a former party leader, and informal conversations with party leaders, strategists and journalists, and both post-hoc (in the case of 2005) and pre-hoc analysis (in the case of 2008). Whilst such research is subject to the usual limitations of qualitative research it provides interesting perspectives on the variability and fluctuation of political marketing strategy in New Zealand.

Political marketing in the 2005 election: Dominance of a sales-orientation?

The 2005 election showed strong elements of a more sales-oriented attitude amongst both major parties and they sought to use marketing techniques to win what turned out to be a very close contest.

Like other parties who have been in power for a long time, Labour focused on its achievements in delivery – such as low unemployment, 10,000 modern apprentices, increased spending on health and education, and the implementation of a new benefits scheme called Working for Families which supplemented low-middle parental incomes if they were working – but added clear new pledges for its proposed third term (see Table 5.3). The tangibility and clarity of the pledges

Table 5.3 New Zealand Labour's 2005 pledges: 'My Commitment to You'

1. No interest on student loans
2. Final date for Treaty claims 2008
3. Increase rates rebate
4. KiwiSaver
5. 250 extra community police
6. More cataract and major joint operations
7. 5,000 more modern apprenticeships

remained therefore, unlike those of the UK Labour Party whose pledges became vaguer over time.

Unusually for a party seeking a third term, Labour's leader remained a strength, at least against the opposition. Clark was willing to show a co-operative approach – necessary to make coalition government succeed – and campaigned with Jim Anderton, leader of the Progressive Party, as well as with the co-leader of the Greens. However a decline in responsiveness was evident from advertising: as Robinson noted in 2005,

> Labour's opening night leadership message has gone from being target-voter oriented with a message of empathy and caring for ordinary Kiwis, to being more detached and product-oriented, focused on selling the inspirational virtues of its leader irrespective of the needs of voters. (2007: 15)

Clark was featured telling the 'camera' why New Zealand was good, rather than listening to voters share their concerns – more of a product- than a market-oriented approach.

Responsiveness in 2005 came in the form of last-minute policy development of targeted campaigning aimed at students and tenants of state houses. Labour attracted the student market by saying interest would be waived on loans, to encourage Kiwi students to stay or return home (previously if they went abroad payments were deferred). To attract and mobilize tenants of state-owned homes, particularly in South Auckland where there were many potential Labour voters who might otherwise not turn out, Labour sent a mock eviction notice, stating that if National won, tenants would be forced out of their homes. Labour sent these notices during the last few weeks of the campaign. Not surprisingly turnout – and Labour votes – went up and helped to secure victory. Labour won the election – but only just. Their use of marketing was more tactical than strategic.

The National Party also demonstrated more of a sales-orientation than market-orientation. Don Brash, leader of the National Party 2003–2005 recalled when interviewed (2007) that 'my gut feel was the thing which determined the major issues on which we would focus'. And [re: market intelligence data] 'I am one of those who think they are less useful than some others. Some people place very heavy store on them. I tend not to'. Similarly John Ansell, his advertiser, noted how he aimed to show distinctiveness rather than responsiveness:

For 2005 [National] badly needed to find ways to show voters that the two main parties were not two peas from the same pod. . . . Don Brash . . . was clearly not going to be mistaken for a Tweedledee to Clark's Tweedledum. I saw it as my job to show the contrast. (2007, interviewed by author)

National abandoned previously electorally unpopular policies on superannuation, anti-nuclear legislation and four weeks' leave; successfully focused internally on the 'Super blues', pensioner-age members; and underwent reorganization after a period of internal consultation (see Joyce 2007: 105). But further policy development was constrained by Brash on becoming leader in 2004. Brash took a more right-wing approach to focus on traditional National issues: economic growth, welfare reform, education, law and order – more generally security, and the Treaty of Waitangi. He gained attention – and an increase in poll support – when he gave a speech in Orewa which argued for all New Zealanders to be treated the same, regardless of race. However, other events generated negative publicity, such as when he struggled to climb into a racing car and when he was photographed 'walking the plank' to board a boat.

National's political communication was successful in gaining media attention and making a clear distinction between the two parties. John Ansell, designed iconic billboards for the party with a '*red/blue* split billboard device' with contrasting Labour and National colours and positions (see Figure 5.1), so 'the voter could see both sides of an argument, not just one' (Ansell 2007).

Brash observed that 'we got a huge amount of television and print media coverage of the billboards, and that multiplied the effect of them . . .' (Brash 2007). Ansell won awards for his work. However what the party failed to do was convey the image of a party ready to govern, capable of taking mature decisions in a constrained situation that government creates. It was more sales-oriented than market-oriented in nature. The campaign was even almost product-oriented and elitist at times. One of National's big mistakes in 2005 was to appear not to think it worth being open to coalition partners prior to the election. Whilst it remains hypothetically possible for a party to win an absolute majority of seats under MMP, no party has so far achieved this. So, for a party to appearing unwilling to even consider that it may not be able to govern alone, can make a party seem aloof and arrogant.

However, National's approach in 2005 got the Party close to winning. Joyce (2007: 114) noted that 2005 was 'the story of the recovery of a major New Zealand political brand'. If it had won, would we be trying to argue it was a market-oriented party that succeeded? Or a sales-oriented party that succeeded and so we would have to re-address our understandings of political marketing? Perhaps not, given that Labour also adopted a sales-oriented approach, as the theory has always argued it was the party closest to the market-oriented party model that would win – and Labour was closer to a market-oriented party even if it was still far from following the model. The key difference between a market- and a sales-orientation is a way of thinking about the electorate. The leader's thinking, as evidenced by an in-depth interview with Brash, was more sales- than market-oriented. But it does

```
┌─────────────────────────────────────┐
│              Welfare                 │
│                                      │
│       Drift Net. Safety Net.         │
│                                      │
└─────────────────────────────────────┘
```

```
┌─────────────────────────────────────┐
│                Tax.                  │
│                                      │
│                Cut.                  │
│                                      │
└─────────────────────────────────────┘
```

```
┌─────────────────────────────────────┐
│           Which school?             │
│                                      │
│       We decide. You decide.         │
│                                      │
└─────────────────────────────────────┘
```

```
┌─────────────────────────────────────┐
│        What's best for your kids?    │
│                                      │
│          Excuses. Exams.             │
│                                      │
└─────────────────────────────────────┘
```

```
┌─────────────────────────────────────┐
│           Violent criminals          │
│                                      │
│   Out in no time. Do the whole time. │
│                                      │
└─────────────────────────────────────┘
```

```
┌─────────────────────────────────────┐
│            Health spending           │
│                                      │
│        Pen-pushers. Patients.        │
│                                      │
└─────────────────────────────────────┘
```

Figure 5.1 Ansell's red/blue split billboard device in the 2005 New Zealand election

show further variability of both behaviour in practice and judgement in academic analysis.

Political marketing 2005–2008[4]

After the 2005 election both major parties demonstrated a desire to become more market-oriented but neither did so comprehensively. Whilst National succeeded in gaining power from Labour at the 2008 election, the win was not substantial and Clark left after the election with her reputation and the party morale intact and having ensured 30 new Labour MPs had got into power.

The new National leader, John Key, appealed to ordinary voters across market segments. His background was a mixture: he is an extremely rich and successful businessman but is the son of a single-mother immigrant. John Key visited the UK Conservative Party conferences in 2006 and 2007 and discussed strategy with David Cameron, as well as other main party figures. Key also received advice from the Australian firm Crosby-Textor (see *Sunday Star Times* 2008). National's focus groups in election year showed voters were strongly against negative attacks and instead wanted National to show a positive product alternative which informed the campaign strategy.[5] After becoming leader, Key reached out to women and Maori and appeared open to different coalition partners. He also visited 'struggle street', a particular area where householders had low incomes – appearing interested in low- as well as high-earning families – and launched the idea of tax relief on charitable donations. In particular he compromised with the Labour Government on a bill controlling physical force used to discipline children. As Robinson (2008) noted, this helped to convey a positive image of leadership competence, capturing public attention because of unusual visuals showing Key behind a podium next to Clark.

Thereafter National tried to respond to voters' discontent by offering a mix of existing 'safe' Labour policies and new National approaches. The Party's overall attitude was more responsive. Murray McCully, National MP and strategist, said when interviewed:

> At the end of the day this is a process that is about having respect for the views of the public. . . . If you thumb your nose at the public and do things to them without seeking their consent then it comes back and bites your backside real quick. . . . You should look respectfully about what you can learn about market research and polling and focus groups and so on. Not slavishly follow the detail but understand the substance of it. (Interviewed by author, 2007)

Other initiatives by the National Party included reaching out to young professionals through under-40s events, utilizing online discussions and Facebook.

National appealed to a range of markets but still lacked differentiation from Labour. They maintained popular Labour policies such as Working for Families and the new pension scheme KiwiSaver introduced in 2007, and latterly focused on youth and crime after a series of serious incidents in South Auckland closer to the election. This approach by National appealed to the party's traditional white conservative voters but also to a new voting bloc of Asian immigrant voters who were particularly attracted to National's hardline policy on crime.

Campaign communication was generally market-oriented. The opening address showed a group of multicultural children followed by a range of visuals of Key amidst varied groups in society and very much at ease with ordinary people. He also talked about his family and background. Shorter election adverts were aspirational and ended with the phrase: 'you've just got to choose it', giving the power to the voter. National's billboards were designed to suit appropriate target markets (see Table 5.4).

There remained a significant weakness in National's political marketing strategy however. As John Campbell, a current affairs presenter, said when he interviewed Key on *Campbell live* in June 2007 'So you're just Labour with tax cuts'. National's overall policy direction was not clear, with the party appealing to conflicting target markets. On one hand, tax cuts favoured high earners and included a special policy for individuals, the independent earner rebate and National talked

Table 5.4 National's targeted billboards in 2008

Billboard wording	Target market
1 in 5 school leavers doesn't pass NCEA	Traditional supporters
We'll smarten up the system	Families
Get them into training	
Not into trouble. National's youth guarantee	
Make our neighbourhoods safer	Traditional supporters
Tougher bail, sentencing and parole laws	South Auckland voters
Wave goodbye to higher taxes	Higher earners
Not your loved ones	
More doctors + more nurses = less bureaucrats	Public sector professionals

about aspiration and reward. On the other hand, their job redundancy programme was less generous than Labour's, being restricted to single-income earners on lower wages and appealed to traditional Labour voters.

The National product remained vague with party strategists arguing that if they had launched more detailed policies, Labour would have stolen or negated them, particularly given that Labour had government facts and figures at their disposal. This also meant that National had mixed success with conveying an ability to deliver. On one hand Key's professional business experience was often discussed leading up to the election and they responded to the changing global economic circumstances by scaling back their promised tax cuts. However, Key lacked political experience compared with Helen Clark. The positive emotive music and changing visuals in the opening campaign address gave movement and suggested an action-oriented party, with the shots of Key behind a desk conveying the image of a strong leader. But the majority of other communications portrayed Key as a nice ordinary friendly guy, which helped convey a market-oriented responsiveness but not that of an action-oriented leader. Whilst National launched a Commitments card in the campaign in response to voters' desire for a clear alternative product (see Table 5.5) it only appeared relatively late in the campaign, and only on the website and in targeted direct mail, and so failed to gain general public awareness.

However it was too detailed and failed to have the same utility of Tony Blair's or Helen Clark's successful pledge cards which were easy to read and remember (see Figure 5.3 for contrast). The opening campaign address was also very unstructured, with policy after policy announced without key points that voters could remember.

The end result of mixed targeting, mixed messages and unclear communication is that the public were left unsure what exactly National was going to do in government. In this situation, voters project their own aspirations onto promised product (see James 2008). Whilst this can help protect an opposition party from attack and ensure a safe slide into power, it causes problems after the election. Market-oriented political marketing was clearly used by National, but not comprehensively.

Labour's approach in their third term was also mixed and whilst it would be easy to dismiss it as sales-oriented, the party did enact some market-oriented

Table 5.5 National's commitments card 2008

---

1. Strengthen the economy, increase after-tax incomes and ensure Kiwis can get ahead under their own steam by **reducing personal taxes on 1 April 2009, 1 April 2010 and 1 April 2011**.
2. Maintain and build New Zealand's asset base by **increasing investment in infrastructure such as roads, broadband and public transport, and by not selling Kiwibank or any other state-owned company.**
3. Ensure government spending is focused on frontline services by **capping the number of bureaucrats and putting real discipline around government spending.**
4. Make our communities safer by **ensuring the worst repeat violent offenders are not eligible for parole.**
5. Confront failure in our school system by **setting National Standards in literacy and numeracy, and requiring all pupils' progress to be assessed and the results reported to parents in plain English.**
6. Tackle our health workforce crisis by **introducing voluntary bonding for new doctors, nurses and midwives, and by boosting the number of funded medical student places by 200 over five years.**
7. Give families financial certainty by **continuing all Working for Families payments at current levels, keeping 20 hours ECE, and keeping caps on doctors' fees.**
8. Give seniors financial certainty by **keeping the age of eligibility of NZ Superannuation at 65 and steadily increasing the amount of Super paid each week as a result of personal tax cuts.**
9. Encourage people to save for their retirement, while making it fairer and more affordable for everyone in these tighter economic times, by **retaining KiwiSaver, with contributions at the 2% plus 2% level.**
10. Provide a safety net for those who are unable to work by **passing a law to maintain and inflation-index all benefit payments, while encouraging those who can work to go back to work.**
11. Encourage students to get rid of debt sooner by **keeping interest-free student loans and offering a 10% bonus on early repayments.**

---

initiatives. Predictably Clark inevitably lost strength; her chief press secretary Mike Munro resigned after two terms and Clark therefore lost a significant source of support and arguably criticism. Despite retaining an image as a strong and capable leader, Clark failed to reconnect with the public. Robinson (2008) noted that polls showed that the number of people thinking she was out of touch with ordinary people had risen from just over 20 per cent in 1999 to just under 50 per cent in 2008.

Nevertheless Clark remained close to Key in the 'most preferred prime minister' poll, reflecting both her strengths but also a weakness in Key, as any competition analysis would have discovered. When she announced the date of the election in September 2008 Helen Clark said 'This election is a choice between a Government which has shown it can make tough choices and an opposition which flip-flops on almost every major issue . . . Labour is ambitious for New Zealand. National is ambiguous on New Zealand.' Labour sought, throughout the communication and campaign period, to highlight changes in National's policy positions and Key's inexperience. The campaign theme was trust, which whilst communicating Clark's positive reputation, was also subtly saying that Key could not be trusted. However US-style opposition research had negative effects. A humorous negative ad during the campaign called 'The Two Johns' showed how Key had changed his mind on various policies, but any impact was probably cancelled out by National's rebuttal negative ads. Attempts to attack Key in September 2007 for alleged discrepancies in his personal financial dealings also backfired. The Labour Party president Mike Williams had travelled to Australia at the end of October to try to dig up evidence linking National leader John Key with financial wrong-doing. When Williams failed to find any such evidence, the media story became one about Labour's campaign methods rather than Key's previous behaviour.

In terms of policy, in June 2007 Labour launched three major policies – the KiwiSaver, extension of Working for Families and the introduction of 20 hours of free child care for three- and four-year-olds.[6] However communication of these policies was very product-oriented: Clark simply told voters her policies were good. For most of the 2005–2008 period the New Zealand Labour Party website and government website was very stark and formal in comparison with UK and US parties:[7] only from mid-2007 did video begin to be used and appear on the government site.[8] Closer to the election, Clark announced a package to cut taxes, but it lacked differentiation, with no particular centre-left vision, and was clearly copied from the opposition.

Clark tried to counteract the disadvantages of her own longevity. In her 2007 party conference speech she said:

> Our party is in the midst of a major programme of renewal and recruitment . . . we must make room for new people and new ideas so we can continue to offer the very best leadership for New Zealand. Many new Labour MPs will be elected next year.[9]

Clark announced reshuffles of her senior team in November 2007, with the aim of rejuvenating the team, including resignations of scandal-embroiled ministers. At the party conference in mid-November Labour publicized the retirement of older MPs alongside the recruitment of new candidates for office.

However the election campaign suggested a sales-orientation. Although Labour's campaign website (labour08.co.nz) was targeted communication, with three pictorially led links, this lacked engagement (see Table 5.6).

Table 5.6 Labour campaign website targets in 2008

Free off-peak public transport for older New Zealanders with the SuperGold card and tax cuts for Superannuitants [with a figure of a bus and elderly man and woman]	Working for families increased from 1 October, calculate changes to your tax credit [with a figure of a single parent and two children]	Tax cuts for working people from 1 October, calculate your tax relief [with a dollar sign]

Late in the election campaign Labour announced a proposal for a redundancy package for households with two incomes not just one. This seemed to be aimed at traditional National voters with higher combined household incomes, which is contrary to support analysis theory within the Market-Oriented Party framework. The 2008 opening address provided a few shots of Clark in shopping malls and even the $2 shop and her voiceover used words of togetherness: 'the key thing is to keep your ear to the ground on what our people are thinking at the grass roots because that enables me to be a better leader'. However this footage was very brief and the remainder of the address – at least ten minutes – was 'Clark on Clark'. The leader gave the viewer a long list of points as to why they should vote Labour, without evidence of support. Similarly with delivery, Labour alleged superior ability without supporting evidence. Their campaign website (Labour08.co.nz) had a picture of Clark with the quote 'I believe that we have shown in government that we deliver on our promises and we keep our word to voters' and another link with the words 'This election is about trust. Vote Labour. A team you can trust to deliver for your family.' This message was entirely logical and sensibly reflected market analysis and targeting, but such competencies cannot just be alleged, they have to be demonstrated.

The overall sense from the case of the Labour Party, therefore, is that of a party that shifted away from a market-orientation during its time in power. There were signs that the party began to use various tools to try to regain a market-orientation, and this may have mitigated potential losses in the election. But these reverse measures were not implemented wholeheartedly through to the actual election, and sales-oriented communication was utilized in the campaign instead. Nevertheless, this suggests that a move away from a market-orientation when in power is not inevitable.

Overall therefore whilst both the major parties in New Zealand tried to be responsive, suggesting an overall trend towards a market-orientation, neither achieved a full market-orientation, and although National was arguably more successful, the lack of differentiation, achievability and clear product may cause problems for the party when it comes to delivering in government.

Political marketing trends and conclusion

There is no doubt that political marketing is being used in New Zealand. However it is limited by resources; constrained by the multi-party system and the need for coalition government; and the major parties move back and forth between sales and market-orientations from one election to the next. Whilst the trend towards the 2008 election was market-oriented; the trend in 2005 was sales-oriented; in 2002 it was mixed and in 1999 one major party was market-oriented whilst the other was more product- or sales-oriented.

This may reflect distinctive features of political marketing in New Zealand. Apart from the systemic factor, that the MMP environment makes appearing willing to work in coalition a part of a market-oriented strategy, another distinction is the reluctance to present policy ideas too soon before the election. This latter factor inhibits clear communication, strategy and product from emerging. Less than a year before the 2008 election, National had yet to launch many clear policy ideas. The reason given was that if they launched them too early, Labour would have a chance to discredit them, copy them, or make them unachievable with the powers of government. This did indeed happen in 2008 with tax cuts: Labour announced their own package then called National's unachievable in the difficult economic conditions. The communication stage is much shorter and less important, with more emphasis put on the campaign. The three-year election cycle also fails to produce enough time for the product side (market intelligence, product design and adjustment and implementation) and communication. As Robertson (2006) noted, 'one of the problems with three-year cycles, you spend the first year sort of getting over the election, the second year doing some work and the third year getting ready for the next one'. In this way, political marketing is influenced by a systemic factor which is specific to political marketing, rather than the generic ones predicted at the start of the book drawn from general political campaign studies.

Another distinct influence is the diverse and ever-changing electoral market indicated by statistical data on voting behaviour and political attitudes. This arguably impacts on the use of political marketing strategy or orientation, and encourages greater focus on techniques which are easier to use, justify and execute. There was a lack of clear product differentiation, design and communication a year in advance of the election in both 2005 and 2008. This meant that emphasis was placed on marketing tools such as market segmentation, with last-minute pandering in policy terms to micro-segments such as state-home owners and students to achieve an overall victory, rather than a whole-hearted, comprehensive and mature market-orientation.

However it is also possible to argue that the variable orientation of party behaviour from one election to the next suggests an emerging trend apparent from other country studies: that alternative non-systemic factors influence the orientation of political parties, such as whether they are in government or opposition, how long they have been there, internal unity, and leadership.

Thus the democratic implications are similarly diverse as they vary with changes in practice; whilst there is little wholesale pandering to voters in New Zealand there is clearly a focus on attracting certain voters at the expense of others via segmentation which may erode overall representation in the political system. In the end, in New Zealand, as with most countries, whether political marketing has a positive or negative impact on democracy depends in most part on how it is used by the politicians, pollsters and advisors and how the voters they seek to follow, persuade or manipulate, respond to it.

Notes

1 I would like to thank Jesper Strömbäck and Chris Rudd for their suggested revisions to various drafts of this chapter. Interviews for this chapter were funded by Auckland University New Staff Grant 2006–2007 and research completion by Auckland University Faculty Research Grant 2008–2009.

2 Source: New Zealand election study; see www.nzes.co.nz.
3 See for example http://www.labour.org.nz/labour_team/labour_in_your_electorate/ index.html, accessed 3 October 2008.
4 Final drafts of country chapters were submitted in May 2008; initially preventing consideration of the election. It would be impossible to pick a time to ensure everyone was able to cover the most recent election given varying electoral timetables around the world. However on advice from reviewers of the manuscript submitted in September 2008 this particular chapter was revised to take account of the 2008 November election.
5 This was conveyed via a secure source but under Chatham House rules.
6 See http://labour.org.nz/news/latest_labour_news/news070701b/index.html, accessed 12 July 2007.
7 See http://labour.org.nz/index.html; http://www.primeminister.govt.nz/ and www.johnkey .co.nz.
8 See http://www.beehive.govt.nz/HomepageFeature.aspx?id=42, accessed 12 July 2007.
9 http://www.labour.org.nz/news/hot_topics/Speech_to_Labour_Party_conference/ index.html, accessed 13 November 2007.

References/further reading

Atkinson, J. (2006) 'Metaspin: Demonization of media manipulation', *Political Science*, 57(2): 17–27.
Boston, J., Levine, S., McLeay, E. and Roberts, N. S. (eds) (1997) *From Campaign to Coalition*, Palmerston North: The Dunmore Press.
Boston, J. et al. (eds) (2000) *Left Turn: The New Zealand General Election of 1999*, Wellington: Victoria University of Wellington.
Cocker, A. (2006) 'New Zealand On Air: A Broadcasting Public Policy Model?', *Political Studies*, 57(2): 43–54.
Comrie, M. and Fountaine, S. (2006) 'On-Screen Politics: The TVNZ Charter and Coverage of Political News', *Political Studies*, 57(2): 29–42.
Hayward, J. and Rudd, C. (eds) (2004) *Political Communications in New Zealand*, Auckland: Pearson Education.
James, C. (2001) 'Campaigning', in R. Miller (ed.) *New Zealand Government and Politics*, Auckland: Oxford University Press. [196–212].
James, C. (2008) 'Brand, Image, Values: Colin James on Political Marketing', *New Zealand Herald*, 31 October.
Joyce, S. (2007) 'National, The Road to Recovery', in S. Levine and N. S. Roberts (eds) *The Baubles of Office: The New Zealand General Election of 2005*, Wellington: Victoria University Press. [105–114].
Lees-Marshment, J. (2006) 'Political Marketing', in R. Miller (ed.) *New Zealand Government and Politics*, Auckland: Oxford University Press.
Lees-Marshment, J. (2008) 'Managing a Market-Orientation in Government: Cases in the UK and New Zealand', in D.W. Johnson (ed.) *The Routledge Handbook of Political Management*, New York: Taylor and Francis.
Lees-Marshment, J. and Rudd, C. (2006)'Anglocisation, Americanisation and Australiasisation of Campaigning in NZ', paper presented at the New Zealand Political Studies Association Conference, Christchurch.
Levine, S. and Roberts, N. S. (2007) 'Mixed Messages: Voting Behaviour in New Zealand in 2005', in S. Levine and N. S. Roberts (eds) *The Baubles of Office: The New Zealand General Election of 2005*, Wellington: Victoria University Press. [359–383].

Maharey, S. (2007) 'Labour: An Historic Third Term', in S. Levine and N. S. Roberts (eds) *The Baubles of Office: The New Zealand General Election of 2005*, Wellington: Victoria University Press.

Miller, R. (2005) *Party Politics in New Zealand*, Auckland: Oxford University Press.

Robinson, C. (2003) 'The Party Vote, Populism and Political Advertising in 2002', in J. Boston, S. Church, S. Levine, E. McLeay and N. S. Roberts (eds) *New Zealand Votes: The General Election of 2002*, Wellington: Victoria University Press.

Robinson, C. (2005) *Advertising and the Market Orientation of Political Parties Contesting the 1999 and 2002 New Zealand General Election Campaigns*, unpublished PhD thesis, Massey University, Palmerston North.

Robinson, C. (2007) 'Images of the 2005 Campaign,' in S. Levine and N. S. Roberts (eds) *The Baubles of Office: The New Zealand General Election of 2005*, Wellington: Victoria University Press. [180–196]

Robinson, C. (2008) 'Presentation on Campaign Imagery', paper presented at the 2008 post-election conference, Wellington, December.

Rudd, C. (2005) 'Marketing the Message or the Messenger? The New Zealand Labour Party, 1990–2003', in D. Lilleker and J. Lees-Marshment (eds) *Political Marketing: A Comparative Perspective*, Manchester: Manchester University Press.

Sunday Star Times (2008) 'Nat's Secret Advisers Accused of Dirty Tricks across Tasman', 29 June. Available: <http://www.stuff.co.nz/the-press/510571> (accessed 1 June 2009).

Vowles, J. et al. (eds) (2002) *Voter's Veto: The 2002 Election in New Zealand and the Consolidation of Minority Government*, Auckland, NZ: Auckland University Press.

Interviews by Jennifer Lees-Marshment

Ansell, John (2007) National advertiser in 2005, interviewed June.

Brash, Don (2007), Leader of the National Party 2003–5, interviewed January.

McCully, Murray (2007) National Party MP and strategist in 2002, 2005 and 2008 elections; interviewed August 13.

Robertson, Grant (2006), Senior advisor to the Prime Minister Helen Clark, interviewed in November.

Smith, Mike (2006), Labour General Secretary, interviewed November.

Williams, Mike (2007), Labour Party President, interviewed 13 August.

6 Australian political marketing

Substance backed by style

Andrew Hughes and Stephen Dann

Australian political marketing is slowly emerging from the long shadow of one-sided elections and market dominance by sales-oriented political parties into a competitive marketplace of ideas, policies and candidates. After a long period of Liberal–National political rule at the federal level, and an equally lopsided representation of Labor at the state level, the Australian political landscape is shifting from a sales orientation of 'pitching and persuading' to a market orientation of 'listening and addressing' the issues that concern the Australian voting public. Parties increasingly understand the value of marketing as a more holistic process. The chapter examines the 2007 Australian Federal Election as a case study of a contest between a sales-oriented incumbent government and a market-oriented opposition party which engaged in a systematic application of marketing techniques. Analysis is based on external observation of the political parties, election campaigning, and informal discussions with members, candidates and staff of major and minor political parties in Australia.[1]

The Australian political market place

The political system

The Australian political system is a constitutional monarchy based on a federal system of three layers of government:

- Federal Government controls most of the national areas of government, such as defence; six state governments (Queensland, New South Wales, Victoria, Tasmania, South Australia and Western Australia) control areas such as police, health and housing;
- three territory governments (Northern Territory, Australian Capital Territory and Norfolk Island).

Australia has two houses of Parliament: the House of Representatives and the Senate. The House of Representatives is very similar to the House of Commons in the UK, and parties need to hold a majority of seats here to form government. The two main parties are the Liberal Party and the Australian Labor Party (ALP); both are mainly centre-right in ideology, but differentiate on key areas such as economics, the environment and industrial relations, which reflects their strong links to the brand communities that gave rise to them.

Australian political marketers operate within a geographically diverse political marketplace, which consists of 150 parliament electorates, and 76 senate positions spread over eight state-based electorates. Australian political marketers have a tactical advantage over most international political marketers insofar as it is one of only 32 political systems that use mandatory voting. Compulsory voting's value to the political marketer is in providing a relatively stable voter marketplace of approximately 95 per cent of the registered and eligible voting population (Evans, 2006). The system also reduces the need for Australian political marketers to expend effort on improving voter turnout amongst the 13.6 million registered eligible voters (AEC, 2007). Voters do not vote for the Prime Minister directly, despite political advertising pitching the federal elections as a choice of Prime Ministerial leadership contenders. Terms for the House of Representatives run for three years, and use a preferential voting system. The Senate has terms of six years, and uses a proportional voting system.[2]

The media system

Australian political campaigns remain heavily reliant upon mainstream media formats to get their message across to the market, although they are exploring new media. The media system in Australia is controlled by four major companies: News Corp, Fairfax, Publishing and Broadcasting Limited (PBL) and the Seven Network. Medium-sized companies, such as Southern Cross Limited, Australian Provincial News (APN) and WIN Network, focus on regional markets. There are many minor companies that operate two or three radio stations or media outlets, but they do not have the mass market appeal of their larger rivals (see Table 6.1).

There are also two major government-owned television and radio networks: Australian Broadcasting Corporation (ABC) and SBS (Special Broadcasting

Table 6.1 Major Australian media operators as at January 2008

Media type	Major operators
Television	Seven, Nine, Ten, ABC (Fed. Govt owned network), SBS (Fed. Govt multi-cultural owned network), Foxtel Pay TV (urban areas), Austar Pay TV (rural areas), WIN (rural network, usually Nine content), PRIME (rural network, usually Seven content), Southern Cross (rural, usually Ten content)
Radio	Austereo Network, Southern Cross Broadcasting, ABC, Nova
Newspapers	News Corp, Fairfax, PBL and APN
Magazines	ACP (owned by PBL), PMP (largely owned by Seven)
Outdoor	Several medium-sized companies, largest being Eye owned by Ten
ISPs	Telstra, Optus, iiNet, TPG, Three, and several other commercial companies

Service). Both are independent and largely free from political influence, although from time to time claims do arise. The ABC forbids all advertising, and SBS has limited advertising. The Australian press is largely free from political influence, although a more common criticism is the influence of the media proprietors on journalistic freedom. Election coverage is extensive for all federal and state elections, particularly by SKY News on the Pay TV networks which has a dedicated parliamentary and election channel, and the internet has also seen an increase in the coverage of elections.

The political consumer

Political consumption patterns in Australia are subject to more speculation than statistical analysis. Williams (2008) analysis of the 2007 election noted several aberrations from the 'traditional' voting patterns, including 53 per cent of voters having decided their preference months prior to the election, and a ten-year record low of 20 per cent for undecided voters in the week before the election. Previous elections have featured higher levels of swinging voters, lower levels of party loyalty, and shorter decision cycles. However, the nature of the continuous electoral campaign conducted by Rudd upon taking leadership of the ALP through to the current campaigning and relationship building whilst in office could prove indicative of voter decision-making moving away from the 'last minute rush' of the official election campaigns. Given that the shifts in voter behaviours in 2007 mirror the shifts in 1996 which led to Howard's election, it remains to be seen if this type of consumer voting pattern is predictive of a change of government, or if longer-term decision making will occur where a Government retains office.

Political marketing techniques in Australia

Australian political parties utilize a number of techniques or elements of the marketing mix such as market intelligence, segmentation and consultants.

Market research

Political parties are using market research more than ever in Australia. This is perhaps due to campaigns becoming more market-oriented policies and less about long held ideology, partly because of the increased use of personal brands and partly because of a move to permanent campaigning. Although no figures exist on market research conducted by political parties, what can be used as support for this theory is the growth of the two major professional political campaign organisations in Australia, Crosby Textor and Hawker Britton. Crosby Textor conducts much of the market research for the Liberal Party and has been accused of using pushy polling techniques as part of their market research. Hawker Britton conducts market research for the Australian Labor Party, alongside other companies such as John Singleton Advertising. Both companies have experienced substantial growth in their operations.

Intra-electorate segmentation

Australian political marketers are able to capitalize on a fortunate combination of compulsory voting, and detailed political pattern analysis provided by the state and Federal electoral commissions (AEC, 2008). Within each electorate, voting patterns per polling booth are available for analysis, and campaigns can be segmented down to a booth by booth analysis of target markets. A combination of compulsory voting and limited population mobility in most electorates ensures a relatively high level of continuity between the booth voting patterns of a previous election. Consequently, swing booths, marginal booths and 'safe' booths can be identified and targeted on the basis of prior voting patterns.

Most major political marketing campaigns in Australia now run localized versions of the national or state campaign. Local issues are identified, with the aim of identifying what local issue is of greatest importance to each target segment, especially those issues that are of most importance to swinging segments. The party's stance on these issues is then highlighted in localized promotional campaigns to make the segments aware of how the party is addressing these issues. Party websites are especially used for this tactic, with the first widespread use in a major campaign being by the ALP in the Queensland State Election of 2004 but since then more widely applied by both political parties at a state and federal level (Hughes and Dann, 2005).

Consultants

Australia's political marketing environment has been influenced by a mixture of in-house political marketing, and external civilian contractors, with mixed success. The use of external providers is usually as discreet as it is effective – barring the occasion where both major political parties retained the same advertising agency to develop competing political marketing communication campaigns. Advertising agencies have also helped political parties understand the need for a more integrated marketing approach to campaigns.

With campaigns becoming increasingly professional campaign managers are moving away from being one of the party faithful to full-time highly paid professional campaign strategists such as Lynton Crosby advising the Howard Liberal Government. The use of a professional marketer in the Kevin Rudd 2007 campaign has been widely credited with making the difference between the two campaigns for it was the marketer who came up with the Kevin07 concept and the merchandising of the campaign, including the successful T-shirt that almost became a must have fashion item on election day. The expertise used by the ALP that decided to use an integrating marketing approach was far more successful than the expertise that decided to use the same personal selling of John Howard approach that had been so heavily relied upon by the Liberal Party for four previous federal election campaigns.

Such consultants are now used not only in Australia, but have also had an influence in the UK, Canada, the United States and New Zealand. This is possibly due to Australian campaigns becoming the first to adopt a more marketing focus to political campaigns, ahead of other nations in the Asia-Pacific region such as New Zealand or Indonesia, and hence political marketing expertise is becoming increasingly sought after by many political parties around the world. Due to the timing of the Australian political cycle, it has also been suggested that the US political marketing community views Australia as the forerunner and beta test market for campaign techniques to use in the American presidential races. Both major parties in Australia have semi-formal ties with the US parties; the ALP with the Democrats and the coalition parties with the Republicans, exchanging staff to work on each other's campaigns and trial new tactics.

Leader as brand, and presidential-style campaigning in non-presidential electoral systems

The major Australian political parties have adopted the party leader – both as a central political product, and as part of a co-branding technique – as a personal brand (Hughes, 2004a, 2004b; Hughes, 2007). Personal branding has also helped independent candidates and celebrity candidates win seats at a federal and state level. For example, at the 2007 federal election the ALP used over 14 celebrity candidates, or nearly 10 per cent of all total candidates. This is an amazing figure and demonstrates the power of a personal brand in the Australian political market.

As the Australian electoral system does not support direct presidential elections, and only the people who live in the electorate of a leader can vote for them directly, presidential-style campaigning has been conducted by repacking voting for a local member as a proxy vote for the nation's leadership. Although the effectiveness of this approach has varied considerably, the Liberal Party's loss of several popular local members in 2007 indicated that the market was willing to consider the nation's leadership as part of their overall voting decision. This 'president by proxy'-style campaign trend is still in its introductory stage, but as campaigns move to the 'permanent' campaign method this is only going to increase in importance (Needham, 2005). This means that the party brand will become less important to the personal brand as it will be the personal brand more than the party brand that acts as the brand position signifier to the target market.

The evolution of permanent leader-based campaigning in Australian political marketing poses a familiar dilemma for political parties: do they choose a leader based on the possibility of electoral success, a market view, or do they choose a leader who best represents the diverse factions and interests of the party, a more stakeholder approach? Overall, the ALP have answered this question from the market view at a federal level, but only time will tell if the other political parties will apply the same perspective across all levels of politics in Australia.

E-marketing

Online forms of communication are increasingly used in Australia. Major political parties are adopting social media marketing techniques for creating connections with the voting public. However, the success of the online campaign has varied widely between candidates – for example, the Facebook profiles of the respective leaders of the political parties are effectively fake profiles maintained by PR staff members. Despite that, the Facebook profile of Kevin Rudd was far more successful than that of John Howard, especially with the Generation X and Y voters (Griffiths, 2007; Wilson, Saunders and Bruns, 2007). At this point in online political marketing, YouTube is being used very heavily by all political parties as a microbroadcast platform for replaying TVC content, talking-head monologues or 'fireside chat' direct-to-camera monologues (Cornfield, 2006). It is also heavily used by political parties and groups during the mid-point of the campaign when spending on TVC is being kept low for the final week of the campaign. There is also an advantage in using YouTube as a tool for market research: the number of hits and viewer comments provide good information for parties on how the campaign is being perceived by the market, although this is again more the case for the Generation X and Y segments than any other segment.

Other forms of online marketing for Australian political marketing are still in beta. Specific purpose campaign messages sites such as Voting Record (http://votingrecord.com.au) are becoming more common as a means to communicate detailed information on the back of traditional media advertising. Whilst some may say that the increasing use of online marketing techniques is due to an increase in the sophistication of marketing strategy by political parties, and this is partly true, the primary reason is perhaps more simply a matter of finance. Australian political parties are not wealthy, and with the typical federal election campaign costing as much as $50 million, political parties will do all they can to minimize their expenditure during the campaign so they can afford to run as many TVCs as possible in the last week of the campaign when many undecided voters make their purchase decision.

Political marketing strategy in Australia

The following section outlines an observational case study of the political marketing strategies of the two major Australian political parties in the lead-up to the 2007 election – the incumbent Liberal–National Party, and the opposition Australian Labor Party. The activities of the Australian Green Party and the Australian Democrats are also discussed in regard to their efforts to retain and attain positions in the Senate. Observational data on the political campaigns, campaign techniques and methods are used as the chapter was written during the election campaign when all of the political parties were unwilling to allow outside observation of their specific techniques, processes and procedurals for strategic and security reasons. For a comprehensive coverage of the issues and developments leading to the 2007 election, see Williams's 2008 coverage of the election campaign.

Major parties: Australian Labor Party and Liberal–National Coalition

The election of Kevin Rudd, and the use of a professional marketing strategist, perhaps supports that there is now a change of attitude towards marketing by political parties. O'Cass (1996) identified that most Australian political parties did not use marketing in their campaigns but would do so if they understood more about it. Perhaps the ALP is one party that made the effort to understand marketing and apply its principles and techniques to a campaign, with the results there for all to see. The 2007 campaign of Kevin Rudd will likely go down in Australian political marketing history as the turning point in the acceptance and use of marketing strategy at a national level by a major political party. It is unlikely that after this campaign major political parties will continue to ignore marketing strategy, but whether this means that parties have resolved to take a market view to their organizations and policies rather than an ideological one is something that only time will tell.

The ALP

Recent elections

The Rudd/ALP victory was the culmination of a movement by the market towards him that began with his appointment as party leader, and that culminated in an average national swing of 5.5 per cent on election day. That said, the ALP only held a relatively small majority on the popular vote with a swing of 2.1 per cent required for government to change hands. The ALP was also faced with a hostile Senate during its first term in office. Pragmatically, this translates into the need for some compromises and alterations to key policies for the passage of legislation through the Senate.

Despite the apparent market orientation exhibited in the 2007 election campaign, the ALP remains divided between the desire to become more market-driven and the desire to remain faithful to the original ideologies of the party: although a combination of both could represent a more comprehensive market-oriented strategy. Ideology is great on a Sunday morning whilst sipping a latte at an inner-city café but unless that ideology represents the needs of the majority of the market it alone would not be enough to win government. Kevin Rudd's leadership of the ALP suggests that the party is willing to become more market-focused to achieve electoral success without feeling a need to sever ties as 70 per cent of the front bench candidates had strong union or party official backgrounds.

The ALP won office because of their broader product, not just policies. From 25 November 2007 onwards the ALP held power in every state and territory. This was reinforced by the emphasis the Rudd Government had placed on early delivery milestones as a means of reaffirming commitment, demonstrating performance to enhance trust, and producing evidence of the reciprocity of delivering reform in exchange for the votes received to take office (Needham, 2005): paying attention to all stages in the MOP process. For example the Rudd Government produced a document on its first 100 days of government, even though there is no formal requirement of any government for such a document (Australian Government, 2008). It is quite simply a communications tool designed to reinforce to consumers that they made the right decision to vote for the ALP. Many commercial companies use similar techniques, such as car companies who contact customers after they have taken ownership of a car. Community cabinets are also being used by the Rudd Government to demonstrate a connection with the grass roots, and are again an effective reinforcement tool.

The Rudd Government's challenge over time will be to maintain a market-orientation strategy whilst in power, including differentiating from its time in opposition, in the changing economic landscape of 2008. The challenge of marketing an Opposition party to that of the Government with the most powerful personal brand name in Australia, that of Prime Minister, is something the Liberal and National Party Coalition is only beginning to realize.

The Liberal Party

Recent elections

Despite the loss in 2007 the Liberal Party was still the reigning champion of Australian politics, having only ever been out of office for 16 years in the modern era of political marketing. If anything the Liberal Party demonstrated that political marketing was not a fire and forget strategy by failing to continually assess the market and address the needs of the voting public and perhaps relying too much on its personal selling approach. After a long period in government the Liberal party failed to recognize the needs of the market, and condemned itself to the Opposition benches by implementing a series of theocratic and ideologically driven pieces of legislation that were not reflective of the views of the voting public. This was best demonstrated by the product-orientation policy approach of the disastrous Work Choices legislation that was far removed from the needs of the middle-class segment (the 'Howard Battlers') that formed the core support base for the Howard Government.

The Liberal party presented itself as a product- to sales-oriented party after the 2004 election victory. This was partially due to the disadvantage of incumbency, and partly due to the belief that the Prime Ministerial brand name would save them again, after rescuing the faltering 2004 campaign. Further, a previous lack of viable alternative governments evidenced through the post-2004 period when the ALP had four leaders in three years created a false sense of security for the Liberal Party.

By the time the Liberal Party faced the electorate in 2007, it was forced to sell the benefits of the WorkChoices legislation to an electorate who had not previously endorsed this approach to workers' rights or employment contracts. Similar problems for the Liberal campaign existed across the board in any areas where they had implemented a previous campaign promise and then failed on its service delivery, or introduced legislation on an issue which they had not had 'validated' by an electoral mandate, such as the indigenous intervention in the Northern Territory, the length of Australian troop deployment in Iraq and proposed changes to the tertiary education sector.

The Liberal Party could have easily identified the failings of its own strategy had it either carried out market research or even listened to the opinion polls that were highlighting legislation in these areas as being out of touch with the majority of the Australian electorate. The Liberal Party campaign also carried the disadvantage of having a long-established historical track record as an indicator of potential future performance (Hughes and Dann, 2006). Prior elections demonstrated to the market that the party would offer 'non-core promises' to counteract ALP offers, and then fail to deliver on these alternative product offers. This hampered a number of the Liberals' possible product modifications such as the promise of alternative leadership candidates, as the offer of a future possible retirement from a Prime Minister with a track record of backing off set retirement dates was a low credibility product to try to sell to a cynical market.

It was always going to be next to impossible to sell the Howard brand as one of renewal and fresh ideas when it opposed signing the Kyoto Protocol, any apology to the Indigenous Stolen Generation and appeared more interested in being seen as a world leader. As an old saying goes 'think global act local', and this was perhaps something the Liberal Party should have been doing much more of in the 2007 campaign.

The Liberal Party under the leadership of Brendan Nelson has shown signs of trying to move from the inward focused, ideologically centred sales orientation of the former Howard government through changes in the operation and administration of the party. The Liberal Party has attempted to implement increased levels of party room consultation, and inclusive policy development in contrast to the policy by authority approach of the Howard administration. That said, elements of the Liberal Party still engage in the introspective 'win at all cost' approach, as evidenced by the generation and development of the strategy documents discussed by Maiden (2008) that centred on damaging the Australian economy in order to weaken the Rudd ALP government and sell the Liberal Party as a viable alternative. The failure of the Liberal strategic think tanks to generate positive market offers of value is notable, and indicates the legacy of seeing the Liberal Party as something to be sold in contrast to the ALP, rather than to create a policy and party platform that engages the needs of the electorate.

Efforts to increase levels of bipartisanship over key national policy issues such as the Stolen Generations Apology, WorkChoices reform and a commitment to hold the ALP to promised policy decisions indicated a potential for greater movement towards the 'party of alternative government'. Repeated failure to deliver effective executions of the attempted bipartisanship platforms, notably the speech in reply to the Apology, continues to maintain the 'Party of Opposition' position in the minds of the voters. Similarly, threatening to block government policy in the Senate whilst simultaneously insisting the Government be held to election promises sends a clear message to the electorate – the Liberal Party is more interested in point scoring and divisive political behaviour than being a viable alternative government.

Minor parties

However whilst the major parties control roughly 85 per cent of the total market, 15 per cent of the market has always been available for minor parties to fight over.

Prior to the 2007 election, the minor parties consisted of the Australian Democrats, Australian Greens, and a selection of independents. The power and influence of the minor parties has fluctuated with the electoral success of the major parties – as the major parties even out in the Senate, the balance of power shifts to the small parties who can form the majority with either major party. However, the perceived misuse of the balance of power will cost the minor parties long-term success. For example, the 1996 decision by the Democrats to support the introduction of the GST led to their steady decline in relevance to their core market culminating in the loss of their remaining Senate position in the 2007 election.

The loss is significant for seeing the end of the continuous streak of political representation by the Australian Democrats party from the 1950s as the Democrats only held Senate representation at the Federal level. The demise of the Australian Democrats has shown that failure to adopt a marketing orientation, especially the use of a personal brand with a high level of brand attribute coherency with the target market, will usually lead to electoral oblivion in the Australian market. It should be noted that the Democrats' most successful era in Australian politics, the early to mid-1990s, was a time when the party had leaders that were coherent with its party brand. As the Democrats lost traditional support, the Australian Greens emerged to take their place as the third viable party in the senate.

The Greens present a higher level of brand attribute coherency with the inner city middle class by appearing as an ideologically driven choice for saving the environment through the Senate. As the Greens increased their share of the political market in the 2004 and 2007 elections, it was at the expense of the Democrats marketshare. The Greens have maintained an issue-driven campaign that is currently focused on a sales orientation, with the Democrats' attempts to push a similar sales approach resulted in them being direct, and unsuccessful, competitors for the mindshare occupied by the Greens.

Whilst some argue that the National Party is a major party, with representation in both houses of federal parliament, the target markets of the party are shrinking and retreating every year and turning it into a minor party. Before the growth of Australia's major cities and the sea/tree change urban drift generations of post-2000, the National Party won as many as 19 seats in the House of Representatives and even held state government in Queensland. In 2008 this is now down to ten, and two of these seats only require swings of less than 3 per cent to fall. The Nationals are fast running out of time to redesign their brand for the post-2007 era of Australian politics.

Even if the party designs policies only for its key target markets of rural Australia, this may not be enough to prevent it becoming a party that rivals the Greens in size, and therefore one that can no longer lay claim to being a coalition partner that can lay claim to the position of Deputy Prime Minister in a coalition government. There is currently some debate that the National Party influence in government can be saved by a merger with the Liberal Party. However from a marketing perspective any merger of the two major coalition parties would be disastrous for the Liberal Party's positioning strategy and therefore is unlikely to happen. It is therefore likely that in the next few elections the National Party will continue to decrease in size and influence with its target markets unless it becomes more market driven.

Across the board, the minor parties are facing common issues of relevance and market viability as demonstrated during the 2004 to 2007 period where the Liberals held a majority in the Senate and effectively nullified any question of the balance of power being held by the independents and minor parties. Survival for the smaller political players in the Senate will come from realigning their campaigns and policies to meet the needs of a market niche, or, by providing a sustainable alternative political product to attract the attention of voters who vote major party in the lower house, and minor party as a 'checks and balances' approach in the Senate.

Political marketing trends and conclusion

Are the parties becoming more or less market-oriented?

Both Liberals and the ALP are demonstrating applications of commercial marketing theory and practice through their post-election transition strategies. Although the major parties are reluctant to embrace marketing publicly due to persistent negativity associated with the approach in the mainstream media, both major parties have actively sourced marketing expertise to improve their campaign performances.

In the 2007 election campaign, the Rudd government made considerable use of the principles of marketing through policy development, product offering and engaging in market positioning through key areas of comparative policy with the Howard Government, and sufficient product differentiation to demonstrate a relative advantage (Dann and Hughes, 2008; Rogers, 1995). One key aspect of the market orientation that can be ascribed to the Rudd Government has been the implementation of a greater level of relationship marketing between government and voters. The ALP can be demonstrated to be using the Grönroos (1994) relationship marketing paradigm of trust, reciprocity and commitment through the rapid implementation of election promise and the delivery of high profile trust-building policy initiatives. The implementation of the indigenous apology as the opening of the first parliamentary session of the new administration has allowed Rudd's government the opportunity to build on the trust shown by the electorate, and to demonstrate a level of reciprocity to the voters through the delivery of promised policy products.

What changes are likely within the next five to ten years?

The authors regard four potential changes as likely to occur in the Australian political marketplace over the forthcoming decade, based on speculation, pattern analysis and trend projection. First, the market for political products has intensified with the success of the voter–customer-oriented independent lobby group GetUp! Australia (getup.org.au). The success of GetUp at the national campaign level has increased their likely participation in state and local politics, and may form a core political service of maintaining electoral interest in the marketplace. Further, the ongoing success of the progressively oriented consumer-lobbyist organization is likely to attract competition from a conservatively oriented consumer lobby group. GetUp is unlikely to hold a monopoly position in the consumer-based lobby marketplace within the next decade.

Second, the decade will see a redivision of the distribution of power in non-Labor political marketing. Instability amongst the Liberal and National parties over a merger may lead to greater divisions of the conservative political parties in Australia, which could result in a period of broader coalitions that eventually see a merger between the smaller conservative elements of the National and minor conservative parties such as Family First or the remnants of One Nation. An extended period in opposition at the national and state level may force a change to market-oriented approach, something that Robert Menzies would be proud of, away from the outdated personal selling approach that lost its effectiveness many elections ago. It is likely that the Liberal Party will become even more dominant in any coalition arrangement at federal and state levels, and it is hard to see the National Party being able to claim the position of Deputy Prime Minister in the future. The Liberal Party will instead use that position in a two-pronged personal brand approach that worked successfully in the 2007 campaign for the ALP, and of course that has been used to varying degrees of success in other political systems. This will enable it to become more market-focused but also more effective in its campaigning against the ALP which now relies heavily upon this approach at a federal level. This will also mean that the party will need to give much more thought to how it selects, integrates and markets candidates, policies and expertise than it ever has before.

Third, there is a strong possibility that the conservative-leaning ALP government will result in the rise of a progressive liberalism movement as a counterbalance to the increased conservatism evident in the Australian political marketplace. Given the cyclical nature of the Australian political cycle which can be mapped at a peak of progressive politics with Whitlam in 1975, and conservative politics with Howard in 2005, the pendulum is likely to swing back to the progressive side in the next decades. The ALP will be faced with the unusual prospect, for it anyway, of how to handle the issue of generational change within its ranks to ensure that incumbency does not become a disadvantage as it became for the Howard-led Liberal Party, and many other long-serving governments around the globe. The party still has not reached a permanent resolution on whether it wants to be market-oriented or ideologically driven. It will probably realize, through a narrow electoral win at the next election or the one after, that being market-oriented is the more successful strategy.

Finally, the niche market that is available for minor parties will become more competitive. The Greens have had a remarkably successful era, but this is unlikely to continue if the Democrats rebrand and reposition. Other minor parties, and even independent candidates such as Nick Xenophon, will challenge the Greens' claim to the balance of power in the Senate. It is unlikely that any one party will ever again control the Senate like the Liberals did in the period 2004–2007, and instead the minor parties and independents will fight bitterly over the claim of keeping the governing party honest. Of all the areas of the Australian political marketplace it is in the niche market that market-oriented policies and candidates are most likely to be used, as this is the most hotly contested area of the market.

In conclusion, the next five to ten years in the Australian political marketplace will demonstrate the increasing use and acceptance of marketing techniques, methods and strategies in Australian politics. The success of third party issue groups such as GetUp.org.au in generating market awareness for issue-based campaigning, coupled with the independent lobby group becoming a source of market information for the major parties will allow for greater market and marketing orientation in Australian politics. The success of the ALP in 2007 represented the first major field test of sales versus marketing orientation. The experiment will be replicated at the various state and local elections that will arise between the 2007 success, and the next federal election, which will provide opportunity for major and minor parties to experiment with marketing strategy for taking or retaining political office in Australia.

Notes

1   The chapter was written during an election year (2007), during which access for formal interview and survey research was naturally limited.
2   More detailed information on the Australian Political System can be found at the Parliament of Australia website at www.aph.gov.au or at the Australian Electoral Commission, www.aec.gov.au

References/further reading

AEC (2007) 'Media Fact Sheet: 2007 Federal Election Key Facts and Figures'. Available at: <http://www.aec.gov.au/Elections/federal_elections/2007/media/key_facts.htm> (accessed 3 June 2009).

AEC (2008) *The Official 2007 Federal Election Results*. Available at: <http://vtr.aec.gov.au/> (accessed 3 June 2009).

Australian Government (2008) *The First 100 Days: Achievements of the Rudd Government*. Available at: <http://www.theaustralian.news.com.au/files/first100days.pdf> (accessed 3 June 2009).

Cornfield, M. (2006) 'Youtube and You', *Campaigns and Elections*, 27(8): 43.

Dann, S. and Hughes, A. (2008) 'Australian Political Marketing after Kevin07: Lessons from the 2007 Federal Election', *Monash Business Review*, 4(1): 34–37

Evans, T. (2006) *Compulsory Voting in Australia, Australian Electoral Commission*, 16 January. Available at: <www.aec.gov.au/pdf/voting/compulsory_voting.pdf> (accessed 3 June 2009).

Griffiths, M. (2007) 'Oxygen: Social Intranets, Collective Intelligence, and Government Practices', *The Electronic Journal of e-Government*, 5(2): 177–190. Available at: <www.ejeg.com> (accessed 3 June 2009).

Grönroos, C. (1994) 'From Marketing Mix to Relationship Marketing: Towards a Paradigm Shift in Marketing', *Management Decision*, 32(2): 4–20.

Hughes, A. (2004a) 'The Branding of Political Parties: A Case Study Approach', paper presented at the Australian and New Zealand Marketing Academy Conference, Victoria University of Wellington, Wellington, New Zealand.

Hughes, A. (2004b) 'The Power and the Passion: The Use of Celebrity Candidates in Political Marketing', paper presented at the Australasian Non-profit Marketing Conference, Australian National University, Canberra, ACT.

Hughes, A. (2007) 'Personal Brands: An Exploratory Analysis of Personal Brands in Australian Political Marketing', paper presented at the Australia and New Zealand Marketing Academy Conference, University of Otago, Dunedin, 3–5 December.

Hughes, A. and Dann, S. (2005) 'Qualitative Case Analysis of the TeamBeattie.com Website', paper presented at the Australian and New Zealand Marketing Academy Conference, University of Western Australia, 5–7 December.

Maiden, S. (2008) 'Libs consider IR U-Turn Ploy to Trap Rudd', *The Australian*, 1 December.

Needham, C. (2005) 'Brand Leaders: Clinton, Blair and the Limitations of the Permanent Campaign', *Political Studies*, 53(2): 343–361.

O'Cass, A. (1996) 'Political Marketing and the Marketing Concept', *European Journal of Marketing*, 30(10/11): 21–31.

Rogers, M. R. (1995) *Diffusion of innovations*, 2nd edn, London: Macmillan.

Voting Record, http://www.votingrecord.com.au [Offline]

Williams, P. (2008) 'The 2007 Australian Federal Election: The Story of Labor's Return from the Electoral Wilderness', *Australian Journal of Politics and History*, 54(1): 104–125.

Wilson, J. A., Saunders, B. J. and Bruns, A. (2007) 'Scoring the E-Lection'. Available at: <http://gatewatching.org/2007/11/23/club-bloggery-the-8th-scoring-the-e-lection/> (accessed 3 June 2009).

7 Political marketing in the United States

From market- towards sales-orientation?

Jonathan Knuckey

The modern election campaign that attempts to brand and market political parties and candidates has in many respects been a product of the American election campaign. Indeed the term the 'Americanization' of elections is often used as a short-hand way of referring to the professionalization of political campaigns, with all that that entails: polling, television ads, focus groups, segmentation and targeting of voters, direct-mailing, and the hiring of a plethora of campaign consultants. Despite the fact that American campaigns pioneered many of the techniques that are essential to a marketing strategy, the application of a comprehensive political marketing framework to American political parties and candidates has been somewhat limited. At the same time, the evidence to support the notion that American parties have become market-oriented is, at best, mixed. This chapter will examine the political and structural factors that both contribute to and limit the applicability of market-oriented parties in the United States. It then assesses the nature and degree of political marketing in recent presidential elections and concludes by examining the future scope of political market-orientation in American elections. The chapter is primarily based on observations of the political parties and candidates and their campaigning, accounts in the news media and on the Internet, the National Election Studies, and an analysis of others' research.

The US political marketplace

The political system

The United States uses the first-past-the-post electoral system. Members of the House of Representatives are elected to two-year terms in single-member districts in each state. Members of the Senate are also elected on a statewide basis, where each state elects two senators for six-year terms, with one-third up for re-election every two years. Presidential elections are decided in the Electoral College, with each state allocated a number of electors that are equal to its representation in Congress. Electors are allocated in every state (except for Maine and Nebraska) by a winner-take-all system. It is possible that the popular vote victor of a presidential election can fail to win a majority in the Electoral College, a situation that has occurred on four occasions (1824, 1876, 1888 and 2000).

The use of single-member districts and a first-past-the-post electoral system has produced one of the 'purest' two-party systems in the world. At each stage in its history, the United States has possessed just two major political parties. Since 1856, these have been the Democratic and Republican parties.

However, it has been usual for one party to dominate politics during different eras. For example, from 1896 to 1932 the Republicans were the clear majority party. The critical election of 1932 ushered in a new Democratic majority, which dominated the electoral landscape until 1968. Since 1968 no party can claim to be the majority, with divided government—where different parties control the legislative and executive branches—the norm. At the same time elections for Congress and the presidency have been very close in terms of popular vote won (see Table 7.1), producing what Barone (2002) described as the '49 percent nation'. The 2008 presidential election might, however, indicate the potential for the 'emerging Democratic majority' predicted by Judis and Teixeira (2008).

Consistent with the median voter hypothesis (Downs, 1957), both the Democratic and Republican parties have historically eschewed strictly ideological appeals to what has long been a large and diverse electorate. However, the disappearance of moderates within both parties—largely attributable to the regional realignments of the Northeast and South—has produced greater ideological polarization at both the elite and mass levels (Black and Black, 2007; Jacobson, 2007). The crowding of the political spectrum by both parties has made it exceptionally difficult for new parties to make an electoral breakthrough.

Although a strong two-party system should create favorable pre-conditions for the emergence of market-oriented political parties, other structural aspects of the American party system suggest that there are limits to the development of both

Table 7.1 Percentage of the popular vote received by the winning candidate in presidential elections and winning party in US House elections, 1992–2006

Election	Winning Candidate/Party	% of the Vote
1992 Presidential Election	Clinton (D)	43%
1992 US House Election	Democrats	50%
1994 US House Election	Republicans	50%
1996 Presidential Election	Clinton (D)	49%
1996 US House Election	Republicans	49%
1998 US House Election	Republicans	49%
2000 Presidential Election	Bush (R)	48%
2000 US House Election	Republicans	48%
2002 US House Election	Republicans	53%
2004 Presidential Election	Bush (R)	51%
2004 US House Election	Republicans	50%
2006 US House Election	Democrats	52%
2008 Presidential Election	Obama (D)	53%
2008 US House Election	Democrats	53%

Source: Compiled by the author from aggregate election returns.

parties becoming market-oriented. First, American parties have historically had decentralized organizations, with weak national party organizations (Epstein, 1986; Beck and Sorauf, 1992). Historically, the center of party activities in the United States was the local and state party organizations. Before the 1970s, the national party organizations—the Democratic National Committee (DNC) and the Republican National Committee (RNC)—were little more than loose confederations of the 50-state party organizations. However, there has been a trend toward stronger national committees over the past decades. Today, the primary functions of the DNC and RNC are raising and disseminating campaign finances and acting as campaign service providers to candidates. On the other hand, the national party organization remains weak. For example, the machinery of the presidential nomination convention is essentially directed by the party's presidential candidate, with the candidate setting the policies and image of the party. Attempts to 'nationalize' congressional elections—with a similar message articulated by all party candidates—also tend to be the exception rather than the rule.

This reflects a second potential check on the scope for market-oriented parties in the United States: the dominance of candidate-centered politics (Wattenberg, 1996). While candidate-centered politics certainly allows individual *candidates* to adopt market-oriented approaches more readily, it makes it exceptionally difficult for a *party* to apply a market-oriented approach. Hence, while a party's presidential candidates may succeed in pursuing a market-oriented approach, candidates for other political offices need not pursue this approach. The rise of primary elections as the dominant method of candidate selection has also compounded the problem of the party being unable to control the type of candidates running in elections, nor the message articulated by those candidates. In a system where executive and legislative power are separated, this problem is perhaps compounded in that American parties are not presented to the electorate as competing 'teams' with coherent policy goals (Downs, 1957). Furthermore, given staggered election cycles in US elections, it might be entirely rational for members of Congress from the same party as the president to distance themselves from the president in midterm elections.

Political parties and campaign financing

More so than other nations, the financing of political parties in the United States is subject to complex regulations (see for example, Anstead 2008). Although a thorough description of these regulations is beyond the scope of this chapter, some parts are essential for an understanding of how campaign financing works and affects political marketing strategies and tactics.

Campaign finance laws date back to the Federal Election Campaign Act of 1971. An amendment in 1974 imposed limits on the campaign contributions and expenditure, although the Supreme Court in 1976 declared much of this legislation unconstitutional in *Buckley v. Valeo*. Following this ruling, only presidential candidates who accepted public funds were subject to a cap on money they could raise and spend. Up until 2000, virtually all major party candidates accepted public funds and hence spending limits. However, in 2000, George W. Bush did not accept matching funds during the Republican primaries, and the same was true for both Bush and the Democratic candidate John Kerry in 2004. Thus, there were no legal limits to the amount of campaign funding they could raise, and fundraising is indeed one of the most crucial means of successful electioneering.

Another aspect of campaign financing concerns 'soft money.' Perhaps the biggest loophole in attempts to regulate campaign financing came in 1979, when the Federal Election Commission (FEC) allowed the national party committees to raise and spend unlimited amounts of money on 'get-out-the-vote' activities. Consequently, the amount of soft-money rose dramatically, and was increasingly spent by both parties on TV advertising for their respective candidates. According to the FEC, the RNC and DNC raised and spent $488 million in soft money in the 2000 presidential election, compared to $263 million in the 1996 campaign.

This soft-money loophole created pressure for further reform, which was realized in 2002 with the passage of the Bipartisan Campaign Reform Act (BCRA). The goal of BCRA was to ban soft money and limit contributions to state and local parties. However, BCRA brought with it a major unintended consequence: the emergence of so-called '527' groups. Following passage of BCRA, several pro-Democratic groups organized under section 527 of the US tax-code, which allowed them to collect unregulated campaign contributions. When the FEC failed to rule against 527 groups, Republican-leaning groups began to form their own 527 groups. Altogether, 527 groups raised and spent $435 million in the 2004 election, money that was essentially unregulated and which, to all intents and purposes, was essentially 'soft money' (Currinder, 2005).

Campaign finance regulations have proved to be a mixed blessing for American parties. Reforms strengthened the national party committees and both party organizations have used money given to them to professionalize their organizational structure and to utilize new campaign technology. Although the candidates hire their own professional consultants, pollsters, media advisers and specialists in direct mail targeting, the national parties have increasingly become more sophisticated. For example, the RNC's 'Voter Vault' encompasses a large database of voters and campaign contributors. This database has allowed the party and its candidates to tailor messages to individual voters and households, using information about the kind of magazines they receive, whether they own guns, the churches they attend, their incomes, their charitable contributions and their voting histories. This makes it possible to specifically address the issues of voter interest and then target individual voters (Edsall, 2006).

On the other hand, campaign finance reform has diminished the role of the national parties in presidential elections. Public funds go directly to the candidate rather than the party, reinforcing a candidate-centered politics and making it more problematic for the re-branding of a political party beyond the presidential nominee. The most recent reforms also present challenges for a would-be market-oriented political party. For example, in the 2004 campaign the candidates and parties had no control over the type of political advertisements that the 527 groups generated (Edsall and Grimaldi, 2004).

The electoral environment

The most important rationale for political parties pursuing a market-orientation is that voters' party loyalties have weakened over time. Party dealignment has created an electoral marketplace where voters can 'buy' the party product without the constraining ties of brand-name party loyalty. Dealignment has also been used to describe macro-level developments in American politics, specifically the incidence of divided government and greater electoral volatility from election to election. For example, Abramson and colleagues (2003: 295) argue that: 'dealignment seems to be an accurate term to describe the American party system. The old party system is in disarray, but nothing has replaced it' (see also Shea, 1999).

The notion of a dealigned electorate appears to have become the conventional wisdom. However, there is considerable evidence that the dealignment perspective may have been overstated and that in the United States, the scope for parties to become market-oriented may be constrained by continuing party loyalty and increasing polarization (Jacobson, 2007).

First, the strength of party attachments has not continued to erode over time, in a manner that much of the 'decline of parties' scholarship of the 1970s and 1980s suggested (Broder, 1971; Nie, Verba and Petrocik, 1979; Norpoth and Rusk, 1982; Beck, 1984). Table 7.2 shows the strength of party attachments for the American electorate for each decade since the 1950s.

While there was a decline in strong partisans from the 1950s through the 1970s, this decline halted by the 1980s and has since rebounded, so that the share of voters calling themselves 'strong partisans' is just three percentage points lower in 2000–2004 than it was in the 1950s. At the same time, while the percentage of those who are independents but lean toward either of the two parties has grown since the 1950s, this exaggerates the number of genuine independents. As Keith *et al.* (1992) argue, independent-leaners exhibit behavioral characteristics more akin to partisans and should thus be classified as such. This is important, as independent-leaners have contributed most heavily to the rise of independent identifiers since the 1950s. The share of 'pure' independents has shown little growth, peaking at 15 percentage points in the 1970s. By 2000–2004, only 10 percent of the electorate could be classified as pure independents.

Table 7.2 Strength of party attachment in the USA by decade (%)

Decade	Strong	Weak	Independent leaners	Independents	N
1950s	36%	39%	15%	11%	6,250
1960s	34%	40%	15%	11%	6,897
1970s	25%	38%	22%	15%	10,339
1980s	29%	35%	22%	13%	9,505
1990s	30%	33%	25%	11%	9,255
2000–2004	33%	29%	28%	10%	4,530

Source: American National Election Studies, cumulative file.

A further indicator that suggests that dealignment may not have been as wide-spread in the American electorate is the relationship between party identification and vote choice. Although the weakening of this relationship has been central to the dealignment perspective, some have questioned whether partisanship has become a less important predictor of vote choice (Miller and Shanks, 1996; Bartels, 2000). Figure 7.1 shows the magnitude of the relationship between party identification and presidential vote choice. As shown by the figure, there has been no decline in the relationship between party identification and vote choice, and party line voting was in fact greater in the 2000 and 2004 presidential elections than in any prior years.

The strengthening relationship between party identification and vote choice is suggestive of less electoral volatility than is frequently asserted by the dealignment perspective. As shown in Figure 7.2, such a finding is given further credence by the decline of split ticket voting since the 1970s. Indeed, the level of ticket splitting in the 2004 presidential election (17 percent) was the lowest since 1964.

One final aspect of the electoral environment is the voter's perception of the two major parties' ideology and the extent to which ideology shapes vote choice. Historically, party conflict in the United States was less driven by ideology, and this is partially attributable to the existence in both parties of 'discordant' wings, that is conservative Democrats and liberal Republicans. However, a process of ideological sorting has taken place since the 1980s, with ideology becoming a stronger determinant of both partisanship and vote choice (Abramowitz and Sanders, 1998; Abramowitz and Knotts, 2006).

As Table 7.3 shows, the American electorate has been able to consistently place the Democratic Party on the liberal end of a seven-point ideology scale, and the Republican Party on the conservative end. Moreover, the level of ideological polarization has increased over each decade, with the ideological gap between the parties being most evident in the 2000–2004 period.

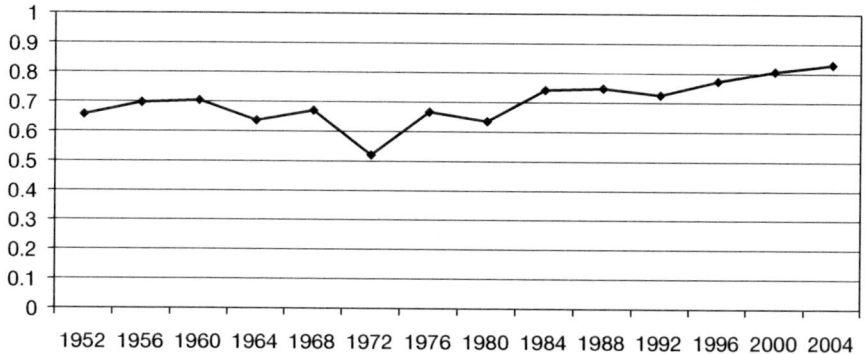

Figure 7.1 Relationship between party identification and presidential vote choice in the USA, 1952–2004

Source: American National Election Studies, cumulative file

Note: The figure shows the Cramer's V statistic to measure the strength of the relationship between party identification and vote choice.

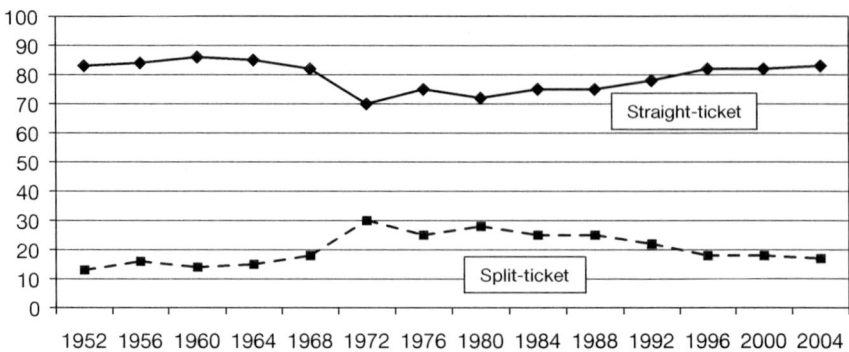

Figure 7.2 Percentage of straight- and split-ticket voting in presidential and US House elections, 1952–2004

Source: American National Election Studies, cumulative file

Note: Split-ticket voting is based on voting for different parties for the presidential and US House vote.

Table 7.3 Ideological placement of parties in the USA by decade

Decade	Democratic Party	Republican Party
1970s	3.1	4.9
1980s	3.3	5.0
1990s	3.3	5.0
2000–2004	3.0	5.2

Source: American National Election Studies, cumulative file

Note: Entries show the mean score for where respondents placed each party on a seven-point scale (1 = extremely liberal, 7 = extremely conservative).

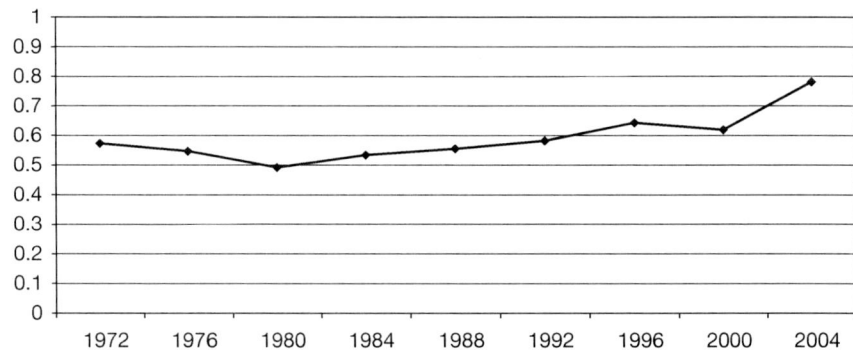

Figure 7.3 Relationship between ideological identification and presidential vote choice in the USA, 1972–2004

Source: American National Election Studies, cumulative file

Note: The figure shows the Cramer's V statistic to measure the strength of the relationship between ideological identification and vote choice.

At the same time, ideology has increasingly come to shape presidential vote. Figure 7.3 shows the size of the relationship between ideological identification and vote choice, with the analysis confined to liberals and conservatives.

These findings, taken together with the declining affect of traditional social group cleavages on vote choice (Levine, Carmines and Huckfeldt 1997), indicate the growing importance of ideology at the individual level. At the aggregate level, state-level ideology is now a stronger predictor of a state's presidential vote than in prior decades (Erikson, 2001).

Political marketing techniques and strategy in the United States

The origins of political marketing in the United States can be traced back to the 1960 presidential election and the campaign of John F. Kennedy. This campaign marked the first time a candidate made extensive use of public opinion surveys in an innovative manner (Jacobs, 1993; Jacobs and Shapiro, 1994). It was also the first campaign where the pollster played a key role and with results from polls used to shape campaign strategy.

Using polls to gather market intelligence in US presidential elections was, however, increasingly utilized more in a manner that suggests a *sales-orientation*. For example, the classic *The Selling of a President 1968* (McGinniss, 1969) describes how Richard Nixon's campaign sought to package and re-brand a 'new Nixon' through the use of television advertising, stage-managed appearances and scripted sound bites. The emphasis on creating and 'selling' a candidate to the electorate has arguably been central to the strategy of presidential candidates ever since, and some have argued this renders American parties—or more accurately candidates—sales-oriented rather than market-oriented (Niffenegger, 1989; O'Shaughnessy, 1990).

However, to suggest that presidential campaigns were entirely sales-oriented may overstate the case. For example, in 1976 Jimmy Carter's pollster adopted marketing techniques to appeal to different segments of the electorate. Moreover, even the campaigns of Ronald Reagan in 1980 and 1984—arguably the template for a sales-orientation—exhibited aspects of a market-orientation (Newman, 1994). The Reagan campaign conducted formal market intelligence to design a product that was consonant with the wishes of a majority of the electorate, promoting policies to reduce the size of the government, lower taxes and projecting strong leadership. This produced significant support beyond the traditional Republican voter base, by appealing to what have been termed 'Reagan Democrats', that is, traditional Democratic identifiers who nonetheless voted twice for Reagan and who remained central to the Republican electoral coalition in electing George H. W. Bush in 1988. This broad coalition enabled the Republicans to win three presidential elections in a row for the first time since before the New Deal era.

While aspects of a market-orientation were evident in US presidential elections from the 1960s onwards, Newman (1994) argues that the 1992 presidential campaign marked a real watershed in the evolution of market-oriented presidential campaigns. The successful campaign of Bill Clinton relied on the sophisticated use of voter segmentation to build a winning electoral strategy, while effectively communicating a message of change together with policies that polls showed voters cared most about—the economy and health care (Newman, 1994: 130). However, the inability of the Clinton administration to deliver on campaign promises led some to question the applicability of political market-orientation in the United States (Ingram and Lees-Marshment, 2002).

The case of George W. Bush's use of political marketing in the 2000 presidential election does suggest however that a market-orientation is possible. For example, Knuckey and Lees-Marshment (2005) suggest that Bush's campaign was consistent with a market-oriented approach with respect to market-intelligence, appealing to voter segments and communicating to the electorate that Bush was a different type of Republican, a 'compassionate conservative.' On the other hand, Shaw (2006) notes that 'the Bush campaign was typically uninterested in tailoring unique campaign appeals for specific jurisdictions' (56), and that Bush himself often expressed disdain for polling (111). Hence, the evidence is somewhat mixed, although it is clear that the Bush campaign made extensive and sophisticated use of various marketing techniques.

Political marketing in the 2004 US presidential election

The final section of this chapter discusses the extent to which the two major party candidates—George W. Bush and John Kerry—adopted a market-oriented approach in the 2004 presidential election. This election can be viewed as an indicator of the extent to which US political parties are market-oriented.

The first stage of a potential market-oriented approach is gathering market intelligence, and in the case of the defeated Democratic Party this meant understanding why Al Gore had lost the 2000 contest to George W. Bush. The internal debate within the party essentially revolved around whether Gore's populist 'people versus the powerful' campaign in 2000 had cost the party support. Those associated with the moderate wing of the party, such as the Democratic Leadership Council (DLC), argued that such a campaign had cost the party middle-class support, the very type of voters that Clinton had assiduously courted since 1992. Moreover, the populist appeal was pitched to blue-collar workers, a segment of the population that was shrinking in size (Judis and Texeira, 2002). According to this diagnosis, Gore lost because he was not able to attract more affluent, white-collar professionals in 2000.

Former Governor Howard Dean articulated a contrasting view. Rather than pursuing a strategy of reaching out to new voters and disaffected Republicans—two important segments from the perspective of the DLC—Dean argued that the Democratic base had to be energized. Dean claimed to represent the 'Democratic wing of the Democratic Party,' and this approach seems more consistent with a product-orientation. Indeed, Dean's criticism of a market orientation was that Democratic core values and ideals were being abandoned. As Dean noted, 'We're not going to beat George Bush by being Bush lite. The way to beat George Bush is to give the 50 percent of Americans who quit voting because they can't tell the difference between the Democratic and Republican Party—give them a reason to vote again.'

The 'energize the base' strategy began to appear sounder as opposition to the war in Iraq began to gain traction among Democratic Party identifiers. Dean had opposed the war in Iraq, and that opposition coupled with his appeal to core party members through innovative use of the Internet elevated him to front-runner status by the middle of 2003, easily overtaking John Kerry who had led polls and fundraising in 2002. Dean's use of the Internet coupled with the rise of the 'blogosphere' has revolutionized political communications in US elections, a development that was perhaps best understood by the campaign of Barack Obama in the 2008 presidential election (see the conclusion for a brief discussion). While the rise of the Internet has allowed candidates and parties to even more finely-tune their message at election time, it has also meant that voters can now find and seek out news about the candidates and the campaigns that best fit their preexisting political persuasions. It is somewhat ironic that a medium that delivers information quickly and easy to voters may, at the same time, reduce the ability of candidates and parties to appeal to opposition partisan supporters.

While Kerry would ultimately triumph in the 2004 nomination race, Dean's candidacy and the movement it spawned within the Democratic Party were nevertheless profound. It ultimately re-shaped the entire strategy of the Kerry campaign, and, again, it was strategy that was adopted and fine-tuned by Barack Obama four years later. In order to understand how the Dean campaign affected the positioning of the Democratic field in 2004, Figure 7.4 shows the *initial*

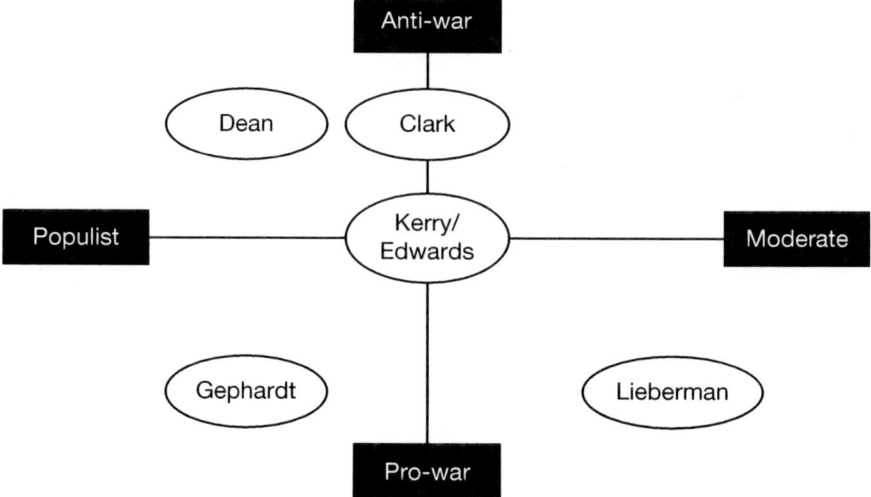

Figure 7.4 Initial positioning of Democratic candidates in the USA on the dimensions of the economy and the Iraq War

Source: Adapted from Ceaser and Busch (2005: 98)

placement of the major Democratic candidates across the dimensions of support for the war in Iraq and general economic policy. Interestingly, although Kerry and John Edwards (Kerry's running mate) supported the resolution to authorize war in Iraq, both increasingly found it necessary to move to the anti-war pole to neutralize Dean. While this helped Kerry win the nomination, it does not suggest a market-orientation but rather a catering to the anti-war base of the Democratic Party. Thus, while Kerry seemed more electable than Dean, because of his stature as a Senator and of his service in Vietnam, he was nonetheless adopting Dean's product-oriented positions and rhetoric.

Compounding Kerry's problem was a general sense that he did not a have a real vision for the Democratic Party. Kerry's movement toward being an anti-war candidate only underscored this, something that Republicans exploited from the moment Kerry became the presumptive Democratic nominee. The Republicans portrayed him as a 'flip-flopper' on the war in Iraq, and used Kerry's own words—'I actually did vote for the $87 million before I voted against it'—to devastating effect in a TV commercial. Kerry, like any challenger to an incumbent president, had to make the case for 'change,' but it was not clear what the nature of such a new direction would be under Kerry. Indeed, in many ways there was no Kerry 'product' or agenda in 2004. Rather, Kerry hoped that opposition to George W. Bush and the war in Iraq together with his own service as a veteran of the Vietnam War would be sufficient to win the election. As Ceasar and Busch (2005: 109) argue: '[Kerry] had served in the Senate since 1985, but he was not a nationally recognized senator . . . his political identity was to many still largely blank.' Even Kerry's pick of John Edwards as the Vice-Presidential running mate did little to amplify the overall theme in the campaign. Edwards differed little to Kerry on policies, and the rationale of Edwards on the ticket—to compete in the South generally and his home state of North Carolina in particular—seemed flawed, given that the Democrats never seriously contested the southern states, except for Florida.

The inability of the Kerry campaign to provide a specific vision was evident at the Democratic convention. While the convention was considered to be well organized and portrayed a more centrist party by deemphasizing socially liberal positions as well as muting more strident attacks on President Bush, the absence of a unifying theme was obvious (Ceaser and Busch, 2005: 117). Indeed, the only theme that seemed to resonate at the convention was Kerry's own war-hero record in Vietnam rather than Kerry's 20-year record in the Senate (Burden, 2005: 37). This record itself came under attack when the Republican group 'Swift Boat Veterans for Truth' launched a series of attacks challenging Kerry's Vietnam record. Thus, although the Democratic convention was well stage-managed, it did little to brand Kerry and the Democratic Party, something that was further evident in Kerry's TV ads in the general election (Tienowitz, 2004).

It is thus not clear that the Democrats ran a market-oriented campaign in 2004. Indeed, it is difficult to apply the sale- or product-oriented label given that there was little in the way of a product to sell or market. As Ceaser and Busch (2005: 117) observe: 'Kerry staked his claim for the presidency on biography to a

greater extent than any presidential candidate since Dwight Eisenhower in 1952.'
Did this explain Kerry's defeat? And did George W. Bush and the Republicans
run a market-oriented campaign?

Unlike the 2000 presidential election, when Bush partly adopted a market-
oriented approach designed to broaden the appeal of the Republican Party
(Knuckey and Lees-Marshment, 2005), Bush's re-election campaign had a very
different goal: mobilize the Republican base. Of course, the events of September
11 had transformed the Bush presidency, and hence the strategy of the Republicans
in 2004. Foreign policy and strong leadership were now stressed over 'compassionate' issues such as health care and education. However, even prior to 9/11
Bush had adopted a 'traditional' conservative agenda of tax cuts, pro-business
regulatory policies, and opposition to partial birth abortion as well as to gay
marriage (Nelson, 2005: 11).

The 2004 Bush campaign was masterminded by Karl Rove, and was based on
Rove's belief that Bush narrowly lost the popular vote to Al Gore by not mobilizing the Republican base. Thus in 2004, an appeal to the Republican base would
be the key to Bush's re-election rather than an appeal to the moderate 'swing
voter.' This strategy was also based on the belief that the size of the electorate
that could be persuaded to vote for either party had dwindled greatly, down to
7 percent according to Rove.

Such an approach seems at odds with a market-orientation, which when applied
by political parties has usually been to attract non-traditional converts to the party.
This highlights the difference between being market-oriented and making use of
marketing techniques (Strömbäck, 2007), as the Bush campaign was very effective
and sophisticated in its usage of marketing techniques while attempting to mobilize
the Republican base. For example, the RNC's database of potential supporters—
Voter Vault—was utilized to target Bush voters. As Matthew Dowd, chief
strategist for Bush's re-election campaign, noted:

> We did a fairly sophisticated analysis of what magazines people read or what
> kind of cars they own or where they live, a combination of what issues they're
> interested in. If somebody thinks that the war on terror is paramount and it's
> very important, they're more likely to be a Republican these days than a
> Democrat. If somebody is against the war in Iraq, they're more likely to be
> a Democrat these days than they are a Republican. So both with where
> people stand on issues today, which you could find out fairly easy [through]
> polling and research, and also their social or household habits will tell you
> a lot. (Quoted in http://www.pbs.org/wgbh/pages/frontline/shows/architect/
> interviews/dowd.html)

In appealing to the Republican base, the leadership qualities of President Bush
were emphasized in early TV commercials. Mark McKinnon, the creative director
of the Bush campaign advertising, noted that: 'We were trying to communicate
strength, trust and values' (quoted in Devlin, 2005: 282). Interestingly, the Bush
campaign placed greater emphasis on 'narrowcasting'—through radio and cable

channels—than through broadcasting on the major TV networks. As Dowd observed: 'If you are active and really put your resources into radio and cable, you have more Republican listeners and watchers on those. . . . So you are actually reaching more Republicans than they are Democrats.' In addition, the Bush campaign relied heavily on negative advertising in 2004, again a strategy designed to reach the GOP than to appeal to swing voters. By one estimation, almost 75 percent of Bush's TV ads in 2004 were negative (Devlin, 2005).

The result of the 2004 election appears to vindicate the Republican's base strategy approach, although Bush only won by less than three percentage points. However, the base strategy seems vindicated by the fact that there was very little fluctuation or volatility in the electorate during the general election campaign (Pomper, 2005: 53). This suggests most voters had made their minds up about the candidates, and the successful candidate would be the one that mobilized more of its base on Election Day. Indeed, the 60 percent voter turnout in 2004—the highest since 1968—suggests that both parties were successful in getting their support mobilized on Election Day. Ironically, had the Democrats nominated Howard Dean as its nominee, a base strategy may have been easier to execute for the Democrats given that Dean, like the Bush campaign, implicitly eschewed a campaign that reached out to swing voters.

Table 7.4 shows that there was exceptionally little crossover support for either candidate, with Bush winning 93 percent of Republicans and Kerry 89 percent of Democrats. Most important is that the relative number of self-identified Democrats and Republicans were equal, which again indicates the success of the Republicans in activating its base. A similar pattern is evident when breaking the vote down by ideology, with few liberals supporting Bush or conservatives supporting Kerry.

Table 7.4 2004 presidential vote choice in the USA by partisanship, ideology and issues

	Size of Group	Bush	Kerry
Party identification			
Democratic	37%	11%	89%
Independent	26%	48%	49%
Republican	37%	93%	6%
Ideology			
Liberal	21%	13%	85%
Moderate	45%	45%	54%
Conservative	34%	84%	15%
Issues: which mattered most?			
Moral values	22%	80%	18%
Economy/Jobs	20%	18%	80%
Terrorism	19%	86%	14%
Iraq	15%	25%	74%
Health care	8%	22%	78%
Taxes	5%	56%	44%
Education	4%	25%	75%

Source: National Election pool exit poll

Moreover, the finding that moral values was viewed by voters as the important issue that decided their vote further reinforces the notion of a Republican base that was energized, given the fact that voters citing moral values gave 80 percent support to Bush.

Political marketing trends and conclusion: Toward market-oriented political parties in the USA?

The potential for a market-oriented approach by political parties in the United States is, at best, mixed. Structural aspects of the American political system, most importantly the separation of power, decentralized political parties and candidate-centered elections, provide limitations for the emergence of market-oriented parties. On the other hand, technological advances in campaigning will—and will continue to—allow parties to engage in the type of market intelligence to allow for the select targeting of voters.

Perhaps the most interesting aspect of contemporary American politics is the strength of partisanship and ideology in shaping vote choice. Much of the political marketing literature assumes that the voters' party loyalties have diminished and that a volatile electorate provides an environment where voters are increasingly critical 'consumers' of politics. In the case of the United States increasingly partisan voting and electoral stability challenge such a perspective.

The 2008 presidential campaign illustrates many of the points made above. While a more complete discussion of political marketing in the 2008 campaign is a topic for future research, one interesting aspect of that campaign is worthy of note. Despite both parties nominating candidates who had the potential to appeal to supporters of the other party—and re-branding the appeal of their respective parties—the evidence suggests that neither Barack Obama nor John McCain made headway among opposition partisans. For example, exit polls reveal that Obama received the support of just 9 percent of Republican Party identifiers, while McCain attracted just 10 percent support from Democrats. This would suggest that Obama's impressive victory—receiving the highest share of the vote for a winning Democrat since Lyndon B. Johnson's landslide victory in 1964—was mainly built around a *mobilization* of Democratic Party identifiers. Of course, the national picture may obscure evidence at the state level that Obama was able to attract crossover support from Republicans in 'battleground' states, especially given that Obama won some states, such as Indiana, North Carolina and Virginia, that have long been in the GOP column. However, even in those states carried by Obama that were Republican states in 2004, the evidence of an appeal to GOP voters is limited. Obama's *best* performance in these states was winning 13 percent support among Republican identifiers in Indiana. He won just 8 percent of the Republican vote in Virginia and only 4 percent in North Carolina.

Again, 2008 illustrates the paradox in the case of the United States where although marketing strategies were certainly deployed—particularly by the Obama campaign, to identify and mobilize potential supporters through 'new media' and technology—long-term forces, such as partisanship, ultimately were decisive in shaping the vote. This, however, may have been less a failure of Obama to execute a market-oriented strategy, and more to do with McCain imitating Bush's 'base' strategy from 2004—illustrated by the choice of running-mate Sarah Palin and the emphasis on tax cuts—which may have even prevented a poor performance by the GOP in 2008 from turning into an electoral rout.

If voters' preferences are shaped long before the election campaign, then the MOP model may seem to be limited in describing and explaining American party politics and elections, given that such a model assumes that election campaigns make a difference. While American parties and campaigns will continue to develop and increase their skills in and usages of marketing techniques, these will probably be used in a manner that suggests a sales-orientation rather than a market-orientation, an approach that emphasizes the mobilization of new voters rather than the conversion of existing voters. The more ideologically polarized the political climate and the electorate remain, the less likely a market-orientation becomes, with a product- or sales-orientation the most likely option for parties to pursue.

At the same time, it is admittedly difficult to classify either the Democrats or the Republicans as simply product-, sales- or market-oriented, and maybe the case of the United States suggests that these classifications are not mutually exclusive. More generally, the example of the United States underscores how the prospects of market-oriented political parties are not just conditioned by the political arena and the electoral environment. Instead the political arena and electoral environment may themselves interact with how a campaign evolves and is ultimately executed.

References/further reading

Abramowitz, A. I. and Saunders, K. (1998) 'Ideological Realignment in the U.S. Electorate', *Journal of Politics*, 60(3): 634–52.

Abramowitz, A. I. and Knotts, H. G. (2006) 'Ideological Realignment in the U.S. Electorate: A Comparison of Northern and Southern White Voters in the Pre-Reagan, Reagan, and Post-Reagan Eras', *Politics & Policy*, 34: 94–109.

Abramson, P. R., Aldrich, J. H. and Rohde, D. W. (2003) *Continuity and Change in the 2000 and 2002 Elections*, Washington, DC: CQ Press.

Anstead, N. (2008) 'The Internet and Campaign Finance in the US and the UK: An Institutional Comparison', *Journal of Information, Technology and Politics*, 5(3): 285–302.

Barone, M. (2001) '49 Percent Nation', *National Journal*, 8 June.

Bartels, L. M. (2000) 'Partisanship and Voting Behavior, 1952–1996', *American Journal of Political Science*, 44(1): 35–50.

Beck, P. A. (1984) 'The Dealignment Era in America', in R. J. Dalton, S. C. Flanagan and P. A. Beck (eds) *Electoral Change in Advanced Industrialized Democracies*, Princeton: Princeton University Press.

Beck, P. A. and Sorauf, F. J. (1992) *Party Politics in America*, New York: Harper Collins.

Black, E. and Black, M. (2007) *Divided America: The Ferocious Power Struggle in American Politics*, New York: Simon and Schuster.

Broder, D. (1971) *The Party's Over*, New York: Harper and Row.

Burden, B. C. (2005) 'The Nomination: Technology, Money and Transferable Momentum', in M. Nelson (ed.) *The Elections of 2004*, Washington, DC: CQ Press. [18–43]

Ceaser, J. W. and Busch, A. E. (2005) *Red Over Blue: The 2004 Elections and American Politics*, Boulder, CO: Roman and Littlefield.

Currinder, M. (2005) 'Campaign Finance: Funding the Presidential and Congressional Elections', in M. Nelson (ed.) *The Elections of 2004*, Washington, DC: CQ Press. [108–132]

Devlin, L. P. (2005) 'Contrasts in Presidential Campaign Commercials of 2004', *American Behavioral Scientist*, 49(2): 279–313.

Downs, A. (1957) *An Economic Theory of Democracy*, New York: Harper.

Edsall, T. B. (2006) *Building Red America: The New Conservative Coalition and the Drive for Permanent Power*, New York: Basic Books.

Edsall, T. B. and Grimaldi, J. V. (2004) 'On Nov. 2, GOP Got More Bang For Its Billion, Analysis Shows', *Washington Post*, 30 December: A1.

Erikson, R. S. (2001) 'The 2000 Presidential Election in Historical Perspective', *Political Research Quarterly*, 116(1): 29–52.

Epstein, L. (1986) *Political Parties in the American Mold*, Madison, WI: University of Wisconsin Press.

Ingram, P. and Lees-Marshment, J. (2002) 'The Anglicisation of Political Marketing: How Blair Out-Marketed Clinton', *Journal of Public Affairs*, 5: 44–56.

Jacobs, L. R. (1993) *The Health of Nations: Public Opinion in the Making of American and British Health Policy*, Ithaca, NY: Cornell University Press.

Jacobs, L. R. and Shapiro, R. Y. (1994) 'Issues, Candidate Image, and Priming: The Use of Private Polls in Kennedy's 1960 Presidential Campaign', *American Political Science Review*, 88(3): 527–540.

Jacobson, G. C. (2007) *A Divider, Not A Uniter: George W. Bush and the American People*, New York: Pearson.

Judis, J. B. and Teixeira, R. (2002) *The Emerging Democratic Majority*, New York: Scribner.

Keith, B. E., Magleby, D. B., Nelson, C. J., Orr, E., Westlye, M. C. and Wolfinger, R. E. (1992) *The Myth of the Independent Voter*, Berkeley, CA: University of California Press.

Knuckey, J. and Lees-Marshment, J. (2005) 'American Political Marketing: George W. Bush and the Republican Party', in D. G. Lilleker and J. Lees-Marshment (eds) *Political Marketing in Comparative Perspective*, Manchester: Manchester University Press. [39–58]

Levine, J., Carmines, E. G. and Huckfeldt, R. (1997) 'The Rise of Ideology in the Post-New Deal Party System', *American Politics Quarterly*, 25(1): 19–34.

McGinniss, J. (1969) *The Selling of the President*, New York: Trident.

Miller, W. E. and Shanks, J. M. (1996) *The New American Voter*, Cambridge, MA: Harvard University Press.

Nelson, M. (2005) 'The Setting: George W. Bush, Majority President', in M. Nelson (ed.) *The Elections of 2004*, Washington, DC: CQ Press. [1–17]

Newman, B. (1994) *The Marketing of the President: Political Marketing as Campaign Strategy*, Thousand Oaks, CA: Sage.

Nie, N. H., Verba, S. and Petrocik, J. R. (1979) *The Changing American Voter*, Cambridge, MA: Harvard University Press.

Niffenegger, P. B. (1989) 'Strategies for Success from the Political Marketers', *Journal of Consumer Marketing*, 6(1), 45–61.

Norpoth, H. and Rusk, J. (1982) 'Partisan Dealignment in the American Electorate: Itemizing the Deductions since 1964', *American Political Science Review*, 76: 522–37.

O'Shaughnessy, N. (1990) *The Phenomenon of Political Marketing*, Basingstoke: Macmillan.

Pomper, G. M. (2005) 'The Presidential Election: The Ills of American Politics After 9/11', in M. Nelson (ed.) *The Elections of 2004*, Washington, DC: CQ Press. [42–68]

Shaw, D. R. (2006) *The Race to 2010: The Electoral College and the Campaign Strategies of 2000 and 2004*, Chicago: University of Chicago Press.

Shea, D. M. (1999) 'The Passing of Realignment and the 'Base-less' Party System', *American Politics Quarterly*, 27: 33–57.

Strömbäck, J. (2007) 'Political Marketing and Professionalized Campaigning: A Conceptual Analysis', *Journal of Political Marketing*, 6(2/3): 49–67.

Tienowitz, I. (2004) 'Kerry dropped the ball on branding', *Advertising Age*, November 8: 6.

Wattenberg, M. P. (1996) *The Decline of American Political Parties, 1952–1994*, Cambridge, MA: Harvard University Press.

8 UK political marketing

A question of leadership?[1]

Jennifer Lees-Marshment and
Robin T. Pettitt

The UK is often considered to be an obvious arena for market-oriented political parties, exemplified by Tony Blair's marketing-driven leadership of New Labour which not only saw great success in 1997, but has been emulated by Labour parties in other countries including Germany, New Zealand and more recently Australia with the election of Kevin Rudd in 2007. The political system, where two main parties dominate, facilitates the adoption of market-oriented strategies; it encourages focus on the median target market, and enables a successful party to dominate legislatures and pass legislation easily. However the overall pattern of political marketing is actually more varied when analyzed over a longer time period, both before and after Tony Blair's victory in 1997. This chapter will explore the nature of the electoral market to provide context for consideration of the systemic effects on behaviour, the use of political marketing techniques, political marketing strategy including historical trends as well as fresh empirical analysis of behaviour 2001–2008, and reflections on the issues raised by political marketing in the UK.

The UK political market place

The political system

National elections are held at least every five years by a first-past-the-post (FPTP) electoral system which has tended to favour the two main parties and single party majority governments. Sub-systems exist at local and European levels and in Wales and Scotland where different electoral systems are used. Nationally however, mainly as a result of the a-proportional nature of FPTP, the parliamentary and especially the governmental arenas are dominated by the two major parties, Labour and the Conservatives. Indeed these two parties have between them monopolized government power to the exclusion of all other parties since 1945. It is true that in terms of votes and to a lesser degree seats, various 'third parties' have increased in strength. Further, devolution has created different party systems outside Westminster. However, as Childs argues:

> Regardless of whether one thinks the electoral system is propping up the two-party system at Westminster, it is still thus propped up, and in the most

important of the various political arenas. Put bluntly, elections to the House of Commons matter more than the election of the Hartlepool mayor. (Childs 2006: 60)

For that reason this chapter will focus its attention on the Labour Party and the Conservative Party.

Although they were historically parties of the left and right respectively, first Margaret Thatcher who served as Conservative Prime Minister from 1979 to 1990 attracted Labour constituencies, mainly skilled workers; and second, Tony Blair, Labour Prime Minister 1997–2007, won support from traditional Tory middle-class voters. Parties that win elections enjoy domination of the legislature, a bicameral parliament, enabling delivery of promises without the need to compromise with coalition partners or non-governmental supporters. The centre ground is therefore the key battleground for most elections, which encourages market-oriented strategies. The disadvantage is that internal supporters within major parties can feel abandoned as their support is taken for granted in favour of targeting floating voters in the centre.

Governments are formed by the party holding the largest number of seats, virtually always amounting to an overall majority. However, as can be seen from Table 8.1 the number of seats won by parties does not relate to their vote share. FPTP leaves small parties with little chance of breaking through. Parties are more effective if they target resources in certain seats rather than the overall vote. The next largest party is the Liberal Democrats, who traditionally occupy an equidistant position from both main parties but in recent years has become more left-wing, picking up alienated Labour voters. Other minor parties include the Greens, Scottish National Party, British National Party and Plaid Cymru but they have limited influence at the national level because of the nature of the electoral system. Whilst the major market oriented parties are offered the chance to secure power and implement change, overall voters can be left dissatisfied. Because of the workings of the electoral system this discontent does not manifest itself with the rise of new parties in parliament as it would in other systems. However recent years have seen a rise in electoral abstention and an increase in votes for losing candidates.

Table 8.1 Recent UK election results, vote share and seat share (%)

Year	Labour votes	Labour seats	Conservative votes	Conservative seats	Liberal Democrat votes	Liberal Democrat seats	Other votes	Other seats
1992	34.4	41.6	41.9	51.6	17.8	3.1	5.9	3.7
1997	43.2	63.4	30.7	25	16.8	7	9.3	4.6
2001	40.7	62.5	31.7	25.2	18.3	7.9	9.3	4.4
2005	35.2	55	32.4	30.7	22	9.6	10.4	4.7

Source: http://www.psr.keele.ac.uk/area/uk/uktable.htm

Electioneering regulations

State support for parties is limited to opposition parties in parliament (so-called Short Money). Parties therefore have to rely heavily on private donations which have to be made public. Parties are entitled to free media in the form of television broadcasts for parties fielding candidates in more than one-sixth of seats. Candidates are also entitled to one free Royal Mail distributed electoral leaflet in their constituency and the free use of public buildings for meetings. Campaign expenditure for general elections at the national level is limited to £30,000 for every constituency where the party fields a candidate, plus around £10,000 to candidates in their seats.

The political consumer

Major parties with an eye on government power need to engage in a difficult balancing act. Both Labour and the Conservative Party have had to reach beyond their traditional markets (working-class and middle-upper class respectively), whilst at the same time protect their core vote from encroachment by competing parties. This reflects the changing electoral market, including falling party identification and increasing electoral volatility, noted in all voting behaviour literature since the 1960s. For example, the British election study and British social attitudes survey indicate that:

- the percentage of those expressing very strong identification declined from 42 per cent in 1964, to 13 per cent in 2001; whilst those with no party attachment increased from 10 per cent in 1983 to 21 per cent in 2003;
- party membership has declined in Labour's case from 1,014,524 in 1952 to 200,000 in 2001; and in the Conservative Party from 2,800,000 in 1953 to 300,000 in 2001; political efficacy has declined; the number of those saying the political system could be improved quite a lot or a great deal has increased from 49 per cent in 1973 to 69 per cent in 1994; and in 2003 62 per cent thought voting in elections was a waste of time; turnout fell 18 per cent between 1992 and 2001, and was the largest decline experienced across other established liberal democracies in Europe, North America or the Commonwealth since 1945.

As the traditional class-based market is eroded, new market segments emerge such as young people, so-called grey voters, women and ethnic groups, each with their own distinctive lifestyle, attitude, political participation and demands. Parties therefore need to ensure they respond to these different segments, arguably with differentiated products whilst still maintaining overall coherence. A number of authors also observe an increase in consumerism, albeit without hard data (Lees-Marshment 2004, Lilleker and Negrine 2004, Scammell 2003 and Needham 2003: 7). Lilleker and Scullion (2008: 1) observe how Gordon Brown's maiden speech as Prime Minister in June 2007 'sets out his stall as a Prime Minister that is required to listen and respond to individuals' concerns and meet their aspirations'. Parties also place greater focus on delivery because the public is more consumerist, but at the same time this leads to greater demands making achieving satisfactory and delivery more difficult.

Communicating with political consumers

The UK media is traditionally dominated by television, particularly the taxpayer-funded BBC, but challenged by commercial channels (ITV, Channel 4, Channel 5), satellite television channels such as Sky News, and increasingly by new media such as the internet. The public gain most of their political information from television. Whilst the UK public also gain information from often very partisan newspapers such as the *Telegraph*, *Guardian* and *Independent* broadsheets and the tabloid *Sun*, *Daily Mail* and *Daily Mirror*, their readership is declining alongside the rise of more instant and up-to-date provision on 24-hour television news coverage and the internet. The growth in communication channels and their multiplicity, independence from government, 24/7 timeframe, and facilitation of consumer participation such as blogging and phone-ins make it increasingly difficult for parties to control how they are perceived by the public.

Furthermore, media studies (see for example Bartle and Griffiths 2001, Corner and Pels 2003, McNair 2005, Scammell 2001) note an increasing tendency to be adversarial, aggressive, combative, cynical, and negative and focused on personalities. The critical nature of the media places great pressure on politicians. In an interview on the chat show *Parkinson* in 2006 Blair likened the media to living with a deranged flatmate against whom neither accommodation nor opposition would work.

Such a negative communicative environment does not help facilitate market-oriented politics and undermines a more mature, reflective, responsive and complex political discussion about public needs, new policy options and delivery. Parties respond by focusing on presentation, and intense media management and bypassing the national media by talking directly to the often less cynical local press. But overall in the UK it is hard to communicate new or changed products, more complex policy, nuance and subtlety.

The next two sections will analyze the use of techniques and strategy. For this, we draw on previous political marketing literature in the UK, as well as fresh empirical analysis of more recent behaviour including interviews with party staff and strategists, analysis of primary party documents and consideration of secondary sources.

Political marketing techniques in the UK

The use of political marketing techniques and consultants has risen rapidly in the UK since the 1980s and most visibly since 2000. Labour and the Conservatives regularly commission market research. Indeed, they continually seek advice from parties and consultants abroad, partly through links with parties in other countries, particularly the United States, as well as shared consultants. Techniques appearing in US elections often come to the UK by the next election. This could be due to Americanization, perhaps reflecting the 'special' relationship, but equally can be interpreted as more a reflection of the overall globalization of political marketing with shared awareness and exchange of ideas and consultants between countries.

The importance of techniques depends partly on the strategy adopted. A more sales-oriented approach elevates the importance of marketing tools. For example, in 2005 the Conservatives employed the Australian public-relations firm Crosby-Textor who had advised the Australia Liberal Party. They made significant use of market segmentation and data analysis, and targeted direct mail and telephone messages from call centres. Voter profiling, heavily utilized by the US Republicans and Democrats as the basis for micro-targeting, was utilized by Labour and the Conservatives in the 2005 election. A Conservative staff member involved with the use of Voter Vault in 2005 recalled how this works:

> We've got all this historic information, canvas codes from people's telephone canvassing or survey canvassing or postal surveys of voters . . . [and] took that data and we went to a private city company who hold a whole load of demographic data . . . and . . . look[ed] at . . . demographic factors that correlated with propensity to vote on the one hand, and affinity with the Conservative party on the other. . . . We built a model that predicted where people would lie on this grid. . . . They range from people who are very likely to vote, but unaligned, to people who are Conservative-inclined, but not certain to vote. . . . For each of our seats we went look, let's say the Conservative vote last time was X, we're going to assume that 90 per cent of those people will vote Conservative again without us doing anything. So we came out along this line here, until we got . . . our target zone. (Conservative staff 1 2007)

Table 8.2 shows Seawright's (2005: 954) outline of the Voter Vault cells.

Labour created a centralized communications and call centre which produced direct mail and DVDs for particular candidates in key seats; and utilized a relationship management tool to track contacts with target voters (Butler and Kavanagh 2005: 55).

Table 8.2 Voter Vault cells used in UK Conservative constituency campaigning in 2005

Highest likelihood to vote	7 Opposition voters	8 Undecided voters	9 Conservative voters
	4 Opposition might voters	5 Undecided might voters	6 Conservative might voters
Lowest likelihood to vote	1 Opposition non-voters	2 Undecided non-voters	3 Conservative non-voters
	Lowest Conservative support → Highest Conservative support		

Source: Seawright (2005: 954)

In addition to private formal research through polls and focus groups, parties engage in informal consultations; e.g. the Conservatives with 'Listening to Britain' in 1997–2001; and Labour with 'The Big Conversation' in 2003. However intelligence is not always used effectively. Nick Sparrow from ICM polling company recalled that whilst working for the leader William Hague 'very often we were brought in to do research on subjects where the policy had already been announced' (Sparrow, interviewed by Lees-Marshment, 2007).

Political marketing strategy in the UK

In 1997 Tony Blair led the Labour Party to a landslide victory after changing the product so significantly in response to market intelligence that the 'New Labour design' was copied by other social democratic parties around the world. New Labour's dominance could lead us to conclude that the general trend in the UK is towards market-oriented parties. However, Lees-Marshment's (2001) comprehensive study of marketing by the two main parties between 1979 and 1997, which readers should refer to for detail, actually suggests a more complex pattern. Whilst first election victories, such as the Conservative Party's win in 1979 with Thatcher and Labour's in 1997 with Blair follow behaviour closely aligned with the market-oriented model, their subsequent behaviour in government tended to move away from an MOP and towards a more leadership-driven, if not sales-oriented approach.

Furthermore, Tony Blair's New Labour Party did not fit the model completely even before 1997. It lacked product differentiation and effective internal reaction analysis. The changes Blair made to the party's product to increase its external support created significant dissatisfaction within the party. As Phillip Gould (2007) later reflected, 'it may be a fair criticism to say in the early days that it was poll-driven or too much . . . public opinion-driven'. New Labour in 1997 was market-driven rather than market-oriented. Market-*driven* means it was motivated and determined by public opinion; the market drove the party. Market-*oriented* however would be where there was more balance; where a party is slanted or tilted towards the public – not wholly driven by it. No doubt Blair himself realized this during the course of his time as Prime Minister, but the market-driven approach could be seen as rational, or at least understandable, given the Party had lost four successive elections.

Furthermore, in opposition both Labour between 1979 and 1992, and Conservatives 1997–2005, for an extended period failed to adopt a market-orientation. Partly this was due to internal implementation difficulties, a lack of public support, and also at times the desire to offer a more conviction-led product. As Lilleker, Jackson, and Scullion (2006) indicated, if anything there was a resurgence of more sales-oriented political marketing in the 2005 election. Analysis of particular case studies since 2001 confirms the overall variety in political marketing orientation.

Attitudes towards political marketing

Indeed, elite attitudes towards political marketing vary over time and from party to party. For example, at the 2004 Labour Party conference Blair argued that in a modern 'opportunity society' the individual and not the state should be in charge. However towards the end of his leadership he noted that he had changed as a politician and had become more concerned with taking long-term, sometimes unpopular decisions and letting history be the judge. The most recent trend is to try to re-connect with voters but not quite in the same way as Blair did it, something which is reflected in party staff attitudes to marketing (see Table 8.3).

It is therefore clear that the attitudes towards political marketing are complex and varied in the UK, and in many ways the behaviour of the two main parties reflects this. Below we examine the approaches to marketing in three case studies, with the leaders Michael Howard of the Conservatives, 2003–2005; Tony Blair and Labour; 2001–2007; and David Cameron and the Conservatives, 2005–2007. Analysis suggests a mixed use of the sales- or market-oriented strategy. Far from being a clear case of successful or failed market-orientation, we see a highly mixed picture of approaches and levels of success.

Case study 1: Tony Blair and Labour 2001–2007

Blair's use of political marketing after 2001 showed a move to sales-oriented behaviour as well as a resurgence of market-oriented responsiveness. In Blair's second term of office, 2001–2005, Labour struggled to maintain a market-orientation and pursued more sales-oriented approaches to many issues including tuition fees and the Iraq war (Lees-Marshment 2008). Perhaps because of the loss of his most trusted aide, Alastair Campbell, or an inevitable increase in arrogance which occurs in office, Blair's ability to remain responsive to public opinion was significantly challenged, which saw him lose support as he moved away from a market-orientation. Additionally interviews with Labour staff suggested that

Table 8.3 Attitudes to and use of market intelligence by the three main parties in the UK

- Will Harris (2004), Director of Marketing for the Conservative Party, described his job as 'presenting policy in an appropriate way'; market intelligence in terms of polling was 'less a source of ideas than a check as to how you're doing'.
- Senior Conservative Staff in Strategy (2004): policy areas were 'very much driven by Michael [Howard], personally . . . policy [was] not driven by polls'; the research department was focused on day-to-day media management rather than long-term strategy and product development; and the policy programme was 'built up using conservative principles and consultation'.
- According to senior Labour Party staff (2004), market intelligence was more to 'inform the way something was presented than the actual policy' and to influence 'language' and 'phraseology' to influence perception; staff said they could not 'think of a major policy position that has been taken on the basis of whether it is popular publicly'.

Source: Interviews with staff by Jennifer Lees-Marshment

market intelligence was viewed more as a sales tool than a market-oriented strategy (see Table 8.3).

Nevertheless, Labour also attempted to re-gain a market-orientation before the 2005 election. The Labour Party conducted continual market intelligence and launched a consultation exercise, the Big Conversation, in November 2003 in response to awareness that the party was beginning to seem out of touch. This facilitated positive, reflective and constructive discussion as a 'way of engaging the public beyond the party' (Karia 2004) although it was criticized as being nothing more than a PR exercise (Wring 2005: 60). In 2004 Labour began a reconnection strategy following advice from the co-creation company Promise (www.promisecorp.com). Promise's analysis connected brand positioning with the Lees-Marshment (2001) product, sales and market-oriented party, acknowledging the success of UK Labour in becoming an MOP with the launching of a new brand, with the reform of Clause IV of the party constitution. However by 2005 the New Labour brand was 'under threat'; 'the brand lens through which people viewed the party had become clouded by the Iraq War and constant attacks on the government' (Promise 2005). Tony Blair's weaknesses affected the whole government because he was 'an icon of the brand'. Promise conducted unusual market intelligence, involving expressive techniques using role play and feelings and action, which enabled people to express deeply held feelings from which to then reconstruct solutions for Labour: see Table 8.4.

This laid the foundations for a reconnection strategy (see Promise 2005 and Scammell 2008). Blair was publicly exposed to intense criticism from ordinary people so that he was seen to face and accept voter discontent. He acknowledged

Table 8.4 Two-chair market intelligence about Tony Blair, 2004

Promise used Two-Chair Work where one of the people in a chair was a voter; and the other one played Mr Blair; first Blair was played as voters saw him; and then as they'd like him to be, where 'he' acknowledged their discontent and was more humble:

> First, as Mr Blair is seen currently by voters: 'I'm afraid you've only got part of the picture. From where I sit the war in Iraq was crucial to the cause of world peace. But I understand that it's difficult to see the whole thing for you. You put me in charge and I just do what I think to be the right thing. I am sure that history will prove us right in the end.'

> Second, Mr Blair as voters wanted to hear him be: 'I understand your feelings and I realize that there are many who do not agree with me over Iraq. I realized this as I listened to more and more people over the past months. I still believe on balance that we did the right thing, though I have been shocked to appreciate the depth of frustration among those who disagree with me. I solemnly promise to spend more time at home in contact with our own people and to debate these issues more seriously before we launch on such an endeavour again.'

There is no difference in policy position in either case. But the difference to role-playing voters was significant; the second comment was much more acceptable. This laid the foundations for the reconnection strategy.

Source: Promise (2005)

criticism on the war and showed respect for public opinion, even if he disagreed with it. This shows that, despite earlier predictions in Lilleker and Lees-Marshment (2005), marketing was only suitable for opposition, there is the potential to re-connect in government. Labour won again in 2005.

Of course, had Blair faced a more market-oriented Tory Party electorate outcomes could have been very different. Furthermore, whilst Blair continued in power from 2005 to 2007 his reputation and the Labour Party as a whole showed signs of being contaminated by the previous SOP behaviour. Blair had already announced his intention to resign before the next election, which prompted intense speculation about his successor. Thus, whilst still in government the Labour Party's ability to set the agenda, show responsiveness and to deliver was severely constrained.

Additionally, the lack of consideration of the internal market and product adjustment in the early stages of New Labour (see Lees-Marshment 2001: 181) began to show its effect. Whilst Labour members have always been rebellious (Pettitt 2006) the highly centralized approach to implementing New Labour is no doubt partly to blame for the membership decline, from 400,000 in 1997 to 200,000 by 2005 (Butler and Kavanagh 2005: 26). This made it more difficult for the party to mobilize supporters. The other long-standing issue which became more of a problem over time was the lack of perceived delivery. Upon winning in 2001, Tony Blair established the Downing Street Delivery Unit to ensure the delivery of election pledges on public service reform (Barber 2007). However, although the government increased investment the effect on overall standards was questioned, for example a poll in October 2006 revealed 'voters think the health service has got worse, not better, during Labour's decade in power and the doubling of investment since 1997 is perceived as having been wasted'.

Support for Blair/Labour still fell after 2005: in October 2006 support for Labour dropped to its lowest level in almost 20 years with the Conservatives opening up a potentially election-winning ten-point lead (*The Guardian*, 25 October 2006). Although Blair was an electorally successful leader and utilized political marketing effectively to win three elections, he did make mistakes, but their impact was limited because he faced an ineffective sales-oriented Conservative Party and responded to market intelligence indicating the need to re-engage with voters.

Case study 2: Conservatives under Michael Howard 2003–2005

In 2003 the Conservatives removed Iain Duncan-Smith who had been trying to reach out to new markets and selected Michael Howard in his place and embarked on a sales-oriented approach (Lees-Marshment 2008). Howard's leadership initiated a return to more right-wing politics to suit their traditional markets. Opinion research was used to test best ways to communicate pre-existing policies and to choose the ones that would resonate most with voters, not to create new ones. Marketing was seen less as a way to produce policies and more as a communication activity, even if one informed by market segmentation and voter profiling.

Marketing communications were employed by the party. At the 2004 conference the party launched its 'ten words' – lower taxes, cleaner hospitals, more police, controlled immigration, school discipline. These matched current topical issues but their simplistic nature gave the impression that the Conservative Party did not have the maturity necessary to deal with the complex reality of running the country (see Lilleker, Jackson and Scullion 2006 for further detail).

The Conservatives lost the election, with only a 0.5 per cent increase in vote share, albeit getting 33 new seats. Polls showed the product was not highly rated by voters. Ashcroft (2005: 85–87) notes how the party's vote share fell in many areas of England as well as amongst professionals. We can therefore see from this case, that although the theory suggests if a party takes a sales-oriented approach and loses, it will adopt a different approach for the next election, this is not always the case. The Conservatives abandoned an MOP strategy between 1997 and 2001, and chose an SOP for 2005. Will Harris argued when interviewed that 'the Conservatives are more principled in opposition than they should have been' (Harris 2006).

Case study 3: The Conservatives and David Cameron 2005–2007

David Cameron was elected after the Tories lost a third successive election in 2005, and embarked on a project to reform and rebrand the party. The party conducted the usual formal research, but also informal discussion through policy groups set up to consult and discuss issues.[2] The policy groups were chaired by Conservatives, but operated somewhat independently from the party (Conservative staff 2 2007) and drew on varied groups of people with different expertise. Mid-term policy reports were produced with new ideas, at times causing a certain level of controversy.

Conservative staff interviewed noted that Cameron 'set about in the first period of his leadership to have a de-contamination of the Conservative brand' to reduce negativity associated with previous party behaviour (Conservative staff 1 2007). Two interesting key themes were communicated effectively which helped to re-brand the party and gain public support: environmentalism and social responsibility. These were conveyed through several symbolic acts such as photo opportunities with Cameron, amongst other places on a Norwegian glacier, a new party symbol (a green tree and a blue sky), actual action to demonstrate caring (senior Conservative MP Oliver Letwin working in Belmarsh prison) and a redeveloped website including the so-called Webcameron feature consisting of brief films with David Cameron.[3] Initial policy ideas including taxes on air travel to tackle global warming and a reduction in inheritance tax have tested the market and been relatively successful in responding to public concerns.

The most interesting aspect of Cameron's marketing is that there has been a fuller and more effective implementation of the MOP concept, with elements of both leading and following, and responsiveness to internal and external markets, and a process of product adjustment. Cameron has appealed both to Tories and to Labour supporters dissatisfied with a perceived lack of delivery on the public sector under Labour by refusing simply to promise lower taxes. New-found support for the NHS was aimed at appealing to voters concerned with potential cuts to public services. In a speech at the Party's spring conference Cameron argued that 'today's Conservative Party backs the NHS, heart and soul'. The party even usurped Labour's traditional position as the party most trusted to run the NHS (ICM poll in October 2006). Conservative staff argued that after market intelligence the focus was on 'putting together a detailed policy platform that reflects Conservative values, but also enables us to win support from the broad-based electorate for the general election' (Conservative staff 1 2007).

The party's new policy document *Built to Last* combined the economy, society and environment, arguing the Party was fighting for a society free from state interference, and for monetary wealth, but also for quality of life and 'making poverty history'. The social responsibility and environmentalism themes hold the potential to attract both traditional and new markets. When interviewed for the *Telegraph* newspaper in December 2006 Cameron emphasized not only the need for change in the Conservative Party, but also how these changes were based on traditional conservative values. The April 2007 party election broadcast showed him meeting and talking to a variety of people, and not just listening but sometimes saying no to what the participants wanted; suggesting a degree of leadership alongside responsiveness, rather than just agreeing with everyone.

However, Cameron's approach has not been without problems. Cameron has also been criticized for being nothing more than presentation. Franz Luntz, consultant, ran a focus group of floating voters on Cameron's first year as leader, published in the *Daily Telegraph* newspaper (4 December 2006), and noted that 'there is an underlying fear of "spin" that could undermine your long-term success. . . . Floating voters believe you are actively engaged in a sincere effort to bring about fundamental change, and they appreciate it . . . [but] they are afraid you'll turn into the Tony Blair of 2006'. Cameron was hit by a defection of a backbench MP, Quentin Davies, who argued in his resignation letter that the Conservative Party has 'ceased collectively to believe in anything, or to stand for anything. It has no bedrock. It exists on shifting sands. A sense of mission has been replaced by a PR agenda'.

Like Labour pre-1997, Cameron is leader of a party which seems to be reluctant to follow him to the centre of British politics where elections are won. The party has been successful in beating back former leadership attempts to introduce a market-oriented approach (Lees-Marshment 2008). The environmentally friendly policies indirectly suggested an attack on business, with greater regulation which did not fit in with the party's usual business-friendly policies. Policy proposals were seen as pandering to the party's right (tax credits for married couples) or have led to a damaging retreat under fire from the party's right (grammar schools). Criticism increased particularly as Brown took over and enjoyed a bounce in opinion polls, although once positions changed back and Cameron regained his positive position it became easier to continue with the MOP strategy.

The main lesson from the Cameron case study is that whilst there is resurgence of MOP-behaviour, he attempted to implement a more comprehensive, adjusted MOP design that could attract new markets and be accepted by the party. This was also partly true of Gordon Brown who took over from Tony Blair as leader of the Labour Party and Prime Minister in June 2007. The timing of this publication prevents a full analysis of Brown's use of political marketing, but similarly to Cameron, Brown has attempted to reach out to new markets, including non- and cross-partisan appointments in his cabinet, eschewing spin, inviting Margaret Thatcher, leader of the Conservatives 1974–1990, to Downing Street and changes to inheritance tax. As a Labour MP said when interviewed 'Gordon has . . . analyzed and saw what worked, what didn't work, what could be improved' (Labour MP 2007): in many ways both leaders learnt lessons from their predecessors showing that political marketing will continue to develop in practice beyond the confines of the Blair New Labour design.

Political marketing trends and conclusion

Political marketing is clearly a strong part of UK politics, but the overall trends are varied, with the MOP dominating only at certain times, and overall it would be argued that SOP behaviour is more prevalent. As such, despite previous criticisms (see for example Ormrod 2006) that the MOP model only works for the UK because of systemic differences, an alternative conclusion is that it only works at certain times in certain conditions unrelated to the system.

The main lessons from the three new case studies are that:

1   Parties do still decide to adopt a sales-orientation; indeed even after losing successive elections internal culture and attitudes may prevent emergence of an MOP;
2   Marketing techniques are therefore as plentiful as the use of marketing concepts;
3   Nevertheless, using SOP strategies and marketing communications to sell an unwanted product will not win an election;
4   Leaders can become sales-oriented whilst in power, but by neglecting consultation with party and public, they lose support;
5   Leaders and parties can move back from a sales- to a more market-oriented approach, even in a third-term government;
6   However, once a leader has a damaged reputation, it is difficult to re-build it – which damages the party;
7   Internal reaction analysis remains crucial: it either lays or erodes foundations for the long-term;
8   Leaders are trying to utilize a market-orientation but in a more balanced, adjusted form than Tony Blair/New Labour offered.

This therefore suggests a more nuanced pattern of political marketing strategy and techniques.

However, it remains to be debated, in conjunction with consideration of all chapters in this book, as to whether this is related to the nature of the system. This analysis suggests that other non-systemic factors also impact on the emergence of an MOP or SOP strategy, such as:

- *attitude and power of the political leader.* Some leaders are more convinced than others of the need for an MOP approach and some leaders may not have sufficient control over their party to pull it in an MOP direction. Arguably William Hague and Iain Duncan Smith wanted to but could not, whereas Michael Howard could have but did not want to. Since 1997 only David Cameron has had both the inclination and the power.
- *the attitude of the party.* In 1997 the Labour Party, having suffered 18 years in opposition, was despite a few vocal critics willing to rethink their entire product in order to win. In the Conservative Party the weakness of Hague and Duncan Smith was compounded by a party not yet convinced of the need for change. Only by 2005 after three stinging defeats was the party willing to elect and follow a leader openly set on changing the party.
- *nature of the competition and their use of marketing.* One of the main reasons Labour slipped from MOP to SOP after 2001 was the continued SOP stance of the Conservatives.
- *responsiveness to market intelligence.* As argued above parties are not always willing or able to act on what the market is telling them.

These made a difference for UK Labour 1979–1992, and for the Conservatives 1997–2005, and New Labour in government 2001–2005. Therefore, while the SOP/MOP pattern is not so clear any more, this is not so much because of the UK political system but individual leadership, electoral conditions, and the state of the competition. Furthermore, the current trend is for major parties to adopt an MOP but in a more comprehensive manner than Blair, with more attention paid to product adjustment in response to both external *and* internal input. This makes the process of adopting an MOP more complex, but potentially more successful long-term.

Notes

1 This chapter was completed 23 April 2008. Lees-Marshment's interviews for this chapter were funded by Auckland University New Staff Grant 2006–2007 and research completion by Auckland University Faculty Research Grant 2008–2009.
2 See http://www.conservatives.com/tile.do?def=policy.home.page (accessed 26 April 2007).
3 See http://www.conservatives.com/Video/Webcameron.aspx (accessed 12 February 2009).

References/further reading

Ashcroft, M. A. (2005) *Smell the Coffee: A Wake-Up Call for the Conservative Party*, London: CGI Europe.
Barber, M. (2007) *An Instruction to Deliver*, London: Politicos.

Bartle, J. and Griffiths, D. (eds) (2001) *Political Communications Transformed: From Morrison to Mandelson*, Houndmills, UK; New York: Palgrave.

Bowler, S. and Farrell, D. M. (eds) (1992) *Electoral Strategies and Political Marketing*, Basingstoke, UK: Macmillan.

Butler, D. and Kavanagh, D. (2005) *The British General Election of 2005*, New York: Palgrave Macmillan.

Childs, S. (2006) 'Political Parties and Party Systems', in P. Dunleavy, R. Heffernan, P. Cowley and C. Hay (eds) *Developments in British Politics*, Basingstoke, UK; New York: Palgrave Macmillan.

Corner, J. and Pels, D. (eds) (2003) *Media and the Restyling of Politics*, London; Thousand Oaks, CA: Sage.

Lees-Marshment, J. (2001) *Political Marketing and British Political Parties*, Manchester: Manchester University Press.

Lees-Marshment, J. (2004) *The Political Marketing Revolution: Transforming the Government of the UK*, Manchester: Manchester University Press.

Lees-Marshment (2005) 'The Marketing Campaign: The British General Election of 2005', special issue of the *Journal of Marketing Management*, 9/10.

Lees-Marshment, J. (2008) *Political Marketing and British Political Parties*, 2nd edition, Manchester: Manchester University Press.

Lilleker, D., Jackson, N. and Scullion, R. (eds) (2006) *The Marketing of Political Parties: Political Marketing and the 2005 British General Election*, Manchester: Manchester University Press.

Lilleker, D. and Lees-Marshment, J. (eds) (2005) *Political Marketing: A Comparative Perspective*, Manchester: Manchester University Press.

Lilleker, D. and Negrine, R. (2004) 'Not Big Brand Names But Corner Shops: Marketing Politics to a Disengaged Electorate', *Journal of Political Marketing*, 2(1): 55–74.

Lilleker, D. and Scullion, R. (2008) 'Introduction', in D. Lilleker and R. Scullion (eds) *Voters or Consumers: Imagining the Contemporary Electorate*, Newcastle, UK: Cambridge Scholars Publishing. [1–11]

McNair, B. (2005) *Introduction to Political Communication*, New York: Routledge.

Needham, C. (2003) *Citizen-Consumers: New Labour's Marketplace Democracy*, London: Catalyst.

Ormrod, R. P. (2006) 'A Critique of the Lees-Marshment Market-Oriented Party Model', *Politics*, 26(2): 110–118.

Pettitt, R. T. (2006) 'Rebellion by the Seaside: How Single Member Plurality has Affected Dissent at the Labour Party Conference', *Representation*, 42(4): 289–301.

Promise (2005) 'Reconnecting the Prime Minister,' Company paper, Promise UK. Available at: www.promisecorp.com (accessed 15 January 2008).

Rudd, C. (2005) 'Marketing the Message or the Messenger? The New Zealand Labour Party, 1990–2003', in D. Lilleker and J. Lees-Marshment (eds) *Political Marketing: A Comparative Perspective*, Manchester: Manchester University Press.

Scammell, M. (2001) 'The Media and Media Management', in A. Seldon (ed.) *The Blair Effect: The Blair Government 1997–2001*, London: Little Brown.

Scammell, M. (2003) 'Citizen consumers: Towards a New Marketing of Politics?' in J. Corner and D. Pels (eds) *Media and the Restyling of Politics*, London; Thousand Oaks, CA: Sage. [117–136]

Scammell, M. (2008) 'Brand Blair: Marketing Politics in the Consumer Age,' in D. Lilleker and R. Scullion (eds) *Voters or Consumers: Imagining the Contemporary Electorate*, Newcastle, UK: Cambridge Scholars Publishing. [97–113]

Seawright, D. (2005) 'On a low road: The 2005 Conservative Campaign', *Journal of Marketing Management*, 21(9–10): 943–957.

Seymour-Ure, C. (2002) 'New Labour and the Media', in A. King (ed.) *Britain at the Polls*, Chatham, NJ: Chatham House. [117–42]

Thompson, K. (ed.) (2005) *British Social Attitudes – The 21ˢᵗ Report: Continuity and Change over Two Decades*, London; Thousand Oaks, CA: Sage Publications.

Wring, D. (2005) 'The Labour Campaign', in P. Norris and C. Wlezien (eds) *Britain Votes 2005*, Oxford: Oxford University Press. [56–68]

Interviews by Jennifer Lees-Marshment

Campbell, Alastair (2005) interviewed by Jennifer Lees-Marshment, 6 October.
Conservative staff 1 (2007) interviewed by Jennifer Lees-Marshment, September.
Conservative staff 2 (2007) interviewed by Jennifer Lees-Marshment, September.
Conservative staff 3 (2007) interviewed by Jennifer Lees-Marshment, September.
Gould, Phillip (2007) interviewed by Jennifer Lees-Marshment.
Harris, Will (2004) and (2006) interviewed by Jennifer Lees-Marshment.
Karia, Kamlesh (2004) Labour Political development project manager interviewed by Jennifer Lees-Marshment, 19 August, Labour headquarters.
Labour MP (2007) interviewed by Jennifer Lees-Marshment, September.
Senior Conservative Staff Strategy (2005) interviewed by Jennifer Lees-Marshment, January.
Sparrow, Nick (2007) ICM pollster interviewed by Jennifer Lees-Marshment.

9 The level of market-orientation of political parties in Greece

Iordanis Kotzaivazoglou and Yorgos Zotos

Since the early 1990s, political communication in Greece has undergone a period of major transformation. Important changes in the Greek and international environment, which began in the mid-1980s, ushered Greek political communication into a 'modernization' phase, whose key characteristics are the blurring of ideological differences between the parties of government and the domination of marketing, professionalization and the media (Negrine and Papathanassopoulos 1996, Yannas 2002). Political marketing strategies and techniques were gradually adopted, primarily in promotional activities but also in product design based on polls.

This chapter discusses the state of the market orientation of political parties in Greece. It mentions the four parties that were elected to Parliament in the 2004 general election, but concentrates on the parties of government, ND and PASOK. The 2004 election was chosen to permit assessment of the post-election performance of the parties. The analysis also covers the first six months after the 2007 election. The analysis is based on observations of the election campaigns, analyses of others research and polls published in the news media. It is argued that none of the Greek parties is fully market-oriented.

The chapter initially provides an overview of the Greek political system, which serves as a background for understanding the preconditions for the market orientation of the country's political parties. Reference is made to the political system, party fundraising, the political market, the media system and political marketing and professionalization. The state of political marketing orientation is then analyzed by applying the Lees-Marshment model.

The Greek political marketplace

The political system

Greece is a Presidential Republic with a 300-seat Parliament. The political system is representative. The party that wins the most seats at the general elections forms the government. While the Greek Constitution does not specify the electoral system, for more than 30 years (since democracy was restored after the seven-year hiatus of the military dictatorship) variants of a plurality system have been used.

Parties receiving less than 3 per cent of the popular vote are not represented in Parliament; three to five parties usually win representation. Two of these, ND (Nea Democratia) and PASOK (Panellinio Socialistiko Kinima) are parties of government. Traditionally, ND is a right-to-centre party and PASOK centre-left. Together they command around 80 per cent of the total vote. The third party that has consistently been elected to Parliament since the restoration of democracy is the communist party, KKE (Komounistiko Komma Ellados). The left-wing SYRIZA (formerly SYNASPISMOS) party has won Parliamentary representation in all recent elections. From time to time other parties also win a few seats (Table 9.1).

The Greek political system may be described as strongly party-centered, although in a peculiar form, characterized by the personal stamp of the original party founders, Konstantinos Karamanlis (ND) and Andreas Papandreou (PASOK), who continued to serve as reference points long after they had retired. It is probably no accident that the present leaders of the two parties are Kostas Karamanlis and Yorgos Papandreou, respectively the nephew and son of the founders of their parties. In recent years the phenomenon has become less marked, but the political system in Greece in general remains substantially party-centered (Samaras 2002).

Party funding

In Greece parties that win parliamentary representation receive state funding proportional to their performance at the last elections. In the past the parties could receive unlimited additional funding from private enterprise or individuals, and spending on promotion was largely without budgetary or legal constraints.

The increasing exorbitance of electoral spending and accusations of interlocking interests between politicians and businessmen, media magnates and journalists, eventually led to laws capping electoral spending (Papathanassopoulos 2002: 67–69). The 2004 elections were the first to be conducted according to legislative provisions that significantly curbed the scope for party and candidate promotion. However, although these laws have not always been complied with, no sanctions have ever been imposed for breaches.

Table 9.1 Results and seats at elections in Greece, 1996–2007

	1996		2000		2004		2007	
	%	*Seats*	*%*	*Seats*	*%*	*Seats*	*%*	*Seats*
ND	38.12	108	42.74	125	45.36	165	41.83	152
PASOK	41.49	162	43.79	158	40.55	117	38.10	102
KKE	5.61	11	5.52	11	5.89	12	8.15	22
SYRIZA	5.12	10	3.20	6	3.26	6	5.04	14
DIKKI	4.43	9	2.69	0	1.79	0	–	–
LAOS	–	–	–	–	2.19	0	3.80	10
OTHER	5.33	0	2.06	0	0.96	0	3.08	0

Percentage of votes and number of Parliamentary seats won in the four most recent elections.

The market

The collapse of 'Existing Socialism', the sovereignty of the free market, the rise of globalization, and Greece's entry into EMU, which forced Greek governments to follow specific policies, modified the ideologies of the two parties of government. The practical impossibility of applying a socio-democratic model led PASOK to adopt largely free market principles. The party's ideological transformation began in the 1990s, under Andreas Papandreou, and was intensified by Konstantinos Simitis with his 'modernization' program (Loulis 2003, Vernardakis 2005, Spourdalakis and Tassis 2006). ND implemented a similar strategy after 1996, shedding its liberal policies in favor of a move towards the centre (Loulis 2003, 2004, Vernardakis 2005, Pappas and Dinas 2006).

The result was the elimination, to a substantial degree, of the traditional demarcation lines between right- and left-wing ideologies. The parties of government have broadened their ideological spectrums and positioned themselves within the broad middle ground. The differentiation between the parties has shifted from ideology to administration (Loulis 2003: 47). The questions the electorate is asked, and upon which the two parties focus their communication strategies, are which has the ablest people, is better fitted to govern, or has the leader most likely to make a good prime minister?

The two parties of government changed from being exponents of a clear political ideology to being largely 'catch-all' parties (Vernardakis 2005). They have become 'loosely ideological formations' embracing a 'mosaic of political, ideological and cultural trends' (Vernardakis 2005: 73) and characterized by positional flexibility and adaptability. Their goal is to garner as many votes as possible from all social groups and classes. Vague, generalized and sweeping statements or fuzzy, flexible, 'feel-good' positions appealing to the pre-electoral demands and wishes of the voters have replaced the clear, well-defined and usually uncompromising old-style party ideology, usually accompanied by direct attacks on the opposing party and its members, featuring highly critical sloganeering and scare-mongering.

The change in the political parties has gone hand in hand with changes in the general political culture. Voter-party identification, traditionally very strong in Greece, has weakened amid growing civic indifference to politics and a significant voter shift to the centre (Loulis 2003, Vernardakis 2005).

The media landscape

The media landscape in Greece comprises public and private broadcasting and newspapers. Privately owned television is the public's principal source of information, although the role of the newspapers and public broadcasting media remains strong.

Privately owned television operates on purely commercial lines; what is newsworthy is what sells. The constant pressure to be first with the news and to increase viewer numbers often leads to exaggeration and reporting of unsubstantiated rumors. These stations tend to pander to popular prejudice by adopting an aggressive hard-line stance towards the political leaders and an engaging manner towards the public.

The logic of the private television stations has also influenced public broadcasting and the newspapers. Public television, traditionally the mouthpiece of the government, became more objective and more commercial, but has remained pro-government (Doulkeri and Terzis 1997, Leandros 2000, Chondroleou 2004). Greek newspapers have always been strongly partisan and politicized. With the introduction of private television, newspaper sales dropped sharply (Leandros 2000, Chondroleou 2004). In response, the press copied the logic of television broadcasting in subject matter and adopted a strong sales-oriented focus in terms of news presentation.

Political communication in Greece today is characterized by the pervasive influence of the media, and particularly private television (Papathanassopoulos 2000, Demertzis 2002). The role of the Internet as a political marketing tool has expanded significantly with each election, as more and more voters come into contact with it. It is, however, difficult to measure its effectiveness and particular role in specific election campaigns (Yannas and Lappas, 2004). Aware of the critical role of the media, parties and politicians seek maximum media exposure, using means of communication compatible with 'media logic'. This adaptation of political communication is evident on three levels: (a) concentration on appearance and image, (b) the use of promotion techniques based on spectacle and the personal element, and (c) the content of political dialogue, which has largely shed political substance for sound bites, slogans and comfortable, vague, general positions. Politics' marked dependence on the media has also led to frequent accusations of interlocking interests between politicians, media magnates and journalists (Frangonikolopoulos 2005, Kontogiorgis 2005).

Political marketing techniques in Greece

Political marketing is another predominant feature of political communication in Greece today. Advertising, poll-based policy shaping and image and news management are obvious in the political reality, particularly in ND and PASOK. Market segmentation has also been applied to the electorate, to permit more precise targeting of the demands of each particular group.

Developments in communications and the technological environment and the manner in which politics is conducted have all played a role in the emergence of a new group of professionals in politics, including marketing consultants, advertising specialists, image makers, PR persons, pollsters, stage managers and IT experts (Yannas 2002). These professionals do not come from the world of politics, nor is it their sole sphere of activity. They are hired by parties and politicians to provide consultancy services (Yannas 2005) and are actively engaged in the planning and promoting of the parties' programs, in many cases taking over the role of the traditional party caucus. Politics is thus often practised by non-politicians whose political decisions are based on non-political criteria. The center of gravity of election campaigns has shifted from ideology to communication. The parties have, with the assistance of their consultants, transformed themselves into 'communication machines' (term used by Mancini 1999: 243) that use political sensationalism and communications bombardment to influence the electorate.

Political marketing strategy in Greece: the main Greek parties in the 2004 election

This unit looks at the parties' level of political marketing in the 2004 election, applying the Lees-Marshment model of product-, sales- and market-oriented political parties (2001a, 2001b, 2003). Reference is made to all the parties elected to the Greek Parliament, but analysis is limited to ND and PASOK. While each stage of the model is used, the emphasis is on the indicators of market orientation. The analysis shows neither party to be fully market-oriented, in terms of this model. Both large parties display features of both MOP and SOP.

The KKE may be described as a product-oriented party and SYNAPSISMOS as sales-oriented. The KKE has for years adhered to a specific Marxist-based policy, accusing the plutocracy, capital and the capitalist world of acting against the people and the worker and calling for a change of system. It is a typical POP, holding firm to its positions in the belief that the voters will come to recognize their justice. SYNASPISMOS focuses on human rights, the social state, ecology and freedom of expression, and tries to 'sell' its arguments to the voters. It uses market intelligence, advertising and communication techniques to persuade voters to choose its product, which is of predetermined design.

The rest of this chapter presents an analysis of the marketing orientation of ND and PASOK in terms of the MOP model.

Stage 1: Market intelligence

Both parties used market intelligence from polling organizations to identify the needs and wishes of the electorate. With professional assistance, party leaders and political planners processed these data and designed their products and communication strategies accordingly.

Stage 2: Product design

The issues that concerned most voters in the 2004 election were things that touched their daily lives – cost of living, income levels, and unemployment – and corruption in the public administration. Table 9.2 tracks the three issues of most concern to the public in 2000–2003.

The electorate was also tired of PASOK, which had governed for 20 of the previous 23 years, and of the existing state of political affairs, and wanted to see new faces and policies (Loulis 2004).

ND designed its electoral product on clearly market-oriented lines. It concentrated on issues that were important to the voters. It held the PASOK

Table 9.2 Public perception of the country's three most important problems in Greece, 2000–2003

	Unemployment	*Cost-of-living*	*Foreign policy*
June 2000	59.2%	14.0%	9.3%
December 2000	58.2%	19.0%	14.3%
June 2001	55.5%	17.0%	9.2%
December 2001	56.4%	15.7%	6.6%
July 2002	64.0%	13.9%	5.0%
December 2002	62.8%	36.4%	9.5%
June 2003	72.0%	46.7%	3.6%

Question asked: What are the three most important problems facing Greece today? (MRB poll, cited in Loulis 2004: 203).

administrations responsible for the situation and poor management of public affairs, and tried to exploit public weariness with the long PASOK regime. It moved even farther towards what Karamanlis insisted was the 'broad social centre'. The party dropped many older stalwarts from its lists, replacing them with younger people, women and familiar public figures, and gave priority to improving the general standard of living and eliminating corruption.

PASOK, led by Konstantinos Simitis, followed a sales-oriented strategy. Contemporary polls consistently showed it trailing ND by a considerable margin (Loulis 2004, Spourdalakis and Tassis 2006). To counter this trend, PASOK adopted a series of populist measures in September 2003, and focused its product design on its strongest points: Simitis himself, who was held to be far more capable than his opponent; Greece's entry into EMU; the economic upturn; the many development projects carried out with EU support; and the country's improved international image, especially in the EU.

It did not work; the polls remained unchanged. Facing the prospect of certain defeat, Simitis resigned the leadership of the party two months before the election, scheduled for 7 March 2004. He was replaced by Foreign Minister Yorgos Papandreou, the most popular of the senior party officials at the time and the son of PASOK founder Andreas Papandreou. The change in leadership brought about a new orientation, geared to the needs and wishes of the electorate: stamping out corruption, a state that cares about the ordinary concerns of the citizen, greater civic participation in public affairs. The new strategy was billed as 'forward flight', focusing on the popularity of the candidate and not the unpopularity of the party. PASOK also repositioned itself in the center ground. It included on its 'national list' (of candidates elected automatically in proportion to the total number of votes cast for the party) former high-ranking ND and left-wing party regulars, following a 'two-ways expansion strategy' towards both left and right (Samaras 2005), and put up young people, women and celebrities as candidates. Papandreou talked constantly about party renewal, in character, name and symbols, and re-oriented its positions towards the daily concerns of the people. This new market orientation seemed to be only superficial, however, adopted to reverse the negative climate and salvage the election. The new positions remained vague and general. The party had no specific program, and frequently swung back and forth between supporting and condemning the old PASOK.

Stage 3: Product adjustment

Although, as the model stresses, an MOP should not 'promise the earth' so as not to fail in performance after the election, both parties indulged in an orgy of promises and attempts to outbid one another, especially in the final days of the campaign. Both parties veered towards more of a sales orientation, attempting to 'sell' their arguments at all costs. This tactic is typical of Greek politics. Both parties obviously knew that they could not fulfill their promises.

In general, both parties faced little internal reaction to their programs. 'United we stand, divided we fall' is a wise maxim, and public dissent would probably lead to expulsion. ND's changes sparked some initial internal reactions (Pappas and Dinas 2006). A number of senior members left, most of them later returning. MP Yorgos Karatzaferis created a more serious problem: expelled from ND, he founded his own party, LAOS, siphoning off substantial support from ND's right wing (Table 9.1).

Both parties also sought to gain the greatest number of voters. They segmented the market and tried to fine-tune their targeting of each group. They drew up party lists including candidates from many ideological, professional and social spheres, plus numerous celebrities, often with little connection with politics, such as athletes, actors, singers and lifestyle figures, in an attempt to win the depoliticized vote. Opting to represent various social groups signaled a shift towards market orientation, but choosing candidates solely for their voter appeal demonstrates an element of sales-orientation.

Stage 4: Implementation

Pursuing these new strategies, both parties elevated new figures to prominence, while shunting others aside. ND worked systematically and persistently to implement its strategy. Despite the isolated initial reactions, ND succeeded in marketing a credible global product. Opinion polls showed that the public believed ND to be more capable than PASOK of addressing major public concerns (Loulis 2004). PASOK's moves were rushed, and did not have the desired result. The party remained essentially unchanged, its positions still unclear.

Stage 5: Communication

Both ND and PASOK take a keen interest in communication. Before the election campaign, Karamanlis engaged in vigorous opposition tactics, although never going to extremes. Being no personal match for Simitis, he concentrated on promoting the party and its positions, adopting an issue-focused, specific-audience-targeted communication strategy (Pappas and Dinas 2006). He toured the whole country, visiting various bodies and organizations and explaining the party's program for each group. Following a newly market-oriented communication strategy, the party focused on promoting its positions, to show the voters that it recognized their problems, had solutions to them, and was ready to govern.

PASOK, by contrast, followed an SOP communication strategy (a) prior to the start of the campaign period, by focusing on its strong points and trying to sell them to the voters, and (b) after the hasty change in leadership, concentrating almost exclusively on the figure of the new leader, but without presenting a clear program.

Stage 6: Election campaign

In 2004, the parties' communication efforts peaked in the pre-election period. The campaign period was hectic, with speeches delivered all over the country, declarations and counter-declarations, accusations and counter-accusations, and advertising both positive and negative. Both parties tried to get maximum media exposure and used slogans focusing on change and a better future.

PASOK's election of Papandreou as party leader just two months before polling day initially created a strong momentum for the party. He adopted socially popular positions, and promised changes, a new ethos and politics more in tune with the voter's needs. He also projected a friendlier image, more 'human' than the usual norm for political leaders, which forced Karamanlis to do likewise. As a result the gap between ND and PASOK dropped from 7–8 per cent to 2.2–8 per cent (Samaras 2006).

After that impressive comeback, an unexpected event dominated the campaign for several days: the 'Pachtas Scandal' involved government MPs trying to force through Parliament a bill favoring a business magnate. The fact itself, the importance attached to it by ND and the media, and the way PASOK handled it caused considerable damage to the governing party, reversing its steady rise in the polls (Samaras 2006).

PASOK never recovered from this setback. It had by this time become abundantly clear that Papandreou had no clear program. His feel-good positions were superficial, designed only to sell the party to the voters sufficiently to secure a victory at the polls. In the sole television debate between the leaders of the parties represented in the outgoing Parliament, Papandreou made a poor impression, appearing nervous and reading from prepared texts. In the final days of the campaign, with the election already lost, he attacked ND as the 'traditional right' in disguise, in a final bid to attract disenchanted voters.

Stage 7: Election

ND won the election with 45.36 per cent of the vote, giving it 165 seats and a solid parliamentary majority. PASOK came second with 40.55 per cent, and after eleven years in government moved into opposition (Table 9.1). Weary of and disenchanted with successive PASOK governments, the voters wanted a change and believed that ND offered a better future.

Stage 8: Delivery

The ND government did not deliver what it had promised. In its three and a half years in power it played a basically administrative role, pursuing essentially the same policies as PASOK, with only minor differences. An opinion poll conducted by ALCO (2007) a few days prior to the 2007 election showed that 76.8 per cent of voters believed that the government failed to deliver on its pre-election pledges of 2004, with just 16 per cent holding the opposite view.

During its administration it tried to proceed with many important structural changes, including a series of privatizations, measures against corruption and tax evasion, pension fund and education reforms and constitutional review. These changes, however, either did not materialize or were less far-reaching than promised.

Often its attempts to impose these changes were met with strong reactions from the opposition parties, the media, labor organizations and other social groups. Powerful minorities resisted vigorously, with protests and demonstrations against the loss of vested interests. The civic majority, however, which in most cases wanted the changes, was by the nature of things unable to express its will equally dynamically. The government's retreat seems to have been due to fear of the political cost.

With regard to the economy and ND's pre-election social and economic promises, the new government promptly announced that its predecessor had concealed the true state of the Greek economy from the country and the EU, and presented figures that resulted in the imposition of EU surveillance. The country was told that the economy would have to be set to rights before any of the promised benefits could be implemented, and assured that the government's program would be put into effect by the end of its four-year mandate, a promise that had not been made before the election. Within its three and a half years the government achieved positive economic results: the EU surveillance was lifted, the public debt was slashed to 2.4 per cent, growth remained buoyant and the official unemployment rate dropped. Once the economic situation began to improve, the government announced that the time had come to implement its election commitments. A series of bills was prepared during the summer of 2007 and they were to be passed once Parliament returned after its August recess. But in the middle of August, which is traditionally holiday month in Greece, the Prime Minister suddenly called a snap election, for 16 September 2007. None of the bills with the announced provisions was tabled, but the government promised that they would be enacted immediately after its re-election, prompting accusations that it was holding large numbers of voters hostage.

Nor did the ND government do anything to tackle price inflation or corruption, issues of particular concern to the electorate and the object of firm campaign promises. Prices continue to rise, making life difficult for the public, particularly those on low incomes. Nothing was done against corruption; on the contrary, major public administration scandals were exposed, tarnishing the government's image.

PASOK was not able to cash in on public displeasure with ND. It failed to keep its campaign promise to institute its proclaimed 'new era of renewal': since the election all key positions have gradually been restored to the traditional old party stalwarts. As the official opposition it sought to exploit various government crises. It followed a harsh opposition strategy, blaming the government for everything that is wrong with the country, forgetting the problems and failures of 20 years of the PASOK government. It called the government incompetent and a menace to the nation, assuming attractive-sounding but vague positions in favor of the social groups concerned. It often blocked government reform measures, and occasionally reversed its own campaign positions, for example on constitutional reform or changes in the education sector.

In a climate of pronounced voter disenchantment, the campaign discourse of both parties in the run-up to the September 2007 election was essentially negative. ND and PASOK accused each other of more corruption, of creating greater problems, of being less likely to honor commitments, and of having more anti-social policies.

Voter disenchantment with the two major political parties found expression at the polls. As Loulis observed (2003: 152), for many years the electorate has not voted for the best party, but for 'the lesser of two evils'. ND managed to secure re-election with an overall plurality of 41.83 per cent, 3.51 points below its previous score. It won a marginal parliamentary majority of 152 seats, which cast doubts over the new government's ability to proceed with the plans for far-reaching and significant change announced by Karamanlis during the campaign period.

PASOK did not succeed in taking advantage of voter disenchantment with the ND administration: on the contrary, it attracted only 38.10 per cent of the vote, a drop of 2.44 points compared to 2004. Its poor performance was largely due to the blurred public image it projected over recent years.

The minority parties received a significant boost (Table 9.1). It is argued that the increase in support for the minority parties had two origins: (i) a certain percentage of their new voters were positive supporters who embraced their views and ideas, while (ii) another percentage were simply expressing their disenchantment for the two major parties.

Six months after the 2007 election, popular dissatisfaction with both parties is stronger than ever. An increasing majority of the population believes that both parties, but especially PASOK, are on the wrong track (Table 9.3).

Following its re-election, the government implemented only a few of its campaign pledges concerning certain social welfare benefits and tax cuts. At the

Table 9.3 ND and PASOK on the wrong track, 2004–2008

	11/2004	*05/2005*	*12/2005*	*04/2006*	*11/2006*	*11/2007*	*02/2008*
ND	29%	39%	45%	51%	45%	47%	64%
PASOK	51%	48%	54%	54%	62%	66%	78%

Percentage of voters who believe that ND and PASOK are on the wrong track
(November 2004–February 2008, *Public Issue* 2008: 10).

same time, it also proceeded to impose a series of other, onerous, measures, not mentioned during the election campaign, in order to boost public revenues. The serious problems facing the country still remain, and are getting worse, despite the government's assertions to the contrary and its desire to deal with them. Adverse international economic developments have further exacerbated the problem. Scandals involving high-ranking government officials delight the media. Most citizens are dissatisfied with the ND administration (Table 9.4).

Table 9.5 presents the results of an opinion poll that asked respondents what in their view were the most serious problems facing the country. The problems cited were the same as before the 2004 election, and the majority opinion was that the ND government had not addressed them successfully.

Another poll demonstrates the widely held belief that both parties of government are dependent on the financial interests of various interest groups, and especially ND (Table 9.6).

PASOK has been unable to cash in on public discontent with the government and finds itself in a protracted crisis. Its defeat at the 2007 election cast doubts over the party's leadership and sparked intense internal conflict. Papandreou was re-elected as party leader with a handsome margin, and promised to bring about change and renewal in the party. The opinion polls, however, remain negative. Most citizens are not happy with PASOK's performance in Opposition (Table 9.7), and do not believe that anything would change if PASOK were to form a government (Table 9.8). Most PASOK supporters feel that its renewal program has made little progress (Table 9.9).

Table 9.4 Satisfaction with the ND administration in 2008

Very satisfied	7.3%
Fairly satisfied	18.8%
Somewhat satisfied	23.8%
Dissatisfied	50.1%

Question asked: How satisfied are you with the way ND is governing the country?

Source: KAPA Research 2008: A4, A.

Table 9.5 Most important problems facing Greece, 2008

	Dec. 2007	*Jan. 2008*
Cost-of-living	24%	22%
Corruption	3%	19%
Unemployment	18%	18%
Poverty, low pay and pensions	17%	16%
Social insurance	16%	4%
Education	5%	4%
National affairs	3%	2%
Health	2%	2%

Question asked: What do you think are the most important problems facing the country at this time?

Source: spontaneous response, VPRC 2008: 10–11.

Table 9.6 Party most dependent on the financial interests of various interest groups in Greece, 2008

PASOK	15%
ND	35%
Both	41%
Neither	2%
Don't know/ No answer	7%

Question asked: Of the two main parties as they operate today, PASOK and ND, which do you think is more dependent on the financial interests of various interest groups, ND or PASOK?

Source: VPRC 2008: 10–11.

Table 9.7 Public satisfaction with the performance of PASOK as Opposition, 2008

Very satisfied	2.3%
Fairly satisfied	8.1%
Somewhat satisfied	26.3%
Dissatisfied	61.6%
Don't know/ No answer	1.7%

Question asked: How satisfied are you with PASOK's performance in Opposition?

Source: KAPA Research 2008: A4, A6.

Table 9.8 Public perception of the potential effect of PASOK in power, 2008

Better	25.3
Worse	28.8%
No different	42.9%
Don't know/ No answer	3.1%

Question asked: If PASOK had won the election, how would things be for the country today?

Source: KAPA Research 2008: A4, A6.

Table 9.9 Public perception of the progress of PASOK's renewal program, 2008

No progress	55%
Slow progress	35%
Rapid progress	7%
Don't know/ No answer	3%

Question asked: How is PASOK getting on with its renewal programme? Question addressed solely to PASOK voters.

Source: VPRC 2008: 10–11.

Voter support for the two major parties has been steadily decreasing since the last election, to the benefit of the smaller parties, and especially SYRIZA (formerly SYNASPISMOS), whose recently elected leader, Alexis Tsipras, is just 33 years old. This change seems to have given the party a new lease of life. Opinion polls currently give SYRIZA 16 per cent to 18.4 per cent of the vote, most of it drawn from the ranks of disenchanted PASOK supporters. The future will show whether the smaller parties can retain this support.

Political marketing trends and conclusion

With regard to the above, it is evident that no Greek party was fully market-oriented in either 2004 or 2007. ND may have largely followed market-orientation principles before the elections, but its performance in certain areas such as making sure its product is achievable and it delivers in government has been poor. PASOK, which has long been acting mainly like an SOP, identified a need for change but does not seem able to design and deliver a product that meets the demands of today's society.

The parties' inability to offer solutions to the country's problems has created strong public discontent and disquiet. The response to a Public Issue poll in February 2008 showed that 75 per cent of citizens believe that the country is on the wrong track, compared to just 14 per cent who believe it is doing well (Public Issue 2008: 10).

This state of affairs is particularly unpleasant and dangerous for the country and for democracy. The MOP model can help redress the situation. Political figures have a duty to listen and respond to real long-term social needs. They must realize that elections are won and lost during a government's term of office, not with a bombardment of campaign messages.

Both major parties have adopted the MOP philosophy in their rhetoric. They proclaim the need for change reflecting citizens' needs and wants. In practice, however, it appears that they do not act on their own convictions. It is doubtful whether they will adopt an MOP philosophy in the future, although it can contribute effectively towards the resolution of policy-related problems in Greece. It must be conceded that implementing policy is often very difficult and can carry considerable political costs. It strikes at rights and interests, runs into powerful reaction from the establishment and the organized lobbies, and kindles social unrest and conflict. The fundamental responsibility lies with the parties, but the implementation of sound policy and the achievement of reform require active support from the citizens. Unfortunately, people often perpetuate a situation that they dislike in others when it suits their own purposes. This culture impedes the achievability of policy implementation and impairs the effectiveness of political reform. As this culture is deeply ingrained in the mind-set of the public, it will be extremely difficult to change it in the near future. Many voters focus on short-term needs and everyday problems – unemployment, over-borrowing, high prices – and pay little attention to issues that are of greater importance for the progress of society. Many are led astray by populist language and fat promises. Voters, as citizens of a democratic society, must also assume their responsibilities.

References/further reading

ALCO (2007) *ALCO Nationwide Survey for ALTER TV*. Available at: <www.imerisia.gr> (accessed August 29 2007). [in Greek]

Chondroleou, G. (2004) 'Public Images and Private Lives: The Greek Experience', *Parliamentary Affairs*, 57(1): 53–66.

Demertzis, N. (2002) *Political Communication: Risk, Publicity*, Athens: Papazisis. [in Greek]

Doulkeri, T. and Terzis, G. (1997) 'Changing Television in Greece: The Commercialization of Greek TV and the Historical, Legal, Economic and Social Environment', *Asian Journal of Communication*, 7(2): 118–131.

Frangonikolopoulos, C. (2005) 'The Mass Media in Greece Today: Thoughts and Preoccupations', in C. Frangonikolopoulos (ed.) *Media, Society and Politics: Role and Function in Contemporary Greece*, Athens: Sideris. [13–34] [in Greek]

KAPA Research (2008) Nationwide poll, *To Vima*, 2 March: A4, A6. [in Greek]

Kontogiorgis, G. (2005) 'Corruption and Political System', in K. Koutsoukis and P. Sklias (eds) *Corruption and Scandals in Public Administration and Politics*, Athens: Sideris. [131–143]

Leandros, N. (2000) *Political Economy of the Media: The Restructuring of the Media Industry in the Age of the Information Revolution*, 2nd edn, Athens: Kastaniotis. [in Greek]

Lees-Marshment, J. (2001a) 'The Marriage of Politics and Marketing', *Political Studies*, 49(4): 692–713.

Lees-Marshment, J. (2001b) 'The Product, Sales and Market-Oriented Party: How Labour Learnt to Market the Product, Not Just the Presentation', *European Journal of Marketing*, 35(9/10): 1074–1084.

Lees-Marshment, J. (2003) 'Political Marketing: How to Reach that Pot of Gold', *Journal of Political Marketing*, 2(1): 1–32.

Loulis, I. (2003) *The Twenty Years that Changed Greece: What Goes, What Comes, and the Next Elections*, Athens: Nea Synora-A. A. Livani. [in Greek]

Loulis, I. (2004) *The End of a Dominance: How and Why PASOK Lost the Elections*, Athens: Nea Synora-A. A. Livani. [in Greek]

Mancini, P. (1999) 'New Frontiers in Political Professionalism', *Political Communication*, 16(3): 231–245.

Negrine, R. and Papathanassopoulos, S. (1996) 'The "Americanization" of Politics: A Critique', *International Harvard Journal of Press and Politics*, 1(2): 45–62.

Papathanassopoulos, S. (2000) 'Election Campaigning in the Television Age: The Case of Contemporary Greece', *Political Communication*, 17(1): 47–60.

Papathanassopoulos, S. (2002) 'Television and Elections in Greece in the Decade 1990–2000', in N. Demertzis (ed.) *Political Communication in Greece*, Athens: Papazisis. [39–94] [in Greek]

Pappas, T. and Dinas, E. (2006) 'From Opposition to Power: Greek Conservatism Reinvented', *South European Society & Politics*, 11(3–4): 477–495.

Public Issue (2008) *I Kathimerini*, 20 Jan: 16. [in Greek]

Samaras, A. (2002) 'Political Marketing, Partytocracy and the Transformations of the Political Communication System', *Journal of Business and Society*, 15(1): 158–173.

Samaras, A. (2006) 'The 2004 Parliamentary Elections in Greece: Chronicle of a Defeat Foretold', in *Election Time: The European Yearbook of Political Campaigning 2004*, Oporto: European Association of Political Consultants. [105–132]

Spourdalakis, M. and Tassis, C. (2006) 'Party Change in Greece and the Vanguard Role of PASOK', *South European Society & Politics*, 11(3–4): 497–512.

Vernardakis, C. (2005) 'Political Parties and Centre: The Ideological, Political, and Cultural Parameters of Contemporary Political Powers', in C. Vernardakis (ed.) *V-PRC: Public Opinion in Greece 2004: Elections, Parties, Interest Groups, Environment, and Society*, Athens: Savalas. [57–85] [in Greek]

VPRC (2008) Nationwide poll, *Ta Nea*, 9–10 Feb: 10–11. [in Greek]

Yannas, P. (2002) 'The Role of Image-Makers in the Greek Political Scene', *Journal of Political Marketing*, 1(1): 67–89.

Yannas, P. (2005) 'Political Marketing in Greece is Ready for Take Off', *Journal of Political Marketing*, 4(1): 1–15.

Yannas, P. and Lappas, G. (2004) 'E-Campaign in Greek Elections: 2000–2004', *WSEAS Transactions in Information Science and Applications*, 5(1): 1332–1337.

10 Political salesmen in Hungary[1]

Balázs Kiss and Zsuzsanna Mihályffy

Hungarian political parties have been experimenting with political marketing techniques since the system change (1990). The first truly marketing-based campaign was the general elections campaign of Fidesz in 1998. The campaign had a clear strategy aimed at selling the new party image, and it was the first campaign that put emphasis on the party leader by positioning him as a competent PM candidate, aided by a marketing advisor. Since the late 1990s, the expression political marketing has become almost fashionable; a party which could not claim that it was using political marketing means did not qualify as professional enough among the political competitors. Parties have been borrowing tricks and tactics from each others' campaigns, they have been learning the lessons from others' successes and their own failures, and they have also been keen on learning from international, in particular British and American, experience.

In the parliamentary election campaign of 2006 Hungarian political parties were more willing than ever to employ marketing techniques and rely on the assistance of external campaign advisors, sometimes international consultants as well. The chapter presents the campaigns of four Hungarian parties, those of the ones that managed to get into the Parliament: MSZP – Hungarian Socialist Party, Fidesz – Alliance of Young Democrats, SZDSZ – the Alliance of Free Democrats, and MDF – the Hungarian Democratic Forum. The analysis is based on external observation of the political parties and election campaigning, including informal discussions with party campaign managers, members, activists, and data gathered through the daily downloading and archiving of party and candidate websites.

The Hungarian political market place

The political system

The basic facts of the Hungarian political system are as follows:

The Hungarian party system shows increasing concentration: in 1990 the two biggest parties received 45 per cent of the list votes, in 2006 the first-placed MSZP and the second-placed Fidesz received 85 per cent. As parties rarely receive absolute majority, coalition governments are formed, which creates the need for

Table 10.1 Overview of current Hungarian political system

Party system	Multi-party system with five parties in Parliament, several minor parties outside Parliament
Parliamentary parties	Government: • MSZP (leader: PM Ferenc Gyurcsány) • SZDSZ (minor party, leader: Gábor Kuncze)
	Opposition: • Fidesz (leader: former PM Viktor Orbán) • MDF (minor party, leader: Ibolya Dávid) • KDNP (minor party, leader: Zsolt Semjén)
Electoral system	Mixed proportional. 176 MPs elected from single member constituencies, 210 from regional and country lists
Party or Candidate based	Strong party identification with major parties, but increasing role of party leaders
Government system	Prime Minister, Ministries
Parliament	Unicameral, 386 MPs, 5 per cent threshold
Funding of parties	Spending limit: HUF386 million/party. (Approx. €1.5 million)
Advertising regulations	Ban on publication of opinion polls from the eighth day prior to polling day; campaign silence period from 0:00 hours on the day prior to polling day

the existence of smaller parties as potential coalition partners. However, small parties are in a difficult situation thanks to the electoral system. There is a 5 per cent threshold, and also a complicated nomination system. Each SMC candidate has to collect 750 nomination sheets as a prerequisite for entering the race, and having a certain number of SMC candidates is a further prerequisite for setting up a list. Only parties with a certain number of regional lists qualify for a national, compensatory list. The filtering elements make it harder for smaller parties to succeed, working against a variety of political marketing orientations. Overall, the political system is more party-centred than candidate-centred, but campaigns are becoming increasingly focused on the party leader. Regulation concerning party and campaign funding is weak, and there is no real sanctioning, which is why parties tend to spend several times more than the official limit.

Hungarian citizens have two votes: one is cast for a local SMC candidate, the other for a regional party list. Parties therefore have to compete for both the SMC and the list votes, which is why they seek to have a candidate in each SMC, and to set up a list in each region. Hungarian voters do not usually split their vote: most citizens vote for the same party in the SMC and the list contest. Consequently, the national campaign is much more important than the local one. Turnout in Hungary is usually not very high; it varies between 65 and 71 per cent for parliamentary elections. In other words, about 30 per cent of those entitled do not cast their vote, which offers a great opportunity for Hungarian parties to focus their strategy on enlarging their base. Volatility in the Hungarian electorate is decreasing, mainly because there are fewer parties, and because it is becoming unthinkable for voters to switch parties, especially across the left–right divide. According to recent data, 46 per cent of Hungarians identify themselves with one party or another (Tóka and Henjak 2007, 210–240). The two major parties have a base of approximately 1.5 million each, while the core support of the two minor parties is roughly around 200,000. Party identification is about 70.1 per cent. There is a significant political distrust in Hungary, and voters are cynical, arguably making it more difficult for parties to convince voters, but increasing their desire for market-oriented politics, especially delivery of the product.

The media landscape

The Hungarian media landscape is as divided as the political elite, and according to the same division: left and right. Two important trends include citizens' increasing reliance on privately owned television channels for public information, and the shrinkages of print media.

As regards television, there are 50 or so channels, most of them are politically unimportant. The public television channels are pro-government; the two big private televisions (*RTL Klub, TV2*) are mostly apolitical, but during campaigns they are anti-right; the two smaller television channels are strongly biased: one is pro-right (*Hír TV*), the other one is pro-left (*ATV*). The biggest public channel (*MTV1*) was also pro-left at the time of the 2006 campaign.

In 2006, three national quality dailies supported the left (*Népszabadság, Népszava, Magyar Hírlap*), and one (*Magyar Nemzet*) supported the right. The tabloids deal with politics very rarely; during campaigns two are pro-left (*Blikk, Színes Bulvárlap*), the third (*Napi Ász*) is pro-right. The public radio (*Magyar Rádió*) has three channels, the first channel (*MR1*) has the greatest reach in peak hours, and was considered pro-right in 2006. One of the private radio stations (*Klubrádió*) is deliberately leftist; it supports the present prime minister's standpoint, while the other private news radio (*Inforádió*) is neutral or slightly pro-right.

The most frequently visited online media are rather neutral; though they have political character, they do not link them to any parties. There are a lot of outlets, and the main print media also have online versions.

The left–right division in the media is sometimes backed by ownership links, but recently one can also say that the media has striven to serve the deeply divided audience. Fewer media deny party sympathy and claim to be neutral.

For the political organizations, no media are free of charge in Hungary: political actors have to pay for political advertisements. It can happen however, that some media are not willing to broadcast any political advertisements. On the other hand, with some exceptions, there is no spending limit to media buying, particularly if one counts posters, direct mail and leafleting among the media. Thus, governments are entitled to advertise their successes well before the campaign period and the parties also use advertisement possibilities offered by papers and magazines (even such as *Playboy* and *Cosmopolitan*) to run long-lasting image campaigns.

Political marketing techniques in Hungary

The marketing arsenal deployed by the parties has been increasing and professionalizing since the first democratic election of 1990. By 2006 the Hungarian parties
had caught up with those of the West – partly because the latter had been
exemplars for them, and partly because, especially the major parties, started to hire
international campaign consultants. The development took place not only in the
techniques but also in the acquisition of marketing consciousness. All the
parliamentary parties build electoral databases, pay close attention to their images,
employ activists for more and more purposes, and implement deliberate news and
media management. Under the aegis of marketing consciousness, the parties
position themselves on the political market, segment the electorate, and not only
according to the more traditional sociological stratification (age, gender,
settlement, education, etc.) but also according to political behaviour (previous
party preferences, the use of political media) as well.

Fidesz was the first to notice that political communication was a field to be
approached professionally. From the mid-1990s until the end of its 1998–2002
government period, Fidesz communicated with specifically chosen electoral
segments in order to win or keep them. The first tendency of personalized politics
can also be credited to the party: Viktor Orbán as prime minister had communicative forums and activities specifically developed around him, and the staff did its
best to position him successfully. Fidesz was the first party that employed
permanent communications advisors, mainly domestic ones.

Their 1998 failure forced MSZP to pay attention to political marketing. In 2002
the socialists won by applying direct marketing: they sent direct mail and activists
to the citizens. In government between 2002 and 2006, MSZP used several
campaign means: government communication was helped by counsel from abroad,
regular training of the many hundreds of activists, the government and the party
strived for centralization of communication, and strategic news and media
management was implemented.

The party's communication activity became extremely intense after the change
of prime minister in 2004. Ferenc Gyurcsány, the new prime minister, as well as
the new image of the party had to be made known. MSZP developed the strategy
of winning back the 2002 supporters (mainly elderly people) and attracting one
new target, the youth vote.

SZDSZ, the Liberal party, has been communicating consciously since 1990 but
the party failed in marketing terms: in the middle of the 1990s it positioned itself
on the market the wrong way and, by 2002, its support had fallen by two-thirds.
The Liberals proved to be able to identify themselves as a small party as late as
2004, during the European campaign period – they achieved remarkable success
and provided an example to all the other parties, namely that political organizations
should run image and identity campaigns regularly.

MDF also became a professionally communicating party in 2004. This was the
first time the party employed domestic consultants and realized that, being small
and having its supporters geographically scattered, it should position itself vis-à-
vis the two big parties.

Political marketing strategy in Hungary

In the following section we will explore the main issues through analysis of how the four parliamentary parties that ran campaigns in 2006 used political marketing strategy, according to whether the given party was product-, sales- or market-oriented.

MSZP

According to its own declarations, MSZP (Hungarian Socialist Party) was product-oriented in 2006. The prime minister and the socialist politicians claimed that the parties in government were supposed to determine the road of development for the country which they claimed it would achieve with the 'New Hungary' programme.[2] The message was that the government and the party did not want to follow and subordinate themselves to the wants and needs of the people and of any interest groups, just the opposite: they were autonomous in their vision. However whilst the party developed its product on its own, sale was planned and designed according to foreign patterns and opinion polls, and the politicians also paid very thorough attention to feedback during the implementation. The design of the product itself was determined by its communicability. The party did not consider whether it was deliverable, or whether it squared with the citizens' wants and needs, but only their own communications wants and needs. This makes the party sales-oriented.

1. Product design according to elite views

Communicability and the opportunities within the political field of force influenced the product design. During the campaign the technical manager of the campaign claimed that their main goal was to offer the electorate policy objectives in connection with which it was impossible to ask why the leftist coalition had not implemented them yet, being in government. The party wanted to design objectives that it hoped to be able to defend in the everyday fights of the political elite and campaign communication; the needs and wants of the people were not taken into account.

Another important factor that determined the product design was the aim to satisfy the local socialist politicians and the relevant business circles that helped and financed the campaign of the party sometimes by illegal means. The 'New Hungary' programme promised several smaller and bigger investments all around the country, anticipating prosperity in every region.

2. Market intelligence to inform communication and campaigning

MSZP's market intelligence focused on perception of the political behaviour and promises of the party and the rivals, particularly the largest rightist party. Polling was carried out not only on national level but in each constituency as well. The results were communicated rather cautiously: by some effort, the party members and the sympathizers were able to get some data but one cannot speak of regular and public information.

The party considered the segmentation of the electorate to be extremely important. MSZP concentrated on its 2002 voters, they had to be regained, and chose one single segment to win: youth. The market intelligence was directed not on the changes required within the party but on the opportunities in communication: what image to show of itself.

MSZP proudly claimed that it used every possible communication channel and means during the campaign.[3] Although in the beginning online campaigning was not cultivated because internet penetration was remarkably low in Hungary, in January 2006, just over two months before the election day, the prime minister himself began blogging. The party published a huge amount of posters, television and radio commercials, and one could find its advertisements not only in newspapers but in magazines like *Playboy* and *Cosmopolitan*. Like the main parties, MSZP also sent direct mail and online newsletters. The presence of party activists was very visible in the streets.

The role of the communications experts was considered so important that the manager of the campaign, who had spent a long time studying the campaigns of the British Labour Party, and therefore the administrative director of the party for a while, was someone outside the party, and in addition to him another non-member sat in the highest managerial board of the campaign. The campaign of the party was long and well-designed and prepared in advance.

- Ever since his election as Prime Minister, Ferenc Gyurcsány concentrated not on governance but on campaigning, that is, on the question of how MSZP could win the 2006 elections.
- The most intensive part of the campaign was also very long: it began as early as the September of 2005, that is, more than seven months before election day.
- The campaign moved through different stages, each with special slogans, posters, advertisements, strategy and tactics.

Many of the messages were negative, criticising Fidesz, the main rival. The negative campaigning was aimed at the mobilization of previous supporters.

3. The success and failure of sales-orientation

The party scored a great success at the elections: it stayed in power, which was exceptional since 1990, moreover, it increased its majority in parliamentary mandates.

After the elections, MSZP and the governing coalition did just the opposite of what it had promised during the campaign. They had suggested an undisturbed continuation, yet the government decreased the standard of living through a series of restrictive measures; they had promised tax cuts, but tax rises followed; the promised rise of pensions was postponed, and so forth. Moreover, all the new political measures were not communicated very well. One explanation is that, although during the campaign the prime minister claimed that they had specific plans as to what to do after the elections, it turned out that they had had no plans at all; therefore everything had to be implemented in a great hurry without preparation. The measures were not leftist at all, one would evaluate them rather as market- and globalization-friendly.

Fidesz

1. Image of a market-oriented party

Fidesz sought to convey the image of a market-oriented party after the 2004 European election. Its main message was that the party listened to people and followed voters' needs. The party carried out a lot of informal market research in 2005 in a series of whistle-stop tours called 'National Consultation'. The aim of the Consultation was to incorporate voters' views in the party's 2006 election manifesto. The party's manifesto was referred to as '3 million people's programme' during the campaign, with which Fidesz also established a sharp contrast with the main opponent, as the MSZP's manifesto was entitled 'Ferenc Gyurcsány's New Hungary programme'.

Fidesz conducted extensive and wide-ranging formal market intelligence before and in the run-up to the 2006 general election campaign. The party used polling for policy developments and to check its existing support, it used focus groups when designing the new party logo and television ads, and it also consulted with media advisors and think tanks. Fidesz commissioned market intelligence mostly on voters' opinion about the party and its policies, and to a lesser extent on what voters wanted changed. The party used the results of market intelligence mostly in campaign formation – in this sense it leaned towards sales-orientation.

2. Product design and differentiation

There was certainly a strong desire among Fidesz's leaders to win the election, to please voters, and to try to change the party, if necessary, to accomplish this goal; however, it was sometimes unclear whether change happened in response to voter awareness, or because the leaders thought it was the right way.

There are at least two obvious examples for the willingness for change. First, the party frequently stressed that it had compiled its election manifesto based on the 'consultation' events. It contained pledges such as the drastic cut of social security contribution, a job creation scheme, a new housing programme, and a family-friendly taxation system. The manifesto, however, was less explicit in *how* the goals could be achieved. Second, Fidesz tried to renew its image. It launched an image campaign before the campaign proper, and sent the message to the electorate that the party was aware of its weaknesses, and ready to change.

Although the party was familiar with voters' needs, it failed to carry out product adjustment to make sure the product was deliverable. To complicate the situation even more, Fidesz's message was not coherent. The party warned voters that if the MSZP formed government, budget corrections would follow, which would imply that the economy was in a bad state, but simply said that 'Fidesz would do it better'. The 'how', again, was not clarified; although the party explained its programme, it did not give details of its economic policy.

As part of the product adjustment, the party tried to find ways in which it appeared distinct from its main opponent. There were some clear policy differences, for example Fidesz opposed the privatization of the health care system. There were sharper contrasts on a symbolic level, for example in their position with respect to the 1956 revolution, the communist period, and to Hungarians living outside the country borders. Fidesz certainly tried to emphasize its strength of being in opposition: it constantly blamed the governing coalition for the country's economic state.

Implementation of the product was successful, despite the fact that the party probably did not carry out internal consultation. The MPs and candidates seemed satisfied with the party's product. There were several rounds of trainings for candidates and activists to ensure that they knew the new product well, however, it is unlikely that members and MPs had the opportunity to be involved in the process of change.

3. Professional communication – with weaknesses

Some elements of Fidesz's communications strategy were decided on and carried out well in advance, for example Fidesz started to build a voters' database in 2004, and had been refining it in various ways since then. The party used all kinds of campaign tools including telemarketing, targeted direct mail, websites, paid media, all kinds of printed material, party souvenirs and so forth. Fidesz was assisted by a number of professionals as well, including international political consultants and a Hungarian PR company.

Before the election of 2006 Fidesz segmented the market to identify target groups of voters who might be persuaded to vote for the party, for example pensioners and those with low income in particular, while it tried to maintain its core voters. The party's campaign was targeted, but also tried to target as much of the electorate as possible.

During the campaign the party appeared united and professional for the most of the time. Problems nevertheless emerged at times of scandals, showing the party's limited capability to handle unexpected situations. This proved to be one of the biggest weaknesses of Fidesz, as quite a few scandals erupted.

The campaign was aimed at increasing the party's support, with a polling-day mobilization intended as a last-minute surprise. Some information about the huge number of activists employed by the party was, however, leaked, and eventually the plan became widely known. Also, the operation was probably not organized effectively enough; at least, the party did not obtain enough votes to win.

4. After the election

Fidesz's strategy proved ineffective – the party did not win the election. Moreover, it won fewer seats in the new Parliament than four years before. Since the election Fidesz has been acting as a very critical opposition. The government–opposition relationship is best described as hostile. Meanwhile Fidesz continues to be responsive to voters; it is trying to force the Prime Minister to resign, which is the will of the majority of the electorate. The party is apparently reflecting on losing the election and has been devoting time for discussion of its future developments and policy orientation. It started to prepare its new programme in early 2007 and published it in December 2007, entitled 'Strong Hungary'. The 100-page document contains some of the elements of the 2006 manifesto, but in a more established way. It contains more elaborate and detailed arguments and gives the necessary conditions for achieving the party's goals.

SZDSZ

1. Retention of unpopular positions

The party's main message since 2004 was that SZDSZ is the third main political force in Hungary, the 'liberal pole', and the sole representative of liberal values. The recognition that the party should recreate its liberal image came after research results had shown that there are some issues towards which 20 per cent of the voters have a liberal approach. Although the accuracy of this opinion research is questionable, the party used its result to pick the policies which were most liked by voters, such as the limited role of the state.

SZDSZ has pursued the same ideology for a long time, although with varying intensity. The party clearly assumes that its product will attract the necessary number of voters. The product design, however, has two significant elements which do not follow the majority of public opinion – one being the central message. The Hungarian electorate is rather conservative – liberalism only appeals to a small circle. The other one is the communication style the party adopted a few years ago. Probably thanks to its creative team, the party's advertisements are humorous and full of great ideas, but also sometimes arrogant and offensive. This provokes aversion in many, because it reflects party politicians' opinion that 'they know best'.

The policy-design included party views rather than the results of market intelligence, as the party had a preconception of its product, and relied on research only to refine this conception. In the 2006 election campaign the SZDSZ offered a limited range of policies, with only a few target fields such as taxation, education and privatized health care. Yet party leader Gábor Kuncze was elected to suit the public: he was popular among people in general, not only among the party's core supporters.

The party has been conducting market intelligence for a long time, and used several methods including focus groups, opinion polls and informal surveys of the supporters, not only in campaign-time. The results are kept closely guarded from the public, with the exception of favourable results, which occasionally appear on the party's website and in other campaign literature, to help strengthen the core support. Market intelligence usually focused on how SZDSZ was doing in the polls, and how the party was perceived, rather than what voters would like to see changed. Results are used to ascertain how best to communicate with the core supporters and the target voters, what communication methods to use and how to persuade.

The party relies on a particular type of segmentation. Almost like a niche party, it identified the liberal voters as its core supporters, and the 'probable liberals' as its target market, who might be persuaded.

2. Sales-oriented communication and campaign

When it comes to campaigning, SZDSZ is also sales-oriented. It spares no effort to lead successful communication and persuade voters to support the party. Its campaigns are usually very expensive; they use all kinds of media and the latest developments and employ several consultants. The party's sales-oriented approach became increasingly obvious towards the end of the 2006 general election campaign, when they came up with an entirely new element in their product: a little chap called Pisti Kovács, the new party 'mascot'.[4]

SZDSZ is very good at communication. The party's communication is designed to persuade voters, rather than just inform them. It uses a wide arsenal of communication tools, especially the most modern communication techniques, and is aided by professional consultants to help with its communication. It conveys the main strengths of the party, namely its policies, and it downplays its weaknesses. For example the party never acknowledged in the 2006 election campaign that it was worryingly close to the parliamentary threshold.

The party communicated the most effectively during the campaign period. There was a well-organized campaign plan with clear structure and timeline, to which the party stuck until it became obvious that their support would not be enough to prevent the party from falling out of parliament. As the campaign is the final sales period and the party was threatened by poll results that it would score below 5 per cent, it decided to use whatever techniques necessary to persuade undecided voters, and dissuade Fidesz's supporters. This was the time when the party introduced a five-year-old child, Pisti Kovács, and positioned him as the main representative of what the SZDSZ stood for. From February onward, the little boy was the key symbol of the party, he appeared everywhere: on campaign literature, in TV-spots, on party souvenirs, etc. He was a truly lovable character, and the idea behind his sudden appearance was clearly to offer voters something they liked without reserve. In the meantime the SZDSZ engaged in attacking and weakening the Fidesz, and even more so during the last few weeks of the campaign.

3. Election success, but poor delivery

Despite previous worries, the party performed well in the election. SZDSZ not only managed to get into parliament, but it was the only party to increase its support: it obtained 38,000 votes more than in 2002. This meant that the party could stay in power as the coalition partner of the MSZP in 2006, which was a great victory, as no other government had been granted a second turn.

Although SZDSZ remained in power, it seemed incapable of delivering its product, which is partly due to the circumstances that limit the opportunities, and partly due to the party's small size. The only element of the manifesto that the party did not give up was the privatization of the health care system; in fact the rigidity of the party cost the government a huge failure at the 2008 March referendum, leading to the termination of the coalition.

MDF

The campaigning and the behaviour of MDF party was constrained by its small size and lack of financial support, not just due to the low income from membership fees or the low state grant to the party, but rather to the fact that MDF is not important enough for the business circles to be supported. One of the corollaries of the situation is that so far MDF was able to obtain rather restricted media influence although it has done its best. Thus the party is forced to position itself vis-à-vis the two big parties, and more precisely in contradistinction to Fidesz, the large rightist party. On the other hand, that constraint also gave them a great opportunity, because MDF has been covered fairly mildly by the overwhelmingly leftist media.

In 2006, the central aim of MDF was to get into parliament, that is, to get in the first round at least 5 per cent of the votes. In order to do that they had to design a product that was really needed and wanted by at least 5 per cent of the electorate. This task was very challenging because in Hungary citizens tend to vote for the two big parties; fewer and fewer people support other organizations.

1. Elite-driven product design

In designing its product MDF was also driven by the political elite rather than the social or economic interests of the population, but it did offer what a specific segment of the electorate wanted politically: an alternative to the big parties. We should not forget the wants and needs of the (leftist) media either, criticising Fidesz from the central right made MDF fairly popular with the greater part of the media. The party also utilized the popularity of the female party president, and organized its 2006 campaign around her. Ibolya Dávid had been very popular for years, and the 2004 European campaign, which was focused on her, resulted in an unexpected success.

While the party product mostly contained image components and political message, its policy aspects were the most deliverable among the party offers. MDF was consistent regarding policy issues. Since 2002, when MDF was the only one in Parliament that did not vote for a series of laws that increased the standard of living of the population, claiming that the central budget would prove to be unable to finance the wage raises and the extra pensions, the party had consistently been against any popular but burdening state measures. In 2006, therefore, it could claim that it had always fought for the 'normal' economic and social policy.

In 2006 the objective of MDF was not to get into government, but to get into the parliament at all; after the first round of the election, when the party thought the left would win, it confirmed what it had previously claimed, that it would not help Fidesz improve the position of the right in the second round.

2. Reactive communication and campaign

The communication of the party had been unified since 2002: it underlined the roughly equal independence and distance from both big parties, and the commitment that this was the only way to create a 'normal' Hungary. The president and the politicians of MDF reiterated parts of that credo in every media opportunity, regardless of the actual topic. This continuous and consistent communication may have reached its goal; enough citizens were able to link characteristic elements to the party that it was in opposition but autonomous on the right. Not being policy issues, the messages did not link to specific sociological categories; therefore it was not worth segmenting the electorate.

3. After the election

It is difficult to assess the results of the political marketing applied by MDF. On the one hand, it managed to get into the parliament despite predictions to the contrary. On the other, however, MDF obtained fewer than 3,000 votes above the minimum, that is, if it had got 3,000 fewer votes, we would now be talking about complete failure. Moreover, the firm nonalignment policy led to the further shrinkage of the party: members, sometimes nationally renowned politicians, left the party claiming that MDF had betrayed the right by not helping Fidesz in the second round.

Since 2006, the party has not considerably increased its support, and is still eclipsed by Fidesz. There is no news of serious internal discussions and elaborations of their political programme, no signs of renewal in communicating with the citizens, and in general, the party is almost imperceptible in the political market.

Political marketing trends and conclusion

As a conclusion, we would like to find out whether there is an evolution of the campaigning from product orientation towards market orientation. First of all, we have to underline that we did not find wholly product-oriented parties among the most important ones. We also do not see any tendencies that would force the parties to return to product orientation. We saw that the parties were sales-oriented in most cases, and some even experimented with methods belonging to market-orientation. That would suggest the evolution premised by the model.

On the other hand, the example of Fidesz suggests that voter-awareness in programme design does not ensure election victory. Of course, it can be claimed that Fidesz did not pay enough attention to the other aspects that a market-oriented party should, such as that the product be deliverable, but this applies to MSZP as well, which was nevertheless able to win. Where MSZP proved to be more responsive was the political, and not the social and economic, needs and wants of the voters: the party thought it important to find and promote a new, extremely dynamic and perfectly communicating leader, while the rival ran the old leader who was much loved in his own camp but rather hated outside it. And although the market-orientation of MDF may have contributed to the success of the party, this success was so uncertain, that it cannot count as evidence of a direct cause–effect relationship between market-orientation and electoral success in the context of the Hungarian general election of 2006.

The last three general elections (1998, 2000 and 2006) seem to verify the thesis that in Hungary it is usually sales-orientation that offers success. In 2006, SZDSZ's behaviour exemplifies this claim most clearly: when the previous, rather product-oriented strategy proved unsuccessful, and the party became fearfully close to falling out of the parliament, it switched to clear sales-orientation, which brought about success. The main reasons for parties' favouring sales-orientation are:

- the 5 per cent threshold, which forces citizens to vote for the parties that will most probably get into the parliament;
- the media landscape, which is dominated by players who are supporting either the left or the right whether in a more concealed or open way;
- the financial conditions, which make it practically impossible for a new organization to enter the political market.

These seem to be the main factors that have let the parties grow more and more independent of the needs and wants of the people. The parties need popular support only during election campaigns, and, with the political culture being rather divided, they can generally obtain it by negative campaigning.

Yet, it would probably be oversimplification to talk about a unique Hungarian model, but the above analysis of Hungarian party campaigns has shown that there is a unique characteristic – which may or may not be exclusively Hungarian – namely that party elites consider voters immature, and easily convincible through appealing policies and pledges. Thus what we have seen for the two decades of democratic campaigning in Hungary is the sophistication of communication: the expanding arsenal and paraphernalia of campaigning techniques and means, procedures and processes, strategies and tactics, activists and managers, advisors and counsels – the constant strengthening of sales-oriented political marketing strategies. The conclusion therefore might be that Hungarian parties have been good at borrowing techniques from abroad, but it seems they still have a lot to learn as far as 'the idea behind' is concerned.

There is one component of party behaviour whose importance must definitely increase in the future, namely delivery. 2006 demonstrated for all the parties that there are limits in promising because there are limits in delivering the promises. If the parties did learn the lesson, they may even realize that if they cannot promise everything to everybody, they have to know what is really important for the people and design their products accordingly. Then a new period may begin in Hungarian politics in general and Hungarian political marketing in particular, the era of market orientation.

Notes

1   This paper is part of a broader research project, funded by the Hungarian Scientific Research Fund (OTKA), Project number: T 049546.
2   This was actually the program of Ferenc Gyurcsány; MSZP had an official program but that was overshadowed very quickly by 'New Hungary'.
3   See the interview with Viktor Szigetvári, who was the campaign manager of MSZP, in *Magyarország Politikai Évkönyve 2006-ról*, edited by Peter Sándor, László Vass and Ágnes Tolnai, Budapest: DKMKA, 2007.
4   An everyday name like Johnny Smith in English. Pisti Kovács was personified by a real five-year-old boy.

References/further reading

Bajomi-Lázár, P. and Sükösd, M. (eds) (2003) *Reinventing Media: Media Policy Reform in East Central Europe*, Budapest: Central European University Press.

Bayer, J. and Jensen, J. (eds) (2007) *From Transition to Globalization: New Challenges for Politics, the Media and Society*, Budapest: IPS of HAS.

Enyedi, Zs. and Tóka, G. (2007) 'The Only Game in Town: Party Politics in Hungary', in P. Webb and S. White (eds) *Party Politics in New Democracies*, Oxford; New York: Oxford University Press.

Haerpfer, C. W. (2006) 'Hungary: Structure and Dynamics of Democratic Consolidation', in H-D. Kingemann, D. Fuchs and J. Zielonka (eds) *Democracy and Political Culture in Eastern Europe*, Abingdon, Oxon [England]; New York: Routledge.

Saradin, P. and Bradová, E. (eds) (2007) *Visegrad Votes: Parliamentary Elections 2005–2006*, Olomouc: Palacky University.

Tóka, G. and Henjak, A. (2007) 'Party Systems and Voting Behaviour in the Visegrad Countries 15 Years After Transition', in P. Saradín and E. Bradová (eds) *Visegrad Votes. Parliamentary Elections 2005–2006*, Olomouc: Palacky University. [210–240]

White, S., Batt, J. and Lewis, P. G. (eds) (2003) *Developments in Central and East European politics 3*, Durham, NC: Duke University Press.

11 The Czech case

A marketing-oriented party on the rise?

Anna Matušková,[1] Otto Eibl[2] and Alexander Braun

This chapter aims to explore ways that parties in the Czech political system use political marketing. The main focus is on the 2006 Parliamentary General Elections, and we take a closer look at the case study of the campaign of the Social Democratic Party (ČSSD) as an example of the country's first real case of party behavior that could be described as a Market-Oriented Party (MOP).

We chose the 2006 campaign because it was considered revolutionary in many aspects. There was an unusual public focus on the campaign, which the media characterized as negative, brutal, aggressive and confrontational (Matušková 2006: 62). In reality, the Czech Republic experienced its first campaign where voter research and political marketing techniques dictated rather than followed the course of the campaign. In this way, the Czech political system for the first time contained all three elements of the JLM Model—Product-, Sales-, and Market-Oriented Parties.

The Czech political marketplace

The political system of the Czech Republic is a parliamentary democracy based on asymmetrical bicameralism where most power is vested in the lower chamber of the Parliament, the House of Deputies, consisting of 200 MPs. Elections to the House of Deputies take place every four years, and the wining party is usually asked by the President to form the government. The government-to-be then seeks a vote of confidence from the House of Deputies in order to assume office.

Following an election, seats are distributed proportionally based on the d'Hondt method, where a party must reach the 5 percent[3] threshold to have members in the Parliament. Given the system, governments in the Czech Republic are typically based on coalitions or are minority governments.

The Czech party system itself is among the most consolidated and stable of the countries of the former Soviet block (see Kopeček and Šedo 2003), and it can be described as mild five-party format pluralism. Most larger parties in the House of Deputies have had a stable electorate, both demographically and geographically.[4] The stability hypothesis is supported by a modified party replacement calculation (for further details see Šedo 2006a: 91–97, Šedo 2006b, compare Birch 2003: 121–126, 185–186) where the modification takes into account the number of seats in the Parliament (as opposed to the percentage of votes in the elections) and distinguishes four types of possible change factors:

1   no change (0)—keeping the name and electoral strategy;
2   minimal change (R0)—partial changes in either identity or electoral strategy;
3   significant change (R2)—substantial changes in either identity or electoral strategy;
4   complete change (RC)—creation of a new actor on the political scene (Chytilek and Šedo 2007: 24–25).

Overall political stability is also reflected in the stable volatility of the electorate. The table below presents both the "classical" volatility (Pederson's Index, V-values) and volatility modified by Birch (for more on Birch see Birch 2001, 2003: 123; Šedo 2005: 127). The modification consists of including only those parties that participated in both the t election and t–1 elections (value Vb in the table below). We also use a modified Pederson index (Vc) to express how much of the overall electorate moved among the existing parties.

The party system is dominated by two competing parties—the right-wing conservative ODS (Civic Democratic Party) and the center-left social democratic ČSSD (Czech Social Democratic Party). These two parties are the main pillars of most coalition governments,[5] and the poles that politically divide Czech society.

In addition to these two parties, seats in the House of Deputies have also always been held by the center-right Christian democrats KDU-ČSL (Christian and Democratic Union—Czechoslovak People's Party) and extreme-left communist

Table 11.1 Party replacement in the Czech Republic

Form replacement	1992		1996		1998		2002		2006	
	*	%	*	%	*	%	*	%	*	%
0	1	7	4	55	4	90.5	3	84.5	3	90.5
R$_0$	2	25	2	45	0	0	1	15.5	1	6.5
R$_2$	1	38	0	0	0	0	0	0	0	0
R$_C$	4	30	0	0	1	9.5	0	0	1	30

* Candidates/candidate ballots winning seats in parliament

Source: Chytilek and Šedo 2007: 27

Table 11.2 Volatility between 1996 and 2006 in the Czech Republic

	V	Vb	Vc
1996	20.94	17.07	20.02
1998	16.06	7.87	8.76
2002	20.74	12.18	12.7
2006	17.95	15.62	16.67

Source: Based on data from www.volby.cz

KSČM (Communist Party of Bohemia and Moravia; the party is a direct descendent of the old Communist Party from before the country returned to democracy in 1989 and has always been excluded from any coalition talks by all other parties).

Since the early elections of 1998, there have always been five parties in the House of Deputies, with the fifth party changing in different elections. Between 1998 and 2006, it was the right-wing Union of Freedom,[6] which was replaced by the Green Party in the 2006 elections. The fact that there have been five parties— the same four parties and a fifth one that changed—is testament to the semi-closed character of the political market in the Czech Republic. It is possible, albeit not easy, for a party to get enough votes to break through and enter the parliament. While the system remains open to new parties, in reality incumbent parties grow stronger in every election (and the two strongest parties—ODS and ČSSD—got almost 68 percent of votes, or 78 percent of seats in the 2006 elections; Eibl and Matušková 2007).

Even though Czech voters behave in a stable and consistent way and mostly stay loyal to "their" parties, parties overall have to deal with low party membership, and with low party identification (voters are much more likely to know with certainty which party they would never vote for than which party they would vote for (Rose and Mishler 1998). Party identification trends in the Czech Republic are shown in Tables 11.3 and 11.4.

The low level of party membership or identification manifests itself in practical financial issues. The main source of party financing is state contributions, which are allocated based on electoral success. All parties that receive at least 1.5 percent of votes in the House of Deputies elections are entitled to a state contribution of about 4 per vote. Those parties that actually get into the Parliament also get about €36,000 a year for each MP. Other sources of income are membership dues and sponsorship by individuals or companies (the latter of which must be officially

Table 11.3 The attitude towards preferred party in the Czech Republic (1995–2005) (%)

| Strong relationship | 61 | 67 | 66 | 72 | 61 | 57 | 60 | 56 | 46 | 42 | 42 | 46 | 49 | 42 | 47 | 49 |
| Weak relationship | 38 | 32 | 33 | 28 | 37 | 43 | 40 | 43 | 53 | 55 | 57 | 53 | 50 | 57 | 53 | 50 |

Source: Kunštát 2005, http://www.cvvm.cas.cz/upl/zpravy/100529s_pv51114.pdf

Table 11.4 Party identification in the Czech Republic (%)

	very strong	strong	moderate	weak	very weak
KSČM	11	42	34	21	5
ČSSD	7	14	70	22	4
SZ	0	2	15	3	2
KDU-ČSL	3	29	27	8	5
US-DEU	1	1	14	2	1
ODS	10	48	123	39	18

Source: ISSP 2004

registered if in excess of €2,000). Additionally, some parties, such as the Social Democrats and Christian Democrats, recovered buildings that were nationalized by the Communist regime and have obtained funding by renting or selling them.

Media and politics in the 2006 elections

After the fall of the Communist regime in 1989, the media market underwent a radical change. The state lost its monopoly power to provide and control information, and the media started to play the role of the "guardians of democracy." The media system became de-centralized and private publishing houses and private TV and radio owners became competitors to the state-run television and radio channels (which, while run and sponsored by the state, are similar to public service media, playing a role like that of the BBC in Britain, for example).[7]

With a few exceptions, the Czech media, both private and public, present themselves as non-partisan and objective, even if there are some clearly discernible politically biased traits in the style of their reporting. This trend towards public neutrality continues in the run-up to elections, when media outlets refrain from publicly endorsing individual parties (with the exception of op-eds).

Press

There were nine published dailies in the Czech Republic in 2006. Five of them were considered "serious-reporting" newspapers (*MF DNES, Právo, Lidové noviny, Hospodářské noviny* and a series of regional dailies, *Deníky Bohemia/ Moravia*), three were tabloids (*Blesk, AHA!* and *Šip, Deníky*) and one focused solely on sports news (*Sport*). The *Blesk* tabloid was by far the most widely read paper, followed by *MF DNES* and the composite of the regional dailies of *Deníky Bohemia/Moravia* (published under regionalized names in different regions).

Despite the stated neutrality of the media, dailies implicitly lean towards different parties in their coverage, as shown for example by a study by Barbora Petrová (Petrová 2006). The following charts from her research show the number and types of mentions of various political parties and their leaders in four of the main "serious" dailies (*MF DNES, Hospodářské noviny, Lidové noviny*, and *Právo*; unfortunately, the regionalized *Deníky Bohemia/Moravia* were not included).

Two findings are apparent from the above: First, the media have almost exclusively focused on reporting on the two main parties, ODS and ČSSD. Second, there are apparent bias tendencies in how the papers covered these parties. At least in 2006, *Právo* was close to the left and/or ČSSD, and *MF DNES* and *Lidové noviny* were close to the right and/or ODS. *Hospodářské noviny* had the most balanced coverage, according to this analysis.

Television and radio

There were three nationwide TV channels in the Czech Republic in 2006—public Czech Television and private Nova and Prima. However, their role in the

Table 11.5 Readership of dailies in the first half of 2006, Czech Republic

Name	Readership
Blesk (excluding the Sunday paper)	1,527,000
MF DNES	1,048,000
Právo	478,000
Sport	312,000
Lidové noviny	232,000
Hospodářské noviny	208,000
Super Spy	77,000
Deníky Bohemia	
Východočeské	220,000
Severočeské	206,000
Západočeské	188,000
Středočeské	125,000
Jihočeské	122,000
Deníky Moravia	
Moravskoslezské	142,000
Středomoravské a Východomoravské (bez Kroměřížského deníku)	132,000
Jihomoravské	118,000
Vysočina	72,000

Source: Media Projekt 2006

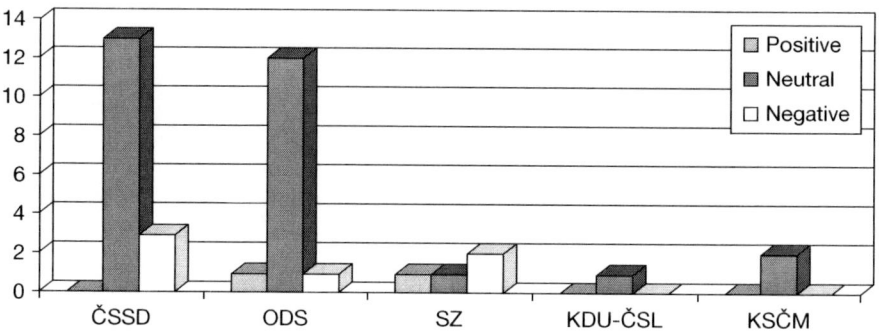

Figure 11.1 MF DNES

Figure 11.2 Hospodářské noviny

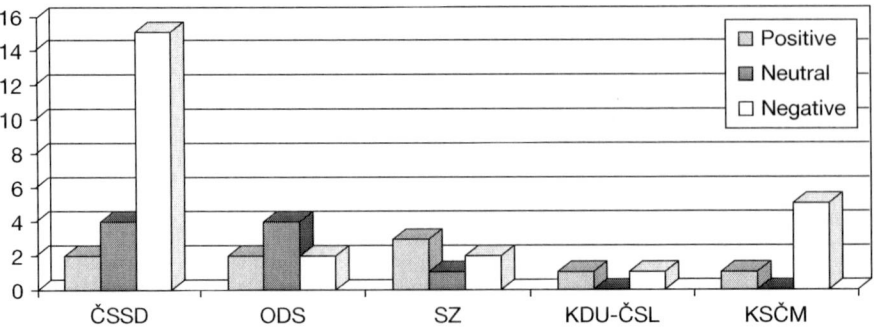

Figure 11.3 Lidové noviny

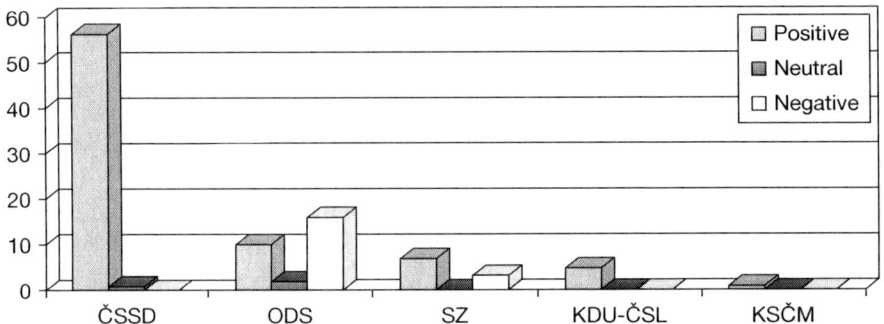

Figure 11.4 Právo

Source: Petrová 2006: 54–55

campaign was somewhat limited, as televised political advertising is significantly curtailed by law and completely forbidden on private television channels. Each party, regardless of strength, is given an equal block of broadcasting time on public television. These blocks are generally televised in less attractive time slots, and include a long series of spots by all parties, limiting the viewership and effectiveness of this type of marketing.

That said, television still plays a crucial role in how parties present themselves to voters, through TV news coverage and televised candidate debates. While the former has in composite probably the most influence on how voters perceive the parties in general, debates, which are shown on all three TV channels, are the most watched political programs, and generate days of other media coverage.

The radio market is fragmented into several nationwide stations (both private and public) and a large number of local broadcasters (or local branches of nationwide stations). The same access restrictions apply to radio as to TV—no air time can be bought by parties, and the public radio stations broadcast party messages in large blocks that are listened to by a very limited number of voters. In general, radio plays little role in Czech election campaigns.

Internet

The internet played a relatively large role in political marketing during the 2006 elections. All larger media outlets created specialized online portals aimed solely at providing information about the elections, and, of course, all parties addressed the elections on their websites. The 2006 election was the first time the parties truly focused on online presentation as a specific campaign tool, and the quality of the campaign websites was generally quite high. The two main parties, ODS and ČSSD, used the internet to the fullest out of all the parties. ODS did a particularly good job in coordinating their online and offline advertising to reinforce the message, and ČSSD was credited with being most interactive and responsive to voters' queries online. While the parties clearly presented their election platforms online and many (especially ČSSD and ODS) aimed parts of it specifically at target groups, the internet was not used to help organize sympathizers, fundraise, or even to help collect email addresses to supplement the parties' email communication.

Voters, party affiliation and its implication for campaigning in the Czech Republic

In terms of geography, party support for the main parties is dispersed quite equally across the country. The exception are KDU-ČSL voters, for which support is largely concentrated in the southeastern part of the country and in rural areas (Chytilek and Šedo 2007, Pink and Kabát 2006), and ČSSD, which tends to do slightly better in the eastern regions of the country.

There are significant differences among the electorate in terms of demography. An age division in the society results in younger voters supporting ODS and the Greens, while older voters favor ČSSD and the Communists (and, to some extent, KDU-ČSL in some rural areas). Additionally, there is an education division between ODS and ČSSD voters, with the former finding greater support among the more educated parts of the society. In terms of income, not surprisingly, higher-income voters tend to vote for the business-oriented ODS, and voters who are more concerned about social issues tend to support the parties on the left side of the political spectrum. Furthermore, ODS and the Greens do significantly better in large cities.

That said, the Czech electorate is also characterized by very low levels of party affiliation and a large number of undecided or swing voters. There is a widespread skepticism toward politics and the political system among Czech voters (as illustrated by all major polls on the subject) and, perhaps as a consequence, election turnout had been declining prior to the 2006 elections (see Table 11.6). The spike in turnout in 2006 has been widely viewed as a result of the forceful and negative campaign of ČSSD, which created a sense of urgency among voters and made them participate in the election in larger numbers than usual.

In terms of party membership, Czech political parties face a long-term difficulty with low numbers of members and activists. The percentage of votes that came from party members in 2006 represented negligible numbers for ČSSD, ODS and Greens: 1.02 percent, 1.57 percent and 0.62 percent respectively. KDU-ČSL

Table 11.6 Czech turnout 1990–2006

year	1990[a]	1992	1996	1998	2002	2006
turnout	96.79%	85.08%	76.41%	74.03%	58.0%	64.47%

[a] The high turnout that year was because it was the first free and democratic parliamentary elections after the fall of the Communist regime.

and KSČM, however, are in somewhat different positions, with members' votes representing 10.71 percent and 12.1 percent of all received votes.[8] This has a natural impact on campaign strategies, and KDU-ČSL and KSČM tend to run campaigns focused on their core members without an extensive use of political marketing techniques (thus both parties fall into the categories POP and SOP). On the other hand, ODS and especially ČSSD cannot rely on members' votes, and are forced to run more general voter-centered campaigns, and thus, they are closer to the MOP model.

This means that there exist large numbers of swing and undecided voters in the country, and the two main parties, ČSSD and ODS, focused primarily on them in their campaigns. At the same time, the potential for each party is limited, as both parties have large unfavorable ratings among significant parts of the population (which was exacerbated by the antagonistic 2006 campaign). In reality, this means that undecideds can either be convinced to vote for the party they "don't hate" or will not turn out to vote at all. Typically only a few choose to switch to smaller parties.

Primary research among candidates

In order to understand how campaigns and political marketing are viewed by those who are their direct actors, i.e. the candidates themselves, we conducted an email survey among the members of the Czech Parliament. Every member of the House of Deputies and the Senate received a survey with 21 closed-ended questions, designed to analyze their attitudes towards political marketing.[9] The response rate was about 15 percent in both chambers of the parliament (30 completed interviews out of 200 surveys in the House of Deputies and 14 out of 81 in the Senate). This survey thus provides a merely directional but at the same time very valuable and unique insight into how the election process is perceived by those whose careers are directly dependent on it.

The majority of respondents displayed a somewhat discrepant view of how campaign techniques should influence the campaign strategy. While 75 percent of the surveyed respondents said that identifying target groups is important, only 34 percent said that opinion polls (the most effective tool for identifying target groups) are indispensible to a campaign. Their answers also illustrated a relatively narrow understanding of political marketing, viewing it only as a tool for preparing a good advertising campaign. Further, 81 percent of respondents said that meeting the needs of their party base is the primary motivating factor in their campaigns, and only 32 percent expressed a willingness to change policy positions (an important aspect of the MOP model). And yet, at the same time, 59 percent agreed that inadequately responding to voters would result in party failure.

While the base size of this survey is limited, it is worth noting that the most positive view of the value of political marketing in campaigns was expressed by ČSSD MPs—candidates from a party that just went through its first MOP experience. For example, unlike members of other parties, ČSSD members are more open to the possibility of adjusting the party platform according to voters' desires.

Independent of the above-described research, we carried out another qualitative survey of campaign managers and professionals across the political spectrum (summer 2006). The responses correlate with the above findings: political marketing in the Czech Republic was, by and large, understood narrowly as just a tool for advertising and, to some extent, conducting a field operation. The only exception was among ČSSD, which for the first time focused fully on research and other political marketing techniques as some of the main driving aspects of their campaign.

Political parties and their classification into the JLM Model

The following section takes a more detailed look at all of the five parliamentary parties as they stood in the 2006 campaign and classifies them into one of the three categories of the JLM Model. We then analyze one of the parties, ČSSD, in great detail to show that it was closest in its positioning, strategy and behavior to the definition of a marketing-oriented party.

KSČM: Product-oriented party

During the 2006 campaign, the Communist Party (KSČM) was in a unique position on the electoral market, with the most loyal voters, skewing towards the older and poorer; and very stable electoral results (10 to 15 percent) but extremely low coalition potential, as all other parties publicly announced they would under no circumstances form a coalition government with KSČM. The party was positioned as a real leftist party, although it actually outsourced its advertising operation to a professional firm rather than handling it in-house. KSČM did attempt to focus its advertising on certain target groups, mainly people in a difficult socio-economic situation such as young mothers or seniors. However, its campaign approach yielded nothing in terms of adapting what the party offered, or even making a serious effort to understand voters' wants and how they would fit with the party platform. The campaign was run in a very centralized fashioned, had little sequencing, and ultimately failed to attract new voters. Indeed, KSČM lost a substantial number of voters in 2006 to ČSSD because of its failure to articulate why it was a better alternative for left-leaning voters.

KSČM is a prime example of a product-oriented party, in that its program offering is based strictly on party ideology and there is great resistance within the party and among its traditional voters against any attempt to adjust it to current voters' desires.

KDU-ČSL: Sales-oriented party

Like the Communist party, KDU-ČSL is a traditional party with a clearly defined electorate to which it tries to cater. However, unlike the Communist party, it made a clear attempt to change its focus to a sales-oriented mode in the 2006 election. In terms of the Product Design phase, KDU-ČSL stuck to its guns of socially conservative, pro-family policies, but its communication techniques were clearly sales-oriented. For example its billboards sought to address specific voter groups with somewhat individualized messages, the party used online communication as part of its offering, and its campaign strategy was sequenced to reach voters in different stages. The tone of the campaign was positive, focused on family issues and Christian democratic values, but the party eventually failed to position itself as a viable option besides the dominant ODS and ČSSD. In the end, its voters remained KDU's traditional base—religious and values voters, older, rural, and heavily concentrated in the south-east region of the country.

At the same time, KDU-ČSL retained its position as a king-maker. Regardless of which of the two main parties won, KDU-ČSL was almost certain to be asked to join the coalition government (and both ČSSD and ODS did indeed try to lure the party to their side in post-elections negotiations).

ODS: Sales-oriented party

ODS was the leader in the polls from the very beginning of the campaign. Its candidates were positioned as economic experts and reformers, and as those who could save the country from a return to power by the Communist party. Additionally, they had an image of a likely winner, as they consistently led in public polling through the campaign. Consequently, the party decided to lead a positive campaign, which opened with the unveiling of the party's core proposal, the flat tax, and then built on the concept while introducing its candidates. ODS clearly targeted younger, upscale and more educated voters, who are more concentrated in large cities. While the campaign was to some extent decentralized, overall its techniques centered mainly on outdoor and print advertising, and also used online marketing and online videos.

In its execution, ODS in 2006 behaved as a sales-oriented party, though it eventually introduced certain elements of a market-oriented party (mostly as a reaction to the ČSSD campaign). ODS initially offered a clearly defined program centered on fiscal reform, and devoted most of its campaign to selling these concepts to the public. The market-oriented elements were introduced after ČSSD managed to discredit the proposed fiscal reforms with a large part of the electorate, forcing ODS to re-focus its campaign away from its core proposal.

Green Party: Sales-oriented party

The Green Party, as a newcomer to the political scene, positioned itself as a party of a new political style and in addition to its traditional environmental focus.

However, the style of their campaign was largely indistinguishable from that of other parties, and the Greens in 2006 could be classified as a sales-oriented party, focused on selling its program to the voters. The party got an enormous publicity boost when, four months before the elections, it crossed the 5 percent threshold in public polls, prompting a sudden burst of media attention. Interestingly, the party's purposefully non-aggressive campaign in fact tried to portray the Greens as a product-oriented party—one focused mostly on ideas, regardless of how voters react to them. Nevertheless, this presentation was merely a campaign technique, and the party in reality behaved as a sales-oriented party, with much of its operation focused on grassroots operations.

ČSSD: Market-oriented party

The most interesting party and one that was closest to being categorized as a Market-Oriented Party was the Social Democrats (ČSSD). Even though it was the incumbent party, ČSSD's horserace numbers hovered around 10 percent a year before the election. Moreover, the party's program was relatively undefined and it had just been through a turbulent leadership change. ČSSD voters tend to be older, less educated, more likely to be female, and more heavily concentrated in the eastern part of the country (Moravia region).

Starting around June 2005, the party underwent two major changes—it acquired a new and very energetic leader (Jiří Paroubek, first as the country's Prime Minister and, from September 2005, also the Chairman of the party), and it made a decision to hire American political consultants from Penn, Schoen and Berland Associates (PSB)[10] to create a campaign plan and drive campaign strategy.[11] Both the new leadership and the consulting company started preparing the campaign by researching voters' needs and wants, molding the campaign message around the research findings, and adjusting the messages and strategy based on regular polling. This marketing-oriented party behavior led to the positioning of ČSSD as a protector of social values and economic prosperity, and as a defender of the country from "ODS experiments." The tone of the campaign was unusually negative and comparative (to ODS), coupled with some positive elements. The campaign was highly centralized, to maintain control of the message, sequenced into several strategy stages and constantly updated based on polling. The tactical focus of the campaign was on outdoor and print ad campaigning, with some online marketing, but most attention was directed towards generating positive media coverage and the televised debates.

The case study: Social democrats

We choose the 2006 campaign of ČSSD as a case study because of its departure from the traditional campaign model in the Czech Republic of running as a POP or SOP, and its movement towards the MOP model. This was something that was previously not tried, and most experts, media and other parties were caught by surprise by this step. The MOP classification stems from the fact that the course of the campaign was not only driven by constant polling, but because the actual "product" of the party—i.e. its policies, proposals and behavior—were driven and influenced by polling. In this regard, the party crossed from its traditional sale-oriented mode, of trying to sell its product, to the marketing-oriented mode, where it was actually adjusting its product based on voters' reactions.

In the summer of 2005, a year before the election, ČSSD was a party in disarray and garnering support levels of only 10–11 percent in public polls. Its leader, Stanislav Gross, was forced to resign, the party was bogged down in corruption scandals, and many leading party members conceded that new ideas were lacking after seven years of being in the government. The new Prime Minister Jiří Paroubek and party Chairman Stanislav Gross (Paroubek assumed Gross's function a few months later) decided that the party needed to turn to professional consultants, and hired an American political strategy firm, Penn, Schoen and Berland (PSB). The company's approach to campaigns is very much rooted in the MOP model, as it is based on detailed polling of the electorate and constant refining of the campaign message or messages based on continuous feedback from polling. The consultants were put in charge of ČSSD's strategy, as well as numerous operational aspects of the campaign, and the Prime Minister led the party based on the direction and advice received from the polls and strategy memos.

Stage 1: Market intelligence

At first, the consultants conducted a number of focus groups in the summer of 2005 to get a deeper understanding of what voters (particularly undecided voters) thought about the political situation, political actors and main issues. The findings from the qualitative research served as a basis for a large quantitative benchmark poll of almost 3,000 likely voters conducted in September 2005.

The benchmark poll created the backbone for the entire campaign strategy, and provided a blueprint for the campaign plan. Its findings focused on several macro-areas of how voters think and what their preferences are, covering many of the following areas:

- political environment;
- party selection;
- party attributes;
- leader attributes;
- government accomplishments ratings;
- policy proposals;
- spending priorities;
- voter profiles;
- voter media habits;
- regional differences.

The results provided detailed insights into the minds of voters and their perception of the political situation and actors, as well as what they expect from them.

Stage 2: Product design

The results of the benchmark poll were analyzed in detail and used to segment voters into groups, craft ČSSD's message to match voters' desires, and set up the campaign plan in general. Important to analysis under the MOP paradigm is the fact that ČSSD's campaign message, slogan and overall plan were created by outsiders solely based on the results of polling voters. While the party's legacy was of course part of the survey design and the tested messages were grounded in possible, realistic offerings, the campaign blueprint was designed not only to retain base voters but to capture as many swing and undecided voters as possible.

The benchmark poll showed that ČSSD's main challenge was to gain undecided voters while also winning over current voters of KSČM on the left and ODS on the right. The poll demonstrated that, despite heading the government for seven years, ČSSD was perceived as an ideologically undefined party, whereas its main rivals ODS and KSČM were clearly defined in voters' minds. Additionally, the analysis showed that both of the rival parties had little room to grow, whereas ČSSD could expand its base significantly.

In terms of issue priorities, 48 percent of likely voters considered social security issues such as healthcare, pensions and unemployment benefits to be the primary influence on their vote, and an additional 38 percent focused on economic issues. This clear focus on a social and economic agenda, and lack of emphasis on areas like crime, education and foreign policy, led to the creation of the party's new slogan "Security[12] and Prosperity."

The implication of this slogan, which was to be reflected in all campaign messaging and advertising, was not only to clearly define the hard-to-read party, but also to differentiate it from other parties. The message to voters was that while the conservative ODS focused on the economy, its social platform would be disastrous, and while the Communist party focused on the social arena, it had no program for economic stability and progress. Since the poll showed that voters overwhelmingly focused on both of these two areas in their decisions, ČSSD was to be presented as the only party that could deliver on both social security *and* economic prosperity.

Stage 3: Product adjustment

While ČSSD had a detailed campaign plan in place by November 2005, ahead of other parties, its product offering was constantly refined through additional polling. On average, the party commissioned one to two large strategic quantitative polls every month until the election, and one to five smaller-scale issue polls or focus groups a month. The research component of the campaign was unprecedented in the Czech Republic, and was similar to major campaigns in large Western countries with sophisticated political marketing techniques, like the USA or UK.

An example of ČSSD's product adjustment based on competition, one of the key elements in defining a marketing-oriented party, was the emphasis put on contrasting the different chairmen of the main parties. Initially, ČSSD leader Paroubek had a significant favorability lead over his ODS prime-ministerial rival, Mirek Topolánek (42 percent—29 percent on a forced choice question who would be the best prime minister). Therefore ČSSD's early strategy aimed at framing the race as a referendum on who would be a better Prime Minister. This was all the more important since polls showed that ODS had higher favorability numbers than ČSSD as a party, but would lose if voters were to consider only the leaders. By spring 2006, however, the data started to show Topolánek catching up with Paroubek, and the ČSSD campaign therefore shifted to talk about the most unpopular of ODS's proposals, rather than pitting the leaders against each other.

Additionally, the election platform underwent some adjustments based on internal reactions of party bodies and ČSSD government ministers. While the plan called for targeting swing voters, many of the party's die-hard loyalists insisted that the program focus primarily on retaining base voters. Consequently, even though the consultants had created a detailed demographic and psychographic segmentation of Czech voters, it wasn't extensively used.

Stage 4: Implementation

Implementing the campaign plan within ČSSD was one of the most difficult parts of the campaign. Many party members were unaccustomed to fast-paced and market-oriented campaign techniques and were resistant to giving up old ways. Others were concerned with loss of power within the organization, and vigorously opposed many of the campaign action steps that they perceived as a threat to their position within the party. Regional candidates often insisted that the situation in their area was so specific that only they knew what would work, and were hard pressed to accept direction from party headquarters. Eventually, most of the party unified behind the campaign and ČSSD's new leader, but it took a good deal of time and effort to reach that point.

Stage 5: Communication

Communicating party messages to voters was the main thrust of the campaign in the six months before the election. Based on the campaign plan, a concerted effort was developed to manage the campaign message in both free and paid-for media. Teams prepped each TV debate participant with talking points and rehearsals, the media department monitored the press every morning and identified opportunities for getting the message out, and daily talking points were distributed to candidates. Additionally, a great deal of thinking and effort was devoted to designing and placing billboards and posters designed to convey particular messages, both positive and negative, and direct mail pieces were sent to voters' homes. While ČSSD did manage to update its website and post most of its materials, the internet was not a major communications tool in the 2006 campaign, partly because internet penetration among ČSSD voters was very low.

Stage 6: Campaign

Once the internal party struggle subsided, a firm 24/7 campaign structure was established. The team consisted of a campaign manager, strategist and pollster, media relations experts, advertising experts and field organizers. Again, everyone worked to persuade voters with communication that was based on and refined by polling and communication with voters.

Stage 7: Election

The campaign naturally culminated with Election Day, when ČSSD moved from the 11 percent of public support it had in polls a year before to 32 percent percent. ODS eventually gained 35 percent, and no other party got more than 20 percent. This resulted in a virtual deadlock, as no single party was able to form the government. It was eventually resolved when two ČSSD MPs left the social democratic group, allowing ODS to form a coalition government with KDU-ČSL (which had gained 7 percent) and the Green Party (6 percent). The Communists remained on the sidelines despite getting 13 percent of the votes.

Overall, most analysts agreed that while ČSSD didn't eventually win the election, its result was a success given its starting position. The main reason for this success was clearly ČSSD's professionally conducted campaign and reliance on modern political marketing techniques. Other political parties certainly took note, and there has been a trend among them to transform their campaigns to resemble more the MOP model rather than the traditional models.

Stage 8: Delivery

Since ČSSD did not eventually form the government, measuring delivery is difficult. However, we can look at its delivery as an opposition party, and there ČSSD clearly continues to behave as an MOP. It leads a virtually constant campaign against ODS, pointing out all of its mistakes and highlighting its every social program change, and continues to adjust its offering through the copious use of polling. All of its subsequent campaigns (for example, senate and regional elections) carry clear signs of the MOP model—candidates are vetted through polling, professional teams of consultants work around the clock to fine-tune the party's message to appeal to as many targeted voters as possible, and the party selects the issues to focus on based more on recent poll numbers than on ideology.

Conclusion

The aim of this chapter was to apply the Lees-Marshment POP–SOP–MOP model to the Czech political scene and in particular to ČSSD. We can conclude that the model can be applied to the Czech context, but only to a certain level. The biggest problems logically stem from the nature of the proportional multi-polar political system in the Czech Republic, which requires the creation of coalition governments.

This makes measurement of the delivery stage of the model difficult, because parties are forced to alter their behavior and goals after the election for reasons related to coalition negotiations rather than voters' interests.

As there is only a short tradition of using political marketing methods in the Czech Republic (since the fall of communism, only five parliamentary elections have taken place), it is difficult to arrive at long-term conclusions about the use of political marketing methods or analyze the development of party communication strategies. Nevertheless, it is safe to say that the 2006 elections represented an important change. It is clear that the trend toward professionalization has started, and political marketing techniques can be expected to be used more in the future.

The application of the Lees-Marshment model was most useful in the case of ČSSD. The party showed clear signs of systematic change by using techniques aimed at analyzing the market, updating their tactics based on the development of the campaign, and devising strategies aimed at specific target groups of voters. It was the first party in the country to base its campaign strategy, message, and programmatic offering on a large-scale survey of voters. Additionally, research and strategy also focused on the weaknesses of ČSSD's opponents, and frequently used this information as much as the positive presentation of the party itself.

Overall, we believe the model represents rather interesting heuristic concepts and provides an excellent framework for further research in this field. Specifically in the case of Czech elections, we are excited to expand and keep testing the validity of the model on the country's political system as it contains elements representing all three stages of the model.

Notes

1 The work of Otto Eibl on this text was supported by the research project "Political parties and interest representation in current European democracies" (code MSM0021622407).

2 The work of Anna Matušková was supported by the Fulbright Scholarship and by the research project "Political parties and interest representation in current European democracies" (code MSM0021622407).

3 The legal threshold for coalitions depends on the number of coalition partners—for two-member coalitions it is 10 percent, three-member is 15 percent, and for four and more members it is 20 percent.

4 KDU-ČSL is the only party that gets a significantly higher proportion of electoral support from one specific region over other electoral regions (see Chytilek and Šedo 2007: 30).

5 The only exception was the period of a ČSSD government existing under the existence of the "Opposition Contract" between 1998 and 2002. The "Contract" was a deal between ČSSD and ODS under which ČSSD's minority government would be "tolerated" (meaning supported) by ODS on key political issues. The Contract was a result of a stalemate following the 1998 election after which none of the parties was capable of creating a government that could garner enough votes for a vote of confidence in the Parliament. The Contract is widely accepted by both ČSSD and ODS as a deal that hurt both parties in the eyes of the public and is unlikely to be repeated.

6 Union of Freedom seceded from ODS but after a relative success in the 1998 elections it started to lose power and virtually disappeared after the 2006 elections.

7 Czech public service media consist of the Czech Television Channel (ČT), Czech Radio (ČRo) and the Czech News Agency wire (ČTK). ČT and ČRo are partly financially supported by the state while ČTK is completely financially independent.

8 At the same time, their party membership has been in a steep decline over the years with Communist Party losing over 75 percent of its members between 1998 and 2008 (the average age of a Communist Party member in 2008 was 70 years; KSČM 2008).

9 The survey was carried out in May and June 2007, and consisted of 44 completed interviews (out of 200 MPs and 81 Senators). Respondents came from all the parties—ČSSD, ODS, KDU-ČSL, Greens and Communists.

10 One of the authors of this article was a PSB employee and served as Chief Strategist on the ČSSD campaign.

11 Hiring professional political consultants, particularly foreign ones, and giving them such a prominent and powerful role in the campaign was something the Czech political scene had not seen before. While there were several overtures to both foreign and domestic consultants, the vast majority of campaign work, decisions and analysis was done by the parties internally. Campaigns were mostly done in an idiosyncratic fashion and focused on a rudimentary poster and billboard creation and distribution. While advertising was often outsourced to ad agencies such as Ogilvy or BBDO, the cooperation between the two subjects was typically rocky as politicians resisted the ideas of the ad people and the ad firms were frustrated with the decision making process of the parties.

12 The word "Security" in the Czech version of the slogan clearly referred to social security.

References/further reading

Birch, S. (2001) "Party System Stability and Territorial Patterns of Electoral Competition in the Czech Republic", paper prepared for presentation at the 97th annual meeting of the American Political Science Association, San Francisco, 30 August–2 September. Available at: <http://www2.essex.ac.uk/elect/database/papers/SBvolatility.pdf> (accessed 5 June 2009).

Birch, S. (2003) *Electoral Systems and Political Transformation in Post-Communist Europe*, New York; Basingstoke, UK: Palgrave Macmillan.

Chytilek, R. and Šedo, J. (2007) "Party System Stability and Territorial Patterns of Electoral Competition in the Czech Republic", in V. Hloušek and R. Chytilek (eds) *Parliamentary Elections and Party Landscape in the Visegrad Group Countries*, Brno: CDK.

Eibl, O. and Matušková, A. (2007) "Introduction of the Election Cycle Model: The Case of the Czech Republic 2006–2007", *Central European Political Studies Review*, 9: 114–138.

Electoral Law 247/1995 Sb., about Election to the Parliament of the Czech Republic.

Electoral Server of the Czech Statistical Office (n.d.) Available at: <http://www.volby.cz> (accessed 5 June 2009).

European Commission: Public Opinion Analysis (n.d.) *Standard Eurobarometer 61–68*, 2004–2008. Available at: <http://ec.europa.eu/public_opinion> (accessed 5 June 2009).

International Social Survey Programme [ISSP] (2004). Citizenship Module. Available via NESSTAR at the Institute of Sociology of the Academy of Sciences of the Czech Republic data archive.

Kopeček, L. and Šedo, J. (2003) "Czech and Slovak Political Parties and their Vision of European Integration", *Central European Political Studies Review*, 5. Available at: <http://www.cepsr.com/clanek.php?ID=12> (accessed 5 June 2009).

Kunštát, D. (2005) *Strany a voliči*, Press Release of the Public Opinion Research Centre, Institute of Sociology of the Academy of Sciences of the Czech Republic. Available at: http://www.cvvm.cas.cz/upl/zpravy/100529s_pv51114.pdf (accessed 5 June 2009).

Matušková, A. (2006) "Volební kampaň 2006: Nástup politického marketingu do České republiky", in D. Čaloud, T. Foltýn, V. Havlík and A. Matušková (eds) *Volby do Poslanecké sněmovny v roce 2006*, Brno: CDK. [62–88]

Media Projekt (2006). *Čtenost českých periodik*. Available at: http://www.median.cz/docs/ MP_2006_1%2B2Q_zprava.pdf (accessed 5 June 2009).

Petrová, B. (2006) "Volební Kampaň v médiích", in D. Čaloud, T. Foltýn, V. Havlík and A. Matušková (eds) *Volby do Poslanecké sněmovny v roce 2006*, Brno: CDK. [42–61]

Pink, M. and Kabát, M. (2006) "Parlamentní volby 2006 a volební geografie", in D. Čaloud, T. Foltýn, V. Havlík and A. Matušková (eds) *Volby do Poslanecké sněmovny v roce 2006*, Brno: CDK. [123–144]

Public Opinion Research Centre (CVVM). (n.d.) Home page. Available at: <http://www.cvvm.cas.cz/> (accessed 5 June 2009).

Rose, R. and Mishler, W. (1998) "Negative and Positive Party Identification in Post-Communist Countries", *Electoral Studies*, 17(2): 217–234.

Šedo, J. (2005) "Přenos kvantitativních metod výzkumu výstupů volební soutěže do odlišných regionálních podmínek: Případ stability a stabilizace systému politických stran v postkomunistických zemích Evropy", in P. Fiala, and M. Strmiska (eds) *Víceúrovňové vládnutí: Teorie, Přístupy, Metody*, Brno: CDK. [121–135]

Šedo, J. (2006a) "Proporcionalita zastoupení a navrstvující smíšené volební systémy", *European Electoral Studies*, 1(1): 61–91.

Šedo, J. (2006b) "Stabilita zastoupení v České republice", in B. Dančák and V. Hloušek (eds) *Parlamentní volby 2006 a Česká politika*, Brno: MPÚ.

Party documents

ČSSD (2006) *Campaign Platform*. Available at: <http://www.socdem.cz/soubory/ 422010/vp%5F29%2E3%2E2006.pdf> (accessed 30 April 2008).

KDU-ČSL (2006) *Campaign Platform*. Available at: <http://www.kdu.cz/default.asp?page =510&idr=10149&IDCl=15076> (accessed 5 June 2009).

KSČM (2006) *Campaign Platform*. Available at: <http://volby.KSČM.cz/document.asp ?thema=3351&category=> (accessed 5 June 2009).

KSČM (2008) *Report of the Central Committee about the Party Activity between the VI. and VII. Congress*. Available at: <http://www.KSČM.cz/viewDocument.asp?document =4197> (accessed 30 April 2008).

ODS (2006) *Campaign Platform*. Available at: <http://www.ods.cz/volby2006/ prispevek.php?ID=110> (accessed 30 April 2008).

SZ (2006) *Campaign Platform*. Available at: <http://www.zeleni.cz/59/rubrika/volebni-program/> (accessed 5 June 2009)

12 Testing the market-oriented model of political parties in a non-Western context

The case of Taiwan

Dafydd J. Fell and Isabelle Cheng

Multi-party politics are a relatively new phenomenon in Taiwan. Its first democratic parliamentary and presidential elections were held as recently as 1991 and 1996 respectively. Taiwan is the sole example of a Chinese multi-party democracy and compared to other new democracies has relatively institutionalized political parties. Moreover, since numerous restrictions on campaigning practices were lifted, Taiwan's parties have rapidly embraced many of the marketing techniques associated with the American model of political communication.

In this study we apply the Lees-Marshment model of market-oriented parties to Taiwan, a country that is culturally and politically worlds apart from the model's British origin. We test whether in the first two decades of multi-party competition the leading parties have become increasingly market oriented. Or have the parties remained either sales- or product-oriented? This puzzle is central to the political science debate over whether parties are primarily motivated by policy, or the desire to gain votes and government office. The second question examined is how can we explain the degree that parties become market-oriented? Lastly, we are interested to see whether Lees-Marshment is correct in her assertion that the market-oriented party should outperform rivals that adopt a sales- or product-oriented approach. The analysis for this chapter was based on our observations and content analysis of election advertising of eleven elections between 1992 and 2008. In addition, we conducted elite interviews in 2001, 2005 and 2008 and an elite opinion survey in 2007.

The Taiwanese political marketplace

The party and electoral system

After almost four decades of authoritarian one-party rule, Taiwan's ruling party, the Kuomintang (KMT) began a process of democratization in the late 1980s. The first opposition party, the Democratic Progressive Party (DPP) was formed in 1986 and a year later, Martial Law was finally lifted.

Tables 12.1 and 12.2 show the pattern of continuity and change in the party system since 1986. In the initial period, Taiwan had a one-party dominant system,

Table 12.1 Party seat shares in parliamentary elections in Taiwan, 1986–2008, %

	1986	1989	1991	1992	1995	1998	2001	2004	2008
KMT	80.8	71.3	78.2	59.6	51.8	54.7	30.2	35.1	71.7
DPP	16.7	20.8	20.3	31.1	32.9	31.1	38.7	39.6	24
NP					12.8	4.9	0.4	0.4	0
PFP							20.2	15.1	0.9
TSU							5.8	5.3	0

Table 12.2 Party vote shares in presidential elections in Taiwan, 1996–2008, %

	1996	2000	2004	2008
KMT	54	23.1	49.9	58
DPP	21.1	39.3	50.1	42
NP	14.9	0.1		
PFP		36.8		

in which the KMT won over three-quarters of the seats. This dominance was challenged in the 1990s by the DPP and a second significant opposition party, the New Party (NP). The 2000 presidential election marked the end of KMT dominance and the start of a competitive multi-party system, with the KMT and DPP as the two large parties and the emergence of two new challenger parties, the People First Party (PFP) and the Taiwan Solidarity Union (TSU). From 2000 to 2008 Taiwan had its first taste of divided government. For though the DPP won the presidential elections of 2000 and 2004 and was the largest party in the 2001 and 2004 legislative elections, the KMT in conjunction with its ally the PFP held a parliamentary majority. Following the KMT's landslide victories in the 2008 elections, Taiwan appears to be returning to a two-party system, with the KMT once again the most powerful force.

After the democratic opening Taiwan operated a mixed electoral system, with a multi-member district system in parliamentary contests and a single member district first-past-the-post system for presidential and local executive elections. Following recent constitutional reforms, Taiwan introduced a new electoral system for the parliamentary elections in 2008. The new system is similar to that used in Japan since 1996. Voters have two votes, one for a single member district candidate and another for a proportional representation political party list.

As for voters, in contrast to the weakening of party ties in many mature democracies, there was an increase in the level of Taiwanese voter party identification during the 1990s. Since 1999, levels of party identification have stabilized at approximately 60 per cent. The patterns of seat shares displayed in Table 12.1 suggest a degree of voter volatility. However, party vote shares show considerable stability over the last 16 years, with the two main parties tending to gain around 80 per cent of the votes.

Issue divisions

Like many other new democracies, the European left–right dimension is not the central dividing spectrum for Taiwanese parties. Instead when Taiwanese analysts talk of a left and right they mean a national identity spectrum in which the far left emphasizes Taiwanese identity and calls for a declaration of independence from China, while the far right emphasizes Chinese nationalist symbols and argues for unification with China. The KMT has tended to be located on the center right and the DPP on the left of this spectrum. In addition to identity, the parties have also competed on policy differences related to democratic reforms, social welfare, political corruption, and economic policy. Survey data suggest that parties would be best advised to take a moderate stance on national identity, and rather than focusing exclusively on identity matters, they should also address other salient issues. Nevertheless, Taiwan's leading parties have a core of supporters, activists and politicians that are more ideologically focused on identity and hold more extreme positions on identity than the average voter. Therefore parties need to find a balance between satisfying the electoral market and maintaining internal cohesion.

Political communication and advertising

Simultaneous with democratization came media liberalization. In the late 1980s restrictions on new newspapers were lifted and in the 1990s there was a huge expansion in the number of cable television channels. By the late 1990s the island had a highly liberalized media market, rated by Freedom House (2007) as the freest press in Asia. A result of the explosion in cable news channels was the advent of politics discussion shows similar to the UK's weekly BBC show *Question Time*. The difference is that in Taiwan these shows are aired every night on up to ten different channels.

Taiwanese political analysts distinguish between the open public face of campaigning, known as the "propaganda battle" and the "private face of the campaign" or "the organizational battle" (Fell, 2007). The latter terms refer to cliental practices in which the KMT factions mobilize their clients to vote KMT in return for economic benefits, and factional vote brokers employ emotional and material persuasion to convince voters to support a party candidate. In exchange for political support candidates are expected to offer voters "service," incorporating diverse areas such as attending weddings or funerals, and even resolving disputes with the police. The liberalization of campaigning restrictions meant that the "propaganda battle" became increasingly influential in determining electoral outcomes. In the late 1980s, it was finally possible to hold election rallies and political demonstrations, and newspaper election advertisements were permitted for the first time. From the mid-1990s, Taiwan adopted a US-style free market in paid television campaign advertising. TV ads soon became the largest item of campaign expenditure. The deregulation benefited the KMT, as its superior financial resources enabled it massively to outspend its rivals. Increasingly large-scale televised election rallies that mixed entertainment and political speeches replaced the small-scale local political rallies. The most recent development in political communication has been the use of the Internet, as the main parties have invested heavily in sophisticated websites. There is no doubt that the importance of the modern methods associated with the "propaganda battle" has risen significantly compared to the organizational battle. Nevertheless in many constituencies, parties still need to find a balance between traditional and modern campaigning.

Political marketing techniques in Taiwan

Over a short time period the resource-rich main parties have professionalized their approach to political marketing. According to advertising expert Hong Ya-hui, "In ten short years, the quality of Taiwan's election ads has overtaken the United States" (interviewed by Fell, 2001). Moreover, while initially the parties' campaigns were designed by party leaders, increasingly they have made use of political consultants, particularly from the commercial advertising industry. As the KMT's Mu Min-chu explained, "It's harder to do propaganda these days, so you have to learn from the advertising companies, to make the ads like Elizabeth Arden" (interviewed by Fell, 2001). The parties have also invested heavily in survey technology since the early 1990s in order to improve their understanding of the product preferences of voters. The results of these polls have been used for the increasingly targeted communication messages adopted by the leading parties.

Political marketing strategy in Taiwan

We now return to the questions set out at the outset, namely, the degree to which parties have become market oriented, how we best account for their market orientation and whether the market-oriented party has a clear electoral advantage. Table 12.3 summarizes the pattern of party market orientation in the 1990s and post-2000 periods.

The KMT in the 1990s

At the outset of multi-party politics, the KMT was still a product-oriented party that was only beginning to learn a more sales-oriented approach. The lack of an opposition party and direct national level elections meant that the ruling KMT was insulated from societal pressures under Martial Law. KMT slogans about "retaking

Table 12.3 Summary of direction of party change in Taiwan on the MOP spectrum, 1991–2008

	Phase 1 *1991–1996*	*Phase 2* *1996–2000*	*Phase 3* *2000–2004*	*Phase 4* *2004–2008*
KMT	SOP→MOP	MOP→SOP	SOP→MOP	MOP→SOP→MOP
DPP	POP→SOP→POP	POP→SOP→MOP	MOP→SOP→MOP	MOP→SOP

POP = Product-Oriented Party; SOP = Sales-Oriented Party; MOP = Market-Oriented Party the mainland (China)" revealed how out of step with public opinion the KMT had become. It was only after the introduction of democratic competition and the growing strength of President Lee Teng-hui's Mainstream faction in the KMT that the party became more responsive to the political market.

The first full democratic election in 1991 revealed how far the KMT had traveled from its earlier product-oriented party position. Regarding policy, the KMT was closer to the median voter than its challengers. Rather than stressing its pro-unification position, it warned voters of the dangers of Taiwanese independence. This was combined with messages about the KMT's economic achievements and its record of gradual political reforms. The KMT's political communication was also superior to its rivals. For instance, its newspaper ads tended to use simple but effective slogans that played on voters' fears of a Chinese invasion. Nevertheless, the KMT's transition to a sales-oriented party should not be exaggerated. Even after the legalization of political advertising, the KMT did not initially invest heavily in these areas. Instead it remained reliant on more traditional campaigning methods known as the "organizational battle." Moreover, the continued strength of the ideologically more conservative Non-Mainstream faction meant that the KMT still needed to give at least lip service to unpopular calls for unification with China.

1993 was a turning point in the transformation of the KMT. That year Lee's last major rival was removed from government office, leaving his Mainstream faction dominant. He not only tried to drag his party closer to public opinion on the identity spectrum but also continued to try to steal popular opposition policies. There was a significant shift in the KMT's communication style, with increasing expenditure on political advertising and conducting surveys rather than the previous over-reliance on the "organizational battle." These measures enabled the KMT to do what most formerly authoritarian parties fail to do, to keep winning elections after the transition.

The KMT was the first party to understand the power of TV ads once the cable TV market was fully liberalized. Being the richest party in the world, the KMT was able to outspend its rivals vastly on TV ads. The party's communication made great use of its number one asset, Lee Teng-hui, who was actually far more popular than the party itself. Also the KMT was becoming increasingly sophisticated in targeting key social groups that it needed to win over. For instance, in the face of stiff competition from the NP for the support of mainlanders in the 1995 legislative elections, the KMT produced a series of TV and newspaper ads designed to convince that ethnic group that it was the best defender of their interests.

On the policy front, as Lee's Mainstream faction came to the fore in the party, they had the flexibility to take an increasingly market-oriented approach that was quite distinct from that when policy was dominated by the out-of-touch elite of the Martial Law era. The KMT tactics showed its awareness of how public opinion was shifting from the center-right to the center-left on the identity spectrum. Although the KMT's adjustment often infuriated party loyalists, it enabled the KMT to continue to win elections. A number of policy shifts reveal the KMT's new approach towards popular opposition policies. After condemning the DPP call for attempting to re-enter the United Nations in the early 1990s, the KMT did a policy flip-flop in 1993 by making this official government policy. By taking a strong line against Chinese military threats, the KMT also won credit from the Taiwanese nationalists, particularly in the 1996 presidential election. The KMT was effective in winning support by taking popular social welfare demands from the DPP, particularly the Universal National Health Insurance program, which featured in KMT ads throughout the 1990s. Therefore by the time of the 1996 presidential election the KMT had reached its most market-oriented point to date.

Despite its electoral success up to 1998, a number of weaknesses in the KMT's product contributed to its eventual loss of power. Although Lee's alliance with local factions enabled him to win the inner party power struggle, it also had serious costs. The local factions were widely associated with political corruption and organized crime. Thus, a number of related scandals involving KMT politicians led to swathes of voters defecting to the DPP or NP. This was ultimately critical in the KMT's loss of power in 2000. As one veteran KMT politician reflected,

> I believe that the main reason that Taiwan's people threw away the KMT at the last election (2000) was not that we had failed with public policies, popularizing education, health insurance, development of high-tech industry, in all these areas we were very successful . . . they wanted change as the KMT had done badly on political corruption. (Ting Shou-chung, interviewed by Fell, 2001)

Despite its superior financial resources there were also weaknesses in its organization and communication. The KMT had the greatest access to market polling of any party, with its own polling center and the resources to commission private polls. However, the hierarchical structure of the party organization meant that such data often failed to permeate the highest levels of the party and thus had little impact on its issue emphasis. There were occasions where the KMT tried to commission surveys that would produce the "desired" results and even refused to accept polls with unfavourable findings (Hsia, 2000). Similarly, though the KMT was able to outspend its rivals in advertising the results were often poor due to the KMT's hierarchal structure. For instance, Hong commented on the KMT's 2000 campaign,

> Lien (KMT's candidate) used a number of advertising agencies and there were so many high level figures to please. When the agency was happy with something, big shots insisted on several revisions. When the KMT was satisfied, the advertising companies were not. (Interviewed by Fell, 2001)

Similarly, well-resourced campaigns produced confused election messages due to poor coordination of multiple campaign headquarters. A former KMT propaganda chief described the party's failed 1998 campaign for Kaohsiung mayor, "It was a five-headed cart. The official residence faction, the wife's faction, city government faction, the PR company faction and the party branch faction. That's why the campaign was such a mess" (interviewed by Fell, 2001).

The DPP in the 1990s

In contrast to the sales-oriented KMT of 1991, the DPP adopted a product-orientation approach. This was the result of an internal shift in the power structure towards the more radical factions. The party focused on radical independence, calling for the declaration of a Republic of Taiwan. While the emphasis on independence and violent actions such as street demonstrations and fights in parliament helped solidify core DPP support, they also scared off middle-class or floating voters, limiting the party's scope for expansion. At this point the DPP still lagged behind the KMT in survey technology and seriously misread the mood of popular opinion.

The DPP's 1991 advertising campaign also revealed its product-oriented approach. For instance, unlike the KMT's short but terrifying slogan ads, many DPP newspaper ads were lengthy full-page essays on why a Republic of Taiwan was right for the island. Few voters would have the patience to get through such academic-style arguments. Unsurprisingly, the DPP's marketing failures of 1991 contributed to a humiliating election defeat to the sales-oriented KMT.

Following the DPP's disastrous 1991 election, the party began a long journey from a product-oriented party to first a sales-oriented party and by the 2000 presidential contest, the closest the party has been to a market-oriented party. Throughout this period the party showed itself to be increasingly able to react to market pressures coming from opinion polls and election results to redesign its product. This was not an easy transition, in fact the title of a book by a DPP insider, *DPP: The Pain of Transition*, paints a picture of how hard change was for the party (Kuo, 1998).

It was to be a shift in the internal party balance of power that enabled the party to make such a painful transition from a radical protest movement to a real candidate for central government. The rise of more moderate party leaders such as Hsu Hsin-liang and Chen Shui-bian contributed to shifting the party in a radically different direction in its issue emphasis, policy positions, party image and political communication.

Under Hsu, Chen Fang-ming was the first propaganda chief to revamp the party's advertising. Thus in 1992 the DPP's TV slots looked highly professional for the first time. This trend was continued under the next and first female propaganda chief of any Taiwanese party, Chen Wen-chien. Her campaign was particularly outstanding in 1997, with systematic TV ads and well-designed election rallies led by the famous *Spice Girls* campaigning troupe that combined entertainment and shorter political speeches. In response to the rise of cable news channels, Chen Wen-chien successfully designed campaign rallies that would be effective for both a TV and rally audience.

There was also a revolution in the issue emphasis that brought the party closer to public opinion. The DPP formed its survey research department in the early 1990s and during the decade increasingly used surveys to design its campaigns. The party began to conduct regular polls on its party image. These surveys were designed to examine the party's issue and image strengths. These surveys found the party had serious weaknesses among middle-class, younger, female, and older voters. In policy and party image the surveys showed voters were uncomfortable with its radical Taiwanese independence position, and its reputation for using violence. These were all areas where the DPP made significant efforts to improve its party image to expand its vote share.

First, the DPP's Taiwanese independence position was moderated and de-emphasized. This involved dropping references to a Republic of Taiwan and instead stressing more electorally popular components of Taiwan independence, such as the United Nations re-entry appeal and attacking unification. But equally important was the shift into a broader issue emphasis on policy areas that were to be critical in its expansion into the middle-class and other social groups where the party was weak. The issue areas were political corruption, social welfare, and gender issues. Surveys showed that these were all areas where the DPP had an advantage over the KMT. Also the DPP was to be increasingly effective at setting the electoral agenda on what surveys told it to be its more favorable election issues.

The DPP's social welfare appeal was begun in the early 1990s and was used consistently throughout the decade. It was effective as almost 60 percent of the population were excluded from the old welfare system. Moreover, even after universal health insurance came into effect, the vast majority of elderly were without pensions and this was to be consistently stressed by the DPP. Once the DPP had a new female propaganda chief, it was able to address its low female support, with heavy emphasis on appeals for child care, child allowances and stress on female victims of crime. Nevertheless, the issue the DPP campaigned most heavily on in the 1990s was political corruption. This appeal was especially effective with urban middle-class voters disillusioned with KMT corruption. In repeated campaigns the DPP was able to discredit the KMT, with accusations of vote buying, contract corruption, and embezzlement by high-level KMT politicians.

In order to improve the party image among younger voters, the leadership attempted to change the tone of the election campaigns. In particular, the party discouraged the use of violent antics that had often been used in the late Martial Law era and also reduced the emphasis on what was known as the "Tragic Taiwanese Appeal." This refers to appeals focusing on the suffering of Taiwanese under Martial Law. By the early 1990s, such appeals were less effective especially among the younger generation of voters who had not experienced the height of "White Terror." Analysts regard the DPP's 1994 Taipei "Hope, Happiness, Chen Shui-bian" campaign as the first to make the break from the "tragic" appeals.[1]

The party also looked different in terms of its leadership and candidates, as all improved their media image radically. In election debates and on the politics talk shows, DPP politicians tended to be far more articulate than their KMT rivals. For instance, in the first televised debate in the Taipei mayoral election in 1994, the KMT candidate was completely upstaged by his DPP opponent. It became common for KMT candidates to refuse to participate in such activities for fear of losing face.

There were of course campaigns when the DPP product failed, as it shifted back to a more sales- or product-oriented approach. The strength of more ideologically oriented factions meant that there were limitations to how far the party could move towards the center. In 1996 the DPP nominated a radical Taiwan independence leader as its presidential candidate. He ran a single-issue campaign that contrasted sharply with the moderate image that the party headquarters had been trying to mold since 1992. As we can see from Tables 12.1 and 12.2, this produced the DPP's worst election result since 1991. Similarly, the DPP was slower than the KMT to grasp the significance of the new liberalized TV ad market. As a campaign manager commented on the DPP's defeat in Taipei in 1998, "We didn't adjust to media developments. We spent too much money on newspaper ads, but ignored two new trends, the TV ads and the 24-hour news channels" (ChangYi-shan, interviewed by Fell, 2001).

Following the DPP's poor electoral performance in 1996 and 1998, it made a number of significant efforts to learn from defeat. First, it improved its TV advertising in the 2000 presidential campaign. The propaganda campaign was highly centralized under one of Chen Shui-bian's youthful advisors Luo Wen-chia, in conjuction with one of the top advertising experts Fan Ke-ching. They created what advertising specialists still regard as the most effective propaganda campaign in Taiwan's electoral history. Second, the party tried to change the content and tone of Chen's speeches in response to the new media environment, creating a special speech writing team. Third, the party needed to adjust its policies to give it a more moderate image. On the critical national identity spectrum it passed the *Resolution on Taiwan's Future*, which for the first time accepted the Republic of China as the national title and the position that there is no need to declare Taiwanese independence as Taiwan is already independent. This was a significant moderation for the DPP and brought it closer to the median voter. These reforms along with an emphasis on welfare and anti-corruption meant that the DPP reached its most market-oriented position in its successful 2000 presidential campaign.

The KMT in the post-2000 era

The KMT's defeat in the 2000 presidential election had a devastating impact on the party and led to its most serious internal soulsearching since it lost the Chinese Civil War in 1949. Being freed from the concerns of being the ruling party gave the KMT greater flexibility to adjust its product. The party embarked on a series of radical reforms to its leadership, campaign style and policy positions. These changes have contributed to the party's gradual recovery and eventual return to ruling party status in 2008. A critical factor in this post-defeat transformation was the changing balance of power away from Lee's Mainstream faction towards politicians associated with the Non-Mainstream faction, such as Ma Ying-jeou.

In terms of party leadership, the KMT's initial post-2000 picture was not encouraging as no one challenged the uncharismatic Lien in the first chairman primary in 2001, which almost guaranteed he would be the party's candidate in 2004's presidential election. Although he joined with his former rival James Soong in a joint presidential team and had a huge opinion poll lead six months before the election, they finally lost narrowly. The hierarchal nature of the KMT meant that party ranking rather than market appeal determined its presidential team in 2004.

The leadership has been more market-oriented since the KMT's first competitive party chairman primary in 2005, won by Ma. Under Ma, the KMT reached its most united and popular state since the late 1990s. A key factor in this recovery has been Ma's willingness to take advice from political consultants and polling experts from outside the KMT. As a result, Ma's presidential campaign was targeted on areas where the KMT had performed poorly since the mid-1990s, particularly the south of the island and rural regions. This targeted approach was visible in two of Ma's key campaign projects. The first was known as the "Long Stay," in which Ma would live in rural people's homes and work in the fields with farmers for several days. Second, Ma led his campaign team on a 675-kilometer cycle tour from the far south to the far north of Taiwan. Once again, polling data was used to target regions where KMT support level was lower when selecting locations for rest stops.

In terms of policy, the KMT tried to learn from the 2000 defeat in adjusting policy positions of the 1990s, though in some cases this made it actually less market-oriented. One positive move was its attempt to change its damaging reputation for political corruption. The KMT passed regulations designed to avoid nominating candidates linked to corruption. Moreover, as the party had lost both central and most local offices by 2000, it was less vulnerable to accusations of corruption. By 2005 it was apparent that the KMT's efforts had paid off, as DPP government scandals ensured the corruption issue was beneficial to the KMT for the first time, contributing significantly to the party's sweeping local election victory that year.

The party has also taken a popular line in attacking the DPP for its poor economic record and reminding voters of the fine economic times under KMT management.

On the crucial national identity issue, the KMT initially moved away from the market, reverting to more orthodox Chinese nationalist symbols and calling for unification. This was closely related to the strong level of competition coming from the PFP and NP to the right from 2000 to 2002. In the run up to the 2004 presidential election the party again seemed to be moving back to the center, stressing its love for Taiwan, and, though referendums are associated in Taiwan with independence, the KMT allowed a referendum bill to be passed in parliament.

Under Ma it is not clear exactly what the party position on identity is, with mixed messages coming out of the party headquarters. For instance, in 2006 it reiterated that the party's ultimate aim is unification with China. Also it has once again placed heavy emphasis on Chinese nationalist symbols such as Chiang Kai-shek, despite their low popularity. Nevertheless, after Ma had received KMT nomination he made efforts to shift the party back towards the center again. In 2007 Ma began to contest the DPP's ownership of the Taiwan identity appeal. For instance, he published a book titled *The Native Spirit: Taiwan's Exemplary Stories* and has endorsed the KMT referendum proposal to apply for United Nations membership.

While Lee's KMT took a mixed approach between the organizational and propaganda battle, Ma is trying to focus on the latter to make the party electable again. The quality of the KMT's party propaganda has improved considerably since 2000. It has been more willing to allow advertising companies to have a free hand in designing products. For instance, in 2001 Fan Ke-ching (who had designed the DPP's advertising in 2000) designed the KMT's election advertisements. The KMT has also attempted to learn from the marketing successes of the DPP. It has invited DPP defectors to advise in KMT election campaigns. For instance, the central advisor to Lien's 2004 presidential campaign was former DPP party propaganda chief Chen Wen-chien. Similarly, like the DPP in the 1990s, the KMT has become increasingly ready to give articulate younger politicians influential campaign positions.

In short, it was the reaction to a disastrous presidential defeat and a shift in the inner party balance of power towards Ma's faction that pushed the KMT towards the more market-oriented approach that contributed to the party's return to power in 2008.

The DPP in the post-2000 era

Like many parties worldwide the DPP struggled to remain a market-oriented party after making the transition from opposition to ruling party. During its 2000 election campaign, it raised unrealistic expectations that it was unable to deliver. Under the DPP, Taiwan suffered its worst economic recession and highest unemployment since the 1940s. It had considerable achievements in improving the social welfare system, particularly in the area of pensions. Nevertheless, the realities of government office made it far less enthusiastic on new welfare pledges than when in opposition.

The DPP also lost ownership of the anti-corruption issue that had been so effective in its rise to power. Particularly after 2004 the DPP was dogged by numerous alleged corruption scandals, some involving the president and his family. Instead the party had often been forced back to rely on the identity issue, despite the fact that opinion polls show voters do not see this as the number one priority. During the DPP's first presidential term (2000–2004) it did attempt to take the center ground on the identity issue, promising not to declare independence and taking a conciliatory line in relations with China. However, in the second term the party returned to radical positions similar to those it had taken in 1991 and 1996, its two most disastrous product-oriented campaigns. For instance, in 2004's parliamentary elections it began calling for "name rectification," a term that can incorporate changing the national title, the names of state-owned enterprises and overseas government offices to Taiwan. Then in 2006 Chen broke one of his inaugural pledges by scrapping the National Unification Guidelines and a year later the party chairman Yu Hsi-kun called for the adoption of a new constitution to redefine Taiwan's official title and territory.

How can we explain the DPP's apparent shift away from the market after 2004? Although the party's access to opinion polls is greater than ever, it would appear that the message was struggling to seep through to those designing party policy. Apart from complexities of being the government party, there were also significant changes in the inner party power structure that contributed to this shift away from a market-oriented party. Firstly, Chen's position as president (and party chairman between July 2002 and December 2004) made him the most powerful DPP leader to date. He has been less accessible to those younger advisors who guided him in the 1990s, such as Luo Wen-chia. In fact there were rumblings about his overemphasis on identity to the detriment of social issues in the aftermath of the 2004 parliamentary election setback.

The factional balance of power was also highly influential on the party's post-2000 fluctuations between more market- and sales-oriented marketing on identity. The two most influential positions were the premier and party chairman. When moderates held these posts the party took more market-oriented positions. For instance, while Hsieh Chang-ting was party chairman in 2000–2002 there was a more conciliatory policy towards China. In contrast, more confrontational tactics such as the anti-Chiang Kai-shek campaign of 2006–2007 coincided with the chairmanship of Yu Hsi-kun. Yu's sales-oriented tactics caused criticism within the party, as they further alienated middle-ground voters in the run-up to the presidential election in 2008.

Despite these moves away from the market-oriented party model in issue emphasis, the DPP continued to perform well in its political communication. The DPP showed remarkable skill in controlling the issue agenda in the run-up to elections. For instance, a year before the 2004 presidential election the KMT had a huge opinion poll lead, but the DPP was able to maintain the media's agenda on its more favorable issues for almost the whole campaign and thus narrow the KMT's lead and eventually win the election. However, during the second DPP term, though the party still dominated the issue agenda and produced quality advertising, this was unable to compensate for the weaknesses in its political product that ultimately led to the series of electoral defeats to the increasingly market-oriented KMT.

Political marketing trends and conclusion

We have examined the market orientation of Taiwanese parties during the first two decades of multi-party competition. Taiwanese parties have been highly adaptable in designing their marketing strategies in these campaigns. They have reacted to messages from election results and surveys to create a unique hybrid style of political communication that incorporates imported techniques but also local issues and campaign practices.

We have shown that there has not been a linear movement towards the market-oriented party model. Instead, the KMT and DPP have fluctuated between more sales- and market-oriented approaches. We found support for Lees-Marshment's assumption that market-orientation will have significant implications for election results. In other words, a sales-oriented party will generally beat a product-oriented party, and a market-oriented party will generally beat a sales-oriented party.

The most consistently useful variable for explaining parties' market-orientation has been inner-party balance of power. When the party is dominated by more election-oriented leaders or factions, parties have tended to take a more moderate and market-oriented approach. In contrast, with more ideologically oriented factions holding the upper hand, priority has been given to ideological orthodoxy, even where this is electoral poison. Another key factor in the degree of market orientation has been the electoral system. Thus for instance, the need to appeal to the majority of centrist voters in single-member district presidential elections has prompted leading parties to take more market-oriented approaches, while they have often reverted to core appeals under the multi-member district parliamentary elections. However, the move to a single-member district system for parliamentary elections after 2008 may prove a further incentive for market-oriented party practices.

The overall trend towards more market orientation for the leading parties has significant implications for the quality of Taiwan's democracy. The market-oriented approach does not necessarily result in identical catch-all parties. It is our contention that in the case of Taiwan, the shift towards market orientation of parties has positive implications. At the outset of multi-party politics, Taiwan's parties were out of line with the electorate in both their most stressed issues and positions on the central issue dimensions. Election results and public opinion trends have forced the parties to adapt their political product radically to suit the electoral market by moderating their positions and adjusting their issue emphasis.

Note

1 Point made by numerous DPP campaign managers in interviews with Fell in 2000 and 2001.

References/further reading

Fell, D. (2005) *Party Politics in Taiwan*, London: Routledge.
Fell, D. (2007) "Putting on a Show and Electoral Fortunes in Taiwan's Multi-Party Elections," in J. Strauss and D. C. O'Brien (eds) *Staging Politics: Power and Performance in Asia and Africa*, London: IB Taurus. [133–150]
Freedom House "Freedom of the Press 2007: A Global Survey Media Independence". Available at: <http://www.freedomhouse.org/template.cfm?page=362> (accessed 5 June 2009).
Hsia, C. (2000) *Sun Set on the KMT*, Taipei: Commonwealth Publishers.
Huntington, S. (1991) *The Third Wave: Democratization in the Late Twentieth Century*, London: University of Oklahoma Press.
Kuo, J. (1998) *DPP: The Pain of Transition*, Taipei: Commonwealth Press.
Rawnsley, G. (2006) "Democratization and Election Campaigning in Taiwan: Professionalizing the Professionals," in K. Voltmer (ed.) *Mass Media and Political Communication in New Democracies*, London: Routledge.
Rigger, S. (1999) *Politics in Taiwan: Voting for Democracy*, London: Routledge.

Interviews by Dafydd Fell

Chang Yi-shan (2001) DPP campaign manager in the 1990s, interviewed October.
Hong Ya-hui (2001) Advertising specialist, interviewed 14 May.
KMT Propaganda Chief (2001), interviewed October.
Mu Min-chu (2001) Deputy Director of KMT propaganda department, interviewed October.
Ting Shou-chung (2001) Senior KMT legislator, interviewed September.

13 Political marketing in Ghana

Kobby Mensah

The unprecedented 2000 election in Ghana, according to Handly and Mills (2001), is often wrongfully characterized as 'a transition from a military to a democratic rule' (5). It was remarkable in many ways, especially being the first time the nation witnessed a transfer of power from one democratic government to another through the ballot box. In fact there had already been two previous elections since the country was returned to constitutional rule in 1992. However, the elections of 1992 and 1996 had both been won by the same party that was once the military administration.

The new political era brought about by the 2000 elections generated a great deal of discussion about the structures, organization and the nature of participation that underpinned the new political system. One particular feature of interest, was the 'newness' of political campaigning offered to Ghanaians by the major political parties, especially the New Patriotic Party (NPP) to engage voters effectively and to outshine competitors using marketing instruments and techniques (Mensah, 2006). The approach was ingenious in the Ghanaian context and truly reflected global trends and, according to electoral observers (Handly and Mills, 2001; Nugent, 2001; Smith, 2002; Ninsin, 2006) these trends seemed positive overall, although they did pose some challenges.

The political system

Ghana has experienced a number of remarkable political transitions: from slavery to colonial rule, to multi-party democracy after independence, to military dictatorship and lastly, a shift back to multi-party democracy in 1992 (Austin, 1961; Monfils, 1977; Anebo, 1997; Handly and Mills, 2001). Earlier constitutions of 1958, 1969 and 1979 were overthrown in military coups in 1966, 1972 and 1981 respectively. The military interventions reflected and weighed heavily on party configurations, the media system as well as other democratic institutions such as the Electoral Commission. Those interventions resulted in the fragility and neglect of political institutions, placing them in a kind of limbo, where they remained until the 2000 elections.

In April 1992, the socio-political landscape of Ghana began to change when the people overwhelmingly voted for a constitutional mandate in a referendum. The constitution that emerged then required the organization of presidential and parliamentary elections by a permanent independent Electoral Commission on 7 December every four years and according to a first-past-the-post electoral system. Voting takes place at local polling stations within constituencies located in 180 districts across the country by secret ballot under universal adult suffrage. By the 2000 elections, well over 90 per cent of eligible voters were registered to vote (Ayee, 1997; Larvie and Badu, 1996) and six political parties had been on the presidential and parliamentary ballots (African Elections Database, 2006).

Since independence, political parties have been major actors in Ghana's democratic process, providing the main platform for political participation, especially for elected office. The evidence for this is in the number of candidates elected as president and members of parliament (MP) on party tickets, as against those elected as independent candidates. Whereas both offices, presidential and parliamentary, have seen a number of attempts by independent candidates to defeat party candidates, it is the latter that have been overwhelmingly victorious, with just four and one independent candidates elected at the 2000 and 2004 elections respectively. The country's constitution combines both the American presidential system of government with elements of the parliamentary system. This makes it possible for the president, selected through party primaries if running on a party ticket, to be elected directly by popular vote in the same way as a member of parliament. Notwithstanding the power of the party, a number of events, including military interventions, have made Ghanaian political parties appear as though they are agents of the few, instead of the masses as intended (Ninsin, 2006).

When Ghanaian political parties first emerged in the 1950s, they were aligned on a left–right, socialist–conservative ideological continuum. They were, however, also implicitly aligned with the characterisation of their leaders, Nkrumah and Danquah, the founding fathers of the nation and the pacesetters in mass party politics in Ghana. Thus, Nkrumah and his 'radical' Convention People's Party (CPP), the first to govern under independence, was social democratic and of the left, while Danquah's moderates, the UGCC party, which later metamorphosed into the New Patriotic Party, occupied the right of the ideological scale with conservative credentials (Anebo, 1997).

In 1992, when the nation was returned to constitutional rule once again, a third party of significance emerged, the National Democratic Congress (NDC). The NDC to a large extent took over the CPP's position as a social democratic mass party and became the new reference point for radical politics (Carbone, 2003: 10). Having won two consecutive elections in 1992 and 1996, the NDC became the main opposition party pushing the CPP to a distant third.

Unfortunately for Ghana, these ideological leanings gradually translated into other subliminal identifications such as tribal, religious and other sectional divisions, as the nation departed further from the early years of independence. Although political parties and their interests are proscribed by the constitution to be formed along these lines, they have replaced left–right ideology as the main divisions around which to mobilize voters (Nugent, 2001; Ninsin, 2006). Ideological debate on policy for campaigning is non-existent. This could be attributed to a number of reasons, including the long absences of political participation as a result of years of military rule. Other factors that stifle political debate are poverty and illiteracy. The illiteracy rate in Ghana is estimated to be about 40 per cent of the electorate (Ninsin, 2006), with most trapped in poverty. This group can make little sense out of abstract left–right, socialist–conservative ideological debates that seem to have little practical relevance for their own daily lives. Rather than on the campaign trail, this ideological debate was to be found in the forums organized by elite communities such as news conferences and seminars.

Hence, subordination of ideology in Ghanaian politics is both party- and voter-bound. Parties implicitly appeal to ethnic, religious and tribal loyalties, leaving few voters to identify with a specific ideology as well. A significant number would vote according to family attachment to political interests and the majority succumb to the 'electoral hype' – voting for parties that appear the most appealing on election day. In fact, this characterisation of voter identification also explains the structure in party membership and in turn, the funding issues, candidate selections and many other party-related issues.

With regard to party membership, Ninsin (2006) identifies two forms in Ghana: formal and informal (12). The former is a committed card-bearer of a party who contributes to the party's activities in the form of dues, attending party meetings and political rallies. The formal member is most likely to canvass for votes for the party either at the local or national level, as well as delivering his or her own guaranteed vote during the election. In contrast, the more numerous informal member does none of the above apart from voting for the party at general elections.

The informal member is thus loosely attached in contrast to the formal member who has ideological, family and economic convictions to bind his or her vote to the particular party. The informal member could be categorised as 'floating', according to Ninsin as their allegiance is volatile. They, just like 'floating' voters, are likely to be swayed in one way or the other based on a number of reasons, including ethnic identification of a party leader or key issues specific to the election as was the case in 2000 (see below).

In the December 2008 elections, for example, the NPP claimed the selection of their presidential running mate, Dr Mahamudu Bawumia, led to a series of defections to the NPP of other party members, especially from the NDC. According to Moustafa Hamid, a spokesperson for the NPP campaign in an interview with a radio station, Joy FM, 'there was virtually no other party in Mamprugu except the NPP. People are defecting in their large numbers from the NDC, including the CPP's Walewale parliamentary candidate' (both Mamprugu and Walewale are towns in Northern Ghana, the NPP presidential running mate's home region) (Hamid 2008; Rand Merchant Bank 2008).

It is important to note however that although party member defections do occur, especially in election time for reasons as explained above, political parties and their allies within the media make headlines out of these defections as a political ploy to achieve two things. First, to deceive the public that they are gaining ground even in the opposing parties' own backyard, even when they have no evidence to support this. Second, political capital is made out of these defections in order to destabilise the support bases of the opposing parties. What was different, and perhaps credible to some extent in the 2008 election however, was how such party defectors were made to denounce their previous party membership on platforms at political rallies of those they planned to join; this was so even for some prominent party officials who sought to cross over from one party to another.

The state of membership also translates into funding problems. Party funding in Ghana is seen as wholly inadequate as it is mostly solicited through membership dues, handouts from party leaders and sympathizers (CDD-Ghana, 2005). In a country where the average worker earns less than a dollar a day and formal party membership is the reserve of the few, political parties are financially dependent on a small number of 'political entrepreneurs' (Ninsin, 2006: 15). These entrepreneurs are people who are economically self-sufficient and who use their wealth to assume leadership positions in the party. Although these political entrepreneurs can claim democratic legitimacy for their positions – they are selected or elected according to transparent party rules – they use their positions to further their own and their supporters' interests. They use material inducements to buy votes and to influence decision making in their favour.

So, notwithstanding, that the party political system in Ghana has seen some remarkable degree of democratic advancements and modernisation (Nugent, 2001; Smith, 2002; Ninsin, 2006), challenges remain and reforms are required to combat what some would regard as unhealthy influence over the political process of ethnicity, religion and, especially, money.

The situation of underfunding has also strengthened the two-party system since independence (Handly and Mills, 2001; Nugent, 2001: 4). Smaller parties find it hard to compete with the membership dues, the logistics, training and tax exemptions given to them by donor agencies, the Electoral Commission and the government. Hence, the political landscape today continues to be dominated by just two parties, the NPP on the right and on the left, the 'new kid on the bloc' since 1992, the NDC.

Electoral volatility

Research suggests a substantial partisan identification in Ghana with about 66 per cent of respondents interviewed by the Centre of Democratic Governance (CDD) in 1999 claiming to identify with a party. It is arguably risky, however, to take for granted such a finding as an accurate measurement of party loyalty amongst Ghanaian voters. In the CDD's 1999 'Afrobarometer', 38 per cent of respondents interviewed identified with the NDC, a mirror image of what the party claims is the size of its membership relative to the total electorate (Ninsin, 2006: 18). On the other hand 25 per cent identified with the NPP. However, this significant lead of about 10 per cent for the NDC did not save the party from losing to the NPP in the ensuing elections of 2000. So, what could account for the polling gap? Although there was a second ballot, which saw all the opposition parties uniting against the NDC, the discussion will focus only on the strength of the parties manifested in the first ballot. For the NPP to survive the first ballot meant the party must have gained ground on either the NDC or other parties or both, making it possible for a run-off between the two parties. How this happened is probably due to the 'newness' of the NPP's campaign and the fragility of the electorate's allegiance with all parties (see Table 13.1).

It is true that in aggregate terms, the two parties have enjoyed some level of stable dominance since 1992. The duo has dominated the electoral market for four consecutive terms, alternating government office between themselves. They have gained almost 91 per cent of the total votes and have influenced the socio-political discourse in many ways (Morrison, 2004: 429). However, individual party dominance is fragile and is vulnerable to competition. The two parties may generously raise their core membership and support stakes (Ninsin, 2006: 18) to look good 'electorally' before the election campaigns.

Table 13.1 compares the electoral performance of the parties and shows their electoral net gains and losses in the presidential elections since 1996 until 2004. While the NDC won the 1996 presidential elections, the NPP's net gain of almost 13 per cent since the 1996 elections is significant. Although Rawlings and his newly formed NDC party had won both the elections of 1992 (not shown in the table) and 1996 based on Rawlings' unprecedented popularity among rural voters and the urban poor (Anebo, 1997), the party's dominance was being chipped away gradually, leading to its major losses at the 2000 elections. By 2004, the party since 1996 had accumulated a net loss of about the same size as the net gain of the NPP in the presidential elections, suggesting that the NPP gains were the NDC's losses.

The above argument is plausible since the other opposition parties have not shown any significant increase in support since 1996, with a peak in support in 2000 followed by their worst result in 2004. Although the figures may not show a significant margin of change between the two major parties, it does show how the electoral market fluctuates in Ghana. The analysis also makes the case about the

Table 13.1 Electoral volatility in Ghana based on valid votes cast in presidential elections 1996–2004 (%)

Party Led by:	NDC Rawlings / Mills	NPP Kufour	Others
1996	*57.4	*39.6	3
2000	(43.1)	(56.9)	(*)
	44.5	48.2	7.3
2004	44.64	52.45	2.92
Net + / −	**−12.76**	**12.9**	**−0.08**

Source: Electoral Commission (EC) of Ghana.

*Note: * Analysis based on parties' own electoral strength when not in any alliance of some sort.* The two main parties, the NDC and NPP in 1996 formed electoral alliances with other smaller ones under the Progressive Alliance (led by Rawlings) and the Great Alliance (led by Kufour) respectively. The PNC led by Edward Mahama, however went alone and got 3 per cent. Figures in brackets represent the second round of results in the 2000 elections since none of the candidates secured more than 50 per cent of the votes in the first ballot.

use of marketing by the NPP, gaining strength from one election to the other although the NDC may exhibit some degree of consistency in its electoral base. However, it should be noted that Ghana is only in its fourth electoral cycle since the constitution of 1992, and it may be too soon to say whether the pattern of electoral volatility and two party dominance will become a long-term feature of the party system.

The Media System

'If a vibrant private press is the hallmark of a healthy democracy, then Ghana has it in abundance' (*The Statesman*, 2006). This quote follows the *Statesman*'s count of almost 30 of its competitors in the market. However, the image of growth as observed by the *Statesman* does not do full justice to the growth of the entire media industry in Ghana. The Ghanaian media industry of television, print, radio, mobile communication and the internet is thriving in its establishment and patronage. Those that have made tremendous impact on the political system since 2000 are radio, television and the print, with mobile phones and internet gradually assuming significance.

Fifteen years ago, Ghana could only boast one broadcasting house, the Ghana Broadcasting Corporation (GBC) and two state-regulated national newspapers, the *Daily Graphic* and the *Ghanaian Times*. The GBC solely operated radio and television programmes throughout the country, whilst the *Daily Graphic* and the *Ghanaian Times* supplied print nationally. In the twenty-first century, the Ghanaian broadcasting industry boasts over 96 FM stations, over 30 newspapers and six television broadcasting houses, and cable networks such as CNN and the BBC.

The media industry has become very competitive since 1996 when it was deregulated and liberalized (Gadzekpo, 2005; Intermedia, 2005). Especially with television and radio, operators are increasingly trying to win the major share of the market through prime time programmes like 'the morning shows' that normally host panels of experts from varied areas including politics to discuss pertinent socio-economic issues; 'drive jams' in the afternoon, which mix music with 'listener-generated' social discussions; and 'evening talk shows' with a moderator and panel of activists on gender, environment, poverty and many other issues.

The distinctive change from a predominantly state-owned media to a thriving liberalized media environment is the departure from a politicized media that served the interests of political incumbents. An independent media system has ensured some degree of freedom and diversity of discussions, making way for citizens in varied capacities to contribute, get informed and make decisions through the public sphere. Listeners of radio and television programmes are offered the opportunity to contribute to discussions through 'phone-in', 'text-in' and 'mail-in' access.

The other change worth noting is the collaborative way through which these discussions are carried out. Radio and television discussions mostly use news articles and stories that appear on the front pages of the print media. This adds to the appeal of television and radio as people get the opportunity to know what is making the news even when they are not able to buy the daily newspaper. Although there is a growing trend in all the three sectors – print, radio and television – radio seems to be the most popular.

In 2005, Gadzekpo observed that about 90 per cent of the Ghanaian population had listened to the radio in the past seven days, whilst 69 per cent listened to it at least once a day (Gadzekpo, 2005). The mixed use of English and the local language is one of the factors making radio the most popular. It is also the cheapest way to become informed as radio sets are shared in open spaces: at home, at work and at commercial places like lorry stations. Although newspapers are also shared in Ghana, they are however predominantly found in regional and district capitals as it is in rural areas where illiteracy rates are highest. Apart from the now deregulated national newspapers mentioned above, some of the most read newspapers are *Insight, Public Agenda* and *Crusading Guide* from the left of the political spectrum, and the *Statesman* and *Accra Daily Mail* from the right (*The Statesman*, 2006).

As for television, a lack of transmission facilities in most of the nation's rural areas and the cost of ownership are major factors in its subordination to radio. The most popular television stations in Ghana are the national broadcaster, Ghana television for its Saturday evening 'talking point' programme aired in English, and the Sunday evening 'Akan Drama' aired in one of the local languages. Metro TV's socio-political discussion programme, 'Good morning Ghana', in English is popular among educated groups while TV Africa's local news bulletins and TV3's 'evening talk shows' aired in different languages, appeal across a number of audiences. On radio, Joy FM, Radio Gold and Peace FM are the most popular, with the latter being well known in its local language broadcasting. Although all are based in Accra, the capital of Ghana, they transmit to other regional, district and rural areas through affiliated radio stations.

Notwithstanding the growth of the media, some observers are concerned by the abuse of the media by self-interested politicians. As the constitution does not limit the purchase of political advertising spots on any media and does not inhibit the setting up of new media channels, it is noted that some politicians are taking advantage of the system (*The Statesman*, 2006), raising concerns about parallelism. Some media houses, especially those in the camp of opposition parties, are accused of granting coverage to only 'opportune witnesses' (Berkel, 2006: 87) whilst they exclude those with whom they disagree.

Reports also suggest that the government is favoured by the media in anticipation of receiving government advertising contracts (CDD, 2005). Although the abuse of the media by political incumbents is low compared to the past, the proliferation of media outlets has, however, ushered in a new kind of abuse, undermining the intended constitutional provision of a level playing field.

Political marketing techniques and strategy

The relative unimportance of ideology for voters, the fragility in voter identification, the chronic under-funding of parties, and the increasing growth of an intrusive media – all these were factors parties had to confront going into the first Ghanaian elections of the twenty-first century. This section of the chapter examines how the parties adapted to these circumstances and the role marketing played in their campaign strategies.

The first part of the analysis deals with how marketing instruments were used by the two major parties; the second part of the analysis considers if the parties can be characterized using the Lees-Marshment framework as product-, sales- or market-oriented parties (Lees-Marshment, 2001). The analysis draws on data derived from three sets of in-depth interviews carried out in 2004, 2007 and 2008. The first round of interviews in 2004 were semi-structured telephone interviews with two electoral observers of the 2000 elections. The second set of interviews was carried out face-to-face in July 2007, again using an unstructured questionnaire, with five campaign officials from the NPP and the NDC. The final round of interviews was with seven academics from the University of Ghana in March 2008. These interviews were supplemented with analysis of media reports. The major question addressed was: what were the changes observed in political party campaigning behaviour over the period in question?

It was noted that changes first began with the NPP when in opposition at the 2000 elections, followed by the NDC in 2004. The NDC suffered two consecutive electoral losses and this undoubtedly was a stimulus for the party to reappraise its electoral strategy. The significant development noted by the electoral observers was the use of the commercial marketing type of paid billboards, advertising slogans and jingles on television and radio during prime time slots such as the seven o'clock evening news:

> Political parties have become a little bit more 'savvier' than before, employing huge monstrous commercial electronic billboards at major intersections as compared to those small sign boards at street sides and corners in the olden days. The developments of video clips, jingles and slogans were heavily utilized. Most of the TV commercials were shown with massive supporters at a rally of their political parties; videos of underdeveloped areas of the nation were shown by the opposition parties. What was again notable was the development of a single message: the 'Positive Change' camp and the 'Continuity' camp.

In the second set of interviews, the NDC respondent intimated that since the party's loss of power at the 2000 elections, it had begun using market research through surveys and focus group discussions to identify the reasons why people did not vote for the party or the candidate. Although he acknowledged that the process was also used in developing the 2004 party manifesto, ideology was still paramount in the way the party developed its policies. The following is part of his response:

> We determine policies based on our ideological orientation as a social demo-cratic party. But I think a fair balance of ideology and market research is

happening now. Based on ideology, the party develops its campaign messages and gives it to the candidate to go out there to present to the people. Market research however determines what other areas people are concerned about.

It appears to be the case that the NDC, as the respondent intimated earlier on in that interview, held the belief that as a social democratic party, and having been in government for a long time (1992–2000), the party possessed some kind of gut-instinct to discern the needs of Ghanaians. While the party may use market research, it is a supplementary method, used only to understand 'what other things could be on people's minds'. One can therefore argue that the marketing principle is subordinated to that of ideology in the NDC party.

In the case of the NPP, the interviewee observed that after 2000, the party began to use segmentation to target voting blocs; to downplay ideology; and to make greater use of the 'free media'. He hinted that due to the party's perceived image as being tribal, dominated by the Ashanti (the major tribe of the majority ethnic group, the Akans, in Ghana), and elitist, some level of targeting and brand endorsement were necessary. The party would select some party leaders from the minority tribes as the 'party's face', and enter into dialogue with such tribes as proof of the party's national character. The NPP distanced itself from party tradition and ideological debates and instead focused on 'good governance' issues such as inclusive government, the repeal of the criminal libel law and zero tolerance for corruption – issues of concern for all voters irrespective of class, religion or ethnicity. The NPP interviewee stated that:

> In 2000 I took a deliberate step to say that we will reduce the mostly Akan face and push forward other ethnic, religious and gender faces, so if you go back to most of our press conferences that we held, you will find people like honourable 'X' [and he mentions some female, GA, EWE (other tribes) and Muslim members of the party] at the front row. And whenever the Akan members are pushing forward, I say to them please hold back, hold back let us show that we have other people inside this team! And that was deliberate. . . .

The party strategist went on to say that another significant strategic change was brought about by the emerging importance of the 'free media'. According to him:

> In 2000 we did not have enough money and I knew that visibility was one critical thing we needed, so when I became campaign manager the first thing I wanted to do was to make sure we were visible . . . fortunately the new radio stations that were being opened up, and you know the radio is a very hungry medium, needed some drama, and you know you cannot have drama if you have only one voice being drummed out [referring to old style political adverts], so invariably on every programme that was being done [referring to the NPP's adverts on radio and TV], there were two voices.

The interviewee did not mention the direct use of surveys and focus group discussions with voters, as was the case of the NDC, to inform party programmes and manifesto development. He did, however, acknowledge the use of radio monitoring to understand the issues people cared about. Consultations were also held with smaller parties going into the second round ballot when the NPP needed the support of the smaller parties. While this consultation did have influence over the content of the NPP manifesto to some degree in areas like health care, for example implementing the national health insurance scheme (NHIS), it did not extend to the party's economic policy which is based on liberal free-market ideas. The smaller parties preferred economic policies based on poverty allevia-tion, but, according to the interviewee, the NPP stood firm on its wealth creation position.

The changes in party organisation as identified above have been acknowledged by other researchers. However, some hold reservations as to what surveys and focus group discussions are designed to tell the parties. Reports from donor agencies, highlighting the plight of the Ghanaian people, are in abundance for parties to consult: 'If political parties will read the many reports, such as the Ghana poverty reduction strategy (the GPRS) like I have done, it is easy for politicians to know what our people want' (interview with Jonah, University of Ghana, March 2008).

Analysis: Marketing instruments and party organisation

It is clear from the interview scripts that some amount of marketing has been conducted by the organisations of the two main parties, the NPP and NDC. However the two parties have differed in instruments used. Although the NDC acknowledges market research at the level of policy development, it is as an 'afterthought', in order to 'unearth' other issues that may be bothering voters and which the party has not picked up on.

Although the NDC respondent hinted the operations of research teams on the ground conducting focus group discussions and surveys, it is however difficult to validate such claims as they are 'secrets of our trade' (NPP interviewee). However, the NDC's newly found 'retail politics' dubbed 'I Care for You' (Myjoyonline.com, June 2007; *Accra Daily Mail*, 2008) is in the public domain. In this programme, the party's candidate meets people on the streets, market centres, hospitals, and commuter stations asking them about their needs and telling what his government will offer them.

However, with the NPP, segmentation, branding and advertising were observed although it was not evident that these were part of an integral strategy for develop-ing party policy. A segmentation strategy akin to Baer's (1995) recommendation that a political campaign strategy should begin with identifying an overall theme, from which other sub-themes could be derived, was developed by the NPP. Baer's 'broadcast message' is used to identify generally the core stance of the party and the 'narrowcast message' is the sub-themes used to identify and target specialized groups that matter to the electoral campaign. Such an approach will invariably identify the segmentation base – geographic, demographic, behavioural or psycho-graphic (Smith and Saunders, 1990) – upon which a political market could be categorised. Thus, the emergence of the NPP's 'Agenda for Positive Change' was a reflection on the general mood of the people. Those who expressed active discontent were to be assured of good economic performance and good governance; and those who entertained fears of electoral chaos were to be reassured of the party's commitment to the relative peace and stability the nation enjoyed as captured in five clear narrowcast messages on policy initiatives.

The messages targeted the interests of five influential segments of the Ghanaian society. These were: a proposed repeal of the criminal libel and sedition laws, targeted mainly at journalists; a dual citizenship bill aimed at the Ghanaian diaspora; an all-inclusive government; a national reconciliation initiative; and zero tolerance for corruption, all of which were of concern to smaller parties and other interests groups. The NPP's stigmatized party image and the relatively less competitive presidential candidate were issues countered with a brand endorsement strategy. In an endorsement, a higher value of an endorser is added to that of the host in order to extend the host's competitive reach into areas where it previously lacked market access. The endorser brand possesses market assets in the form of credibility and reassurance (Aaker, 2002; Mottram, 1998; Kapferer, 2004) to be passed on to the host to assure customers of the host brand's certainty to deliver the promise. The NPP thus identified and created 'endorsers' who became the mouthpiece of the party in areas where they were weakly represented. These endorsers were party members and officials of good reputation and popularity within their electoral areas.

Other mundane attributes of the presidential candidate, such as his build, height and calm demeanour, were to be summed up into a composite political asset in the well popularised slogan, 'Gentle Giant' (NPP respondents, 2006). Finally, all the above messages were to be 'dramatised' for the 'sensational' media with the hope that upon being exposed to the entire drama that comes with it, people will come to own the campaign and will spread the word. Hence, the skillfully developed 'J. A. Kufour song' which pummeled the Ghanaian airwaves as advertising commercials leading up to the 2000 elections. Though the NPP respondent did not mention how much the party spent on paid advertising during the campaign, it is reported that the party spent close to $2 million on the media campaign alone, a phenomenal amount by Ghanaian standards (http://moforiatta.blog.com).

Conclusion

Through market intelligence of some kind, the market-oreinted party tries to identify and understand the needs of voters in the design, communication and distribution of political programmes. Both the major Ghanaian parties made significant use of marketing techniques. And both parties recognize the importance of communicating with voters to try and elicit their support. As such, neither the NDC nor the NPP are product-oriented parties. Nevertheless, both parties retain some commitment to an ideology, more explicit for the NDC but still evident for the NPP in its support for a free-market economic policy. Neither party, however, could be categorised as market-oriented. The NPP used marketing to help change the party's image without this having much impact on developing party policy. In the case of the NDC, marketing intelligence was used more towards finding out party weaknesses rather than what were the policy needs of citizens. This places both parties in the category of sales-oriented. Yet the situation is far from static and the parties have shown an awareness of various techniques associated with a market-oriented party – targeting, focus groups, polling, brand development. Future developments may see the parties use such techniques to develop policy rather than just to sell policy.

Acknowledgement

My profound gratitude to Dr. Baffour Agyeman-Duah, formerly of the Ghana Centre for Democratic Development (CDD-Ghana) and now UN Senior Governance Advisor in Dar es Salaam, Tanzania. His advice led to my interest in political marketing research. Thank you, Dr. Agyeman-Duah.

References/further reading

Aaker, D. (2002) *Building Strong Brands*, New York: Simon & Schuster.
African Elections Database (2006) 'Ghana Detailed Election Results'. Available at: <http://africanelections.tripod.com/gh_detail.html> (accessed 5 June 2009).
Anebo, F. K. G. (1997) 'Voting Pattern and Electoral Alliances in Ghana's 1996 Elections', *African Association of Political Science*, 2(2): 38–52.
Austin, D. (1961) 'The Working Committee of The United Gold Coast Convention', *Journal of African History*, 2(2): 273–297.
Ayee, J. R. A. (1997) 'The December 1996 General Glections in Ghana', *Electoral Studies*, 16: 416–427.
Baer, D. (1995) 'Contemporary Strategy and Agenda Setting', in J. A Thurber and C. Nelson (eds) *Campaigns and Elections American Style*, Boulder, CO: Westview Press. [47–61]
Berkel, B. (2006) 'Political Parallelism in News and Commentaries on the Haider Conflict: A Comparative Analysis of Austrian, British, German, and French Quality Newspapers', *Communications*, 31(1): 85–104.
Carbone, M. G. (2003) 'Developing Multi-Party Politics: Stability and Change in Ghana and Mozambique', Working paper no. 36, London: Crisis States Programme, Development Research Centre, DESTIN, London School of Economics.
Centre for Democratic Development (CDD) Ghana (2005) 'Financing Political Parties in Ghana: Policy Guidelines'. Available at: http://www.ndi.org/files/1883_ghcdd policyguidelines.pdf (accessed 10 June 2009).
Gadzekpo, A. (2005) 'Ghana Country Assessment Paper', submitted to Ghana Draft Audit-1, Accra: School of Communication Studies, University of Ghana, Legon.
Hamid, M. (2008) 'Bawumia's Selection Triggers NDC and CPP Defections'. Available at : <http://www.myzongo.com/2008/08/26/bawumias-selection-triggers-ndc-and-cpp-defections/> (accessed 5 June 2009).
Handly, A. and Mills, G. (2001) 'From Military Coups to Multiparty Elections: The Ghanaian Military – Civil Transition', Working Paper Series, The Hague: Netherlands Institute of International Relations 'Clingendael'.
InterMedia (2005) *Ghana: Media and Opinion Survey Data for Developing Countries*. Washington, DC: InterMedia.

Kapferer, J.-N. (2004) *The New Strategic Brand Management: Creating and Sustaining Brand Equity Long Term*, London: Kogan Page.

Kwesi, J. (1998) 'Political Parties and Transition to Multi-Party Politics in Ghana', in K. A. Ninsin (ed.) *Ghana: Transition to Democracy*, Dakar: CODESRIA.

Larvie, J. and Badu, K. A (1996) *Elections 96 in Ghana*, Accra: Friedrich Ebert Stiftung.

Lees-Marshment, J. (2001) *Political Marketing and British Political Parties*, Manchester: Manchester University Press.

Mensah, K. (2006) 'Theme Talk: Well On Target in Ghana', *Newsletter for Political Marketing Group p.s.a. (Political Studies Association) Specialist Group, UK*, 10: 4–6.

Mensah, K. (2007) 'Kwame Nkrumah and Political Marketing: Locating Osagyefo's Campaign Strategy in Modern Political Campaigning', *Journal of Pan African Studies*, 1(8): 93–113.

Moforiatta.blog.com (n.d.) 'Ghana – The New Kid on the Block', weblog entry. Available at: <http://moforiatta.blog.com/492764/> (accessed 5 June 2008).

Monfils, B. S. (1977) 'A Multifaceted Image: Kwame Nkrumah's Extrinsic Rhetorical Strategies', *Journal of Black Studies*, 7(3): 313–330.

Morrison, K. C. (2004) 'Political Parties in Ghana Through Four Republics: A Path to Democratic Consolidation', *Comparative Politics*, 36(4): 421–442.

Mottram, S. (1998) 'Branding the Corporation', in S. Hart and J. Murphy (eds) *Brands: The New Wealth Creators*, Maidenhead: Palgrave Macmillan. [63–71]

myjoyonline.com (2007) 'Ayariga Defends Prof. Mills' Door-to-Door Campaign Strategy'. Available at: http://news.myjoyonline.com/politics/200706/5431.asp (accessed 5 June 2009).

Ninsin, K. A. (1996) 'Ghana: Beyond Crisis and Adjustment', *Africa Development*, XXI (2 and 3): 25–42.

Ninsin, K. A. (2006) *Political Parties and Political Participation in Ghana*, Accra, Ghana: Konrad Adenaur Stiftung. Available at: <http://www.kas.de/wf/doc/kas_9821-544-2-30.pdf> (accessed 5 June 2009).

Nugent, P. (2001) 'Ethnicity and Recent Democratic Experiments in Africa', *African Issues, African Studies Association*, 29(1/2): 2–7.

Oquaye, M. (1995) 'The Ghanaian Elections of 1992: A Dissenting View', *African Affairs*, 94: 259–275.

Rand Merchant Bank (2008) 'Ghana elections: Will ruling party reign supreme?' *Vuka Africa Special Edition*. Available at: <https://www.fnb.co.za/downloads/economics/VukaSpecialEdition06nov08.pdf> (accessed 5 June 2009).

Smith, D. (2002) 'Ghana's 2000 Elections: Consolidating Multi-Party Democracy, Notes on Recent Elections', *Electoral Studies*, 21: 519–526.

Smith, G. and Saunders, J. (1990) 'The Application of Marketing to British Politics', *Journal of Marketing Management*, 56: 1–17.

The Statesman (2006) 'Golden Age of the Press?'. Available at: http://www.thestatesmanonline.com/pages/news_detail.php?section=1&newsid=1566 (accessed 5 June 2009).

Vieta, K. T. (1999) 'The Flagbearers of Ghana.' Available at: <http://www.ghanacastle.gov.gh/president/castle_newsp_details.cfm?EmpID=681> (accessed 10 January 2007).

14 Political marketing in a weak democracy?

The Peruvian case

Pedro Patrón Galindo

Peru is a developing country, experiencing severe economic and social difficulties with almost 40 per cent of the population suffering poverty and 60 per cent some form of unemployment (INEI, 2008). Peru is also a country with a weakly consolidated democratic system, one that has been interrupted by several military and civil coups.

In the 1980s, Peruvian politics was dominated by four parties: the centre-right *Acción Popular*-AP (Popular Action), the liberal *Partido Popular Cristiano*-PPC (Popular Christian Party), the centre-left *Partido Aprista Peruano*-APRA (Peruvian *Aprista* Party), and the left-wing *Izquierda Unida*-IU (United Leftist Parties). These four organisations, referred to by Meléndez (2007: 216) as 'old' or traditional parties, together won almost 90 per cent of the votes between 1978 and 1989; in 1989 this percentage fell to 71.5 per cent and in the presidential elections of 1995 it was a mere 6.3 per cent (ONPE, 2008).

This decline in support reflected the failure of the traditional parties to adequately represent the wishes of Peruvian voters, who progressively started to vote for independent candidates and new political movements such as the *Unidad Nacional*-UN (National Unity), *Partido Nacionalista Peruano*-PNP (Peruvian Nationalist Party) and the *Alianza por el Futuro*-AF (Alliance for the Future). Peruvian analyst Martín Tanaka argues that this incapacitation of the traditional parties was due to the ideological polarisation of the party system as well as the presence of 'anti-system' terrorist movements, the *Sendero Luminoso* (Shining Path) and the *Movimiento Revolucionario Tupac Amaru*-MRTA (Tupac Amaru Revolutionary Movement) (Tanaka, 2005: 8). Effective government, therefore, has been a long-term problem in Peru.

The failure of the traditional parties provided the opportunity for the populist leader Alberto Fujimori to occupy the presidency throughout the 1990s, drawing support from most social groups. However, in 2000 some of the traditional parties returned to the political arena with revitalised organisational structures. In particular, the APRA, AP and PPC relaunched their organisations while working together to oppose the Fujimori regime. Nevertheless, citizens still seem to be more attracted to independent candidates and new political movements than to the traditional parties. As a result, short-term, populist policies tend to dominate the political marketplace and these do little to address the deep-seated economic and social problems confronting ordinary Peruvian voters. This in turn feeds back into the disillusionment voters have with politicians given their inability to deliver on their promises or for their promises to have little practical benefit for citizens.

The Peruvian political system

This chapter will examine the major contemporary Peruvian parties to see how well they can be characterised by the Lees-Marshment (2001) typology of product, sales- and market-oriented parties. A distinction will be made between parties that may adopt marketing techniques, and be market driven, but which do not in other ways reflect a market-oriented party. Before looking at the parties in detail, some key features of Peruvian political parties and the party system will be outlined.

Peru has a presidential, candidate-centred, majoritarian political system. As in other Latin American countries, political rights are incorporated into electoral legislation that, amongst other things, establishes political parties as legal entities.

In Peru, the 1933 Constitution was the first one in the country that recognised political parties as such, but it was not until 2003 that the first electoral law was passed by the Peruvian Parliament. As Tuesta claims, 'it was a law that enforced the presence and real life for political parties, providing rights but also obligations they did not have before. The objective was clear and declared: the law should create the conditions for the constitution and strengthening of a democratic political system' (Tuesta, 2006: 771). However, in the 2006 presidential elections in Peru, of the 23 'political movements' that ran (JNE, 2008), some of them faced charges of unlawful procedures under their registration with the Electoral Authority.

With regard to the financing of the political parties' activity, this is set out in the 2003 Electoral Law. There are two types of financing, public and private. In the former, the state provides 3,450 Peruvian *soles* for each vote obtained in the last parliamentary elections. As for private financing, this has always existed in Peru but until 2003 was unregulated. According to the 2003 Electoral Law, private funding corresponds to the membership fees, funds obtained through the activities undertaken by the party, benefits from properties, income from other sources authorised by the law and, in general, any donations. These regulations have forced the parties to create new internal bodies responsible for private funding. In terms of external regulation, a new entity within the Electoral Authority was created with the new electoral law; it requests financial reports from the political parties for control and audit of the funding.

The media arena is a fertile ground for the development of political marketing in Peru. In this regard, Peruvian mainstream news media are highly commercialised (only one television and radio station, as well as one newspaper, are state-owned) and independent from the parties (in the sense that none of the former belong to the latter). They are quite critical of all politicians and parties, and are very active in searching for corruption scandals. Thus, the media in Peru tends to frame politics as a strategic game in which the political agenda is defined as a result of the confrontation between the media and the parties.

As indicated above, before the 2003 Electoral Law there were few references to the regulation of the activities of political parties in Peru. With regard to campaigning and political propaganda, the 1979 Constitution stated in Article 71 that registered parties had free access to state-owned mass media. The 1993 Constitution introduces a slightly different approach, stating that free access to state-owned mass media for political parties would be dependant on the last general election results.

The 2003 Electoral Law regulates, among other aspects of the political parties activities, their right of free access to mass media. Article 37 covers the so-called 'Electoral Frame', which is a means for political parties to have free access to private and public radio and television stations between 30 and 2 days before the elections (political advertising is forbidden in Peru 48 hours before an election).

As compensation, the state reduces the transmission fees paid by television and radio stations in proportion to the air-time given to the parties. The state also provides its radio and television facilities for production purposes. Time is allocated as follows: 50 per cent is distributed evenly across all parties and the other 50 per cent is allocated according to how many MPs the parties have. Parties that run for the first time have the right to the same amount of time as the party that obtained the least number of parliamentary seats. Time not used by parties can be utilised by the electoral authority for informational/educational purposes.

With regard to paid advertising, the legislation indicates that the rates charged cannot exceed the average used for commercial advertisements. Political advertisements can only appear between 60 and 10 days before the election day and cannot last for more than five minutes in total, per day. There is also a regulation of political advertising when parties are not campaigning: each party with parliamentary representation can only advertise for five minutes per month to promote their policies and proposals.

It is quite significant that, in the context of a country where political institutions and democracy are meaningless concepts for most of the population, organisations involved in political action avoid using the term 'party' in their communication – although they are legally registered as such – since the word has a very negative connotation among citizens. In Peru, as Tanaka argues, 'the real problem is not the formal rules of the system but the players in the political arena: political parties, or more precisely, the lack of parties with a minimum structure and, as a consequence, a political party system' (Tanaka, 2005: 9).

Political parties in Peru, therefore, operate in an environment where there is considerable distrust of politicians and while this may encourage parties to appear to 'listen' to voters in order to seem responsive and trustworthy, it also means that if parties fail to deliver on promises made, support can quickly evaporate. There is little reservoir of goodwill towards parties that helps them to see out hard times.

Another feature of the party system is the relatively weak organisational structure of the parties. In the case of the old parties, such as the APRA, party structures atrophied during the 1990s at a time when the parties were excluded from power during the Fujimori era. For the new parties, they are primarily electoral vehicles for political entrepreneurs and as such, the parties lack an extensive grassroots organisation. This lack of a strong organisation often forces parties to use professional marketing techniques to try and communicate with voters as they lack the members and structure to reach out to voters in a more indirect way.

Moreover, part of Peru's political culture embraces the presence of messianic discourses that concentrate power in one person, normally the party leader-candidate. Indeed, the political and economic instability of the region seems to provide fertile ground for political leaders with redemptory discourses. As Tuesta argues: 'Leaders that emerge beyond the margins of the political system must assume a discourse of redemption and a mandate for social change. Their arrival to power expresses the discredit of the representational institutions and the non-existence of stable political identities' (2002: 144). This is a trend adopted by the traditional parties as well, as they sometimes fall into the 'populist' category in order to compete with new movements.

A final notable feature of the Peruvian political system is the extremely low levels of party identification; this is reflected in the high levels of voter volatility as shown in Table 14.1. Even the APRA lost most of its voters in the mid-1990s, when it obtained just 4.1 per cent of the votes at the 1995 presidential elections.

Table 14.1 Votes in Peru by parties, 1978–2006

Year	AP	PPC	FREDEMO	APRA	IU	CAMBIO 90	PNP	Independents
1978 (A)	NP	23.8	–	35.3	29.4	–	–	11.5
1980 (Pr)	45.4	9.6	–	27.4	14.4	–	–	3.2
1980 (M)	35.8	11.1	–	22.5	23.3	–	–	7.4
1983 (M)	17.5	13.9	–	33.1	29	–	–	6.7
1985 (Pr)	7.3	11.9	–	53.1	24.7	–	–	3
1986 (M)	–	14.8	–	47.6	30.8	–	–	7.8
1989 (M)	–	–	31.2	20.4	20.2	–	–	28.2
1990 (P1)	–	–	32.6	22.6	13	29.1	–	2.7
1990 (P2)	–	–	37.5	–	–	62.5	–	–
1992 (A)	–	9.7	–	–	5.5	49.2	–	35.6
1993 (M)	11.6	5.7	–	10.8	3.9	NP	–	64.7
1995 (Pr)	1.7	–	–	4.1	0.6	64.4	–	29.2
1998 (M)	3.8	–	–	4.8	–	32.7	–	91.4
2000 (P1)	0.4	–	–	1.4	–	49.9	–	48.3
2000 (P2)	–	–	–	–	–	74.3	–	25.7
2001 (P1)	–	24.3	–	25.8	–	–	–	49.9
2001 (P2)	–	–	–	46.9	–	–	–	53.1
2002 (M)	–	39.9	–	–	–	1.8	–	58.3
2006 (P1)	–	23.9	–	24.5	–	7.5	30.8	13.4
2006 (P2)	–	–	–	52.6	–	–	47.37	–
2006 (M)	1.4	47.8	–	12.0	–	4.0	4.3	30.52

Sources: Tuesta Soldevilla (1995) and ONPE (2008).

Notes: (M): Municipal elections.
(A): Constitutional elections.
(P1 and P2): First and second electoral round.
(Pr): Presidential, one round only.

High electoral volatility and weak party loyalty push parties towards vigorous campaigns for voters at each election – parties have little core vote that they can rely on to receive regardless of the campaign effort. Indeed, as shown in Figure 14.1 these voters still seem to be more attracted to independent candidates and new political movements, based on their effectiveness in the short-term rather than on structured policies and proposals. Thus, according to Rafael Roncagliolo, there is a growing disaffection toward democratic systems, which have not been able to provide an effective response to the problems citizens consider most critical, such as poverty, inequality and security. Within this context, political parties, which are considered to be responsible for managing [Latin American] countries, are mostly blamed for the crisis. This makes political parties and politicians lose, or seem to be losing,their credibility and legitimacy quite quickly (Roncagliolo, 2007: 13).

This, combined with a weak party structure, makes the use of marketing techniques even more vital to inform, convert and mobilise voters.

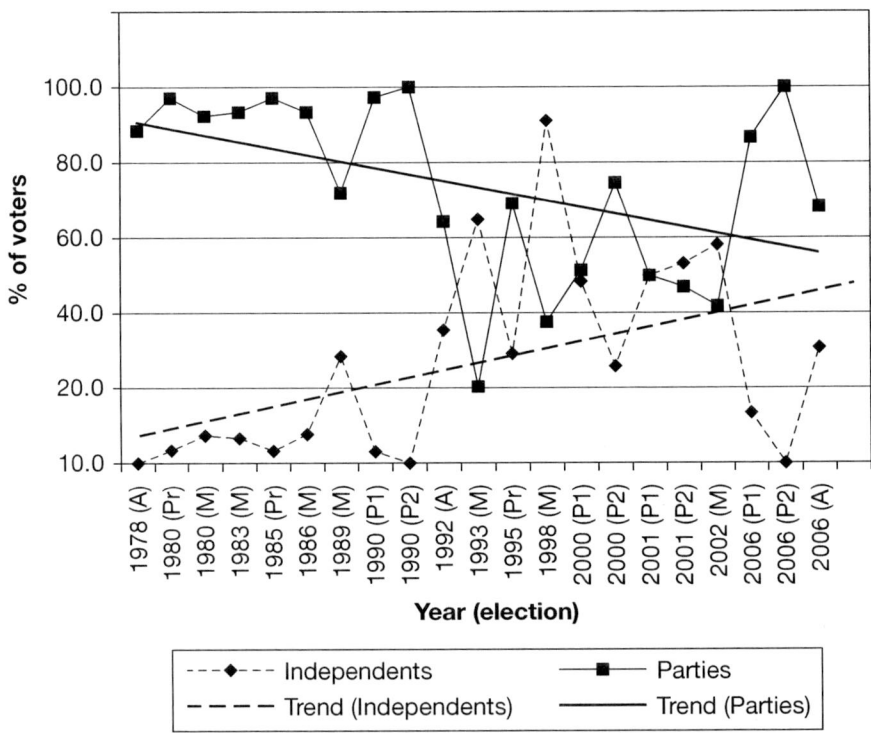

Figure 14.1 Trend in vote: Parties vs. Independents

As Vergara (2007) shows in Figure 14.2, in order to understand the behaviour of Peruvian voters, it is important to take into account what he calls the 'discretional' axis, which classifies parties depending on their more or less authoritarian

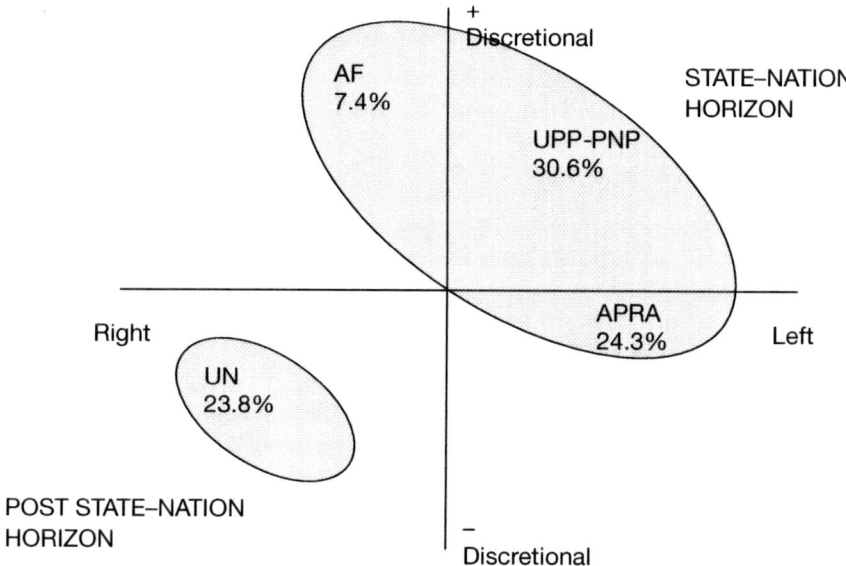

Figure 14.2 Mapping Peruvian political parties

Source: Vergara (2007: 32), based on the 2006 election results (first round).

style. With regard to the 'horizons', these are related to the historical-social dimension of inclusion of the population in the modern state. As mentioned before, more than half of the Peruvian population does not have a solid relationship with the State: they are not 'formally' employed, nor do they pay taxes or social security or receive public services in exchange.[1]

Furthermore, it was not until the 2006 election that the consulting and communication group Apoyo carried out polling nationwide. Most people in rural areas do not have access to a telephone and mailing service is limited. Therefore, even if parties had the resources, the effectiveness of such as phone polling and direct mailing would be restricted. Yet with voting compulsory in Peru, and rural voters accounting for approximately 25 per cent of the electorate, communicating with such voters is important for parties. How do they do so? This will be examined in the next section of this chapter.

The APRA: a market-oriented party?

The APRA was founded as a movement in 1924 in Mexico by Víctor Raúl Haya de la Torre. Since its foundation it has been one of the most important and influential parties in Latin America. According to Barnechea (2001: 47), it became the prototype of a popular party, a mass-organisation model. It was registered as a party in Peru in 1931.

After an intense political life, being banned and re-legalised several times, in 1978 the APRA obtained a majority in the Constitutional Assembly, formed by the military government (1968–1980) to draft a new constitution. However Haya de la Torre died in 1979, and because the party had been so focused around him, this significantly damaged the performance of the APRA in the presidential elections in 1980. In 1982, though, the APRA became the most important opposition party, mainly because of the efforts of its young leader, Alan García. He created in just a few years a new image for the party as a modern political party with a social democratic ideology, renewing the party elite with a new generation of *Apristas* (Tanaka and Zárate, 1998: 142). In 1985, the APRA won the presidential elections and García began his term in power with 96.1 per cent support.

This positive start gave García the political power to implement the policies he had put forward during the presidential campaign. However, economic, social and political problems created a crisis of governance for García. Between September 1988 and the beginning of 1989, there was a popular demand for García's resignation as well as rumours of a possible military takeover (Tanaka and Zárate, 1998: 163).

García's loss of popularity – and along with it that of APRA – reinforced the view among Peruvian citizens that the traditional political parties, epitomised by the APRA, could not solve the pressing social and economic problems facing the country. This provided the opportunity for apolitical candidates, such as the world-famous writer Mario Vargas Llosa, to enter the political arena and challenge the monopoly of power held by the traditional political parties.

During the 1990s the APRA failed, as did the other traditional parties, to respond to citizens' expectations and needs. The low point for the APRA came in 1995 when the party obtained just 4.1 per cent of the vote in the presidential elections. However in 1996, Alan Garcia and the APRA's Secretary General, Jorge del Castillo, initiated a process of re-launching the party (Patrón-Galindo, 2005). The major electoral setbacks for the APRA during this decade were undoubtedly catalysts for self-reflection by the party leaders. Since the turn of the century, the APRA's electoral performance has improved significantly and a major contributing factor for this has been the revamping of the party organisation, a modified brand image, and greater use of marketing techniques. Garcia has boasted about the APRA's use of marketing research methods, especially electorate segmentation and voter targeting, which he considers a positive development for the party being able to meet people's expectations. Programme development is now far more objective, founded on public opinion integrated with ideology rather than on ideology alone. This is highlighted by García's statement that 'the polls are as important as the elections in determining political behaviour, and that is also why [other] associations are so important to us' (APRA website, 2008).

The APRA has tried to project its vision of a Peruvian society based on social justice. This has offered a clear contrast to the autocratic style of government under Fujimori. The APRA's New Minimum Programme attempts to modernise the party while at the same time ensuring that the party's traditional ideology is not completely abandoned. This has involved the party embracing the economic and technological changes associated with globalisation but at the same time maintaining a discourse that is anti-imperialist and critical of neo-liberalism. The party 'product', then, offered by the APRA is an adaptation of Haya de la Torre's doctrine, which seeks to satisfy the demands of the 'orthodox' or purists in the party who feel that little of the party's core discourse should be changed, and the 'heterodox' or realists who wish to see a more modernised programme that will have appeal and relevance for ordinary voters.

In addition to the party's programme, there have been wide-ranging changes to the party organisation. The National Executive Committee (NEC) of the party has been divided into several national secretariats, specialising in key subject areas such as education, public health, labour, agriculture and international relations. A new School of Training in Municipal Issues has been set up to offer training as a means of acting as a think-tank in which politicians and academics participate and thus gain the party support from the political and academic elite. These new party units are charged with producing updated documentation for policy making and preparing party members for lobbying, negotiation and governing.

According to Meléndez (2007: 250), for the 2006 elections the APRA, through its Political National Directorate, created the Social Front, as a series of participative discussion forums with specialists on issues such as agriculture, education and the non-governmental sector. The party elaborated its proposals based on these meetings. This was a clear demonstration of how the APRA was using market intelligence to assist in the formulation of policy. This was not an opportunistic following of public opinion for short-term gains as García tried to develop policy within an ideological framework that harnessed widespread dissatisfaction with the neo-liberal prescriptions (epitomised by the 'Washington Consensus') being imposed on developing countries such as Peru. In the Lees-Marshment framework, therefore, the APRA approximates in some respects a market-oriented party. Alone among Peruvian parties, the APRA has the resources to adopt marketing techniques on a consistent and nationwide scale. The party's structure is also sufficiently centralised to allow a leadership committed to some degree of modernisation, to implement change over any opposition amongst the rank-and-file.

Finally, it is worth noting that the APRA has made efforts to improve the ways the image of the party is communicated. As noted above, voters are distrustful of politicians in general but the poor performance of García during his first presidency means there is particular antipathy towards him and his party. García has tried to counter this negative image by projecting the image of an experienced politician who has learned from the mistakes from the past and someone that has become 'centred', in a country highly polarised between the mainstream right-wing policies and the radical proposals of the nationalist left.

Nevertheless, the APRA has faced problems with policy delivery. Since his election as president in 2006, Alan García has lost nearly one-third of his support, as measured in opinion polls.[2] This is largely due to his government implementing right-wing policies despite what the APRA had promised before the election. Some of the ministers in his cabinet actually belong to conservative parties, but they were called to participate in the government to project an image of stability towards the elite economic and financial groups in the country and abroad.

The PNP: product- or sales-orientation?

Like other countries in Latin America, the 1990s was dominated by the so-called 'neo-liberal' ideology. After its re-launch in 1996, it was the APRA who led the leftist movement and presented an alternative to the prevailing political and economic trend of neo-liberalism. However, in 2005 Ollanta Humala, a former Peruvian Army Colonel, became the leader of the Peruvian Nationalist Party (PNP) and launched his candidacy for the presidential elections of 2006 with a political programme that was more radical and leftist than that of the APRA.

Humala could not register the PNP (due to the limitations of the new Electoral Law) and so formed an alliance with the Union for Peru, a party founded in 1995 by former Secretary General of the United Nations, Javier Pérez de Cuéllar. Pérez de Cuéllar, after losing the presidential elections in 1995, had left the party he founded. Since then, the Union for Peru has been 'used' by different leftist groups until 2006, when its members decided to form the alliance with the PNP. The alliance gathered different leftist initiatives and combined these with a nationalist ideology based on Humala's father's ideas related to the need for a revolution to be carried out by people of dark skin (indigenous population) against white people (European descendants).[3]

Nevertheless, with time Ollanta separated his discourse from his father's, leaving the more revolutionary positions to his brothers Antauro and Ulises (also leading a party that ran for presidency in 2006). Ollanta's own ideas were based on his opposition to neo-liberalism and the influence of the United States over Peru. According to a party member, Ollanta's disavowal of a more revolutionary course 'was due to the need of obtaining more acceptance from voter segments that rejected the initial radical propositions'. However, the party member carried on to say that

> within the party there is a constant debate on whether our proposals should be more attached to our ideology or whether they should be 'adapted', in order to become more appealing and thus make a move to the centre. Budgetary constraints are also a barrier to implementing marketing techniques.

On this latter point, it should be noted that for Peruvian political parties, marketing techniques are considered too expensive to conduct other than sporadically.

Ollanta's presidential candidacy raised, amongst the conservative sectors of society, the issue of an authoritarian style in Peruvian politics and the fear that the improvements in the economy since 2000[4] would be harmed by a president ideologically related to Bolivia's Evo Morales and Venezuela's Hugo Chávez. In fact, during the 2006 campaign there were some accusations and journalistic investigations about the Venezuelan president actually funding Humala's campaign, which was denied by the PNP. On the social side, Ollanta was in favour of legalising abortion (which is forbidden in Peru), which met with vigorous opposition from the Catholic Church.

In spite of these question marks against his economic and social policies, Ollanta Humala obtained 30.7 per cent of the votes in the first round of the 2006 presidential elections, while Alan García obtained 24.3 per cent. Lourdes Flores of the right-wing UN came last with 23.8 per cent. This result seemed to confirm that the shift to the left observed in other Latin American countries,was also occurring in Peru.

With regard to the use of political marketing, being a new political organisation but with strong ideological underpinnings, the PNP had neither the resources nor the willingness to fully develop a market orientation. Nevertheless, the party was quite successful in the second round of the 2006 elections: Humala obtained 47.4 per cent of the votes, not too far behind Alan García's 52.6 per cent.

In terms of market intelligence, the PNP does not admit openly to have gathered data on people's expectations regarding proposed policies. However, when comparing its discourse during the campaign and the one used before he launched his candidacy (especially through the *Ollanta Magazine*, edited by his brother Antauro), it is clear that Ollanta Humala projected a less radical, nationalist image in order to attract more voters from the centre of the political spectrum. This is evidence, therefore, that the party saw the need to try and 'sell' itself to voters, to make the party more electable.

When it came to organisation, the PNP was quite effective at capitalising on the expectations of some left-wing leaders that joined it under the ideological umbrella of the struggle against poverty and neo-liberalism. The party has a national reach with delegations from all regions of the country and even abroad.

In terms of policy making, according to Meléndez (2007: 250), the PNP has a team of professionals and specialists that elaborate a government plan that has then to be approved by a wider commission. In this case, the government plan becomes a guideline for the governing bodies to be ratified in the field.

Although the PNP has a majority in the unicameral Peruvian Congress, the party's poor showing at the 2006 municipal elections (see Table 14.1) exposed the inability of the party to retain a core of loyal support. While the party has made some efforts to persuade voters to accept what it has to offer, the party still remains wedded to an ideological orientation that restricts its appeal to a niche group of voters.

The UN: the most product-oriented party

National Unity was founded in 2000 by Lourdes Flores Nano and is Peru's third largest party. He participated in the 2001 presidential election and obtained 24.3 per cent of the vote. At the legislative elections held on the same day, the party won 13.8 per cent and 17 out of 120 seats in the Congress. The party is an alliance of other political parties. Its members were initially the Christian Popular Party (PPC), National Solidarity (SN), National Renewal (RN) and Radical

Change (CR), but the latter two left the coalition around the time of the 2006 national election. The alliance led by Lourdes Flores participated in the 2006 national election. Flores came third in the presidential vote and the alliance won 15.3 per cent of the votes and 17 seats in Congress.

Ideologically speaking, the UN is located on the conservative right within the Peruvian political spectrum, the polar opposite to the PNP. Its president, Lourdes Flores Nano, began both presidential campaigns in 2001 and 2006 as the favoured candidate. However, in both contests, Flores was portrayed by her opponents as representing the 'rich people's interests'. In a country suffering widespread poverty, such an image of elitism quickly lost Flores support during the campaigns.

The SN was founded in 1999 by Luis Castañeda Lossio, a former member of Acción Popular. SN joined the UN electoral alliance following the municipal elections of 2002, when Castañeda became the Mayor of Lima. Castañeda used to be Director of the Peruvian Social Security Institute, and used this as a platform to enter the political arena. Casteñeda was re-elected mayor of Lima in 2006 with an increased majority (see Table 14.1).

In terms of the use of political marketing, as Meléndez (2007: 250) points out, the UN has a slightly different approach to that of the APRA. The 'Plan of Government' is a body formed by specialists corresponding to each of the Peruvian ministries. This cabinet holds meetings with external professionals to elaborate a governing programme that is later debated with the leaders of the party.

According to interviews with political communication consultants Gustavo Rodríguez and Sandro Venturo (both 2008), 'the strategy for Luis Castañeda's campaign in the municipal elections was based on the perceived idea that the citizens in Lima are looking for a "sheriff", someone with an authoritarian image that may guarantee security on the streets'. Another key element in the UN's government programme is the scrutiny of the effectiveness of carrying out public works, especially in poor neighbourhoods. Nevertheless, for Rodríguez and for Venturo (2008) these two policy proposals were not based on systematic use of marketing techniques and a market approach, but is 'actually a subjective perception probably based on public polling and the public opinion expressed in the mainstream media'.

After this analysis, it can be argued that the UN is the most product-oriented party in Peru. While the PNP does not have the resources to carry out market intelligence, the UN does not seem to be willing to use its funds to carry out marketing techniques to gather information on what voters' demands are. This is probably the reason why Lourdes Flores has not been able to win any elections; although she has begun every campaign as the favourite, she has lost each of the elections in which she has participated.

AF: a market-driven party?

The AF's origins began with Cambio 90, a political movement founded in 1989 by Alberto Fujimori. Fujimori won the 1990 presidential elections and two years later led a civil-military coup and called elections for a Constitutional Assembly to draft a new constitution.[5] Cambio 90 also won the 1995 and the 2000 presidential elections. However, due to corruption scandals the president left the country after being re-elected for a second time in 2000 and went into exile in Japan until 2007. AP's Valentín Paniagua, president of the Peruvian Parliament at the time, became president of the country in a 'transition' term between 2000 and 2001.

In recent elections Fujimori's party has adopted different labels, such as Vamos Vecino (Let's go Neighbour), Solución Popular (Popular Solution), Perú 2000, Sí Cumple (Keep Promises) and Alianza para el Futuro (Alliance for the Future, whose initials symbolically coincide with Alberto Fujimori's).

Peruvian society was profoundly divided while Cambio 90 and Fujimori were in power. For most citizens Fujimori and his party were quite effective in fighting terrorism at the beginning of the 1990s although charges of violation of human rights also date from this period. Fujimori also presided over the revival of the economy which had been virtually destroyed by hyper-inflation during the period of APRA government in the 1980s.[6]

Meléndez (2007: 250) argues that the AF is a peculiar type of party. It has a body called the National Coordinator of the government plan, which works as an external consulting committee that is not part of the organic structure of the AF but elaborates government proposals that are then coordinated with the National Executive Committee of the party.

Unlike the traditional parties, AF does not have a clear ideological basis or a group of founders with a common political project. According to Vergara (2007: 82), the identification between the citizens and Fujimori was strengthened during his term in office by the marketing of himself and his party as 'a Peruvian like you'. This was an implied reference to Fujimori's main opponent at the time who was the white-skinned and world-famous writer Mario Vargas Llosa.

The AF continues to base its appeal on the image and legacy of the party leader, although it has been harmed by the trial of Fujimori since 2007 on charges of corruption and violation of human rights. Fujimori's daughter, Keiko, has taken over leadership of the party and the AF obtained the highest number of votes in the 2006 parliamentary elections. The discourse of the party is still constructed around limited issues such as the need for more authority in the country (Patrón, 2004: 116). These are aspects that make the party market-driven rather than market-oriented.

Political marketing in a new democracy

A major problem that all political parties face in Peru is the lack of a developed democratic political culture which could underpin the prevailing political institutions. This not only constitutes a barrier to voter engagement, but is also a threat to the very consolidation of democracy in the country. Romeo Grompone points out that when the Fujimori regime collapsed in 2000 the opposition parties and social movements that fought against his autocracy were not ready to take over (Grompone, 2001: 10). According to Grompone, this was different to other countries such as Brazil, Chile, Uruguay, Argentina, Portugal and Greece in their transitions to democracy. In Chile, for example, the political parties analyzed their own mistakes instead of just blaming the regime during the dictatorship of Pinochet. They renewed their ideological proposals and understood the importance of reaching strategic agreements among themselves (Grompone, 2001: 11). Such a strategy showed sensitivity to what the people wanted and an awareness that the parties had inadequately listened to these demands in the past.

Grompone argues that in other transitions to democracy, parties kept their communication structures, which could be activated when they returned to democracy. The parties tried to widen their support bases and projected the image of adapting their discourses to the new times. This did not happen in most Peruvian political organisations with the possible exception of the APRA and, according to Tanaka (2005: 9), even this old party lacked a solid infrastructure and an organisation able to connect with voters' demands.

A market-oriented organisation has as its goal the satisfaction of the consumer. It tries to understand those whom it intends to serve and deliver a product that reflects their needs and wishes. It is willing to change its behaviour in order to obtain more support. In this sense, no Peruvian party fully fits Lees-Marshment's market-oriented party model.

But despite Tanaka's reservations, the APRA does come closest to being market-oriented. This might be one of the reasons why this party won the elections in 2006. Of all the political parties analysed in this chapter only the APRA has the resources to adopt marketing techniques on a consistent and nationwide scale. The party's structure is also sufficiently centralised to allow a leadership committed to some degree of modernisation to reach out and try and meet voter expectations, in spite of any reservation rank-and-file members may have towards such a strategy.

With regard to the other parties, the AF is market-driven or populist while the other two parties remain ideologically driven or product-oriented. The AF as well as the UN and PNP have all been formed with short-term objectives in mind.

In terms of market intelligence, the PNP does not admit openly to have gathered data on people's expectations regarding proposed policies. However, when comparing its discourse during the 2006 presidential campaign, it is clear that Ollanta Humala tried to project a less radical image (in terms of nationalism) in order to attract more voters from the centre of the political spectrum. Unlike the PNP, the UN does have the resources to carry out market intelligence, but does not seem to be willing to use such resources to implement marketing techniques to gather information on what voters' demands are. Thus it can be argued that the UN is the most product-oriented party in Peru.

The AF continues to base its appeal on the image and legacy of the party leader, former president Alberto Fujimori. The discourse of the party is still constructed around limited issues such as the need for more authority in the country (Patrón, 2004: 116). These are aspects that make the party market-driven rather than market-oriented.

Finally, it needs to be emphasised that Peru's political culture is based on messianic discourses that concentrate most power in one person, normally the party leader-candidate. As Vergara (2007: 54) argues, populism has become the pact between the new political society and the leaders in order to accelerate its access to modernity. Also, most political parties in Peru lack solid organisation and grass-roots support. The challenge for the parties to survive is to become something other than just populist – whether this be a market-oriented, sales-oriented or product-oriented party.

Notes

1 As a reference, the Peruvian tax burden is approximately 15 per cent of the GDP, in 2006 figures.
2 According to the Public Opinion Institute at the Catholic University of Lima, García's popularity has dropped from 56 pe rcent, since the first opinion poll after he was elected, in September 2006, to 39 per cent in February 2009.
3 Isaac Humala Núñez is a labour lawyer and nationalist from Ayacucho (Southern Peru) and is the ideological leader of the Movimiento Etnocacerista, a group of ethnic nationalists. He is a former communist leader who served as the model for a colourful character in Peruvian novelist Mario Vargas Llosa's novel *Conversation in the Cathedral*. He was Vargas Llosa's teacher of Marxism-Leninism when the writer became a member of a university Communist cell.
4 The Peruvian economy has experienced an unprecedented growth since 2000, at an average of 5 per cent of the GDP, with exports tripling, inflation as low as 3 per cent and significant reductions in poverty (INIE).
5 This is a common trend in some countries with unstable democracies in Latin America: in 2007, Bolivia's Evo Morales, Ecuador's Rafael Correa and Venezuela's Hugo Chávez took similar initiatives in their respective countries.
6 According to Barnechea (1995: 62), during the APRA's first term in power inflation went up to 1,722 per cent, production fell 7.3 per cent and both private and public incomes decreased –30.8 per cent and –9.6 per cent respectively. In 1989 inflation was 2,775 per cent and the GDP fell 13.8 per cent. Unemployment rose to 8.3 per cent in 1990 and sub-employment to 86.4 per cent. In July 1990 the critical poverty index was 49 per cent, greater than in 1985.

References/further reading

Barnechea, A. (1995) *La República Embrujada*, Lima: Editorial Nuevo Siglo.
—— (2001) *Para Salir del Laberinto: Del Neoliberalismo a la Nueva Socialdemocracia*. Lima: Editorial Santillana.
Barreda, J. (2001) 'Relanzamiento y Refundación', *Diario Correo*, 9 August.
Basadre, J. (1994) *Perú: Problema y Posibilidad*, Lima: Fundación M. Bustamante.
Cuestión de Estado Magazine. (2001) 'Elecciones otra Vez: Entre las Opciones y los Deseos', Lima: Instituto de Diálogo y Propuestas, (N° 27–28).
Daeschner, J. (1993) *The War of the End of Democracy: Mario Vargas Llosa versus Alberto Fujimori*, Lima: Peru Reporting.
De Soto, H. (1987) *El Otro Sendero*, Lima: Instituto Libertad y Democracia.
Degregori, C. I. (2000) *La Década de la Antipolítica: Auge y Huida de Alberto Fujimori y Vladimiro Montesinos*, Lima: Instituto de Estudios Peruanos.
García Pérez, A. (2000) *La Década Infame, Deuda Externa 1990–1999*, Cali: Fundación para la Investigación y la Cultura.
García Pérez, A. (2003) *Modernidad y Política en el Siglo XXI: Globalización con Justicia Social*, Lima: Editorial Matices.

Grompone, R. (2001) 'La Obligación de una Transición Audaz', *Revista Cuestión de Estado*, Lima: Instituto de Diálogo y Propuestas.

Haya de la Torre, V. R. (1936) *El Antiimperialismo y el APRA*, Santiago de Chile: Ediciones Ercilla.

Instituto Nacional de Estadística e Informática. (n.d.) Home page. Available at: http://www.inei.gob.pe (accessed 5 June 2009).

Jurado Nacional de Elecciones del Perú (2002) Home page. Available at: http://www.jne.gob.pe (accessed 5 June 2009).

Lees-Marshment, J. (2001) *Political Marketing and British Political Parties*, Manchester: Manchester University Press.

Meléndez Guerrero, C. (2003) '¿Adiós a los Outsiders?', *Revista Quehacer*, 140, March–April. Available at: <http://www.desco.org.pe/qh/qh140cm.htm> (accessed November 2003).

Meléndez Guerrero, C. (2007) 'Partidos y Sistema de Partidos en el Perú', *La Política por Dentro: Cambios y Continuidades en las Organizaciones Políticas de los Países Andinos*. Lima: Ágora Democrática.

Oficina Nacional de Procesos Electorales (2003) Home page. Available at: <http://www.onpe.gob.pe> (accessed 5 June 2009).

Patrón Galindo, P. (2004) 'Symbolism and the Construction of Political Products: An Analysis of the Political Marketing Strategies of Peruvian President Alejandro Toledo', *Journal of Public Affairs*, 4(2): 115–124.

Patrón Galindo, P. (2005) 'The Relaunch of the American Popular Revolutionary Alliance', in D. Lilleker and J. Lees-Marshment (eds) *Political Marketing: A Comparative Perspective*, Manchester: Manchester University Press.

Roncagliolo, R. (2007) 'Los Partidos Andinos: Entre la Crisis y el Cambio', *La Política por Dentro: Cambios y Continuidades en las Organizaciones Políticas de los Países Andinos*, Lima: Ágora Democrática.

Tanaka Gondo, M. (2005) *Democracia sin Partidos: Perú 2000–2005*, Lima: Instituto de Estudios Peruanos.

Tanaka Gondo, M. and Zárate Ardela, P. (1998) *Los Espejismos de la Democracia: El Colapso del Sistema de Partidos en el Perú*, Lima: Instituto de Estudios Peruanos.

Tanaka Gondo, M. and Zárate Ardela, P. (2002) *Valores Democráticos y Participación Ciudadana en el Perú 1998–2001*, Lima: Instituto de Estudios Peruanos.

Tuesta Soldevilla, F. (1994) *Perú Político en Cifras: Elite Política y Elecciones*, Lima: Fundación Friedrich Ebert.

Tuesta Soldevilla, F. (1995) *Sistema de Partidos Políticos en el Perú: 1978–1995*, Lima: Fundación Friedrich Ebert.

Tuesta Soldevilla, F. (2002) 'El Liderazgo Político en el Perú', in W. Hofmeister (ed.) *Liderazgo Político en América Latina*, Rio de Janeiro: Fundación Konrad Adenauer.

Tuesta Soldevilla, F. (2006) 'Los Partidos Políticos en Perú', in *Regulación Jurídica de los Partidos Políticos en Perú*. México: IDEA and Instituto de Investigaciones Jurídicas de la UNAM.

Universidad Católica del Perú (2009) 'Poll on Alan García's Popularity', Lima: Instituto de Opinión Pública.

Vergara, A. (2007) *Ni Amnésicos ni Irracionales: Las Elecciones Peruanas de 2006 en Perspectiva Histórica*, Lima: Ed. Solar.

Interviews

Rodríguez, Gustavo (2008) Peruvian Political Communication Consultant, 1 May.
Venturo, Sandro (2008) Peruvian Political Communication Consultant, 1 May.
Peruvian National Party Member (2008) 24 May.

Official party websites

Alianza por el Futuro: <http://www.fujimoristas.com>
Partido Aprista Peruano: <http://www.apra.org.pe>
Partido Nacionalista Peruano: <http://www.partidonacionalistaperuano.com>
Partido Popular Cristiano: <http://www.ppc.org.pe>

15 Political marketing techniques in Russia

Derek S. Hutcheson

In the decade-and-a-half since the first free multi-party elections in Russia, both the political system and the political consulting industry have developed substantially. In recent years the political system has come to be dominated by the so-called 'parties of power' – parties set up by the incumbent elite and strongly backed with administrative and other resources. But to what extent can their success be attributed to successful marketing alone? This chapter analyzes the development of the political consulting industry and the marketing techniques used by Russian political parties in the context of the framework elaborated elsewhere in this volume. Russia is often referred to as a 'managed' democracy, in which there is heavy influence by the political elite on the institutional framework of elections, but within which competition still exists. As will be seen below, the country differs from many of the other cases in this book on a number of aspects.

The analysis in this chapter is based on a variety of sources: author interviews with political consultants and party managers; analysis of campaign documents and advertisements; and accounts of electoral campaigns from informed observers and participants. Additionally, some results are reported from post-election surveys in 2004 and 2008, the latter co-commissioned by the author. Given the centralized nature of the Russian party system, which is dominated by one party (United Russia), the book's framework political marketing survey was not undertaken, but related questions were asked of the interview respondents and have been borne in mind in the analysis.

The Russian political marketplace

The institutions of the Russian political system derive from the December 1993 constitution, which until late 2008 had remained essentially unaltered since its adoption, despite significant political change around it. Table 15.1 gives an overview of key features of the Russian political system. In summary, it has:

- A strong president, hitherto directly elected every four years, with a wide range of executive and appointment functions. Powers include the requirement to dissolve the lower chamber of parliament, the State Duma, if it fails to approve his choice of prime minister three times in a row, and a right to veto legislation.

- A relatively weak bicameral parliament. The lower house, the 450-seat State Duma, has been elected on a four-year cycle since 1993, using a mixed unconnected PR system from 1993 to 2003 and list PR in 2007. The upper house, the Federation Council, consists of two appointed representatives from each of the (currently 83) subjects of the Russian Federation.
- Following constitutional amendments in late 2008, the president's term will last six years, and the State Duma's five, from the next elections onwards. In the longer term, this will decouple the timing of the parliamentary and presidential elections which have traditionally followed in quick succession and effectively formed one long campaign in recent cycles.
- The president and the government undertake the executive functions of the state dually, with the prime minister nominated by the President subject to the approval of the State Duma. The prime minister is institutionally subordinate, serving at the president's discretion, but Vladimir Putin's move in May 2008 from the presidency to the chairmanship of the government, and his clear participation in areas which go beyond the immediate domestic scope of his portfolio, have strengthened the political weight of the former office.

Table 15.1 Summary of the Russian political system

Party system	Multi-party. Four parties currently represented in the State Duma.
Electoral system	List-based PR, distributed by Hare method, with 7 per cent threshold.
Party- or candidate-based	Mainly candidate-based until 2003; now more party-based.
Government system	Semi-presidential: powerful directly-elected president nominates Prime Minister, subject to approval of State Duma (which is dissolved if it fails to confirm the president's choice three times in a row).
Parliament	Bicameral: State Duma (450 seats, directly elected); Federation Council (166 seats, two nominees from each region representing executive and legislature).
Main parties (Leader, stance, % vote in 2007)	United Russia (Vladimir Putin*, pro-government, 64.3 per cent) Communist Party of the Russian Federation (Gennadii Zyuganov, left oppositionist, 11.6 per cent) Liberal Democratic Party of Russia (Vladimir Zhirinovsky, nationalist-patriotic/populist, broadly pro-government, 8.1 per cent) Fair Russia (Sergei Mirinov*, social-democratic pro-government, 7.7 per cent).
Main media outlets (% watching news daily, 2008)	First Channel (73 per cent) Russia (61 per cent) NTV (45 per cent).

Sources: Russian Constitution 1993, State Duma Election Law 2007, *Rossiskaya Gazeta*, 11 December 2007: 10; Russian Research Survey 2008

Notes: * = Neither Vladimir Putin nor Sergei Mironov are members of the State Duma.

There are a number of aspects which potentially impact on political marketing:

1. Elections and the executive: Article 97.3 of the Constitution proscribes members of the State Duma from simultaneously holding government office, which has limited the direct influence of parliamentary parties, and even election results, on the composition of the government. The hypothesis that a party's marketing strategy in parliamentary elections will be driven by its likelihood of being part of the governing coalition is thus rendered moot.

2. Electoral system: For the 2007 State Duma election, Russia shifted from the mixed unconnected electoral system used since 1993 to a party list-based proportional system with a 7 per cent threshold. This no longer enabled candidates to enter parliament via any route other than through inclusion on the lists of the strongest parties; and the high threshold reduced the number of significant party actors in the electoral process, strengthening the party apparatus (Buribaev *et al.* 2006: 14–19).

3. The role of parties: The party system in Russia differs from that of most of the other case studies in this book in that throughout the post-communist period it has suffered until recently from a lack of institutionalization. The varying menu of parties on offer at successive elections arguably has made it harder for parties to develop long-term relationships and strategies to voters.

4. The nature of parties: Elections in recent years have witnessed the decline of programmatic parties (such as the Communists and the liberal Yabloko party), and dominance by more amorphous 'parties of power' – relatively ideology-free 'virtual' parties whose main unifying policy is support for the presidential administration and government. This, as well as points 2 and 3, should theoretically render parties relatively open to a marketing approach.

5. Lack of public trust: Public trust in the institutions of the state has traditionally been comparably low with that in central Europe, and much lower, in general, than in Western Europe. Having said this, the gap is narrowing: the proportion of citizens trusting political parties was at an all-time high of 17 per cent in 2008 (Russian Research Survey 2008: q.B14), having rarely been more than one in ten of the population since the start of multi-party politics. Any politician or party that is trusted gains a substantial advantage – a tactic used successfully by United Russia in 2007 when it included the popular Vladimir Putin (trusted by 69 per cent of the electorate) at the head of its list.

6. Political orientations of voters: The traditional ordering of politics into a left–right dichotomy does not work particularly well in Russia: fewer than a third (28 per cent) of respondents in the 2008 survey were able to place themselves anywhere on such a scale (Russia Research Survey 2008: q.C7). The relative lack of self-identification of voters should allow parties greater scope to reposition themselves between elections. Moreover, voter preferences are comparatively unfrozen: in 2003, only 44 per cent of voters had made their choice before the campaign started, and in 2007, 49 per cent (Russian Research Surveys 2004: q.C18, 2008: q.C15).

7. The financing of election campaigns: Like two-thirds of post-communist countries, there are limits on maximum donations in Russian elections (Walecki 2003). These increased substantially from about US$2.4m in 1995 to US $16.4m in 2007. In practice, there is reasonable anecdotal evidence that the low official permitted expenditure figures of the 1990s were the tip of a much larger iceberg, and that the proportion of campaign funding which is visible in official figures has increased more than the overall sums spent, even it is still probably below 50 per cent (Barsukova and Zvyagintsev 2006; Kurtov and Kagan 2002: 110; unattributable interviews with Moscow-based political consultants).

8. Party political broadcasts: Each party running for election is allocated an equal number of party political broadcasts and advertisements in state television, radio and press outlets. However, since 1999, parties which have used their 'free' advertising but failed to win a minimum share of the vote (2 per cent in 1999 and 2003, and 3 per cent in 2007) have been obliged to repay the costs of these broadcasts within twelve months, the cost of which can dwarf their actual campaign turnovers and render a marketing-based campaign more risky. This also makes it easier for major parties or candidates to stay in power with less need to be or remain market-oriented.

9. Other media coverage: Analysis of media coverage during election campaigns shows that, notwithstanding the rules on equality of airtime for party political broadcasts, pro-Kremlin parties and candidates dominate in the television news. The ownership of the media and press in Russia is a complex web of interdependence between different holding companies, many of which are privately owned – particularly in the print media (RBK 2006). Successive waves of election media monitoring have shown that the coverage given to the 'parties of power' in the state television news programmes has been disproportionately large and positive, and that to their main opponents usually negative or negligible (e.g. CJES 2007). Once again, this has important implications for marketing strategy. For the 'parties of power', the main means by which their image is defined is through the airwaves. For more programmatic parties, particularly the Communists, access to the airwaves is both editorially difficult and financially expensive. Consequently, their marketing strategies tend to rely on more traditional techniques such as leafleting, canvassing and holding street meetings.

Political marketing techniques in Russia

Russian political marketing – or, to use the Russian term, 'electoral technology' (*izbiratel'naya tekhnologiya*) – is not a straightforward transfer of American or even West European expertise. There is a multi-billion dollar political consulting market with its own techniques and values. As Andrew Wilson (2005) has demonstrated, the Russian model, which has been copied in other post-Soviet states, builds on an indigenous political culture that extends back to the pre-communist era and combines it with more recognisable forms of modern marketing. A significant number of Russian campaign professionals have produced handbooks about the unique aspects of their work (e.g., Berezkina 1997; Egorova-Gantman and Mintusov 2002; Lisovsky and Evstaf'ev 2000; Lyzlov 1999; Maksimov 1999; Malkin and Suchkov 2008; Panarin 2004; Sorokina 2003; Tsuladze 2000; Yanbukhtin 2008), although with the exception of Wilson's and Oates's (2006) studies, little comparative academic attention has been paid to the phenomenon in the Russian context.

The use of Western campaigning techniques enjoyed a difficult baptism, detailed analysis of which can be found elsewhere (Hutcheson 2006; Wilson 2005). Its first notable victory was Boris Yeltsin's second presidential election victory in 1996. For the first time, a clear strategy of market segmentation was used successfully in a Russian campaign, and it resurrected his poll rating from single figures (Mickiewicz 1999; OSCE/ODIHR 1996). The following four years marked a period of 'unlimited flights of fantasy' for Russian political marketers (Sanaev 2005: 8): elections were characterized by innovative campaign methods in a relatively under-regulated environment, where the creativity of the consultants was constrained mainly by their ethical codes and financial restraints. The 1999 State Duma campaign and 2000 presidential elections marked the zenith of this 'creative and dirty' phase, since when the independent political consulting market has become more constrained and institutionalized into party structures.

The changes to electoral legislation during the Putin years, and the development of the political system under 'managed' (or, as the authorities prefer to denote it, 'sovereign') democracy, have had a significant effect on the political consulting market. Considerable legislative tightening has narrowed the market for independent consultants. As a result, middle-sized companies which had previously derived much of their income from single-member district and regional gubernatorial and legislative campaigns face an increasing challenge for survival and many are moving into the sphere of business PR (Bekker 2006; Filimonova 2005; Kochalov 2006; Mintusov interview 2006). Related to this has been a professionalization of the industry *per se*; more people employed within it nowadays have had academic training in marketing theory, and 'one-man band' election consultants have been replaced by more multi-vectored companies. Furthermore, whereas previously businesses tended to split their funds across a number of parties, only the 'parties of power' are now in a position to deliver policy results consistently, further strengthening their resource base and weakening that of other parties.

The absolute level of resources put into elections has arguably declined less, since financial-industrial groups are now prepared to devote more resources to other regional legislative and municipal election campaigns (Mintusov interviews 2006, 2008). Moreover, at the level of elections to the State Duma, candidates now face two marketing challenges *within* the party structures themselves. The first is to get themselves sufficiently high up a list to stand a chance of election in the first place (Buribaev *et al.* 2006); and the second is to ensure that their regional list markets itself sufficiently well relative to other regions. (Seats within a party's overall total are allocated across different regional lists according to each region's relative share of the party's overall votes.)

Perhaps most significantly, the increasing predictability of politics in the Putin era, and the reduction in the number of electoral organizations involved, has led to more consulting being done 'in-house' by political parties, whose primary interest is now in having permanent structures throughout the country rather than using professional non-partisan consultants on a one-off basis (Mintusov interview 2008; Yanbukhtin 2008: 48–9). Many of the staff of these party campaign units are former employees of the larger independent companies.

Political marketing strategy in Russia

The 1999 State Duma election saw the creation of successful 'broadcast' parties (Oates 2006: 66–88) – parties created on the basis of little infrastructure, with a heavy emphasis on the promotion of an image. Subsequent elections have witnessed the eventual domination of the electoral arena by such parties and the decline of programmatic ones. In part this is due to an increasingly sophisticated understanding of the needs and wants of the electorate. However, if a market-oriented party is considered to use political marketing as a means of understanding the public, rather than manipulating it (see Chapter 1), the degree of administrative resources used to back these campaigns make it hard to argue that the 'broadcast' parties fulfil the criteria for being considered purely market-oriented parties.

Table 15.2 gives a preliminary attempt to classify the major parties in Russian elections since 1993 according to the Lees-Marshment Model. Arguably, true market-oriented parties are still relatively rare in Russia. There have been a number of successful attempts to formulate new political parties from scratch based on finding an electoral niche. However, few parties have succeeded in adopting a true market-oriented 'permanent campaign' approach from election to election. The possible exception to this is the populist Liberal Democratic Party of Russia, which has won representation in all five Duma elections. The dominant pro-Kremlin United Russia party may also be considered a partial exception to the rule, as will be seen below. However, the fact that its attempts at product adjustment are accompanied by a very strong administrative effort to sell the party probably render its approach something of a hybrid between the market- and sales-oriented approaches.

Parties of power

An understanding of the Russian party system begins with the role of the 'party of power'. 'Parties of power' have been successive political structures formed *from within* by the entrenched establishment to consolidate and legitimize its rule

Table 15.2 Party orientations and percentage of votes in Russia, 1993–2007

	1993	1995	1999	2003	2007
'Parties of Power'					
Russia's Choice	SOP (15.5)	SOP* (3.9)			
Our Home is Russia		SOP (10.1)			
Bloc of Ivan Rybkin		SOP (1.1)			
Unity			MOP (22.3)		
Fatherland-All-Russia			MOP/ SOP (13.3)		
United Russia				MOP/SOP (37.6)	MOP/SOP (64.3)
Leftist Parties					
Communist Party of the Russian Federation	POP (12.4)	POP (22.3)	POP (24.3)	POP (12.6)	POP (11.6)
**Motherland				MOP (9.0)	
**Fair Russia					MOP/SOP (7.7)
Nationalist/Populist					
Liberal Democratic Party of Russia	MOP (22.9)	MOP (11.2)	MOP (6.0)	MOP (11.5)	MOP (8.2)
Liberals/Democrats					
Union of Rightist Forces			MOP (8.5)	SOP (4.0)	SOP (1.0)
Yabloko	SOP (7.9)	SOP (6.9)	POP (5.9)	POP (4.3)	POP (1.6)

Sources: Post-election publications of the Central Electoral Commission of the Russian Federation

Notes: * Russia's Choice evolved into Russia's Democratic Choice in 1995, and ceased to be the main 'party of power'. ** Motherland and Fair Russia could also be considered 'parties of power', as noted below.

through a party façade (Overloot and Verheul 2000). Their party platforms have lacked ideological foundation, and their identities have been defined through market-oriented, media-driven television campaigns to position themselves within gaps in the electoral market. These virtual structures have in turn been given a public face through the presence of prominent national politicians, regional governors, and numerous middle-ranking state officials to the party's regional leadership organs. It is this which differentiates the Russian phenomenon of the 'party of power' from that of dominant political parties in more traditional democracies, which have first used political marketing to reposition themselves and then had to gain elected office from a position of opposition.

As the vote shares shown in Table 15.2 illustrate, attempts to set up dominant 'parties of power' in the mid-1990s – Russia's Choice in 1993 and Our Home is Russia in 1995 – largely failed against the more traditional product-oriented marketing of the left-wing opposition. The pro-Kremlin parties' early attempts to use marketing in the mid-1990s focused too much on the 'outputs' – professional-looking advertisements – and neglected real marketing features such as product assessment and product adjustment in the 'inputs' (Malkin and Suchkov 2008: 88–89; Oates 2006: 91–102). As a result, a sales-oriented approach was inadvertently adopted which sought to sell unpopular government policies and leaders to a sceptical electorate, rather than reflect its aspirations. However, the situation has reversed since 1999, and the 'party of power' has been the dominant electoral form in the second decade of Russian independence.

The success of the 'parties of power' is based on a variety of factors, not the least of which is the tremendous administrative capital advantage that comes with the backing of the federal and regional administrations, domination of television news coverage, and the reflected popularity of a popular president. These aspects probably render the approach partially sales-oriented. Indeed, the advertising strategy of the main party of power in recent elections – United Russia – has been very centralized and disciplined, concentrating on message saturation by focusing on a narrow range of issues, deliberately simple messages, and a unitary style across the whole country (Yanbukhtin 2008: 89–108). This is in contrast to earlier post-Soviet elections in which there was a very regional focus to election campaigning in such a vast country (Hutcheson 2001).

Nonetheless, the United Russia exhibits several traits of a marketing-oriented party. First, its primary target in each election has been to augment its core electorate of centrist non-ideological voters – a potential 35 per cent of the electorate when its predecessor Unity was established in 1999 (New Russia Barometer VIII 2000) – with pro-Putin voters from other parties. This is a classic 'catch-all' party aim, and its main campaign strategies have focused on de-emphasizing ideology and linking its brand with that of the president (Yanbukhtin 2008: 44). In each election, it has been careful to avoid creating a 'product' on which its delivery could be tested. In emphasizing its freshness and desire for a strong, safe and non-corrupt Russian state (Lisovsky and Evstaf'ev 2000: 282–89), it hoped in 1999 that voters from different sectors of the electorate would project their own image onto it (URF interview 2002). More recently, it has sought to define itself as the party of the national interest, conflating its identity with that of the state itself. Indeed, so successfully was this achieved in 2003 that much of its distinctive advertising literature for a 'strong and united Russia' did not even feature the party's name or logo (Yanbukhtin 2008: 103). Moreover, it has sought to capitalize on its support from Vladimir Putin both implicitly (such as in its slogan 'Together with the President' in 2003, when Putin officially stood aloof from the contest) and more explicitly in 2007, when Putin headed its party list and the party sought to redefine the election as 'a national referendum on Putin' (*Rossiiskaya Gazeta*, 17 October 2007: 1). In rebranding him as the 'national leader' (United Russia manifesto 2007), its attempt to polarize the electorate carried the subliminal message that anybody not voting for his party was implicitly unpatriotic. Two-thirds of United Russia's voters said that they had voted for it because Putin was heading it, rather than for its programme (Levada survey 2008).

Second, United Russia's choice of campaign issues, candidate selections, and strategic decisions have been determined by market research. Interestingly, the party has preferred to use sociological firms from different regions to the ones they are reporting on to ensure their objectivity from local politics and influences (Yanbukhtin 2008: 36, 55–63). Moreover, its positioning within the political arena has been carefully calculated: for example, it decided on a very narrow list of six themes on which to concentrate its entire 2003 campaign (chosen in response to research), and attached the presentation of each to a particular person in the party leadership, the aim being to position each at a particular point between the centre-left and centre-right electorates and personify the party's political position as that of the broad centre (ibid.: 66).

The third element of the Kremlin's success in recent years has been successful segmentation of the electorate. While Unity/United Russia have targeted the pro-Putin centrist voters, other satellite 'parties of power' have been established on the ideological territory of main rivals to harness other sectors of the electorate – the liberal-oriented Union of Rightist Forces in 1999; the 'virtual' left-wing party Motherland (*Rodina*), formed in 2003 to draw left-wing voters from the Communists (Sagareva 2004); and the social-democratic Fair Russia formed for the same purpose in 2007. Admittedly, the segmentation strategy faltered slightly on that occasion after the decision was made to polarize the election around Vladimir Putin's own involvement in the United Russia campaign, which left its centre-left partner to carry out the difficult balancing act of being 'in opposition to the ruling liberal United Russia party but supportive of Vladimir Putin', its leading candidate (Mironov 2007).

The success of the 'party of power' model in the last decade gives several important indications. The rise of United Russia and other satellite 'parties of power' has been reinforced by the consolidation of the elite, such that 'administrative resources' in Russian election campaigns have become a unipolar resource. United Russia's primary advantage, as Putin himself has noted, is that it is 'close to the power structures' even through it still lacks any unifying ideology (*Kommersant'*, 14 November 2007: 1). The 1990s showed, however, that being close to power does not in itself guarantee success if the product is not designed properly. In other words, a 'party of power' cannot be created without effective segmentation, market research, and targeting of the electoral middle ground. Nonetheless, the increasingly overt use of administrative pressure at all levels makes it doubtful that we can refer to the 'parties of power' as true market-oriented parties; they have not only adapted their policies and images to the market, but adapted the market itself through their domination of it. As a result, it would probably be more accurate to describe them as hybrid marketing- and sales-oriented parties.

Communist Party of the Russian Federation

Alongside the Liberal Democratic Party of Russia, examined below, the Communist Party of the Russian Federation (CPRF) is the longest-standing actor in the Russian party system. It considers itself the official successor to the Soviet ruling party, although its ranks are primarily those of the ideological 'true believers', as many key personnel from its Soviet predecessor continued to occupy elite positions in the 1990s and were to be found amongst the various 'parties of power' rather than in the communist opposition. In the 1995 and 1999 State Duma elections it came in first place in the party list vote, basing its appeal on the dual pillars of ideologically driven left-wing voters and protest voters disenchanted with the reform process, but has performed less well since the turn of the century.

Its electoral strategies and party platforms have tended to follow fairly similar lines on each occasion. The party has entered each election campaign with essentially the same platform: opposition to the ruling class, socialism and pro-Russian nationalism, indicating a tendency towards product orientation. Aside from the free party political broadcasts, it has spent noticeably less on television advertising than its main competitors. Instead, its focus has been on mobilizing a defined electorate through grass-roots activities. Moreover, lacking access to state television and resources to buy additional access, it has concentrated on distributing information through its own newspapers, such as *Pravda* and *Sovetskaya Rossiya* (Zyuganov 2004: 75).

Until the early 2000s, this was consistent with the paradox it faced as the dominant actor in the crowded bloc of the leftist opposition groups: it could not move towards the centre without risking the loss of potential supporters to smaller, more hard-line left-wing parties (Robinson 1998: 165). The converse was also true; it could not expand its electorate substantially by moving further towards the extremes, as it gained many of its votes from this wing already. Since then, it has faced additional problems, primarily that Putin's emphasis on a strong state and the defence of Russian national interests has echoes of its own rhetoric, leaving it, in the words of one commentator, 'politically unemployed' (*Vek*, 24–31 August 2001: 4).

Nonetheless, in the context of managed democracy, and as the only party of a left-wing oppositional stance that stands a realistic chance of winning more than 7 per cent of the vote, it now has an effective monopoly of that sector of the electorate, which is smaller than in the 1990s but still accounts for a relatively consistent share of voters (12.6 per cent in 2003 and 11.6 per cent in 2007). The CPRF's benign but vocal opposition is useful to the establishment in demonstrating the maintenance of political pluralism, which it keeps in check through competition from the left-wing 'sub-parties' of power – Motherland in 2003 and Fair Russia in 2007 – whose voters are less entrenched in their opposition to the regime (Wilson 2005: 235–6). As such, although the CPRF talks optimistically of recapturing its late 1990s electorate and adding 15 per cent to it (Zyuganov 2005: 88), the fact that it is a programmatic party with a distinct electoral niche mitigates against adopting a market-oriented approach, as its scope to reach beyond its own electorate is somewhat limited.

Liberal Democratic Party of Russia

The only party apart from the CPRF to have been represented in all five State Dumas is the populist-nationalist Liberal Democratic Party of Russia (LDPR). In the sense that it has carefully honed its campaigns and platforms between elections, the LDPR is probably the closest Russia has to a true market-oriented party, albeit a charismatic one which has engaged in the process to maintain an electoral presence, rather than to develop into a 'catch-all' organization. Led by (and essentially the party of) the flamboyant Vladimir Zhirinovsky, it was initially founded in March 1990 as the Liberal Democratic Party of the Soviet Union (LDPSU), and its greatest success came when it unexpectedly won the party list vote in 1993. In the remaining elections of the 1990s its support roughly halved at every subsequent election, but in 2003 and 2007 it maintained a presence.

The party's name is somewhat misleading: for most of its existence, it has not advocated liberalism, but rather imperialism, nationalism, and protectionism. Nor is it a party in the traditional sense of the word, but essentially the political infrastructure of its leader and his entourage. Using careful research, Zhirinovsky and the LDPR have mastered the art of aiming their pitch at a specific sector of the electorate. The typical LDPR voter is less likely to approve of the government's work than the average voter (Russian Research Surveys 2004, 2008), and the party attempts to appeal to this anti-establishment sector of the electorate. It has focused its fire in successive elections on different 'enemies' of Russia, according to whichever has appeared most dangerous at the time (which in turn is established through careful market research). Nonetheless, its overtly oppositionist stance masks the fact that in reality it often votes with the establishment it publicly opposes. Some of Zhirinovsky's more outlandish ideas, such as the legalization of polygamy as a means of solving the country's demographic crisis (*Kommersant'*, 26 October 2000: 9), are aimed at maintaining this anti-system image whilst masking the close relationship between the LDPR and pro-government forces.

Liberals and Democrats

Two parties are of interest in the traditional liberal wing of the Russian party system: Yabloko and the Union of Rightist Forces. Although they are often perceived as feeding off the same electorate, they do have slightly different positions and approaches to political campaigning.

Yabloko was the only party apart from the CPRF and LDPR to win election to the first three State Dumas in the 1990s, but its support has since dwindled. Like the CPRF, Yabloko has consistently eschewed a market approach to campaigning, although it did manage to tap into public disenchantment over the war in Chechnya in the 1995 election and benefited from favourable links with Vladimir Gusinsky, the owner of the leading non-state TV channel at the time. Its approach might have been considered sales-oriented in the first two State Duma elections. Since then, however, it has arguably moved towards a product-oriented strategy, espousing essentially the same platform of a 'socially oriented market economy' and opposition to Putin in successive elections, and failing to adapt to the changed political landscape around it (Manikhin 2003: 89–105). Despite falling below the 5 per cent party list threshold for the first time in 2003, it continued to refuse co-operation with other liberal-right organizations despite the changed institutional circumstances surrounding it, and crashed to an even more ignominious defeat in 2007. Deeper collaboration which would impinge upon the party's independent identity has been resisted by the party leader Grigorii Yavlinsky, indicating also the fact that Yabloko, despite having had a consistent liberal ideology throughout its existence, is another party to be dominated by its leader. It was only in the face of its apparently terminal electoral decline that Yavlinsky stood aside as party leader in June 2008, having headed the party since its foundation, and he remained on its political council.

The Union of Rightist Forces (URF), formed in September 1999, came into existence in response to the collapse of the 'old right' (including the remnants of 1993's 'party of power', Russia's Choice), which had formed the backbone of the government from the collapse of the USSR until the financial crash of August 1998. It sought to consolidate and reinvigorate the moribund and fragmented liberal wing of the party system. Whereas the 'old right' had concentrated on a sales-oriented approach, from the beginning the Union of Rightist Forces' campaign was explicitly market-oriented. It carried out extensive research and sought to appeal to two constituencies: the traditional liberal electorate, and the younger sector of the electorate. Its image was constructed to emphasize youth and 'coolness', a strategy which took its support from below 4 per cent to 8.5 per cent, helped also in part by implicit backing from the Kremlin. However, in the longer term its attempt to straddle the pro-Kremlin and liberal divide created great problems for it, and its initial success as a market-oriented organization has waned. In 2003 it returned to the sales-oriented approach used in earlier elections, depicting its party leaders (including the unpopular Anatolii Chubias, head of the United Energy Systems and architect of the Russian privatization programme) working on a laptop computer in a private jet, demonstrably out of touch with the life of the average voter. By 2007 the party had been completely marginalized, and sought to depict itself as a persecuted liberal minority. Its 0.96 per cent of the vote confirmed that at least the latter part of its assessment was true.

Political marketing trends and conclusion

This chapter has presented some preliminary findings about the Russian political consulting market and the nature of market-oriented politics in the Russian Federation. The era of 'managed democracy' has witnessed changes in the electoral and political consulting markets. Greater legislative specificity combined with more restricted electoral opportunities have resulted in a concentration of the market at the top and bottom of the sector, with an increasing diversification of political marketing firms into other forms of public relations. At the same time, the pro-Kremlin political parties have moved more of their political marketing inside their own structures.

The restricted competition of the 'managed democracy' era has placed a premium on the identification of gaps in the electoral market. These have been effectively filled by specially formed 'broadcast parties' or 'parties of power' – administratively backed structures which rely on the twin pillars of establishment support and effective media strategy, even in the absence of a grass-roots organization. The electorate has become increasingly polarized into pro- and anti-Kremlin blocs, the latter of which accounts for approximately one-quarter of the electorate.

For the 'parties of power', something approaching a market-oriented strategy has been a useful way of creating a 'catch-all' product utilizing their core asset – Vladimir Putin – by conflating support for the president with pride in the Russian state. However, the overwhelming use of administrative resources and legislative engineering in the process mean that it is not only the parties which are adapting to the market; the market is itself being adapted by the parties, and the 'parties of power' have grafted a market-based approach onto a strongly sales-based approach based on Putin's repuation. Balanced against this, the parties competing for the other quarter of the electorate – generally more programmatic in their nature – have limited access to state resources, and small scope for electoral expansion as their key voters are in relatively distinct niches. This creates a disincentive towards market-orientation, as their greatest chance of electoral success lies in the successful mobilization of core supporters based on a consistent programme. The pure product-oriented approach chosen by some parties has arguably been less successful than the more sales-oriented version chosen by others.

The institutional framework of the Russian electoral market has created a situation in which pure market-orientation is relatively rare. Parties are relatively polarized in their campaigning techniques depending on their place in the party system. Arguably, the 'parties of power' have developed a market-sales hybrid model which serves simultaneously to sell a product and to define the marketplace in the first place. Programmatic parties display attributes of more traditional campaigning methods but these are a logical response to the framework of the party system. In contrast to the more distinct differences in campaigning methods seen in other countries in this volume, the combination of political marketing and managed democracy has led in many cases to blurred boundaries between the three campaigning models in the Lees-Marshment framework.

Acknowledgements

Various grants have contributed towards fieldwork and data materials for the current study, in particular British Academy Small Research Grants SG-35159 and SG-40918, and UCD Seed Funding Grant SF-149.

References/further reading

Primary and Secondary Literature

Barsukova, S. Y. and Zvyagintsev, V. I. (2006) 'Mekhanizm "politicheskogo investirovaniya", ili kak i zachem rossiisskii biznes uchastvuet v vyborakh i oplachivaet partiinuyu zhizn', *Polis*, 2: 110–21.

Bekker, V. (2006) 'Politkonsalting ili agitprop?', *Politicheskii Zhurnal*, 19 June. Available at: <http://www.nikkolom.ru/2006/10_07_06_31iarticle.htm> (accessed 5 June 2009).

Berezkina, O. (1997) *Kak stat' deputatom ili prodat' sebya na politicheskom rynke*, St Petersburg: Izdatel'stvo Bukovskogo.

Buribaev, A., Pis'mennaya, E. and Guseva, D. (2006) 'Dumasedy i tol'ko', *Russkii Newsweek*, 3–9 July: 14–19.

CJES [Centre for Journalism in Extreme Situations] (2007) 'Vtoroi otchet o rezul'tatakh monitoringa SMI v ramkakh vyborov v Gosudarstvennuyu Dumy Rossiiskoi Federatsii 2007 (1 oktyabrya – 22 noyabrya 2007)'. Available at: <http://www.memo98.cjes.ru/?p=3&sm2=on&reports=200711> (accessed 5 June 2009).

Egorova-Gantman, E. and Mintusov, I. (eds) (2002) *Politicheskoe konsul'tirovanie*, 2nd edn, Moscow: Nikkolo M.

Filiminova, V. (2005) 'Piarshchiki "v zakone" ', *Politicom.ru* [online journal]. Available at: <http://www.politcom.ru/2005/prsoob38.php> (accessed 5 June 2009).

Hutcheson, D. S. (2001) 'Campaigning in the Russian Regions: The Case of Ul'yanovsk', *Journal of Communist Studies and Transition Politics*, 17: 70–93.

—— (2003) *Political Parties in the Russian Regions*, London/New York: Routledge Curzon.

—— (2006) 'How to Win Elections and Influence People: The Development of Political Consulting in Post-Communist Russia', *Journal of Political Marketing*, 5: 47–70.

Kochalov, M. (2006) 'Transformatsiya PR-rynka i PR-industrii v putinskie vremena', *Sovetnik*, 1, 30 January.

Kurtov, A. and Kagan, M. (2002) *Okhota na drakona: Razmyshleniya o vyborakh i politicheskom konsul'tirovanii*, Moscow: GUVShE.

Lisovsky, S. F. and Evstaf'ev, V. A. (2000) *Izbiratel'nye tekhnologii: Istoriya, teoriya, praktika*, Moscow: RAU-Universitet.

Lyzlov, V. E. (1999) *Pobeda, tol'ko pobeda!*, Moscow: PAIMS.

Maksimov, A. A. (1999) *'Chistye' i 'gryaznye' tekhnologii vyborov: Rossiiskii opyt*, Moscow: Delo.

Malkin, E. and Suchkov, E. (2008) *Politicheskie Tekhnologii*, 7th edn, Moscow: Russkaya Panorama.

Manikhin, O. (2003) *Rossiiskaya demokraticheskaya partiya Yabloko: Kratkii istoricheskii ocherk*, Moscow: Integral-Inform.

Mickiewicz, E. (1999) *Changing Channels: Television and the Struggle for Power in Russia*, 2nd edn, Durham NC; London: Duke University Press.

Mironov, S. (2007) 'Address of the Leader of "Fair Russia" Sergei Mironov to Voters', Interfax Press Conference, 30 November. Available at: <http://www.spravedlivo.ru/first_face/203.smx> (accessed 5 June 2009).

Napolitan, J. and Hutcheson, D. (2004) 'Vremya universalov ukhodit', *Sovetnik*, 2(98): 23–5.

Oates, S. (2006) *Television, Democracy and Elections in Russia*, London/New York: Routledge.

Overloot, H. and Verheul, R. (2000) 'The Party of Power in Russian Politics', *Acta Politica*, 35: 123–45.

OSCE/ODIHR (1996) *Final Report on the Presidential Election 1996*, Moscow: OSCE.

Panarin, I. N. (2004) *Informatsionnaya voina: Pobeda v Bashkirii*, Moscow: Gorodets.

RBK (2006) 'Rossiiskie SMI', *RBK*, April: 64–5.

Sagareva, O. (2004) *Eto 'Rodina' moya: Khronika genial'noi avantyury*, Moscow: Kraft+.

Sanaev, A. (2005) *Vybory v Rossii: Kak eto delaetsya*, Moscow: Os'-89.

Sorokina, E. (2003) *Kommunikatsiya v Period Izbiratel'noi Kampanii: Keis Stadis*, Moscow: Avanti.

Robinson, N. (1998) 'Classifying Russia's Party System: The Problem of "Relevance" in a Time of Uncertainty', *Journal of Communist Studies and Transition Politics*, 14: 159–77.

Tsuladze, A. (2000) *Bol'shaya manipulyativnaya igra*, Moscow: Algoritm.

Walecki, M. (2003) 'Money and Politics in Central and Eastern Europe', in R. Austin and M. Tjernström (eds) *Funding of Political Parties and Election Campaigns*, Stockholm: IDEA. [71–93]

United Russia Manifesto (2007) *Plan Putina: Dostoinoe budushchee velikoi stran*, Pre-Election Programme. Available at: <http://www.edinros.ru/news.html?id=124255> (accessed 2 October 2007).

Wilson, A. (2005) *Virtual Politics*, New Haven, CT; London: Yale University Press.

Yanbukhtin, E. (2008) *Edinaya Rossiya: Tekhnologii uspeshnoi izbiratel'noi kampanii*, Moscow: Vershina.

Zyuganov, G. (2004) 'Politicheskii otchet TsK KPRF X S"ezdu Kommunisticheskoi Partii Rossiskoi Federatsii', in *Materialy X S"ezdu KPRF*, Moscow: ITRK. [7–87]

—— (2005) *Bol'shchie ispytaniya: KPRF pered novym izbiratel'nym marafonom*, ITRK: Moscow.

Interviews

Igor Mintusov (2006 and 2008), Chairman of the Board of Directors, 'Nikkolo-M', 6 July 2006; 14 March 2008.

URF (2002) Senior Union of Rightist Forces campaign manager, 22 April (name unattributable).

In addition, the author has spoken to political consultants between 2002 and 2008 from several Moscow-based consulting companies who requested anonymity.

Surveys

Levada Centre post-election survey: Available at: <http://www.levada.ru/press/2008010901.html> (accessed 5 June 2009).

New Russia Barometer VIII (2000) Conducted by VTsIOM (All-Russian Centre for the Investigation of Public Opinion) on behalf of the Centre for the Study of Public Policy, University of Strathclyde, fieldwork 13–29 January 2000, N=1,940. (Used here with permission)

Russian Research (2004) 'Inclusion without Membership? Bringing Russia, Ukraine and Belarus closer to "Europe" ', National representative survey conducted by Russian Research Ltd (London/Moscow). ESRC funded (RES-00-23-0146). Fieldwork 21 December 2003 – 16 January 2004, N=2000. (Used here with permission)

Russian Research (2008) National representative survey conducted by Russian Research Ltd (London/Moscow). Part-funded by British Academy Small Research Grant BA-40918, held by the author, with support from the UK Economic and Social Research Council under grant RES-000-22-2532 to Ian McAllister and Stephen White. Fieldwork 30 January – 27 February 2008. N=2000.

16 Political market-orientation in Japan

Masahiko Asano and Bryce Wakefield

Japanese politics has long been dominated by the Liberal Democratic Party (LDP). This chapter seeks to address whether the LDP's political marketing strategies or those of its opponents have played a role in the ruling party's success, and whether these strategies have changed in light of new electoral laws introduced in the 1990s. After briefly outlining the Japanese political system and media in Japan, we turn our attention to political marketing strategies in the post-war period before providing an analysis of post-1993 strategies for each major non-LDP party in Japan. As the LDP's recent political marketing strategies and techniques have been in a state of flux, they are addressed in a case study on the 2005 election at the end of the chapter. The study is based on analysis of secondary and primary sources, and interviews with staff from Japan's three largest political parties.

The Japanese political marketplace

The Japanese electoral system

The Japanese National Diet (*kokkai*) is bicameral, however, the LDP has dominated both of Japan's houses since the party's inception in 1955. The Constitution of Japan allows the House of Councillors (*sangi'in* – Japan's upper house) to vote down non-budgetary legislation passed by the House of Representatives (*shūgi'in* – Japan's lower house), though until recently, LDP dominance of both houses has ensured that this prerogative was largely a nominal check on lower house power. Most analysis of electoral performance in Japan has therefore focused purely on the House of Representatives (see Kamijō, 1991; Tanaka, 2005).

One of the distinct characteristics of Japanese politics from 1925 until 1993 was its single non-transferable vote, multi-member district (SNTV-MMD) electoral system. Japanese voters cast a single vote for the candidate of their choice and depending on district magnitude the top three to five finishers gained a seat in each district. As there were only 130 districts delivering some 500 members to the House of Representatives, the LDP had to field more than one candidate in each district in order to capture an outright majority. The ability to capture more than one seat in each district skewed results radically towards the LDP and was a major cause of one-party dominance. As the system encouraged competition between

LDP members for multiple seats in each district, it also contributed to the emergence of party factions (Wada 1996: 10–11, 14–15).

The government of Japan abolished the SNTV-MMD system in January 1994 in response to public concerns about a string of political finance scandals and public accountability. The House of Representatives now consists of 480 members elected for a term of four years under a mixed member majoritarian (MMM) electoral system. Three hundred members are elected from regional constituencies by popular votes in plurality contests, and 180 (originally 200) members are elected from ranked party lists in large proportional districts across the country. Unlike mixed-member proportional (MMP) systems in Germany and New Zealand, however, the list is not corrective, and parties merely receive a proportion of members on the list that corresponds to their party vote, regardless of how many seats they win in the plurality districts.

Media in Japan

Japan has five national daily newspapers, with a total combined daily circulation of 69.1 million in 2007 (World Association of Newspapers, hereafter, WAN 2007).[1] The *Yomiuri Shimbun* and the *Asahi Shimbun* both maintain far higher circulations than any other newspaper in the world with a circulation of 14.08 and 12.2 million respectively. The centrist *Mainichi Shimbun*, the financial broadsheet the *Nihon Keizai Shimbun (Nikkei)* and the conservative *Sankei Shimbun* garner 4.0 million, 4.6 million and 2.7 million respective daily sales (WAN 2004). Newspaper readership has, however, declined in recent years (WAN 2007), due partly to the growing influence of the Internet. In addition to the 'Big 5' national newspapers, Japan has local and regional newspapers and daily mass-circulation party newspapers, such as the Japan Communist Party's *Akahata* (Red Flag). Although some studies show that a certain degree of self-censorship and elite 'capture' of the media takes place (Freeman 2000), no party has formal links with the major national dailies. Indeed, newspapers have often been highly critical of the government and its leaders, some (such as the *Asahi*) more than others.[2]

Nippon Hōsō Kyōkai (NHK), the state-run Japanese broadcaster, has been the primary source of television information in Japan since 1950. Nevertheless, NHK has increasingly lost more of its audience to the 'Big 5' commercial stations, each of which has organizational and financial links to Japan's major daily newspapers. Content analysis conducted on NHK news coverage in the 1980s and 1990s found no consistent bias towards any one party (Krauss 2000: 33). However, Krauss argues that NHK's decline in popularity coincides with changes in Japanese society after World War II. The late 1980s through to the 1990s witnessed increasing rates of political cynicism and public disgust with official corruption and malfeasance (Krauss 2000: 9). Allegations of corruption impacted heavily on the NHK after 2004, when it was revealed that its employees had embezzled funds from the corporation. At the same time, the broadcaster was alleged to have given in to pressure from conservative politicians to censor a documentary dealing with Japanese sex slavery in World War II (*Japan Times*, 11 February 2005). Viewers responded with their wallets, and by 2005 more than a million subscribers had refused to pay their annual NHK receiver's fees (IHT/*Asahi*, 24 February 2005), which are often collected by NHK employees going door-to-door.

Despite the NHK's woes and declining newspaper circulation, newspapers and television are still an important source of political news in Japan. A 2007 *Yomiuri* poll showed that most respondents (69.6 per cent) still think the NHK 'plays a large role' in 'quickly communicating the events of the world' (*yo no naka no dekigoto*). Most viewers (63.8 per cent) turn to 'regular newspapers' for background and details related to news stories, whereas commercial stations were considered the best source (58.8 per cent) for addressing 'injustice in society or of those in power'. The Internet scored much lower than newspapers, the NHK and commercial television channels in these three categories (33.1, 10.7 and 10.6 per cent respectively). Also, 92.5 per cent of respondents claimed to read newspapers and 53.6 per cent read them for an average of half an hour or more per day (*Yomiuri* Poll, conducted 6–7 October, 2007). The influence of national dailies and the television networks on political opinion should therefore not be underestimated.

There are, however, strict restrictions on political advertising in Japan. Japanese electoral laws originally prohibited political candidates from buying space in newspapers or magazines, or time on television and radio. Following the revision of the law in 1975, political parties have been able to advertise more freely, but advertisements cannot mention the candidacy of particular party members (Pharr 1996: 7). As long as party advertising stays within the domain of 'political activity' by advocating policy or focusing on the leadership, however, there are no restrictions on using the mass media even during the campaign period. Nevertheless parties must not step into the domain of 'electoral activity' by advertising for a particular candidate on television or in newspapers.

Political marketing strategy in Japan

In order to understand recent changes in the way parties have marketed themselves to the Japanese public, it is useful to examine the historical context within which they have developed their political marketing strategies. In the post-war period, the Japan Communist Party (JCP) and the Socialist Party of Japan (SPJ) maintained strong positions on ideological issues at the expense of highlighting concerns closer to voters' daily lives. Both parties were particularly wary of the US–Japan Mutual Security Treaty that saw American forces based on Japanese soil. In addition to opposing the treaty, the left-wing parties prevented conservative governments from amending the nation's constitution which, written after Japan's defeat in war, banned the use of force as an instrument of state policy.

The way the two major left-wing parties communicated with their voters highlighted their role as product-oriented parties. The parties chose to argue their point of view through associated elites in the media, unions and academia who were more receptive to their message than the general public. The SPJ, in particular, relied on *Sōhyō*, a giant federation of industrial unions. However, the party's dependence on this organization 'dictated a doctrinal orthodoxy of sorts' (Tani 1992: 89), alienating many mainstream voters. In addition to its own contacts with unions, the JCP communicated to members through *Akahata*. Left-wing leaders thus 'claimed the authority *as professional politicians* to control and direct the organization and ideological content of the movement against' the security treaty and placed opposition to US bases within the frame of the Marxist principles of their parties (Sasaki-Uemura 2002: 83). They were less concerned with building mainstream support and more concerned with communicating their message from above, as is typical of product-oriented parties.

Moreover, many on the left were satisfied with their place outside government because, partly due to the SNTV-MMD voting system, they consistently garnered enough votes to deny the LDP the two-thirds majority necessary to revise the constitution. While many Communist and Socialist candidates were thus aware that a product-oriented approach would not bring electoral success, they nevertheless held the 'product' to be more important than popular support (Aspinall 2006: 78). As a result, the SPJ's share of the total vote peaked in 1958 at 32.9 per cent (32 per cent of the seats) and declined almost continuously until 1990, although the JCP made gains during this time (Kamijō 1991: 41, 54).

LDP members, in contrast, understood the importance of conducting market intelligence, designing and adjusting their policies accordingly before implementation, and communicating their policy messages to potential voters. The LDP's initial platform included conservative goals such as constitutional revision and changes to liberal education policies implemented under the post-war American occupation, but these were downplayed from 1960 as the ruling party, responding to public opposition to constitutional change, focused on the more immediate economic concerns of voters. The avoidance of a strong ideological platform was also a result of the multi-member district electoral system. As the system placed members of the same party in competition, ruling party candidates had to make use of their personalities and connections rather than attempt to formulate a coherent party platform based on a set of common principles.

Candidates therefore nurtured *kōenkai* – private support organizations affiliated with individual candidates rather than the LDP. *Kōenkai*, which still exist, are also a response to the strict advertising regulations, as members engage in campaign activities – such as door-knocking and distributing leaflets – that are illegal if conducted by the party or candidate (Christensen 1998: 991). The *kōenkai* also act as a conduit for information between the candidates and their constituents, their broad membership constantly providing a source of market information at the local level (Woodall 1996: 90). Communication between the candidates and the public is thus a continuous process. It is not separated into discrete steps as in Lees-Marshment's description of a market-oriented party. Nevertheless the *kōenkai* incorporate important elements contained in the market-oriented model.

Kōenkai are not merely an avenue for information. Because contributions to *kōenkai* were not included in official party fund totals, they provided an important revenue source for candidates' campaigns. As LDP representatives came to rely on these funds after the war, they become beholden to private interests at the local level (Kitaoka 2000: 180–182), resulting in a system where LDP candidates would use their influence with the bureaucracy in Tokyo to secure lucrative public construction projects, government assistance for loyal constituents in sectors such as agriculture and other favours. As concrete flowed to LDP districts, loyal voters were rewarded with jobs while local contributors were rewarded with contracts and subsidies. Post-war development thus continued apace and the system ensured that communication with voters was highly region-specific. At a national level, meanwhile, the party emphasized the economic gains felt by the voter, and on occasion showed great flexibility in dealing with voter demands, particularly in the areas of environmental policy and lifestyle improvement during the 1970s (Stockwin 1999: 145). General elections almost became a matter of course as voters responded positively to the economic inducements offered by LDP candidates.

Such a system, however, was contingent on the delivery of policy promises made by local candidates to their constituents. While the system of patronage at the local level was well suited to a nation engaged in post-war reconstruction, it depended on the central government's ability to manage the economy in order to provide funds for subsidies and public protests. In the early 1980s manipulation of the exchange rate precipitated a real-estate bubble which deflated early in the 1990s, throwing the economy into a decade-long recession. In the context of economically leaner times, the corruption that had arisen from close working relationships between the government and business interests eroded public faith in the LDP. The system that the party had built in the post-war period was inadequate to deal with new challenges before the nation. The government fell to a vote of no-confidence and was replaced by an unwieldy eight-party coalition made up of traditional opposition parties and LDP offshoots in 1993. The SPJ left the coalition less than ten months later and in a move that shocked all observers joined the LDP in forming a new government. The LDP–JSP coalition revised the electoral system in 1994 in order to check single-party dominance, but the LDP has nevertheless remained the dominant party in government by negotiating coalitions and support deals with minor parties.

Party strategies since 1993

Despite Japan's economic problems, LDP politicians were reluctant to change their policies to suit the new economic and electoral conditions. However, other parties in Japan were still attempting to come to terms with the new electoral system and no clear challenger to LDP dominance emerged until the end of the 1990s. Since then, changes to party marketing strategies have seen most parties moderate their platforms to a certain extent.

The DPJ

Since 1998 the main challenger to the LDP has been the Democratic Party of Japan (DPJ). The DPJ has drawn its members from factions that split from the LDP and the Socialist party during the 1990s and has grown through a series of amalgamations. It is not surprising then that the DPJ has factions of its own. Although the party leadership has attempted to stem public criticism of the party as disjointed (Hyde 2006: 110–111), it has occasionally faced criticism even from within its own ranks for its attempts to create a unified party image at the expense of substantive policy platforms that will inspire public trust (*Yomiuri Shimbun*, 15 January 2007).

Concerns about unity notwithstanding, the DPJ has improved its performance by importing concepts employed overseas by market-oriented parties. Prior to 2003, *kōyaku* (lit. 'pledges') issued by Japanese political parties to the electorate were often vague and were largely a statement of party goals without an explanation of policy strategies to achieve them. Nevertheless, public demands for greater political accountability soon prompted at least one gubernatorial candidate to adopt a manifesto outlining his specific policies in addition to his objectives, and by 2003 academics and civil society groups were increasingly advocating that Japanese political actors present detailed manifestos as part of their campaigns (Tanaka 2005: 227–228). The same year, the DPJ became the first party in Japan to adopt the technique for use in a national election, and publicised their '*manifesuto*' as representing a new type of contract between the public and a political party. While the DPJ's campaign communication focused more on explaining the notion of a manifesto to the Japanese public and less on the policy product contained therein, the party's approach signalled that its leaders were beginning to understand key aspects of the market-oriented strategy.

It was clear that the DPJ strategy was, in part, an import from Britain. Party leader Kan Naoto, aware that the British Labour Party had effectively used manifestos in its 1997 and 2001 campaigns, even dispatched DPJ members to the United Kingdom to study Labour's election strategy (*Kyodo News International*, 3 November 2003). When Prime Minister Koizumi Jun'ichirō attacked the DPJ's manifesto in the Diet as 'just a *kōyaku*, even if you change its name', Kan mentioned Blair's 2001 'Contract Delivered' campaign slogan, and noted that unlike the LDP's *kōyaku*, the British public could check Labour's performance against specific promises made in past manifestos (National Diet Records, 156th Session, National Basic Policy Committee Joint Council, No. 7, 11 June 2003). Later, on the eve of a state visit by the British Prime Minister, Kan even said that he wanted Koizumi to 'exchange views with Prime Minister Blair' so that he could come to 'acknowledge the differences between the ruling parties' [pledges] and the opposition's manifestos' (National Diet Records, 156th Session, House of Councillors Budget Committee, No. 26, 18 July 2003).

The DPJ's techniques worked well in 2003. Although some in the mass media criticized the factionalized nature of the party and 'thermometric differences' between its headquarters and its candidates (*Nishi Nihon Shimbun*, 6 October 2003) the party raised its share of the total vote by 7.41 per cent in the plurality seats and gained 50 more seats than it had after the previous election (Tanaka 2006: 235–236). Other parties have recognized the DPJ's success and even the LDP under Koizumi adopted a more detailed set of 'promises' for the 2005 election, as discussed below.

The JCP

Nevertheless, some parties still adhere strongly to product-oriented principles. It is clear, for example, that the JCP, historically the most product-oriented party on the Japanese political spectrum, remains proud of its record. Ichida Tadayoshi, the JCP's Chief Secretary believes that the party's message is needed now more than ever with what he sees as attempts by conservatives in the LDP to redefine the nation's 'constitution, pacifism and democracy as old fashioned (*furukusai*) and return to the pre-war' conception of the Japanese state (Ichida 2007). Ichida believes that even despite an 'allergy' towards communism in Japan, the party should not change its brand, because 'carved into the party name is a history of opposing war and constantly [supporting] popular sovereignty under oppression' (*Akahata*, 14 May 2008). Even one of the most prominent members of the Japanese right has praised the Communists for keeping to their original stance, albeit somewhat implicitly. In 1999, Tokyo's ultraconservative governor-elect Ishihara Shintarō criticised the factional splits and mergers that defined Japanese politics throughout the 1990s, yet singled out the Communist Party as the only political group that remained coherent and true to its message (Berton 2000). Their ideological rigidity carries a high price – the party received 7.4 per cent of the proportional vote in 2005 – and the JCP will remain a fringe party for the foreseeable future.

New Kōmeitō

New Kōmeitō, which has served as the LDP's coalition partner since 1998, stands in the centre of the political marketing framework as a sales-oriented party. New Kōmeitō is unofficially affiliated with the lay Buddhist organization *Soka Gakkai*, many of whose members seem to vote for the party irrespective of its policy position. However, because Soka Gakkai's religious practices have sometimes been controversial, there is some scepticism towards New Kōmeitō's links to the organization. Opinion polls taken around the time New Kōmeitō entered into the coalition with the LDP showed that 51 per cent of the Japanese public were wary of the party's involvement in government (Tolbert 2000).[3] Public scepticism of the party has provided an incentive for New Kōmeitō to reach out to mainstream voters and since 1998 it has tried hard 'to shed its image as the political arm of *Soka Gakkai*' (Tolbert 2000). For example, the party is willing to entertain policy positions that do not reflect the pacifist leanings of its largest support group. In 2004 tensions emerged between New Kōmeitō and *Soka Gakkai* when the former supported the LDP's decision to send troops to Iraq (*Asahi Shimbun*, 10 January 2004). Also, although the party's official website acknowledges that the Buddhist organization provides an 'electoral endorsement to the party' it is careful to note that the 'relation between the two entities is no different from that of a political party and any civil group' and that 'Soka Gakkai has not provided any degree of oversight to the Komei Party or its current successor, New Kōmeitō' since 1970 (New Kōmeitō, n.d.).

The SDP

The Social Democratic Party (formerly the Socialist Party) stands as an example of a political organization that has lost its share of the vote despite greatly moderating its policy agenda. Although the SPJ's announcement in 1994 that as part of the ruling coalition it would no longer oppose Japan's post-war security architecture shocked many observers, as early as 1983 party chairs Ishibashi Masashi and his successor Doi Takako had attempted to move the Socialist Party away from its doctrinaire Marxist roots. Voters initially responded favourably and the party increased its share of seats in the 1989 upper house election before a series of scandals as well as in-fighting between the moderates and the left-wing of the party eroded public confidence. The coalition with the LDP lost the Socialists whatever traditional support they had left. The party continued to moderate its platform and image, changing its name to the Social Democratic Party (SDP) in 1996 and supporting the LDP from outside the Cabinet between 1994 and 1998. However, the emergence of the DPJ as a more 'realistic' market-oriented opposition party continues to hinder the party's success at the polls. The SDP won only six seats in 2003 and seven seats in 2005. The former party of 'permanent opposition' (*man'nen yatō*) has thus become a minor player in today's electoral landscape.

Case study: the LDP's political marketing techniques and strategy in the 2005 election and beyond

Background to the 2005 election

Throughout the 1990s, participation rates in general elections declined as Japanese voters became dissatisfied with the failure of the LDP and other parties to articulate policies that dealt with Japan's growing economic problems. While new parties emerged during this time, they were generally offshoots of the LDP and SPJ, and as the largest party in the Diet there was little incentive for the LDP to change its electoral strategy. The LDP did respond to voter dissatisfaction by instituting a series of reforms aimed, among other things, at strengthening the political executive vis-à-vis factional and bureaucratic elites and allowing for greater transparency in government. However, dissatisfaction with the selection – behind closed doors – of gaffe-prone Prime Minister Mori Yoshirō (1998–2001) led to demands for better leadership and more political reform at the same time as the DPJ was emerging as a challenger to the LDP.

After reforming its leadership selection rules to allow greater input from prefectural offices, the LDP chose Koizumi Jun'ichirō, a charismatic political maverick, as its new leader in 2001. Koizumi campaigned on a strong platform of 'structural reform' (*kōzō kaikaku*), ignored the factional power structure within the LDP and challenged the links between politicians, the bureaucracy and business that many blamed for Japan's economic problems. However, Koizumi's reform agenda was soon overshadowed by his response to the 9/11 terror attacks, including the establishment of a legislative framework to respond to terrorism, and his support for the Iraq War. During the 2003 election, his party only slightly increased its margin, while the DPJ, with its market-oriented electoral strategy, made large gains. By 2005, though, Koizumi was again ready to focus on reform, and in particular, the privatization of the national post office, which held some 340 trillion yen (approximately US$370 billion in 2008) in its savings scheme. Koizumi held that a privatized post office could be more efficiently structured and that capital from the savings scheme could act as an important source of private investment funds which would help revitalize the economy.

Koizumi faced dissent, however, from within his own party. The prime minister had already threatened vested political interests by reforming a programme of government loans drawn from the postal savings scheme by Ministry of Finance bureaucrats. The legal framework surrounding these loans meant that they did not need to be mentioned in the national budget and were thus a major source of capital for LDP members' post-war pork-barrel projects (McCormack 2001:43). Koizumi's agenda had targeted this programme, although there was some concern that his reforms did not go far enough to wrest the savings scheme from bureaucratic control (*Japan Times*, 5 March 2005). Privatization would also lead to restructuring within the postal service, much to the dissatisfaction of many of the postal workers who had historically been an important constituency for LDP members due to their prominent place in rural communities (MacLachlan 2004: 308). Although Koizumi convinced the House of Representatives to pass postal privatization legislation, 37 members of his own party voted against it. The Prime Minister held firm, threatening errant LDP members with an early election if his legislation did not pass the House of Councillors. On 8 August 2005 the upper house rejected his bills by a margin of only 17 votes, prompting the Prime Minister to call a snap election to gain a mandate for his reforms.

LDP techniques in the 2005 election

Koizumi used four main techniques in his 2005 campaign: (1) direct communication with voters, using a variety of marketing techniques; (2) the act of framing the election as a battle between a new 'reformist' LDP and 'anti-reformers' originating from the party's own ranks; (3) a strong mass media campaign focused on Koizumi as leader of the LDP and postal privatization as the single most important issue of the election; and (4) use of a detailed list of clear election promises.

First, the LDP showed that it was willing to listen to the electorate at the national level. The party used a greater variety of techniques to communicate with potential voters than did other moderate parties (Table 16.1). The DPJ and the LDP both conducted more extensive opinion polling of voters than did New Kōmeitō, indicating that these parties both used these marketing techniques to sound out the views of voters rather than just communicate their policy platforms.

Next, Koizumi's most controversial strategy was to pit errant members of his own party against a 'reformist' LDP. As party president, Koizumi refused to endorse the candidacy of the 37 members of the LDP who had voted against

Table 16.1 The use of marketing techniques in the 2005 Lower House election in Japan

	LDP	New Kōmeitō	DPJ
Telemarketing	0	0	0
Direct mail	0	0	0
PR/media consultants	1	1	1
Voter databases	2	0	0
Opinion polling	2	1	2
Focus groups	0	0	1
Opposition research	1	0	0
E-newsletter	1	1	0
Extent HQ	0	0	0
Total	**7**	**3**	**4**

Notes: Each number in the cell represents the following: '0' = 'not used at all', '1' = 'partly used', '2' = 'much used', '3' = 'systematically used'.

Telephone interviews were conducted by Asano Masahiko with relevant 'managers' of the three party campaign committees, Igata Koichichi (LDP), Takagi Yosuke (New Kōmeitō) and Suzuki Kenichi (DPJ), January 8–18, 2008.

privatization. Thirty-three of the incumbents nevertheless chose to contest the election, which only helped Koizumi to cultivate his image as an embattled reformer. Koizumi selected young, attractive and often female candidates whom the mass media took to calling 'assassins' (*shikaku*) to challenge the postal 'rebels' (*zohan*) running in the election, many of whom were former LDP ministers and faction heavyweights.[4] The Prime Minister's manoeuvering, which became known as 'Koizumi theatre' (*koizumi gekijō*), and the sense of a Manichean battle between 'rebels' and 'assassins' generated immense public interest in the contest and led to the highest voter turnout (67.5 per cent) since 1990.

Rid of those who had opposed him, Koizumi could now present the 'new' LDP as a party with strong leadership that was committed to delivering reform. Television was an effective medium for communicating this message, and in LDP advertisements Koizumi simply stood before the camera and, without music or special effects, stressed the importance of privatization in the space of a few sentences:

> Four years ago I made a promise to all of you: Even if I destroy the LDP, I would bring about reform. Postal privatization is a promise to all of the people. [Text: Don't stop the reforms *(kaikaku wo tomeruna)* – LDP]

Koizumi thus again highlighted his message that the rebels had been responsible for delays in reform and his 'new' LDP was now ready to deliver. During a similar spot, Koizumi focused his attention on the inefficiency associated with the post office, an issue that was easy for voters to understand:

> Postal privatization is the core of reforms. What kind of reforms can ever take place, while we protect the special interests of the 270,000 civil servants within the postal system? Postal privatization is connected to all reform. [Text: Don't stop the reforms – LDP]

Koizumi's ads, which focused on his ability to deliver, were thus clear, simple and effective.

In contrast, the DPJ, already competing for attention against Koizumi's fight with the rebels, ran a lacklustre television campaign. DPJ advertisements featured a shot of leader Okada Katsuya accompanied by an audio montage of his speeches. At the end of the advertisement, Okada stressed that the party would not 'give up on Japan' (*nippon wo akiramenai*). Voters found the DPJ campaign – which stressed that the party was not against privatization *per se*, but opposed the LDP's plans – 'abstract' and 'hard to understand' (*Asahi Shimbun*, 19 August 2005). Despite their success in using television to publicise their manifesto in the previous election, the DPJ's 2005 campaign came up somewhat short in this area.

Koizumi, on the other hand, appeared to have learned important lessons from the DPJ's performance in 2003. The LDP's pledges (still called *kōyaku*) were far more detailed than they had been before. The party listed 120 'promises' (*yakusoku*) that it would keep in order to fulfil its vision of small government, and outlined each promise in greater detail in an Internet document (LDP 2005). Standing out conspicuously as the first promise on the list was passage of the six postal privatization bills the upper house had previously rejected. Although these were not explained in full in the document, the legislation had already been debated at length in public, and diagrams on the same website clearly depicted postal privatization as essential to bureaucratic reform and 'small government'.

Some commentators were not easily impressed by the LDP's 'manifesto'. *Genron NPO*, a non-profit organization established in 2001 to analyze party policy and information about election promises, criticized the LDP for 'not sketching out a roadmap' including clear 'targets' and 'systems for policy implementation' (Genron NPO 2005). Nevertheless, the *Asahi Shimbun* noted that 'the two large parties had greatly changed their strategies' since previous elections by issuing 'manifestos . . . and competing on policy execution "timetables (*kōteihyō*)"' which voters could use as 'an index to measure the ability of getting things done' (*Asahi Shimbun*, 12 August 2005). For many then, the LDP had adopted key aspects of a 'conventional' party-wide market-oriented electoral strategy. Figure 16.1 indicates the comparative political market orientation of the different parties in 2005.

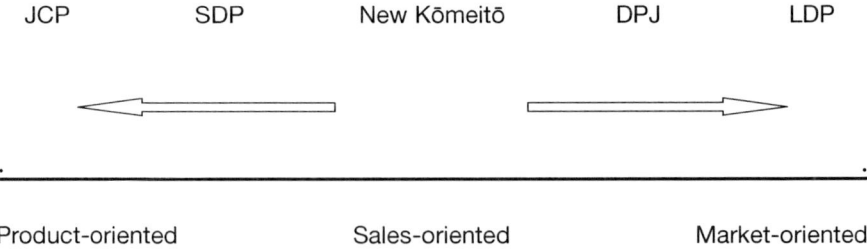

Figure 16.1 Party location in political marketing framework in Japan (2005 election)

Koizumi's campaign was extraordinarily successful. Although many had assumed that the LDP would win in 2005, few predicted that it would increase its margin by 59 to a total of 296 seats. New Kōmeitō lost three seats for a total of 31; however, the ruling coalition gained a two-thirds majority in the lower house and could now override the upper house when it rejected legislation, guaranteeing that Koizumi's bills would pass the Diet. Most of the LDP's gains were wrested from the DPJ, which lost 64 seats for a total of 113, the poorest showing for the party since 1998. Perhaps more important for the LDP, however, was the poor performance of the postal rebels. Of the 33 that ran, only 15 retained their seats, 4 losing to the DPJ and 14 to the ruling parties (*Kyodo News International* 2005). The LDP landslide was, however, amplified by the fact that many of its gains were in the single member districts where it garnered only 38.18 per cent of the popular vote yet won 73 per cent of the seats available. Despite the addition of the list seats, then, the MMM system is far from proportional. Indeed, the 2005 election yielded a total overall skew of 23.49 per cent in favour of the LDP once the proportional vote was taken into consideration (FairVote 2005). Such an outright majority may therefore be difficult to sustain in future when contested by a reinvigorated opposition.

The aftermath of the 2005 election

In 2005, the LDP demonstrated that it could adopt 'conventional' political market-oriented techniques successfully. However, there is little evidence that Koizumi's successors have learned from his campaign. Following party rules regarding term limits, Koizumi stepped down in September 2006, and though his successor, Abe Shinzō, promised to focus on Koizumi's reforms, his actions demonstrated otherwise. Abe attempted to return the party to the nationalist principles enunciated at its foundation by focusing on an agenda including reform of the education system, a more muscular defence policy and constitutional revision. Although his cabinet implemented a number of Abe's preferred policies, the prime minister's explanation of his agenda was far from clear (see Abe 2006). His tenure was also beset by a series of minor scandals that cast doubt on his competence, and perhaps most controversially, Abe invited the postal rebels to rejoin the LDP subject to their support for the party's privatization agenda. This last move raised doubts about his commitment to reform.

Meanwhile, the DPJ was re-evaluating its own performance. While it faced minor scandals of its own after the 2005 election, by April 2006, it had elected political heavyweight Ozawa Ichirō as its leader. Ozawa had been well known prior to taking the post, and had played an instrumental part in the coalition that defeated the LDP in 1993. Ozawa highlighted the differences between the DPJ and the LDP, criticizing in particular the government's handling of a scandal that saw 20 million of the nation's pension records go missing. As a result of the public's dissatisfaction with the government over the pension scandal, Ozawa led the DPJ to victory in the 2007 House of Councillors election and its largest ever win in the upper house. As the DPJ now holds the upper house, the LDP will be unable to claim that it can deliver on its promises in the next election, due by September 2009. Even if the ruling coalition wins a simple majority, it is unlikely to maintain the supermajority needed to circumvent the upper house's prerogative to block bills. This will no doubt be exploited by the DPJ, which will position itself as the only party capable of delivering on its promises.

Since Koizumi's departure, the LDP has therefore been in freefall. Citing health problems, Abe resigned shortly after the 2007 upper house election and was replaced by Fukuda Yasuo, a competent behind-the-scenes politician who nonetheless did little to show that he can replicate the strong market-oriented approach adopted by Koizumi. Perceived as a weak leader who failed to address the pension problem, Fukuda's support rate quickly dropped and he resigned in September 2008. Asō Tarō, Japan's prime minister at the time of writing, has been no more successful in outlining a clear strategy for addressing the nation's problems, and with the onset of the global financial crisis has indicated a reluctance to implement Koizumi's reformist policies, exposing tensions within the party by angering supporters of privatisation and prompting criticism from Koizumi himself. With a lack of talented leaders able to forge coherent policy proposals, the prospects for an LDP victory at the next election are looking ever dimmer.

Political marketing trends and conclusion

Political marketing strategies are evolving in Japan. As Koizumi demonstrated, the change in electoral rules in the lower house has helped to strengthen the power of the party leader vis-à-vis factional interests. There is little scope for party members to strike out on their own as independents if the party refuses to nominate them as candidates (Asano 2006; Takenaka 2006). The presence of a large single-member district component in the electoral system will mean that the tendency towards competition within parties will likely continue to weaken, because candidates no longer contest elections against their own party colleagues in the same plurality districts. Since the end of the 1990s interparty competition has become more prominent, meaning that the public is now more responsive to effective political marketing by party leaders, rather than promises made by regional candidates. Koizumi showed that he understood these aspects of the MMM system by simplifying usually complicated political issues into punchy phrases on television in order to catch attention, communicating policy detail through other media and focusing on his competition with the 'rebels' so that voters hungry for innovative solutions to Japan's decade-long financial turmoil could easily understand his vision as an alternative to politics as usual. The 2005 campaign marked a departure from traditional 'Japanese-style' attempts to mobilize the 'personal' vote cultivated by local candidates and the arrival of 'Koizumi-style' marketing: emphasizing the leader and national issues. Nevertheless, the LDP has yet to prove that it has learned from Koizumi's strategy.

Notes

1 Where applicable, these figures represent morning and evening sales combined.
2 For example, the *Asahi* and *Yomiuri* engaged in an editorial dialogue critical of Prime Minister Koizumi Jun'ichirō's visit to Tokyo's Yasukuni Shrine, which some maintain is a symbol of Japan's militarist past (Watanabe and Kawamiya: 2006). Also, the Japanese media can be extremely critical of public 'gaffes' by politicians (see *Asahi Shimbun*, 15 May 2000).
3 This may also be because of a general ambivalence towards religion in Japan. Although many Japanese will observe religious customs on holidays and special occasions, 71.9 per cent claim no religious belief (*Yomiuri* Poll, 17–18 May 2008)
4 Kamei Shizuka, one of the 'rebels' himself, originally used the terms 'rebels' and 'assassins' to criticize Koizumi (*Asahi Shimbun*, 10 August 2004). They were picked up as 'fun' phrases by the media and ironically played to Koizumi's advantage by highlighting the divide between the 'old' and 'new' LDP.

References/further reading

Abe, S. (2006) *Utsukushii kuni e* (Towards a beautiful country), Tokyo: Bungei Shinsho.

Asano, M. (2006). *Shimin shakai ni okeru seido kaikaku: Senkyo seido to kōhosha rikurūto* (Institutional Reform in Civil Society: Electoral Systems and Candidate Recruitment). Tokyo: Keio University Press.

Aspinall, R. W. (2006) 'The rise and Fall of Nikkyōso', in R. Kersten and D.Williams (eds) *The Left in the Shaping of Japanese Democracy: Essays in Honour of J. A. A. Stockwin*, London: Routledge. [65–81]

Baerwald, H. H. (1986) *Party Politics in Japan*, Boston: Allen and Unwin.

Berton, P. (2000) 'The Japanese Communist Party and Its Transformations', *JPRI Working Paper*, 67. Available at: <http://www.jpri.org/publications/workingpapers/wp67.html> (accessed 6 June 2009).

Christensen, R. V. (1998) 'Putting New Wine into Old Bottles: The Effect of Electoral Reform on Campaign Practices in Japan', *Asian Survey*, 38: 10.

Fairvote (2005) *Japanese Parliamentary Elections*. Available at: <http://www.fairvote.org/?page=1596> (accessed 6 June 2009).

Freeman, L. A. (2000) *Closing the Shop: Information Cartels and Japan's Mass Media*, Princeton: Princeton University Press.

Genron NPO (2005) *Jimintō Shinmanifesuto Hyōka* (New LDP Manifesto Evaluation). Available at: <http://www.genron-npo.net/forum_policy/000906.html> (accessed 6 June 2009).

Hyde, S. (2006) 'The End-game of Socialism', in R. Kersten and D. Williams (eds) *The Left in the Shaping of Japanese Democracy: Essays in Honour of J. A. A. Stockwin*, London: Routledge. [97–113]

Ichida, T. (2007) 'Itsu Made Mo Hantai Dake No Kyōsantō De Wa Nai' (Not a Forever-Opposing Communist Party), interview on *Videonews.com*, 10 February. Available at: <http://www.videonews.com/nagata/011020/001167.php> (accessed 6 June 2009).

Japan Audit Bureau of Circulations (2008) Document issued on 18 January.

Kabashima, I. and Broadbent, J. (1986) 'Referent Pluralism: Mass Media and Politics in Japan', *Journal of Japanese Studies*, 12(2): 329–361.

Kamijō, S. (1991) *Sengo Nihon no Sōsenkyo: Deita no Jikeiretsu Bunseki* (Japanese Post-War Elections: A Time Series Analysis of Data), Tokyo: Hokuju.

Kitaoka, S. (2000) *Futsu no Kuni e* (Towards a Normal Nation), Tokyo: Chūō Kōron Shinsha.

Krauss, E. S. (2000) *Broadcasting Politics in Japan*. Ithaca, NY and London: Cornell University Press.

Krauss, E. S. (1996) 'The Mass Media and Japanese Politics: Effects and Consequences', in S. J. Pharr and E. S. Krauss (eds) *Media and Politics in Japan*, Honolulu: University of Hawai'i Press. [355–372]

LDP (2005) 'Jimintō no Yakusoku' (The LDP's Promises). Available at: <http://www.jimin .jp/jimin/jimin/2005_seisaku/120yakusoku/> (accessed 6 June 2009).

MacLachlan, P. L. (2004) 'Post Office Politics in Modern Japan: The Postmasters, Iron Triangles and the Limits of Reform', *The Journal of Japanese Studies*, 30(2): 281–313.

McCormack, G. (2001) *The Emptiness of Japanese Affluence*, rev. edn, Armonk, NY: East Gate.

New Kōmeitō (n.d.) *Views on Politics and Religion*. Available at: <http://www.komei.or.jp/ en/about/view.html> (accessed 6 June 2009).

Pharr, S. J. (1996) 'Media and Politics in Japan: Historical and Contemporary Perspectives', in S. J. Pharr and E. S. Krauss (eds) *Media and Politics in Japan*, Honolulu: University of Hawai'i Press. [3–18]

Sasaki-Uemura, W. (2002) 'Competing Publics: Citizens' Groups, Mass Media and the State in the 1960s', *Positions*, 10:1.

Stockwin, J. A. A. (1999) *Governing Japan*, 3rd edn, Oxford: Blackwell.

Tanaka, Z. (2005) *Nihon no Sōsenkyo 1946–2003* (Japan's General Elections 1946–2003), Tokyo: Tōkyō Daigaku Shuppan Kai.

Tani, S. (1992) 'The Japan Socialist Party before the Mid-1960s: An Analysis of its Stagnation', in T. Kataoka (ed.) *Creating Single Party Democracy: Japan's Postwar Political System*, Stanford, CA: Hoover Institution Press.

Takenaka, H. (2006) *Shushō Shihai* (Domination by the Prime Minister), Tokyo: Chuko Shinsho.

Tolbert, K. (2000) 'Japanese Voters Wary of Party tied to Sect', *Washington Post*, 26 May.

Wada, J. (1996) *The Japanese Election System: Three Analytical Perspectives*, London: Routledge.

Watanabe, A. and Kawamiya, Y. (2006) *Yasukuni to Koizumi Shushō* (Yasukuni and Prime Minister Koizumi), Tokyo: Asahi Shinbun Ronsetsu Shukan.

Woodall, B. (1996) *Japan Under Construction: Corruption, Politics and Public Works*, Berkeley, CA: University of California Press.

World Press Trends (2004) *World Association of Newspapers*, Paris.

World Press Trends (2007) *World Association of Newspapers*, Paris.

Akahata, 14 May 2008.

Asahi Shimbun (*Asahi Newspaper*). Various issues.

International Herald Tribune/Asahi. Various Issues.

The Japan Times. Various Issues.

Kyodo News International, 12 September 2005.

Yomiuri Shimbun (Yomiuri newspapers). Various issues.

Yomiuri Shimbun Polling Data, various polls.

17 Implementing and interpreting market-orientation in practice

Lessons from the UK

Roger Mortimore and Mark Gill

Many commentators, both in academia and the media, and some politicians, see the adoption of political marketing and its lessons by parties as a threat to honest politics and good government, amounting to the abandonment of principles for populism. Developments such as the introduction of spin doctors, triangulation of policy and the 'permanent campaign' are seen as undermining traditional political virtues such as adherence to moral or ideological principles, as leading to barely distinguishable parties or candidates that make a mockery of the purpose of elections to offer the public a choice between alternatives, and as encouraging governments to behave irresponsibly for short-term gains in popularity rather than exercising judgement. Even the parties' use of opinion research to guide their decisions is demonised.

Such criticisms are not necessarily expressed as relating to 'market-oriented parties' (MOPs), a phrase which has not yet crossed into the mainstream of political debate. But some of those who *are* aware of political marketing models pin the criticism more explicitly to the theory: one British political scientist, recently reviewing a collection of essays on political marketing, argues that 'defining New Labour as an MOP implies that it has abandoned its principles for popular support' (Coleman 2007: 182, reviewing Lilleker and Lees-Marshment 2005).

As a case study to counter these arguments, Britain seems to offer useful scope. The primary empirical inspiration for the Lees-Marshment model of Market-Oriented Parties was 'New Labour' under Tony Blair before and after winning the 1997 British general election, and these aspects of the Labour government's behaviour since then have been a focus for attack. Blair is charged with having abandoned the Labour Party's historic identity and established ideology in favour of populist policies attractive to floating voters. A leading British political journalist recently summed up the strategy as 'commission polling evidence and focus groups to find out what people wanted. And then to offer it to them' (Paxman 2007): this was viewed as a scathing attack.

As practitioners, we are wary of trying to generalise too incautiously across different political systems. National differences in institutional arrangements, electoral rules and the cultural bases of party competition must inevitably affect the extent to which a model of campaigning behaviour is directly translatable from one country to another. (Indeed, Lilleker and Lees-Marshment (2005: 205) find that the Lees-Marshment model 'requires development and refinement before it can be considered generally applicable'). This will tend to be truer the more sophisticated the model becomes.

Therefore, for the sake of citing specific examples and showing directly how the scope of the model might be widened, we have mainly confined our discussion to Britain, to the recent experience of the Labour Party and the historical context in which that stands. Although as practitioners we have understanding of political marketing in practice in countries other than the UK, and MORI's approach to political research and advice to political parties, based on many of the principles outlined in this paper, has been used internationally for Westminster-based political systems (with a strong party base) and Presidential-style systems (with a weak party base) in work by the co-author (Gill) and Sir Robert Worcester, given the confidential nature of this work such examples cannot be cited in this chapter. Nevertheless the principles of our argument should hold, even if the detailed refinements that would be needed to best adapt the model to other political contexts would call on the expertise and specialist knowledge of researchers fully familiar with their particular circumstances.

At the heart of opposition to Britain's parties becoming market-oriented seems to be the presumption that it is only a party's policies (and the presentation of them) that can or should be researched and reformulated in adopting a market orientation. We believe this is a mistake. It underestimates the subtlety of the market. But because models of market-oriented behaviour do not always explicitly take into account the importance of factors such as ideology, long-term consequences of short-term decisions and the interaction of public opinion with elite and media opinion, it is apparently assumed that a market-orientation must entail a party abandoning all these considerations in favour of purely pragmatic short-term grubbing for votes. Models are inevitably simplified reflections of reality; but public opinion is complex, and to be effective – whether as an analytical tool for academics or as a prescriptive blueprint for political marketing practitioners – the model must allow for this.

We argue therefore, first, that it is a mistake to take too narrow a view of what a party's election offering consists of, and that there is a place for ideological considerations within the core mechanism of a market-oriented model.

Second, both the volatility of public opinion and its occasional wrongheadedness necessitate the incorporation of leadership responsibility into the MOP model. Judgement is also required in deciding what policy pledges are achievable to the satisfaction of the voting public and what the practical outcome of particular policy choices would be.

Further, parties may need to consider more than a single 'market', the voters. The opinions of various internal party groups, from front-bench MPs to grass-roots members and activists, have a knock-on effect on wider public opinion. External campaign funders must be appeased (an even more crucial consideration in the USA and some other countries than in Britain). Influential journalists must be won over. A truly market-oriented party will be monitoring all of these markets and trying to find the best way to reconcile them, not merely allowing some a veto and ignoring others altogether.

We are firmly convinced that any theory of market orientation that omits these factors will be liable to produce a sub-optimal campaigning strategy, but that it should also be perfectly possible to incorporate them, and that all are susceptible to research by parties and candidates. We believe that it is right for politicians to take public opinion into account, not only in their own interests of maximizing their chances of electoral success, but also in the interests of good government. This should involve no need to compromise on principles, to abandon the exercise of responsible judgement and leadership, or unnecessarily to narrow the choice facing the electorate.

The pedigree of polling

There is nothing new in parties and government paying attention to public opinion, in Britain any more than in most other democracies – it is not purely a character-istic of a 'post-ideological' age. Polling for the parties has been established for more than half a century,[1] but governments were taking public opinion into account long before that, even if their methods of divining it were necessarily cruder. The Prime Minister Stanley Baldwin described how his parliamentary colleagues between the wars kept in touch with public opinion during weekends in their constituencies: 'How they do it, I don't know. I suppose they talk to the stationmaster' (Young 1952: 242). Winston Churchill's government during World War II relied on Mass Observation as well as Gallup polls to gauge public opinion and morale, an indispensable consideration to the direction of the war effort.

Baldwin's government offers a clearer case of policy driven by fear of the electoral consequences against a Prime Minister's better judgement than any in the age of more scientific opinion polling. He described his decision to appease Hitler in the 1930s with (in his own words) 'appalling frankness': 'Suppose I had gone to the country and said that Germany was rearming and that we must rearm. . . . I cannot think of anything that would have made the loss of the election from my point of view more certain' (Baldwin 1936).

'Focus groups' (qualitative research) are a slightly newer tool in British politics, but were well established by the 1960s and were a fundamental part of Labour Party planning from the 1980s (Wring 2007). Yet they have been an especial bugbear of New Labour's critics, seen as the epitome of the change that Tony Blair brought to the practice of British politics. A widely read Conservative columnist went so far as to comment in 2002: 'There are, it is too often said, only two certainties in life: death and taxes. New Labour has added a third: focus groups. Dig deep enough into any issue and you will find a focus group at the bottom of it' (Pollard 2002).

It is certainly true that focus groups, unlike quantitative polling, are not an objective measuring tool, and it could be argued, as Savigny (2007) does, that this makes them unscientific. But this would be to misunderstand their value. They offer a degree of insight which more structured polling does not into the way voters think and how they relate the various issues and circumstances to themselves, to each other and to the parties. They may be 'unscientific', but politics remains an art and their value when used in conjunction with quantitative polling is considerable – the things a party strategist needs to understand about the state of public opinion are not all numerically measurable.

We believe parties and leaders should know what public opinion is saying: efficient electoral campaigning, and indeed good government once elected, are easiest with a proper understanding of public opinion and a willingness to take it into account. In achieving this, both quantitative polls and qualitative research have a value.

Nevertheless this should not, and need not, degenerate into 'government by opinion poll' or the rudderless populism in policy formulation which its opponents rightly oppose. Of course this involves risks, but the problem is hardly new. Butler and King (1966, quoted in Worcester 1991: 32) were already arguing more than forty years ago:

> In the short run, public opinion sets limits to the politically possible and it is useful to know these limits. But public opinion can be fickle. . . . It is worth remembering that democratic politicians have always conducted affairs with an eye on public opinion. They now have more accurate tools for measuring what public opinion really is. What they will need is education in how to use these tools – and how not to use them.

With this we entirely concur – and it is to suggest developments to the basic MOP model which make better use of these tools that we now turn.

The nature of the 'product'

While we believe that a political party can both morally and usefully make use of public opinion to help design the 'product' it offers the public, we would suggest that a perfect market orientation would go further than this. One way of expressing it is to argue that the market should shape the producer as well as the product, but it may be a simplification to attempt to distinguish between the two.

Lilleker and Lees-Marshment (2005) define the product as 'quite simply how a party behaves – in terms of both the past and the present, and in terms of future promises'. An earlier exposition of the model more clearly allows for this to encompass a wider field than pure policy: 'a party's product includes the leadership, MPs (and candidates), membership, staff, symbols, constitution, activities such as party conferences and policies' (Lees-Marshment 2001: 694). But this still omits much that in our view is essential (and towards which in practice much of a party's research would be directed). Because voters' decisions to support a party are not only affected by what a party says and does but also by what it *is*, this also must be responsive to the market. A party's offering to the electorate includes both the character of the party itself, as perceived by the voters, and the qualities of its leader and candidate for Prime Minister, and the capacities and capabilities of both.

Politically, this factor would probably be described as 'image', but we cannot separate out the 'image' from the 'product'. Worcester and Baines (2006) have argued the importance of political positioning, aimed at 'the development and maintenance of an emotional and intellectual connection with the electorate', and that this must unite message development and policy development components. Therefore, a market-oriented party strategy should not force abandonment of consistent ideology, party tradition or any other factors that give a political party its distinct identity and generate loyalty from its members and voters. On the contrary, these constitute part of the value of the product just as a trusted brand-name enhances product value in the economic market. For some voters supporting some parties indeed, as for some customers buying some products, the brand may *be* the value. The survival of ideology in MOPs will depend on its being something that enhances parties' appeal to their supporters.

The relationship between ideology and policy choice can be a subtle one. Philip Gould (1998: 129) relates how John Smith included in his 1992 'Shadow Budget' tax proposals he did not intend to implement – a party promising tax increases it never expected to impose, and which it knew would be unpopular with key voters, to enhance its ideological image.

Of course, party image encompasses many other elements; voters prefer parties to be consistent, competent, honest and united, and many have a stable identification with a particular party. Recently published analysis of British Election Study data from 1992 to 2001 finds that long-term partisan loyalties and ideology as well as more general measures of party and leader image influenced voters' perceptions of both major parties; judgement of recent economic performance was also a factor, though only in the evaluation of the incumbent (Butt 2006). The public themselves assert the relevance of an even wider set of criteria (Table 17.1).

Furthermore, the voters must trust prospective governments to deal with the unexpected as well as the expected. Therefore factors such as the perceived competence of a party's leader and (proposed) team of ministers and the soundness of its underlying ideological character for dealing with the unknown future may be quite as important to voters as the details of the manifesto: being 'good in a crisis' is high on the list of qualities they value in a Prime Minister (Worcester and Mortimore 2001: 23). Promises must be practical as well as popular, and they must maintain a long-term brand image of the party as competent and honest.

One additional complication is that the 'marketing' will itself inevitably become part of the 'product'. A party seen as sensibly responsive to public opinion will be better regarded than one considered 'out of touch', and to systematise the two-way communication between politicians and voters into a formal consultative mechanism may enhance that. The Labour Party has been alive to this possibility in recent years: an early initiative of Gordon Brown after he took over as Prime Minister in 2007 was towards 'new rights for the British people to be consulted through mechanisms such as 'citizens juries' on major decisions affecting their lives',[2] intended to emphasize that he is receptive to public opinion.

Moreover, parties have no monopoly on opinion polling. They must now operate in a world where the measurement of public opinion is routine, where

Table 17.1 Qualities most valued by British voters in political parties

Q. From this card, how important, if at all, would you say the things I am going to read out will be in helping you decide whether to vote for a particular party?

That the party . . .		Very important	Fairly important	Not very important	Not at all important	Don't know
. . . understands the problems facing Britain	%	80	15	1	2	2
. . . keeps its promises	%	76	18	2	2	2
. . . is concerned about the people in real need in Britain	%	76	18	2	2	2
. . . represents all classes	%	75	18	3	2	2
. . . looks after the interests of people like us	%	74	18	3	2	3
. . . has sensible policies	%	73	21	2	2	2
. . . has a good team of leaders	%	71	23	2	2	2
. . . is not out of touch with ordinary people	%	70	24	2	2	2
. . . is professional in its approach	%	65	28	3	2	2
. . . does not promise anything to win votes	%	60	28	6	3	3
. . . is not divided	%	55	32	7	3	3
. . . is not extreme	%	54	34	6	3	3
. . . is not too dominated by its leader	%	42	44	8	3	3
. . . is moderate	%	39	46	8	3	4

Source: MORI

Note: Base: 1,928 British adults aged 18+, interviewed face-to-face, in home, 24–30 May 2001

'responsiveness' is almost universally regarded as a positive (even by those who value ideological integrity), and where campaign groups, the press and commercial interests will all exploit polling evidence to put pressure on governments and candidates. A party that fails to take public opinion into account in its decision making suffers not only when its decisions are unpopular in themselves, but also from the criticism it will receive for defying the public will. Conversely, should the process of 'consultation' come to appear cynical or insincere, this can be greatly counter-productive, as can any perceived culture of 'spin'.

There is no lack of practical evidence that party and leader image as well as policy substance can be powerful in affecting voting intentions. It can be seen most easily in the fact that although the public is frequently polled on what they consider the most important issues and which party they believe to have the best policies on each, multivariate analysis finds that this can explain only a fraction of the variation in voting intention. The most recent analysis of the British Election Study (Clarke *et al.* 2004) has found leader image to be, consistently over many years, one of the most significant predictors of voting behaviour in Britain. And it is clear that party image can add to or detract from the effect of a party's policies: for example, during the 2005 election, several polls found that Conservative policies were less popular with the public if explicitly associated with the Conservative Party than when tested without any mention of the party proposing them.[3]

The need to protect or regenerate party and leader image may, indeed, legitimately take priority over the development of a policy programme. David Cameron's first 18 months as Conservative leader (2006–7) were widely described as 'policy lite',[4] but there is strong argument that the most urgent task was to develop credibility and trustworthiness. This would lay the foundations for a fair reception for policy announcements, so that they would not be routinely damaged by the knowledge that they were Conservative proposals, as seemed to be the case under his predecessor Michael Howard.

Party and leader image have been among the key factors measured in the parties' private polls in the past, and presumably still are. MORI's research programme for the Labour Party in the 1970s and 1980s, designed by Robert Worcester, was built round his 'political triangle' model that simultaneously considered the effects of party image, leader image and the parties' standings on specific issues, resting on the foundation of voters' values derived mostly from their backgrounds (Worcester and Mortimore 2005).[5] Party image was central to Philip Gould's thinking at the outset of New Labour (Gould 1998: 211–12), identifying 'the extent that the confidence and consistency of fifteen years of Conservative government . . . has established the framework through which these voters see the political world'. More recently he has recounted how in 2005 Labour concentrated on how 'to make explicit the leadership contrast between Tony Blair and Michael Howard' as a key pillar of its election strategy (Gould 2007: 21).

A well-run market-oriented strategy, therefore, is not simply a policy pick-and-mix. Party identity is central to it. However, it may involve development of a modified party identity and evolution of its ideology, in response to long-term as opposed to short-term forces. But in any case, ideology cannot stand still and unresponsive to the circumstances of the day, or British elections would still be fought on attitudes to Catholic Emancipation and the Corn Laws. The transition from 'Old Labour' to 'New Labour' may have been facilitated by the use of political marketing techniques, but it can hardly be assumed that it was an evolution that would not have occurred in any case.

Judgement and the leadership function

Leadership judgement is also indispensable to an MOP. Even a party with no ideological principles would need sometimes to defy public opinion when public opinion was wrong. The public can be wrong about the practical consequences of the policy choices they espouse (but would hold responsible the politicians that implemented them); they can be fickle in their preferences (which a successful party needs to predict); and they can be unfair in their judgement of government performance (so that the criterion for achieving popularity is not delivery but the public perception of delivery).

Public opinion always has to be interpreted rather than being read raw. The operative question is not simply what would be popular 'if there were a general election tomorrow', to use the hypothetical opinion poll question, unless there is a general election tomorrow. In Britain, general elections occur only every four or five years, and second-order elections are generally of little significance except as a weathervane.[6] Mid-term popularity carries no direct electoral pay-off, and for the market model to make sense it must always be directed to election performance. A responsible Prime Minister will frequently need to take decisions unpopular in the short-term which will have borne fruit by the end of the Parliament.

To achieve electoral credit for success in government, the criterion is not delivery on promises to any objective standard, but delivery to the subjective satisfaction of the voter or consumer. Public judgement of government performance is not necessarily fair: people disbelieve government statistics, and persist in believing that national standards are poor even when their own local experience is positive (Page 2007: 449–58). MORI surveys for the British Cabinet Office in 2004 found that satisfaction with how public services were 'provided in your local area' was higher for every one of seven named services than was satisfaction among the same sample with 'the way each service is provided for Britain as a whole' (Worcester *et al.* 2005: 117).

Similarly, the public were shown 26 statements on the outcome of specific government policies (each of which the government stated was true at the time of the survey and for which 'objective performance data of delivery exists'); 22 of the statements were positive and 4 negative. The 7 statements believed by the highest number of respondents included just 3 of the 22 positive ones and all 4 of the negative ones. Seven statements were disbelieved by 60 per cent or more of respondents, including objectively verifiable ones such as 'There are thousands more doctors and nurses working in the NHS [National Health Service]', 'There are thousands more teachers', 'There are stricter penalties for persistent offenders' and 'More people are using buses' (Worcester *et al.* 2005: 118–19). Clearly a government can get no electoral benefit from such achievements if three in five of the public do not believe in them.

It is worth noting, also, how public pessimism about the future of the economy and public services temporarily fell sharply when Gordon Brown replaced Tony Blair as Prime Minister[7] – not because of any announced changes of policy, or perceptions among the public that policies had changed overnight, but presumably solely a reflection of attitudes to the government and Prime Minister which were also evident in polls on other political subjects. Perception of delivery, too, will be affected by more general sentiments of trust or distrust in the government.

Unfortunately for governments of all colours, people are not naturally inclined to believe that things are getting better: we frequently find a sort of 'nostalgia' effect in polling (in many different subjects, not just political ones). Indeed, there is plenty of evidence that public opinion can be simply perverse, and that the public are capable of simultaneously holding mutually contradictory opinions, not only collectively but as individuals. This puts a very real restraint on the ability of an unsophisticated market-oriented strategy to secure continuing electoral success. A party may need to aim not simply at achievable policy objectives which would be popular if successful, but at objectives whose success can be effectively and credibly communicated to the voters once achieved. This, like the achievability of the objectives, may be more a matter of judgement and experience than something which can be drawn directly from the opinion research.

But judgement applies not only to understanding and allowing for the capriciousness of public opinion, but also to anticipating the practical outcomes of policy decisions. Historians will surely consider the defining policy of the Blair premiership to be the invasion of Iraq in 2003, ironically one taken in defiance of public opinion.

Blair's decision whether to invade Iraq had to be built around his beliefs about the consequences of invading and of not invading; only in the light of those could he factor in public opinion. With the next general election anything up to three years away, the critical question even for an utterly cynical and irresponsibly market-led party would not be whether the invasion would be popular at the moment the troops landed, but how it would be viewed in the future; of that decision, predictions of the military outcome would be an essential part.

If the troops had found weapons of mass destruction in Iraq and had been able to install a stable new regime in Baghdad within six months, it would probably have been a decision that would have helped Labour win the 2005 election rather than nearly losing it. Blair's decision is now considered almost universally to have been an error; but it was a failure of military intelligence not market intelligence.

Reconciling multiple 'markets'

Finally, a wise MOP will not confine its opinion research to the voting public. Political parties, like companies, are dependent on various stakeholders and suppliers and, even if their ultimate aim is to maximise general election votes and their performance in no other 'market' matters, they must reconcile the demands of these various groups or eventually find their position in the election market damaged. It is not enough merely to co-opt these groups into the decision-making process.

In British politics, key groups include the grass-roots membership in general and the party's local councillors and activists in particular (who will do the campaigning on the ground and be the every-day ambassadors of the party between elections), the media (through which their message to the voters will be filtered and perhaps distorted), and those whom the parties want to fund their campaigning (without whose support they may be helpless). Party staff will be vital to implementation. Senior members of the parliamentary party – cabinet ministers or shadow cabinet members in particular – may punch above their weight in determining the political atmosphere. In other political systems, party office holders in other tiers of government or coalition partners from other parties, for example, might also be crucial. A truly market-oriented party will be monitoring all of these markets and trying to find an optimum reconciliation of all forces that will act on the eventual election outcome.

The media in particular are absolutely crucial; the party's image is strongly dependent on how journalists portray it. Tony Blair well understood this and made it central to New Labour's strategy for campaigning and for government – hence the importance of his spin doctor Alastair Campbell as a central figure in Blair's inner team. Campbell knew about the decision to drop Clause Four from the Labour Party constitution (perhaps the key symbolic moment of the Labour Party's adoption of the 'New Labour' agenda) before most of the shadow cabinet (Campbell 2007). Furthermore, once the party is in government the media may have direct impact on the success of policy, especially in the economic field – everything from wage claims to confidence in the banking system is liable to be driven by the tone of media coverage. More broadly, all groups with 'opinion leader' functions deserve consideration and probably justify separate research.

Satisfying the internal market of party members can also be especially demanding, not least because it will impact on the decision-making process itself. It is not sufficient to give party members an institutional right of veto: because of the damage that the appearance of internal division can do to party image, the reconciliation of opinions is much better done at an early stage than publicly through a party's formal decision-making mechanisms. In the case of Tony Blair's abolition of Clause Four, the decision could only be taken by a vote of the party conference. As is made clear in Alastair Campbell's diaries (Campbell 2007), Blair and his team had considerable apprehension about reaction to the Clause Four proposal, not because they feared it might be defeated but because even a large but vocal minority might have damaged both the leadership and the party's standing.

Furthermore, Blair accepted that he could only pursue decisions which were acceptable to the 'big three' of Gordon Brown, Robin Cook and John Prescott; without at least their private acquiescence and public support, Blair could not act on his own judgement of the party's best interests (Campbell 2007: especially 7–21).

Conclusions

A successful market orientation does not entail a party being led by the nose by its pollsters. The optimal strategy will involve taking into account ideology and party traditions, the historical context of the political and party system and broader considerations of party and leader image – unless the voters themselves reject these as irrelevancies. In most circumstances these will be, and certainly in modern Britain are, immensely influential on voting behaviour.

If holding a market-orientation necessitated ignoring all these factors, then so much the worse for political marketing. But of course it does not. These are just as much conditions of the market as the raw policy desires of the voters, and it is fully within the scope of a political marketing model to allow for them. We should not be misled by the particular circumstances of the British Labour Party in the 1990s, which happened to be undergoing an ideological evolution at the time that a successful marketing model was constructed around it, into assuming that this is the norm.

Politics, and political strategy, is an art not a science, and nobody is likely to be able to develop a foolproof formula for campaigning by numbers. The leadership function is crucial, and that leader must exercise judgement when to follow the dictates of the market and when to defy it. This is true even within the confines of the market model – when the voters are misguided, the leader's best strategy for long-run success can often be to accept short-term unpopularity. But further, of course, we accept a moral imperative that may require a leader on occasions to reject the promptings of the market altogether. But the weakness here is not in the marketing model but in democracy itself: an MOP is no more than the most efficient expression of the democratic will. If there is a danger here, it does not rest in the possibility that parties might become market-oriented but that the will of the voters might cause market orientation to lead to wrong choices. In other words, democracy is dangerous because the public is not always right; and we knew that already.

This means that many of the criticisms of political marketing in practice are unfounded. Though it may be a tool used by cynical politicians, it is not in itself cynical. A more valid criticism is that following a market-oriented strategy may encourage parties or candidates to concentrate only on a minority of key voters rather than public opinion as a whole. This may be of particular concern in electoral systems of the Anglo-American type, where not all votes exert equal weight, and votes in key states or marginal constituencies are more valuable than others. Whether this ends in all parties fighting over the same tiny group of pivotal voters or should lead to each party identifying a different key segment of the electorate, it is certainly true that parties will not aim to satisfy the electorate as a whole. But that is a direct consequence of the electoral system: if a political system tends to reward campaigning tactics which are not conducive to the public good, perhaps it is the system and not the campaigning that needs to be changed.

But finally, we would caution against forgetting the difference between a theoretical model and reality, not least in the ability to take decisions in the first place. The obstacles that institutional structures may put in the way of conducting and implementing the findings of good research should not be underestimated.

Again, the British experience is a case in point. Philip Gould (1998: 44–5) and Robert Worcester (Worcester and Mortimore 1999: 15–16) have both described the Labour Party's decision-making structure in the mid-1980s, which led (in Gould's words) to 'a chaos of indecisiveness, one-upmanship, hedging and ultimate stagnation'. Worcester has explained how internal tensions within the Labour Party's National Executive Committee influenced the direction of his research: in 1973, the left-winger Tony Benn attempted to prevent him from including any questions on 'personalities'; in 1986–7 it was questions on the party's elec-tion broadcasts that Peter Mandelson wanted to avoid.[8] That situation was perhaps mirrored in the Conservative Party before the 2005 election when a major party funder, Lord Ashcroft, became so frustrated with the campaigning strategy of Central Office that he commissioned his own research programme and independently funded the campaigns of certain Conservative candidates (Ashcroft 2005).

Further, it has always been the case that many politicians are unreceptive, and disbelieve the research findings if they contradict their own gut instincts or prejudices. Worcester quotes the case of Tony Benn in 1982, who cited several hundred letters that had been sent to him as evidence of public opposition to the Falklands War: more objective polling indicated that the great majority of the public took the opposite view (Worcester 1991: 129).

The effectiveness of research, therefore, must be dependent on the communications between decision makers and researchers, and also on how much autonomy individuals and institutions within the party are allowed in their campaigning and other political activities. Worcester makes clear that he considered that best use was made of him by Prime Minister Harold Wilson, a professional statistician by training with whom he could deal directly on occasions, circumventing the party mechanisms. New Labour's adoption of an apparently market-oriented approach in the mid-1990s may owe less to any wholesale transformation of the party than to Philip Gould's being a trusted member of Tony Blair's inner circle with direct access to the leader.

Notes

1   For the history of private polling in Britain, see Worcester (1991) and Moon (1999). For more detail on the Labour Party, and a wider view of its development of marketing techniques, see Wring (2005).
2   Statement by the Prime Minister in the House of Commons, 3 July 2007, retrieved from the Prime Ministerial website (http://www.pm.gov.uk/output/Page12274.asp) on 18 October 2007.
3   An ICM survey in February 2005 for BBC *Newsnight* comparing results from matched samples found that while 82 per cent of the public said they supported 'the idea that immigration should be controlled more strictly', only 65 per cent said they supported 'Conservative policy to control immigration more strictly'. There were similar findings in the Populus surveys reported in Ashcroft (2005).
4   For example, Sylvester (2007) and Stuart (2007). Simon Jenkins (2007) used the term more sympathetically, suggesting that Cameron was also 'conviction-heavy'.
5   See also Worcester and Baines (2006). The Political Triangle concept has also been used by MORI as the underlying structure for its published political polling for the media, and more recently successfully transplanted to Trinidad and Tobago, where Ipsos MORI has conducted the private polls for the People's National Movement in general elections since 2002.
6   Though it is perhaps an over-simplification to dismiss second-order elections altogether, even in Britain (where they include local government elections, elections to the devolved assemblies and European Parliament elections). Even if the national leadership were concerned with nothing but general elections (and in practical terms they would not last long if they were), the need for success at second-order elections feeds into the general election campaign, producing healthy morale, vibrant local parties with campaigning personnel and sources of funding. And in many other countries, of course, these elections are of more direct significance and must be factored into the equation.

7 See trends in the Ipsos MORI Government Delivery Index, http://www.ipsos-mori.com/polls/2007/mdi070513.shtml
8 Personal communication from Sir Robert Worcester.

References/further reading

Ashcroft, M. A. (2005) *Smell the Coffee: A Wake-Up Call for the Conservative Party*, London: CGI Europe.

Baldwin, S. (1936) Speech in the House of Commons, 12 November, quoted in Jay 1999.

Butler, D. E. and King, A. (1966) *The British General Election of 1966*, London: Macmillan.

Butt, S. (2006) 'How Voters Evaluate Economic Competence: A Comparison Between Parties In and Out of Power', *Political Studies*, 54: 743–66.

Campbell, A. (2007) *The Blair Years*, London: Hutchinson.

Clarke, H. D., Sanders, D., Stewart, M. C. and Whiteley, P. (2004) *Political Choice in Britain*, Oxford: Oxford University Press.

Coleman, S. (2007) 'Review', *Parliamentary Affairs*, 60(1): 180–6.

Gould, P. (1998) *The Unfinished Revolution*, London: Little, Brown.

—— (2007) 'Labour's Political Strategy', in D. Wring, J. Green, R. Mortimore and S. Atkinson (eds) *Political Communications: The General Election Campaign of 2005*, Basingstoke: Palgrave Macmillan.

Jay, A. (1999) *The Oxford Dictionary of Political Quotations*, Oxford: Oxford University Press.

Jenkins, S. (2007) 'The Next Prime Minister can't Bow to the Tweedies', *The Guardian*, 25 July.

Lees-Marshment, J. (2001) 'The Marriage of Marketing and Politics', *Political Studies*, 49: 692–713.

Lilleker, D. G. and Lees-Marshment, J. (eds) (2005) *Political Marketing: A Comparative Perspective*, Manchester: Manchester University Press.

Moon, N. (1999) *Opinion Polls: History, Theory and Practice*, Manchester: Manchester University Press.

Page, B. (2007) 'Culture and Attitudes', in A. Seldon (ed.) *Blair's Britain 1997–2007*, Cambridge: Cambridge University Press.

Paxman, J. (2007) James MacTaggart Memorial Lecture, August. Available at: <http://www.bbc.co.uk/blogs/newsnight/2007/08/the_james_mactaggart_memorial_lecture.html> (accessed 6 June 2009).

Pollard, S. (2002) 'Politics Killed Top-Up Fees', *The Daily Telegraph*, 8 December. Available at: <http://www.telegraph.co.uk/opinion/main.jhtml?xml=/opinion/2002/12/08/do0809.xml&sSheet=/opinion/2002/12/08/ixop.html> (accessed 6 June 2009).

Savigny, H. (2007) 'Focus Groups and Political Marketing: Science and Democracy as Axiomatic?', *British Journal of Politics and International Relations*, 9: 122–37.

Stuart, M. (2007) 'Where is David Cameron's New Vision for the Conservatives?', *Yorkshire Post*, 4 September.

Sylvester, R. (2007) 'What Brown has in Store for Cameron', *Daily Telegraph*, 26 June.

Worcester, R. (1991) *British Public Opinion: A Guide to the History and Methodology of Political Opinion Polling*, Oxford: Basil Blackwell.

Worcester, R. and Baines, P. (2006) 'Voter Research and Market Positioning: Triangulation and its Implications for Policy Development', in P. J. Davies and B. I. Newman (eds) *Winning Elections with Political Marketing*, New York: Haworth Press.

Worcester, R. and Mortimore, R. (1999) *Explaining Labour's Landslide*, London: Politico's Publishing.

—— (2001) *Explaining Labour's Second Landslide*, London: Politico's Publishing.

—— (2005) 'Political Triangulation: Measuring and Reporting the Key Aspects of Party and Leader Standing Before and During Elections', *Journal of Political Marketing*, 4(2–3): 45–72.

Worcester, R., Mortimore, R., and Baines, P. (2005) *Explaining Labour's Landslip*, London: Politico's Publishing.

Wring, D. (2005) *The Politics of Marketing the Labour Party*, Basingstoke: Palgrave Macmillan.

—— (2007) 'Focus Group Follies? Qualitative Research and British Labour Party Strategy', *Journal of Political Marketing*, 5(4): 71–97.

Young, G. M. (1952) *Stanley Baldwin*, London: R Hart-Davies.

18 Political marketing, party behaviour and political science

Mick Temple

Introduction

This chapter will critically examine theories of political marketing, with particular reference to the three-stage model as developed by Jennifer Lees-Marshment (2001a). The analysis will concentrate on what is arguably the major weakness in the operationalisation of approaches rooted in marketing theory, in that the media appear to be merely an agent for the transmission of the messages of both 'sales-oriented parties' (SOPs) and 'market-oriented parties' (MOPs). Both the methods of political marketing (such as focus groups) and the normative elements of the Lees-Marshment model also pose problems for traditional conceptions of democratic accountability. Despite such criticisms, the Lees-Marshment model has been an important contribution to the literature and, as the country studies in this book demonstrate, a valuable aid for comparative study.

I need to confess that I am not an expert in the discipline of political marketing. My perspective is that of a political scientist, whose work has ranged across the spectrum from theoretical to empirical work and points in between (including published work on coalition formation, public sphere theory, central-local relations, Third Way theory and media history), and who now finds himself in a Journalism department teaching university courses on the relationship between the media, journalism and politics. Political marketing is one aspect of this relationship. So my role here is to cast an interested political scientist's eye over the debate.

Political marketing: what is it?

There is little dispute that political marketing is an integral part of modern politics: indeed, Newman (1994: 21) has asked whether it is now possible for parties or candidates *not* to market themselves like any other product. However, the first thing to strike the non-specialist reader is, as Strömbäck notes in this volume, the absence of any consensus as to what the study of political marketing entails. There are a number of approaches, drawn from media studies, communication studies, political science and marketing literature, which take different starting points for study. Although political marketing is generally informed by assumptions and models adopted from management studies, and the ontological and analytical suppositions of political marketing literature are that parties and voters act in way that is analogous to businesses and consumers (for example, Reid 1988; Newman 1994; Kavanagh 1995; Butler and Collins 1996; see Savigny 2008a, for a fuller discussion on these issues), there is no 'single, unambiguous answer' to the question 'what is political marketing?' (see Scammell 1999: 718). Some studies (for example, Newman 1999) decline to give any formal definition of the concept. As Strömbäck details in Chapter 2, in the broadest sense of the term, 'political marketing' is concerned with the communication of politics and as such has always been a feature of any political system. However, political marketing is about more than managing the media via tactics now commonly known as 'spin'. The term is now generally used to describe the use of marketing techniques such as consumer (voter) research, focus groups and advertising: that is, selling a political product in much the same way as any other manufactured product or service.

The seminal work of Kotler argues that marketing 'is a relevant discipline for all organisations' in that all organisations have 'customers and products' (1972: 46). Furthermore, Kotler (1981) argues that election campaigning has 'an inherently marketing character' and 'similarities of salesmanship in business and politics far outweigh the differences' (in Scammell 1999: 718–26). Newman maintains that 'the same principles that operate in the commercial marketplace hold true in the politics marketplace' (1999: 35). In essence, election campaigns are seen as 'a condensed consumer-product marketing campaign' (O'Shaughnessy and Henneberg 2002: xi). So, political marketing is informed by assumptions derived from academic management and marketing studies: the political marketing literature confidently asserts that business marketing techniques can be applied to marketing political parties and candidates.

Within what is essentially a sub-field of political communication – although Scammell (1999) points out that for those versed in marketing theory, political communication is a sub-field of political marketing and merely a tool in the political marketing locker – there is a basic assumption that voters choose parties rather as consumers choose products. It is argued that weakening party allegiance (although Knuckey convincingly demonstrates in his study that partisan attachment has become stronger in recent American elections) has contributed to this shift in power relations from political parties to the new 'consumers'. For example, Lilleker posits that the study of political marketing is in large part a reaction to 'the rise of political consumerism and the collapse of partisanship' in Western democracies (2006: 151). Arguably, political marketing has been a contributor to that collapse, its techniques wooing political parties into believing they must adopt its methods and colonise the middle ground, as Anthony Downs' economic theory of democracy (1957) had proposed was the rational strategy for any party seeking power, at least in a two-party majoritarian system.

From this highly debatable Downsian starting point, the normative bias of sympathetic scholars like Lees-Marshment is not only that following a marketing template is essential for electoral success but that political marketing is a 'good thing' (apologies to Sellar and Yeatman, 1930), as is political parties following consumer demands. There are a number of claims that the application of marketing techniques keeps politicians accountable and responsive to voters' demands (Harrop 1990; Scammell 1995; O'Cass 1996; Kotler and Kotler 1999; Lees-Marshment 2001a). In short, political marketing is seen as good for democracy (Lilleker and Lees-Marshment 2005).

As many have pointed out, the use of marketing in politics – at its most basic, persuading others of your right to attain and hold office – is not new (see Wring 1996; Franklin 2004). One could see Machiavelli's brilliant handbook for rulers, *The Prince*, as an early example. However, political marketing as a modern phenomenon in democracies begins with the twentieth century's extension of the electoral franchise to the masses and the selling of parties and candidates to a mass audience. Its modern practice can be directly related to the use of television as a direct marketing tool by American political candidates (Savigny 2009). In Britain, the image of Conservative leader Margaret Thatcher was moulded and 'softened' by advertising men Gordon Reece and Tim Bell in response to public opinion polls. Intensive coaching to lower the pitch of her voice, careful selection of power clothing, a series of 'pseudo-events' and a ground-breaking series of posters and party political broadcasts ensured that British politics would never be the same again. However, the policies themselves remained relatively sacrosanct. As Lees-Marshment (2001c) convincingly demonstrates, Tony Blair's New Labour went beyond image to change the very nature of the product in response to 'consumer' feedback: at the core of political marketing models is the idea of 'reciprocity', with voters' views actually influencing the product via feedback from polls and focus groups. Marketing has now been applied to many other areas of public life besides influencing voters, with quangos, pressure groups and local government departments all employing techniques developed from business marketing.

The three-stage model

Theoretical frameworks have been developed to 'model' the marketing process that parties or candidates go through, providing a template of stages a party needs in order to achieve a market orientation – implicit in these models is that following these stages will lead to electoral success (for example, Egan 1999; O'Cass 2001; Lees-Marshment 2001a). Keith's (1960) three-stage evolutionary model has been widely adopted and adapted in the political marketing literature (for example, Smith and Saunders 1990; Newman 1994; Wring 1997, 2005; Lees-Marshment 2001c). Wring's (1997) seminal work on reconciling political science and marketing – in which he set out a theoretical framework for analysis – and Newman's (1994) important American work, use essentially the same three-stage marketing framework as Lees-Marshment. But neither of these influential writers on the application of marketing techniques to political campaigning has their insights considered in Lees-Marshment and Lilleker's examination of the UK (2005). Likewise, the potential contribution of these studies to the development of the Lees-Marshment model remains undetailed and relatively unacknowledged. There is a serious point to be made here. The barriers between the different approaches of study into political marketing identified by Scammell (1999) may be encouraging the different approaches to political marketing to be operating in isolation from each other. Similar barriers in other areas developed from rational choice theory – for example, the development of models of political coalition formation and duration – have acted to inhibit understanding of the processes involved. Insights from empirical studies into coalitions failed to inform theoretical models and vice versa – with the result that coalition studies as an academic field has arguably became essentially moribund (Temple 1996). Studies of political marketing need to ensure they remain open to the many different approaches.

The three-stage model as put forward by Lees-Marshment charts the development of political marketing or, perhaps more accurately, 'electoral marketing'. Crudely, the three stages move from: (i) 'this is the product, take it or leave it' (a product-oriented approach – POP); to (ii) 'this is the product, isn't it lovely' (a sales-oriented approach – SOP); to the final stage, the triumph of political marketing, (iii) 'you've told us what you want, now here it is, vote for it' (a market-oriented approach – MOP). Lees-Marshment's model is both concise and elegant and the movement from POP to SOP to MOP is an extremely useful aid which convincingly illuminates New Labour's genesis. However, as the chapters in this book indicate, its usefulness in other political systems is less clear. As acknowledged by Lilleker and Lees-Marshment (2005) the model may be more applicable to opposition parties in non-PR systems, especially those seeking office after a lengthy period of electoral failure.

The media are the message?

Business organisations are assumed to identify consumer demand, feed this back into the product and refine it accordingly. The next stage is then to tell the consumer that this has been done. The final stage is the delivery of a refined product that satisfies consumer demand – and therefore produces a profit for the company. In the political environment, parties use opinion polling and focus groups to find out what voters (who are assumed to act as consumers) desire and then refine their product. However, communicating those refinements and selling your product to your customers – in this case, the voters – is crucially different for politicians than for companies. Marketing models differ from political marketing models, in that most commercial marketing is via paid-for advertising. Communication by politicians, even in the USA where paid-for advertising eats up millions of dollars from even the lowliest congressman, is predominantly through 'free' media forms such as photo-ops, pseudo-events, press releases and the attempted manipulation of the news agenda by spin doctors. Communicating the political 'product' to voters is perhaps the most important stage for political actors. As a Labour spin doctor said in 1997, 'communications is not an afterthought to our policy. It's central to the whole mission of New Labour' (Gaber 1998: 13).

In 1988, the Conservative government's Trade and Industry Secretary, Lord Young, infamously pronounced, 'the government's policies are like cornflakes – if they are not marketed they will not sell' (Franklin 2004: 5). Widely seen then as a cynical comment, Young was merely stating what now seems common sense in a media-dominated environment. The Phillis Report into government communications accepted that 'communications should be an equal and equally respected third in the trinity of government policy making, public service delivery and communications' (Phillis 2004: 31). However, while acknowledging the need for effective communication, Phillis argued the negative impact of political spin and public relations had contributed to a 'three-way breakdown' in trust between politicians, the media and the public. The more prescriptive political marketing literature disputes this, maintaining that the use of political marketing techniques, by listening and responding to the concerns of voters, can help to rebuild voter trust. However, for many observers, it is the dominance of marketing techniques, especially the seemingly pathological desire by spin doctors such as Alastair Campbell to manage the news and ensure 'the message' is delivered as the party wishes, which is primarily responsible (as Phillis notes) for the lack of public trust in politicians. Indeed, in Australia, the 'persistent negativity' transmitted by the media towards marketing techniques has meant a reluctance by parties to admit they are adopting a market orientation (Hughes and Dann, this volume).

Despite Phillis's recognition that media and communications strategies play a central role in marketing political policies, key aspects of the media–political party relationship remain unaddressed or peripheral in the political marketing literature, most notably the framing role played by the mass media. In all political systems the media are not only shaping and influencing the political 'message' candidates wish to transmit, their activities are impacting upon the democratic process more broadly (Street, 2001). The media (including the BBC in the United Kingdom, which likes to trumpet its supposed lack of political bias) are *not* neutral actors. As Kotzaivazoglou and Zotos point out (this volume), the Greek media generally take an 'aggressive hard-line stance' towards political leaders, with newspapers being 'strongly partisan': also, despite being more objective than the press, public television in Greece remains 'pro-government'. Mensah (this volume) also reports the Ghanian media as favouring government parties. Hutcheson's examination of Russian electioneering graphically demonstrates the importance of media preferences. Although access to party political broadcasts is apparently equitable, pro-Kremlin parties and candidates dominate in terms of news coverage. Putin's pogroms against 'opposition' media ensure that coverage given to the 'parties of power' in the state television news programmes is 'disproportionately large and positive, and that to their main opponents usually negative or negligible' (Hutcheson, this volume). The implications for opponents of Russia's ruling elites is that their marketing strategy has to rely on more traditional techniques, ensuring their opportunity for a market-oriented approach is limited.

So, the relationship between political parties and voters is mediated by institutions with their own policy and party preferences – clearly, the processes of political marketing are more complex than the models, including Lees-Marshment's, assume. To be fair, Strömbäck's research propositions (this volume) recognise the impact different media systems and journalistic cultures might have on the market orientation of parties, but the impact of the media is perhaps far more crucial than acknowledged. New Labour's ability to portray itself to the electorate as having fundamentally changed was facilitated by a print media who, despite their largely Conservative sympathies, were unable to support John Major's sleaze-ridden and error-prone government. The sense that it was 'time for a change', accompanied by a young and charismatic leader who was able to convince media owners and editors of his correspondence to their own ideological concerns, were perhaps equally as crucial as New Labour's market-oriented strategy.

The final stage in the marketing process, according to management models, is delivery, where political actors need to be seen to have delivered on their promises, but again, this is not a straightforward process when it is the media who play a key role in interpreting government success. According to liberal theory, the media function in order to hold political elites to account. Politicians can tell voters that they have delivered on their promises, but the role of the Fourth Estate is to scrutinise such claims. However, the partiality of most media ensures that voters will receive a complicated picture of just how effective parties have been in delivering their stated aims. In all countries, the media clearly have their own agenda. Whatever the rhetoric about 'the protection of democracy' or operating as a Fourth Estate ensuring citizens receive accurate and relevant information – and many journalists do see themselves as embodying such a role – the media are also businesses operating to make a profit, with the aim of attracting an audience of both the public and advertisers. This applies even to many state-sponsored broadcasters, including the BBC in the United Kingdom. The tension between the media's roles in a democracy and their position in the marketplace brings conflicts which have been largely unacknowledged and unrecognised in the political marketing literature (Savigny 2008a).

The media's influence, of course, goes far beyond its interpretation of party messages at election time. Voters' perceptions and understanding of politics in general are also largely derived through the filters of the media. The media do not, in any political system, confine themselves to a 'neutral transmission function' (Kuhn 2007: 212). The media helps both to form and mobilise public opinion and it clearly has agenda-setting and reporting roles which constrain the approaches political candidates and parties can take. The majority of media are predisposed towards politicians or parties expressing viewpoints that chime with their own ideological or market preferences. Enoch Powell once said that for politicians to complain about the media is like sailors complaining about the sea (Soley 2005: 35): essentially, it's the environment you operate in, so get on with it. Powell's comparison, as with so many of his pronouncements, is wide of the mark. The difference is that, while both the media and the ocean are capricious, the media can also be malicious and is nearly always partisan – a political party will not be allowed to sell its product in the same way as Heinz. Although Maier *et al.* (this volume) report that newspapers in Germany have weak political bonds, in most political systems print media especially are notably partisan. Given this, all dimensions of the political marketing strategy are clearly not without problems, yet in Lees-Marshment's examination of the genesis of New Labour (Lees-Marshment 2001c: see also Lilleker and Lees-Marshment 2005: 14–38) one crucial set of actors is missing from the analysis. At no stage is there any systematic examination of the role and power of the media. The centrality of the modern media to political campaigning and marketing, while often acknowledged in the literature – for example, Lees-Marshment has noted that 'negative media' can inhibit the ability of successful parties to communicate their delivery to the public – is rarely seriously considered. Indeed, despite its overwhelming importance, the media is generally regarded as just one of many methods of conveying a message to the voters (Mauser 1983; Lees-Marshment 2001a; Henneberg, 2002).

Even when the importance of the media is conceded (for example, Butler and Collins 1994; Henneberg 2002) they are afforded a largely instrumental role and, at least implicitly, assumed to comply with the wishes of the political actors involved. To reiterate, a fundamental weakness of these models is a failure to appreciate fully that the conduit of messages is not neutral as it is in the presentation of marketing messages. So, for approaches rooted in marketing and management literature, as Lees-Marshment's model undeniably is, the media appear to be merely a tool in the marketing campaign. This poses no problems for the traditional marketing in a capitalist society of normal commercial products such as beans, computers and car insurance. With very rare exceptions, the media are effectively neutral in their attitude to such products. But political parties are not cans of beans. No one shouts at the television their hatred of Heinz baked beans and their commitment to Crosse & Blackwell's alternative product. The television channels and newspapers carrying such advertisements may have consumer programmes and lifestyle sections in which aspects of a product (for example, hidden charges or inaccurate information) are criticised but such criticism is specific and not aimed at the process of advertising or the capitalist system. Politicians and political parties have a much tougher and fundamentally different ride in the media. On current affairs and news output, the representatives and messages of political parties are subject to intense scrutiny and criticism, while on British television, entertainment programmes such as *Have I Got News For You* and *The News Quiz* hold up politicians as figures of fun who cannot be trusted – similar programmes exist in all established democracies.

This is not the place for an analysis of media power and effects, but one does not have to believe in Herman and Chomsky's 'propaganda model' to acknowledge the media are, if not 'manufacturing consent', playing a powerful role in the way messages are transmitted to the electorate. The ownership and profit orientation of the mass media, their dependence on advertisers (and hence support for the existing system), their reliance on the powerful and their unwillingness to face 'flak' (negative responses) from groups with resources, together with their general ideological preferences (Herman and Chomsky 1988) will all impact on any political marketing campaign. Although still peripheral, approaches founded in more general 'political communication' approaches at least acknowledge the importance of the media in setting the agenda and factor the importance of 'news management' into their analysis: indeed, political communications scholars see modern politics and media as 'inextricably entwined', with the activities of one 'inevitably affecting the other' (Scammell 1999: 721). By contrast, Lilleker and

Lees-Marshment's communication stage fails even to mention the role the media will play, let alone the problems of navigating a hostile press (2005: 224).

The anti-democratic tendencies of political marketing?

Given that it is the media through which politicians market their policies – indeed through which they *have* to market their policies – and that it is 'difficult to overstate the centrality of media to politicians' identity' (Franklin 2004: 5), such an oversight in any model which claims to offer a template is surprising. Politicians themselves are well aware of the media's power over their ability to communicate with citizens. As the Labour MP John Battle put it, politicians are seeing themselves as just 'another consumer product' and 'there is a temptation for my whole political existence to be determined by media coverage' (Franklin 2004: 5). As Franklin has also noted, the packaging of politics poses a number of challenges to democracies, including the possibility that the relationship between government and media becomes essentially collusive. If so, the media's role in informing the public sphere may be 'substantially diminished' by their failure to alert the electorate to the widest range of policy options (Franklin 1999: 9).

Consumers are firmly at the centre of marketing models (Keith 1960). Once consumer demands have been identified (which assumes that preferences are expressed, identifiable and able to be accommodated), they are fed back into the product offering, and as noted above, the product is refined accordingly. In politics, this is evidenced in the political marketing literature though the extensive use of opinion research to inform the construction of the political 'product' (Lees-Marshment, 2001a). This for many is viewed as a relatively straightforward process. However, the normative claims of much of the literature – that marketing 'ensures accountability and responsiveness and is a beneficial force for democracy' (Savigny 2009) – need to be challenged. The empirical evidence in the majority of Western democracies shows declining electoral turnout and an increasing lack of trust in politicians and the very processes of politics (Hay 2007). Arguably, marketing has failed to provide answers to the problem of mobilising the electorate and may be in large part responsible for increasing public cynicism about the motives of politicians. If politicians really do regard voters as the political marketing literature does – as relatively easily manipulated actors, uninterested in the minutiae of policy and lacking deep political beliefs – then it is unsurprising that many voters are being turned off by politics. The increasing volatility of electorates, with partisan attachments being weakened in many democracies, has also been presented as a problem that marketing can help solve by introducing new ways of connecting with disaffected voters – for example, building 'brand' rather than partisan loyalties. However, the claims made in political marketing for the democratic benefits of marketing lack both theoretical sophistication and empirical support (Savigny 2009).

The utilisation of focus groups to determine policy is also problematic. There are a number of fallacies in the assumption in much of the political marketing literature that the use of focus groups is good for democracy: for example, New

Labour's polling and election guru Philip Gould asserts they enable politicians 'to directly hear the voters' voices' (1998: 326). Savigny points out that MOPs, as represented by Lees-Marshment, seem to be extraordinarily selective in their use of such voter feedback. Gould's search for what Mondeo Man and Worcester Woman wanted indicates an essential truth: that New Labour's reliance on focus groups to deliver the electorate's message challenges the 'normative claims to democracy' made for democracy (Savigny 2007: 122) because it is only the views of those key voters which matter. In 1997, Labour had identified 90 key target seats. By 2001 there were 'no key seats only key voters' (Seyd 2001: 54) and by 2005 only a tiny minority of the electorate – Wintour (2005) says 2 per cent – were considered strategically significant by Labour. Such 'stratified electioneering' devalues the role of voters who are permanently aligned to a political party (Wring 2005: 179) and undermines assertions that the voter as consumer is at the centre of political marketing approaches.

So, the claims for 'responsiveness' to public opinion have to be treated sceptically. Labour's rapid ideological move rightwards following Blair's accession was largely based on the views of swing voters: such a development 'undermines the very ideal of liberal democracy' (Savigny 2007: 134). Not only did Phillip Gould's 'interventionist approach' inhibit some opinions being expressed in focus group sessions, but also carefully selected focus groups mean a small and unrepresentative sample of the electorate become paramount, thereby weakening notions of democratic responsiveness and accountability. As noted, Labour's campaign in 2005 continued the narrow focus on a very small and closely targeted section of the electorate, adding weight to claims that the use of marketing is challenging democratic ideals (Savigny 2005: 21). Coleman argues that the use of focus groups means that MOPs are 'populist' – that is, feeding 'popular prejudices in return for votes and power' (2007: 181).

Political marketing has also been accused of subverting democracy's ideal of an engaged and politically active citizen, although Lees-Marshment's idea of the 'citizen consumer' (see also Scammell 2003; Schudson 2006; Lilleker and Scullion 2008) answers some of the criticisms. Lees-Marshment argues that parties should not treat voters solely as consumers, but as both consumers and citizens – but it is difficult to accuse even New Labour of not at least paying lip service to this. There is the need for further debate as to whether, current practice not withstanding, customer needs and a programme for cohesive citizenship are really alien to one another. For example, Scullion (2008) suggests that consumer sovereignty gives the public power, perhaps more power than as a citizen, which meets rather than erodes democratic ideals. Consumerism gives people a stronger voice, empowers them and increases their efficacy. Citizenship can exist within a consumer culture and consumerism in politics can create avenues for the public to take on civic qualities, consider broader public issues and accept responsibility for shaping their own lives (see Savigny 2008b for an alternative argument).

Indeed, several of the issues that political marketing raises need more complex analysis in future. The primacy often ascribed to marketing approaches of winning office by meeting the needs of a few key voters at almost any cost (including ditching key beliefs) does not describe Labour's actions even at the height of its pre-1997 marketing blitz. Whether for show or not, Labour's electoral messages were cleverly designed to indicate a commitment to both change and to its historical roots; the party's traditional values still had to be integrated into a manifesto aimed at attracting back those key swing voters – tough on crime, yes, but also in line with Labour's history, tough on the causes of crime. Despite Peter Mandelson's assertion (in 1990) that Labour was prepared to abandon any policy for electoral expediency (Temple 2000: 304), New Labour did not ditch its philosophical and ideological 'baggage' from the past (Lees-Marshment and Lilleker 2001). This is partly reflected in models of market-orientation by Lees-Marshment and by Ormrod (2005) that suggest that a market-oriented party must not simply follow public opinion but adjust it to suit a range of other factors.

The relationship between politicians and voters is more complex than the marketing models acknowledge and the preferences of traditional voters, interest groups, other political leaders and, as argued, the media, must be taken into consideration. 'Market-oriented' parties may tailor policies according to focus group prejudices but they ignore other actors at their peril. And the ideology of their core supporters needs to be considered and may inhibit adapting policy to attract floating voters. Knuckey's examination of the USA highlights the continuing importance of ideology, as does the country study of Germany here. As the country studies in this book demonstrate, and Strömbäck's research propositions makes plain, the nature of the political systems is also a major factor. Proportional representation systems make it less imperative for ideologically committed parties such as the Greens and Communists to tailor their product to fickle floating voters. Hutcheson's analysis of Russia's brief 'managed democracy' experience (this volume) suggests that campaigning costs inhibit smaller parties and make it less essential for the 'parties of power', who can rely on bureaucratic and media support, to adopt a market orientation. In addition 'the overwhelming use of administrative resources and legislative engineering' to seek voter support means that in Russia the market is itself being adapted by ruling parties. Market-oriented parties are not a logical or natural outcome in many political systems.

An appraisal of the Lees-Marshment model

Lees-Marshment's three-stage model comes directly from the application of marketing and management ideas to the study of politics and, as such, reflects the positivist assumptions underpinning most of the management marketing literature (Savigny 2009). For critics, this more prescriptive political marketing literature commits a 'logical fallacy' by 'conflating evidence consistent with its models as evidence of its normative contribution to political practice'. The paradoxes of such assertions, given the positivist/empiricist nature of such studies and the emphasis in positivism upon observer neutrality, have also been noted (Savigny 2009).

Any criticism of the Lees-Marshment model and the approaches in this collection needs to acknowledge that Lees-Marshment has always accepted that the MOP model does not provide all the answers. Indeed, Lilleker and

Lees-Marshment (2005) were remarkably open about the flaws in the model, acknowledging that more work is needed on the model for it to be truly useful as a comparative tool. Lees-Marshment and her collaborators have not been afraid to address weaknesses in the model and remain remarkably open as to its general utility or even to the question of whether political marketing can ever provide even partial solutions to key problems for liberal democracies. A number of the studies in their 2005 book (for example, Brazil) challenged the idea that market approaches are 'good for democracy' and Lilleker and Lees-Marshment accept the potential conflict between marketing and democracy, recognise the continuing importance of leadership and ideology, question whether a market-oriented approach is possible for governing parties and concede the many difficulties of producing a general explanatory model. The problem is that these important issues are treated as essentially minor gnat bites on the veracity of the model, which can somehow be incorporated to make the model more 'realistic'.

Lees-Marshment's model is effectively a Weberian 'ideal type' which abstracts and simplifies 'reality': such models can be used to highlight some aspects of political behaviour but, arguably, should not form the basis for prescriptive templates (Savigny 2008a). While Lees-Marshment acknowledges that ideology and leadership are important in deciding the actions a party will take, adding these and other factors to the model only succeeds in weakening its analytical value. It becomes merely a description of an observed 'reality' rather than the simple and analytically useful model Lees-Marshment (2001a, b) first offered to explain the genesis of political party strategies. The same strictures apply to all rational choice models which are gradually adjusted to make them more 'realistic' or to make them more accurate predictors of outcomes. For example, the problems of applying a narrow model of rationality in which parties are driven solely by a desire for office, is apparent in the development of predictive coalition theories – but the attempt to broaden the coalition formation model to include ideological closeness and policy preferences weakened the model's explanatory power. The elegant simplicity of economic rational choice theory was lost, and the same caveat applies to Lees-Marshment's model. If MOPs are a permanent feature of modern democracies – and the evidence from the studies in this volume suggests otherwise, despite a perceived movement in the direction of market orientation in (for example) Hungary, Ghana and Australia – then we must attempt to offer a realistic analysis that provides the possibility of comparative studies. But loading down the model with ever more factors is not the way.

As Coleman notes, the three-stage model as offered by Lilleker and Lees-Marshment (2005) fails to address the 'most significant normative question' around their analysis: that is, the extent to which democratic parties should 'see their role as being to satisfy consumer needs rather than supply a programme for cohesive citizenship' (Coleman 2007: 185). Savigny (2009) agrees, arguing that rather than enhancing democracy, marketing politics means that something has been lost. The emphasis on key voters and short-term goals means that the public sphere is less informed, inhibiting the ability of the polity to hold political elites to account, and decisions are no longer taken in the interests of society as a whole. The modelling and prescribing of political behaviour from models and assumptions founded in product marketing is, in effect, subordinating politics to marketing (Savigny 2009). And when everyone is marketing himself or herself, changing beliefs or policies at the drop of a hat in order to attract votes, politics risks descending into populism – further alienating the electorate.

Conclusion

At the core of Lees-Marshment's studies is a belief in the democracy-enhancing capability of marketing. There has been considerable criticism of this and of her model's normative tendencies and failure to consider adequately the role played by the modern mass media (Savigny 2008a). However, this is not to argue that the work of Jennifer Lees-Marshment (or indeed, others working in her sub-field of political marketing) has been ill considered or in vain, as a hostile reader of this chapter might assume. I would argue the Lees-Marshment model is a valuable heuristic device. Having seen a seminar room full of the political classes engrossed by her outlining and exploration of the model, and listened to the spirited debates that followed, it is clear that the adoption of marketing techniques (if not their subjugation of ideology) by political parties is seen as essential and that the approach Lees-Marshment adopts resonates with many politicians. Lees-Marshment's work has been criticised for what it is perceived as claiming – a 'comprehensive theoretical framework' – rather than for the considerable potential insights it offers into not only New Labour's genesis but also the development of marketing perspectives by parties in other political systems. Based around the common framework of the Lees-Marshment model, the fascinating country studies in this book are a valuable addition to our knowledge and give, for the first time, a truly comparative picture of the scope and development of political marketing.

However, the main impact and importance of Lees-Marshment's work may well be the debate it has engendered about the role of political marketing in modern democracies. From personal experience, it is clear that the divide between the different schools of political marketing has acted as a barrier to communication between academics broadly pursuing the same area of study, who have sometimes overlooked work by 'rival' approaches. Any mention of 'market-oriented parties' among a crowd of political communications experts is guaranteed to create a lively atmosphere. Whatever the perceived weaknesses in the market-oriented approach, no study of party political marketing can now fail to address these issues.

However, what the country studies here generally suggest is that the simple stages of 'development' from POP to SOP to MOP, while a potentially valuable aid to understanding the processes of modern mediated politics, fail to delineate the process of politics in most systems. Parties cannot just ditch long-held ideological beliefs in order to meet perceived (and possibly short-term) swings in public opinion. Even commercial organisations have to be careful not to misread consumer feedback – the debacle of 'New Coke', when changes alienated 'traditional users' and led to a massive public relations disaster for Coca Cola, demonstrates this. No party can (certainly not yet, anyway) be a 'true' market-oriented party. In effect, political parties are not purely product-oriented, sales-oriented or market-oriented. They must be both product- and market-oriented if they are to prosper in a mediated political environment.

Finally, in any model of political marketing, the media must be more than one of the many factors impacting on the likelihood of parties or candidates becoming market-oriented, as in Strömbäck's research propositions. When the interaction between parties and 'consumers' is mediated by actors arguably more powerful than either politicians or voters, those actors (press and broadcasting) need to be central to any convincing model of political behaviour.

References/further reading

Butler, P. and Collins, N. (1994) 'Political Marketing: Structure and Process', *European Journal of Marketing*, 28(1): 19–34.

Butler, P. and Collins, N. (1996) 'Strategic Analysis in Political Markets', *European Journal of Marketing*, 30(10/11): 32–44.

Coleman, S. (2007) 'Review of *Political Marketing: A Comparative Perspective*, D. Lilleker, and J. Lees-Marshment (eds)', *Parliamentary Affairs*, 60(1): 180–6.

Downs, A. (1957) *An Economic Theory of Democracy*, New York: Harper.

Egan, J. (1999) 'Political Marketing: Lessons from the Mainstream', *Journal of Marketing Management*, 15: 495–503.

Franklin, B. (ed.) (1999) *Social Policy, The Media and Misrepresentation*, London: Routledge.

Franklin, B. (2004) *Packaging Politics: Political Communications in Britain's Media Democracy*, London: Arnold.

Gaber, I. (1998) 'A World of Dogs and Lamp-posts', *New Statesman*, 19 June: 13.

Gould, P. (1998) *The Unfinished Revolution*, London: Little, Brown and Company.

Harrop, M. (1990) 'Political Marketing', *Parliamentary Affairs*, 43(3): 277–91.

Hay, C. (2007) *Why We Hate Politics*, London: Polity.

Henneberg, S. C. M. (2002) 'Understanding Political Marketing', in N. J. O'Shaughnessy and S. C. M. Henneberg (eds) *The Idea of Political Marketing*, Westport, CT: Praeger.

Herman, E. S. and Chomsky, N. (1988) *Manufacturing Consent: The Political Economy of the Mass Media*, New York: Pantheon Books.

Kavanagh, D. (1995) *Election Campaigning: The New Marketing of Politics*, Oxford: Blackwell.

Keith, R. (1960) 'The Marketing Revolution', *Journal of Marketing*, 24: 35–8.

Kotler, P. (1972) 'A Generic Concept of Marketing', *Journal of Marketing*, 36(2): 46–54.

Kotler, P. (1981) 'Business Marketing for Political Candidates', *Campaigns & Elections*, 2: 24–33.

Kotler, P. and Kotler, N. (1999) 'Political Marketing: Generating Effective Candidates, Campaigns and Causes', in B. Newman (ed.) *Handbook of Political Marketing*, London: Sage.

Kotler, P. and Levy, S. (1969) 'Broadening the Concept of Marketing', *Journal of Marketing*, 33: 10–15.

Kuhn, R. (2007) *Politics and the Media in Britain*, Basingstoke: Palgrave Macmillan.

Lees-Marshment, J. (2001a) *Political Marketing and British Political Parties: The Party's Just Begun*, Manchester: Manchester University Press.

Lees-Marshment, J. (2001b) 'The Marriage of Politics and Marketing', *Political Studies*, 49(4): 692–713.

Lees-Marshment, J. (2001c) 'The Product, Sales and Market-Oriented Party: How Labour Learnt to Market the Product, Not Just the Presentation', *European Journal of Marketing*, 35: 1074–84.

Lees-Marshment, J. and Lilleker, D. (2001) 'Political Marketing and Traditional Values: "Old Labour" for "new times"?', *Contemporary Politics*, 7(3): 205–16.

Lees-Marshment, J. and Lilleker, D. (2005) 'Political Marketing in the UK: A Positive Start but Uncertain Future', in D. Lilleker and J. Lees-Marshment (eds) *Political Marketing: A Comparative Perspective*, Manchester: Manchester University Press. [15–38]

Lilleker, D. (2006) *Key Concepts in Political Communication*, London: Sage.

Lilleker, D. and Lees-Marshment, J. (eds) (2005) *Political Marketing: A Comparative Perspective*, Manchester: Manchester University Press.

Lilleker, D. and Scullion, R. (eds) (2008) *Voters or Consumers: Imagining the Contemporary Electorate*, Cambridge: Cambridge Scholars Publishing.

Lloyd, J. (2004) *What the Media are Doing to our Politics*, London: Constable & Robinson Ltd.

Mauser, G. (1983) *Political Marketing*, New York: Praeger.

Newman, B. (1994) *The Marketing of the President: Political Marketing as Campaign Strategy*, London: Sage.

Newman, B. (ed.) (1999) *Handbook of Political Marketing*, London: Sage.

O'Cass, A. (1996) 'Political Marketing and the Marketing Concept', *European Journal of Marketing*, 30(10/11): 45–61.

O'Cass, A. (2001) 'Political Marketing: An Investigation of the Political Marketing Concept and Political Market Orientation in Australian Politics', *European Journal of Marketing*, 35(9/10): 1003–25.

Ormrod, R. P. (2005) 'A Conceptual Model of Political Market Orientation', *Journal of Nonprofit & Public Sector Marketing*, 14(1/2): 47–64.

O'Shaughnessy, N. J. and Henneberg, S. C. M. (eds) (2002) *The Idea of Political Marketing*, Westport, CT: Praeger.

Phillis, B. (2004) *An Independent Review of Government Communications*. Available at: <http://archive.cabinetoffice.gov.uk/gcreview/News/FinalReport.pdf > (accessed 6 June 2009).

Reid, D. M. (1988) 'Marketing the Political Product', *European Journal of Marketing*, 22(9): 34–47.

Savigny, H. (2005) 'Labour, Political Marketing and the 2005 Election: A Campaign of Two Halves', *Journal of Marketing Management*, 21: 1–17.

Savigny, H. (2007) 'Focus Groups and Political Marketing: Science and Democracy as Axiomatic', *British Journal of Politics and International Relations*, 9: 122–37.

Savigny, H. (2008a) *The Problem of Political Marketing*, New York: Continuum.

Savigny, H. (2008b) 'The Construction of the Political Consumer (or Politics: What Not to Consume', in D. Lilleker and R. Scullion (eds) *Voters or Consumers: Imagining the Contemporary Electorate*, Newcastle, UK: Cambridge Scholars Publishing.

Savigny, H. (2009) 'Political Marketing', in C. Hay, M. Kenny, M. Flinders and A. Gamble (eds) *The Oxford Handbook of British Politics*, Oxford: Oxford University Press.

Scammell, M. (1995) *Designer Politics: How Elections are Won*, London: Macmillan.

Scammell, M. (1999) 'Political Marketing: Lessons for Political Science', *Political Studies*, 47(4): 718–39.

Scammell, M. (2003) 'Citizens Consumers: Towards a New Marketing of Politics?', in J. Corner and D. Pels (eds) *Media and the Restyling of Politics*, London: Sage.

Schudson, M. (2006) 'The Troubling Equivalence of Citizen and Consumer', *The ANNALS of the American Academy of Political and Social Science*, 608: 193–204.

Scullion, R. (2008). 'The Impact of the Market on the Character of Citizenship, and the Consequences of this for Political Engagement', in D. Lilleker and R. Scullion (eds) *Voters or Consumers: Imagining the Contemporary Electorate*, Newcastle, UK: Cambridge Scholars Publishing.

Sellar, W. C. and Yeatman, R. J. (1930) *1066 and All That*, London: Methuen.

Seyd, P. (2001) 'The Labour Campaign', *Parliamentary Affairs*, 54(4): 607–23.

Smith, G. and Saunders, J. (1990) 'The Application of Marketing to British Politics', *Journal of Marketing Management*, 5(3): 295–306.

Street, J. (2001) *Mass Media, Politics and Democracy*, Basingstoke: Palgrave.

Soley, C. (2005) 'The Public is Sick of us Both', *British Journalism Review*, 16: 35–9.

Temple, M. (1996) *The Development of Coalition Theory: A Non-Technical Introduction*, Staffordshire University: Papers in Politics and International Relations, No. 25.

Temple, M. (2000) 'New Labour's Third Way: Pragmatism and Governance', *British Journal of Politics & International Relations*, 2(3): 302–24.

Wintour, P. (2005) 'Campaign Planners Buy into Supermarket Tactics'. Available at: <www.spinwatch.org>

Wring, D. (1996) 'Political Marketing and Party Development in Britain: A "Secret" History', *European Journal of Marketing*, 30: 100–11.

Wring, D. (1997) 'Reconciling Marketing with Political Science: Theories of Political Marketing', *Journal of Marketing Management*, 13: 651–63.

Wring, D. (2005) *The Politics of Marketing the Labour Party*, Basingstoke: Palgrave Macmillan.

19 Global political marketing

Analysis and conclusions

Jennifer Lees-Marshment,
Chris Rudd and Jesper Strömbäck

Political marketing is a global activity: political parties around the world all utilize marketing techniques and concepts, but the extent to which marketing is used to design the political product as opposed to sell it not only varies from one country to another, but from one election to the next. This global study has revealed that the overall trend in political marketing is diverse and fluctuating; it is not simply the case that major office-seeking parties in developed democracies successively move towards the market-oriented party model and that parties in developing democracies eventually will follow. Indeed there are times when parties move closer to the market-oriented party model in new democracies while parties in established democracies remain or move towards the sales-oriented party model. Whilst political marketing is an important tool for parties to consider, and there is no doubt that practitioners are aware of its potential and share both tools and product concepts, it is by no means a quick fix or guarantee of success, given the complex range of activities it involves.

The chapters included in this book have provided a rich and complex picture of political parties and their behaviour and the degree to which the parties are sales- or market-oriented. Each chapter has also described a number of structural and semi-structural characteristics of each country that were singled out as potentially being important in the framework for comparing political market-orientation proposed by Strömbäck in Chapter 2. These are summarized in Table 19.1.

Based on the country chapters, the main purpose of this chapter is to revisit and analyze those systemic factors identified by Strömbäck as likely to facilitate or prevent the process of political parties becoming more market-oriented. We then continue by assessing the degree to which parties, in general, tend to be product-, sales- or market-oriented and what the results imply with respect to the concept of market-orientation and market-oriented parties. We also reflect on the practical complexities of a market-orientation by revisiting the practitioner perspective provided by Mortimore and Gill in Chapter 17 and the democratic implications raised by Temple in Chapter 18.

The political system

As in all comparative analysis, the formal arrangement of the political system is expected to impact considerably on political behaviour. However our empirical study challenges this assumption. Surprisingly, the electoral and party systems seem to have only a limited impact on the extent to which parties are market-oriented. For multi-party systems, as predicted, these tend to foster sales-oriented parties as the multiplicity of parties makes for a crowded political landscape, making it harder for parties to 'shift to the centre'. But even in those countries dominated by two parties (UK, Australia, USA, Taiwan, Germany, New Zealand, Ghana, Japan) there was no clear pattern for these dominant parties to be predominantly market-oriented. There was, however, evidence that these major parties shifted back and forth between sales- and market-orientations, with the main factor pushing a party towards market-orientation being successive electoral defeats/prolonged periods in opposition, while the shift back to a sales-orientation usually resulted from a long period of incumbency.

Few contributors looked closely at minor parties but those that did found some use of market intelligence. This would seem to contradict the expectation that minor parties tend to be product-oriented and thus have little need for finding out what voters think and want. Even the small left-wing Greek Synaspismos party used market intelligence to try to 'sell' its predetermined product to the voter. This finding, however, should not surprise us, as all parties, even those which cater only to a niche market, need to have some idea as to who their likely voters are, where they live and so on. The Hungarian SZDSZ used market intelligence to target its niche market and this was part of the party's sales-oriented strategy. The Australian Democrats and Greens used market intelligence to help design the short-term election campaign rather than for the long-term design of policies.

In fact, gathering information about their potential market would seem to be even more important for small parties who need to use their limited resources effectively. The *priority* given to market intelligence, however, is less for minor parties who have a product/sales-orientation than if they were more market-oriented. The German Greens and FDP, for example, abandoned altogether the use of focus groups for the 2005 election when the surprise early calling of the election probably left these parties with insufficient funds to cover such an activity. This highlights that market intelligence can be used for a range of purposes, not just to find out what voters want. Such purposes include the strength and location of current support for a party; potential support for a new strategy or product; and existing and potential activities of volunteers and members. The information can inform not just product development and strategy but the communication and allocation of resources, and the selling of a new policy, and be used at different stages in an electoral cycle.

In general, therefore, adopting marketing *language* ('door-to-door canvassing' becomes 'voter ID profiling'; 'discussion groups' become 'focus groups') and marketing *practices* (branding, positioning . . .) does not in itself constitute adopting a market-oriented approach. There is an important practical and

Table 19.1 System checklist against research propositions in original comparative framework for political marketing analysis

System characteristics	Hungary	Peru	Taiwan	Germany	Ghana	UK
Candidate- or party-centred	Party	Candidate	Party	Party	Candidate	Party
Majoritarian or proportional electoral systems	Mixed proportional	Majoritarian	Combination (worked proportionally until 2008)	Combination but mainly proportional	Majoritarian	Majoritarian
Strength of left–right ideological dimension	Strong	Weak but strengthening	Weak in traditional European terms	Strong but weakening	Strong	Weak
Two-party or multi-party system	Multi	Multi	Few but two major parties dominate	Multi but two parties dominate	Multi	Few but two parties dominate
Few or many competing parties	Many (five in parliament)	Many	Still two main ones; two smaller ones	Many	Few – two parties dominate	Few
Low or high degree of party identification	High	Very low	Medium	Declining – high	Declining – high	Low
High or low electoral volatility	Low	Very high	Medium	Higher than in the 1960s, still increasing	High	High
Highly or less commercialized media system	Highly commercial	Highly commercial	Highly commercial	Mixed	Highly commercial	Mixed
Adversarial or less adversarial journalistic culture	Less adversarial	Adversarial	Adversarial	Less adversarial	Adversarial	Adversarial
Deep or weak social or political cleavages	Deep	Very deep	Deep divide on national identity	Declining – but still on economic lines	Deep	Weak
Egalitarian or hierarchical political culture	Hierarchical	Still in development	Egalitarian	Egalitarian	Egalitarian	Egalitarian
High or lower level of political distrust	High	High	High	High	High	High
News media independent of or form part of the party-political system	News media form part of the political system	Independent	Independent (now)	Independent but biased	Party influences media	TV independent; newspapers partisan but independent

New Zealand	Australia	Sweden	US	Russia	Greece	Japan	Czech
Party	Party	Party	Candidate	Party (now)	Party	Mixed	Party
Proportional	Proportional	Proportional	Majoritarian	Proportional	Majoritarian	Proportional	Proportional
Weak	Weak	Strong	Strong	Weak	Medium	Weak	Strong
Multi but two dominate	Multi but three dominate	Multi	Two	Multi but one party dominates	Multi but two parties dominate	Multi but two parties dominate	Multi
Few	Few	Many	Few	Few	Still two main ones; two or three smaller ones	Few	Many
Low	Low	Declining – medium	Medium – but has increased	Low	Strong but declining	Very low	Low
High	High	High	High	Low (High 1993–2003)	Low but increasing	Low but increasing	Low
Commercial – state broadcaster works like commercial with adverts	Mixed	Mixed	Highly commercial	Less commercial	Highly commercial	Mixed	Highly commercial
Adversarial	Adversarial	Less adversarial	Adversarial	Less adversarial	Adversarial	Less adversarial	Adversarial
Weak	Weak	Weak	Weak	Weak	Medium – weak	Historically deep	Declining
Egalitarian	Egalitarian	Egalitarian	Egalitarian	Hierarchical	Egalitarian	Hierarchical	Egalitarian
High	High	High	High	Low	High	Low but increasing	High
Independent	Independent	Independent	Independent	Independent of party politics *per se* but not of Kremlin	Mainly independent but newspapers partisan	Independent newspapers with mild ideological differences	Independent

conceptual difference between the usage of marketing techniques and being market-oriented (Lees-Marshment, 2001; Ormrod, 2005; Strömbäck, 2007). All parties may employ marketing techniques, irrespective of party size or position on the left–right spectrum. Being market-oriented involves the transfer of a mindset, of a way of thinking about politics – policies, the policy process and political actors. This is a point to which we will return later.

There is some evidence to support the proposition that where a left–right cleavage is pronounced, it is less likely to find parties that adopt a catch-all appeal (and vice versa). In Peru, for example, major social and economic problems (poverty, unemployment) have tended to polarize politics and push parties to adopt (or at least appear to adopt) appeals to either the radical right or left. In other countries (for example, the UK, New Zealand, Australia, Ghana) where a left–right ideological cleavage is (or has become) less pronounced, we see the tendency for some parties to become more market-oriented in adopting a centrist, catch-all appeal.

The parliamentary arena

Within the parliamentary arena, evidence from a number of countries (the UK, Australia, New Zealand, Taiwan, Sweden, Ghana, Peru) does confirm that parties that suffer successive electoral defeats are more likely to become more market-oriented as a means of recovering lost support. Furthermore, a long tenure of government incumbency, just like a long spell in opposition, can weaken a party's market-orientation. There seem to be at least two possible reasons for this.

First, the party was/is office-seeking and only paid lip service to market-orientation when in opposition, showing it was gathering information about what people wanted but when in office, the party failed to follow through on its promises (weak delivery). Examples might be the ND in Greece after its winning office in 2004; the Hungarian MSZP following its success at the 2006 election; and the DPP in Taiwan after it won power in 2000. Also the 'parties of power' in Russia have used marketing techniques to win office, but once there, have used state resources to make sure they have remained in power irrespective of their government performance.

Second, a party faces the constraints of being in office. It is difficult to deliver and/or keep using market intelligence only to cater for those wants and needs of those it 'consulted' in order to win office; a governing party is now faced with the responsibility to consider a much wider group of voters. Parties may also find themselves in a government with coalition partners, and to retain the support of such partners, a party may need to compromise on some of its pre-electoral promises. Parties that find themselves in these kinds of situation have increasingly to use persuasion in order to retain support, especially amongst core supporters. In a sense there is a 'curse of incumbency' where governing parties are placed into a position where logic dictates they must defend those policies that they have been responsible for implementing and overseeing – irrespective of whether market intelligence tells them that the policies are (or are no longer) popular with voters.

Examples of where long periods of incumbency have pushed parties towards 'selling' rather than 'listening' would be the Labour parties in the UK and New Zealand; the Liberals in Australia; PASOK in Greece; the KMT in Taiwan; the LDP in Japan, and the APRA in Peru.

There are, however, instances where governing parties have tried to reverse this drift away from a market-orientation. In the UK, the Labour Government regained responsiveness in 2005 following a period, epitomized by the decision to join the USA in the invasion of Iraq, when the party seemed to disconnect from its supporters. In New Zealand, the Labour Party also showed signs of resurgent responsiveness in 2007–2008 after a succession of opinion polls suggested the party and its leader were out-of-touch and 'arrogant'. Yet in both these cases, the parties appeared to be simply reacting to a resurgent (and more market-oriented) opposition and lacked sincerity – and did little to revive the flagging electoral fortunes of either party. The New Zealand Labour Party lost office in 2008 after trailing in the polls for over 18 months to its main rival, the National Party. As for the UK Labour Party, there was an initial boost in its support after Gordon Brown took over as leader in June 2007 but by the start of 2009, Labour was 20 points behind the Conservative Party. The Czech Social Democrats were in power from 1998 until 2006. The party had not adopted a market-orientation in order to win power, but it did so in order to try to retain power. Again this was a reactive strategy in response to a massive loss of public support, internal party disunity and alleged corruption – but it was not a response to the emergence of a more market-oriented opposition. And despite becoming more market-oriented, the ČSSD still lost power at the 2006 election.

If we turn to the type of government – single-party or coalition – it is certainly the case that single-party majority governments are in a better position to deliver on election promises than coalition governments (whether majority or minority ones). This ability to deliver on promises is reinforced where there is strong party discipline in the sense that members of the governing party(ies) in the legislature can be guaranteed to support government legislation. However, this proposition holds for all types of parties in government – not just market-oriented ones. Its significance lies more in the internal party arena, where members of the legislature are viewed as just one of the stakeholders who must be brought on board *if* the party leaders should seek to become more market-oriented. In our country studies, we find that most countries have party-centred political systems where loyalty to the party is strong and 'revolts' by government members of the legislature are rare. In Japan, some members of the ruling coalition party, the LDP, did oppose the party leadership's intention to deregulate the postal service – as a result, parliament was dissolved and the party refused to give party endorsement to the rebel members and instead successfully ran officially sanctioned candidates against them.

While coalition governments are common, a dominant party is usually present and while minor coalition parties do gain policy concessions, the perception of the 'tail wagging the dog' is the exception rather than the rule. The one example in our country studies where a *single* ruling party has significantly altered its policy programme from the very start when it was elected is the Peruvian APRA. Ironically, this was not because the APRA had to form a coalition government following the 2006 election, but because it decided to co-opt members from the conservative parties in order to calm fears in economic and financial circles, and it was this that brought about policy change.

Electoral arena

With only a few exceptions, almost all countries are experiencing a decline in the number and strength of party identifiers, declining party membership, greater electoral volatility, declining turnout in elections, a growing distrust of politics and politicians, and a weakening of left–right ideology as a basis for voting. The consequences of all this are that:

1. the parties can no longer rely on unconditional loyalty to retain past support;
2. the party organization no longer has the resources or the ancillary organizations (unions, farmers' associations) to act as eyes and ears for the party – hence an increasing need to employ 'outside professionals' and/or their associated marketing techniques, including polling and focus groups;
3. there appears to have been at least somewhat of a shift from *position* issues to *valence* issues around which political competition occurs – and this competition is based on which party or leader is perceived as the most competent, honest, trustworthy – all qualities that are intangible and susceptible to manipulation by spin doctors, media managers and consultants.

However, the above does not automatically lead to more market-oriented parties. A party, for example, can respond to the above developments by intensifying its use of marketing techniques in order to hard-sell its product. But if it is a product that was originally designed for traditional voting blocs such as 'workers' or 'farmers' or 'small businesses', it is going to be difficult to sell to a more heterogeneous electorate. Even if social groups can still clearly be identified, it is likely that membership of such groups is no longer a strong predictor of political orientation. So, parties now may need to engage more sophisticated methods of voter segmentation (for example, using psychographic or behavioural variables) with which to target voters *within* social groupings. Narrowcasting and micro-targeting thus becomes more important, at the expense of – but by no means replacing – broadcasting communication strategies (Hillygus and Shields, 2008).

The above developments can certainly create the *potential* for a shift towards market-oriented parties. Peru is an example of very weak institutionalization of parties and low levels of party affiliation – fertile ground for the development of market-oriented parties. Yet only the APRA in Peru seems to have gone in this direction with the other parties using a sales-oriented approach. Hungary, on the other hand, is an example where the left–right cleavage still has high political relevance and yet even here, the parties have not really developed into market-oriented ones.

The high levels of public distrust of politicians may not be a recent phenomenon. Nevertheless, when taken in conjunction with declining partisanship and party membership, it reinforces the pressure on political parties to make efforts to at least *appear* to be solicitous of voters' wishes. Furthermore, parties recognize the need to let voters know what they have achieved – delivered on promises – when part of government (it also encourages parties to 'under-promise' and then, hopefully, 'over-achieve').

Overall, our country studies suggest that electoral dealignment is a *necessary* condition for the development of market-oriented parties. If parties still compete along the socio-economic cleavage, drawing their support largely from clearly identified and stable social groupings, where party choice is largely the product of childhood and family socialization, then a market-orientation would seem unnecessary if not even counter-productive. Yet electoral dealignment is clearly not a *sufficient* condition for parties to become more market-oriented – in fact, the evidence suggests more of a widespread shift to sales- rather than market-orientation.

Internal party arena

It was indicated above that if parties endure electoral defeat(s), and this leads to being thrown into opposition or remaining in opposition, then this can push parties into taking a more market-oriented strategy. This may be less the case for policy-oriented parties than for office- or vote-seeking parties. Yet even for vote-seeking parties, the internal party arena may impose constraints on the party's room for manoeuvre. On the one hand, the German experience points to how the strong internal culture retards the development of market-oriented parties, with an active rank-and-file resistant to the kind of top-down changes that a market-orientation would require. The hierarchical culture of the Swedish Moderate party, on the other hand, helped facilitate the changes proposed by the new leader in 2003 and onwards. Parties in newer democracies without firmly established party cultures and traditions might have greater flexibility to introduce radical change in the party direction, as the examples in Peru, Ghana and the Czech Republic demonstrate.

In the UK, the Conservative Party is a good example of how difficult it can be for parties with a long history and clearly identifiable core voters, even when defeated on three successive occasions, to change policy offerings and redesign brand image. Many Conservative Party activists, members and even some of its own elected legislative members were not convinced that the party product was at fault. Other examples of internal party struggles over whether a party should be more market-oriented are the LDP when Koizumi became leader in 2001 and the KMT and DPP in Taiwan. The case of the KMT is interesting in that, while a centralized party structure enabled the party to impose radical changes towards a more market-orientation, this was done at the cost of causing defections from and dissatisfaction at the local levels of the party. This undermined the effectiveness of the changes introduced and highlights that even for centralized and hierarchical parties, there is a need to incorporate the lower echelons of the party into the change process in order for such changes to 'stick'.

In general terms, the more centralized and hierarchical the party, the easier to make the shift in orientation; the more decentralized, the harder. For a party to successfully shift towards a market-orientation, it seems that a party leadership must be able to impose or at least win over those within the party who think this is abdicating leadership/ being poll-driven/abandoning core principles/abandoning core support groups or some combination of these. The product adjustment and implementation stages are therefore crucial in facilitating this.

Media arena

We found with the media, that there was little variance in this variable on the level of analysis applied in the country chapters. All but Hungary could claim to some degree, a media that was highly or increasingly commercialized and independent of political parties – although in the case of the latter, newspapers in particular can still be partisan. Even in cases where there was some state control of television broadcasting, the state channel was increasingly expected to perform in a commercial manner (accepting advertising as in the case of Television New Zealand) or open to competition with private broadcasters (as in the case of Japan's NHK). Similarly, there seems to be a widespread adversarial culture amongst journalists and news reporters across all our country studies. Exactly how adversarial the journalistic cultures are varies, but over time there appears to be a general trend towards increasingly adversarial journalistic cultures. This means, as Temple suggests in his chapter, that the role of the media is 'crucially different for politicians than for companies'. In essence, the media cannot be assumed to be neutral: while the media might not display partisan bias in the strict sense of the word – although some media in some countries do – they are structurally biased in the sense that the media output is shaped by the circumstances of news production, commercial news values, journalistic norms and values, and the competition for people's attention. Although on the level of analysis employed in this volume there is little variation, this should not be understood as if the role of the media is minor (Strömbäck and Kaid, 2008).

Hence, we find that all parties in our study placed emphasis on the use of the free media with which to communicate with voters and, as pointed out in the case of Ghana, in a highly competitive and deregulated media market, there are a multitude of media channels available for politicians to use. While the media may invariably adopt a critical attitude towards politicians and politics (reinforcing – even creating – the distrust amongst citizens noted above), politicians do have the opportunity to play media outlets against one another. The discussion of whether the media are as dependent upon politicians for information as politicians are dependent on the media for communicating with voters – i.e., are politicians or journalists holding the upper hand in this relationship – is not resolved and there may be variations across countries (Esser, 2008; Hallin and Mancini, 2004). However, there is broad consensus in the research literature that journalists and politicians are symbiotically linked and that both parties need each other in the ongoing 'negotiation of newsworthiness' these are involved in (Cook, 2005). Both political parties and journalists might dislike their dependence on the other, but they are, nevertheless, interdependent and symbiotically linked.

It is unlikely that an independent adversarial media is more likely to persuade parties to be market-oriented than sales-oriented; in both cases, parties are put in a position where they need to employ media managers ('spin doctors'). In fact, parties that seek to claim they are following and responding to what citizens say they want can produce more negative coverage from the media, than parties that do not make such a claim. For example, the Labour Party in the UK received much media ridicule for what was perceived as its obsession with focus groups. Precisely because of the cynical stance the media takes towards politicians, this leads journalists to look for ulterior motives and 'hidden agendas' for parties that claim their policies are in line with the wishes of the public. Parties that are more product-oriented and adopt policies that run counter to prevailing public sentiment are likely to be ignored rather than criticized by the media, although this depends on a number of other factors, including the size and importance of the party.

Overall trend in market-orientation

As the above survey of our results show, it is difficult to discern any clear pattern in the behaviour of parties with regard to our dependent variable – market-orientation. Specific characteristics of the political (parliamentary, electoral and party) or media systems did not seem to be strongly linked to the likelihood that a party would opt for more or less market-orientation. The main reason for this, however, is that there were mixed trends in strategy and orientation and, not least important, few cases where the parties are truly market-oriented. Instead, the results clearly show that there is a prevalence of sales-oriented parties over market-oriented ones in most countries. This may be due to a variety of factors: there are still a significant number of party identifiers, even if not strong ones; there are still party members who are needed to mobilize voters, deliver party literature and raise funds; and the left–right cleavage is still of broad significance – for example, few voters would have difficulty positioning the German Social Democrats, Swedish Social Democrats, Australian Labour, UK Labour, US Democrats etc., to the left of the other major party in the political system. Where we do find evidence of a party behaving in a market-oriented fashion, being market-oriented seems more of a tactic to *win* office but not to *maintain* office – for the latter, parties seem to revert to being sales-oriented. We have noted that some governing parties have returned to market-oriented approaches when they started to lose public support; yet this did little to reverse their declining electoral fortunes. Virtually all parties make use of marketing techniques, if to varying degrees and with varying sophistication and dedication, but at the end of the day, few parties can truly be characterized as market-oriented. Most parties use marketing techniques to facilitate the selling of the party, its policies, its image or its brand. Hence, it appears as if there are significant barriers to adopting a marketing-oriented strategy or to become market-oriented, not least with respect to the design of the political product or offering.

Barriers to and facilitators of a market-oriented party

Regarding barriers to adopting a market-oriented strategy or becoming market-oriented, the most significant seems to be the internal market. A party's history means the party cannot approach an election as if it had a blank sheet on which to write party policy. If the party strays too far away from its historically defined image, it runs the risk of losing credibility, of being viewed as opportunistic and of both losing its core voters while failing to attract new ones. If we assume core voters are always situated to the left or right of the median voter for the party, this is a constraint on moving to the centre. If the core group declines for reasons unrelated to party activity (for example, fewer farmers or manual unskilled workers) this reduces the risk the party faces in trying to shift or appeal to new blocs of voters.

There may be a tipping point at which the costs to a party of being more market-oriented are outweighed by the perceived benefits. This may happen when a party has suffered electoral defeats of such a magnitude and/or with such frequency that this is not viewed as a temporary setback; or it may be that the party has little core vote to lose or its core support is so loyal, that a party can risk a revamp and repositioning without fear of losing many stalwart supporters; or the party may have a party organization sufficiently centralized or sufficiently demoralized by lack of success, that party leaders are able to impose more market-oriented measures despite any opposition from the rank-and-file. Examples of where an external shock of successive electoral defeats pushed parties towards a *more* market-oriented strategy would be the UK Conservatives (2001–), Swedish Moderates (2003–); and New Zealand National Party (2005–). In all these examples, however, and in the case of most of the parties examined in this volume, the parties appear to be motivated by goals of vote- or office-seeking. Smaller parties that do not aspire to be catch-all parties and which are most interested in policy advocacy (Gibson and Römmele, 2001; Harmel and Janda, 1994) are less likely to embark on radical change to party strategy in the face of a lack of electoral success.

However the Swedish Moderates suffered losses in just one election before adopting a more market-oriented approach. This suggests that it is important to understand how electoral defeats are perceived and processed by parties – what is seen to have caused the defeat: policies? leaders? a poor campaign? lack of funds? Is the defeat viewed as a temporary setback or the start of a long-term decline? Or might it even be the case that an *absence of electoral victories* can have an effect similar to electoral defeats? A party in successive elections may have expected to perform well but in reality, it did not manage to expand its vote share. Such a party may react as if it had in fact suffered electoral defeats. To address these questions requires further investigation. Certainly there is evidence that electoral defeats bring about change in party leadership (Andrews and Jackman, 2008) and this can be a catalyst for change in party orientation (see below).

For most party activists, the idea of deviating from what is perceived as the core ideology, core values or basic 'evaluation system', is at odds with the reasons for why they once became active in politics. Most people – some pure careerists notwithstanding – join parties because they have a goal to change society in a particular way. To abandon that goal simply based on the argument that some voters want something else may be difficult for an activist to accept. Becoming more market-oriented might be a necessary evil, but it is only acceptable as long as it is perceived as necessary. This returns us to the above question of how electoral defeat or a decline of support in opinion polls is interpreted by the party.

As originally argued in the market-oriented party framework, a market-oriented strategy adopted by a political party has to include consideration of the internal market. David Cameron in the UK and Kevin Rudd in Australia both attempted to appeal to external *and* internal markets while trying to shift their respective parties towards more of a market-orientation. Helen Clark, the New Zealand Labour Party leader, also showed an awareness of the need to adjust the party product in response to internal party demands in the years preceding her successful bid for power in 1999. Therefore being more market-oriented need not mean abandoning internal supporters; and the more effective party leaders are at managing the demands of the different markets, the more successful they can become at implementing a market-oriented strategy. This, however, draws attention to a variable that may be significant but which is hard to measure – leadership.

The leadership factor

We did not mention the role played by party leaders when setting out the various independent variables. It is clear, however, that in many of the country studies, the role of a new leader – often but not always in conjunction with poor electoral performance – was a critical factor in bringing about major change in a party's market strategy. Examples include Tony Blair (UK Labour), David Cameron (UK Conservatives), Kevin Rudd (Australian Labor), John Key (New Zealand National), Alan García Perez (Peruvian APRA), Junichiro Koizumi (Japanese LDP), Jiri Paroubek (Czech ČSSD), George Papandreou (Greek Pasok), Fredrik Reinfeldt (Swedish Moderates) and Ferenc Gyurcsány (Hungarian MSZP). Change in leadership of the DPP and KMT in Taiwan also lends support to the crucial role of leaders although in the case of the DPP, it was a new leader that shifted the party *away* from a market-oriented approach.

With the issue of leadership, there is the time factor to consider, reinforcing the point that party change is usually a long-term process. It is often forgotten that Blair's two predecessors, Neil Kinnock and John Smith, both started the move to 'modernize' the Labour Party and that Blair was building on these foundations rather than starting *de novo*. But the UK experience provides a counter-example that new leaders appointed in the wake of heavy electoral defeats bring about major change in party orientation. The Conservative Party had three leaders spanning three electoral defeats between 1997 and 2005, and yet none were able to 'modernize' the party in a way that the three Labour leaders had between 1992 and 1997.

One final word of caution needs to be given regarding the role played by leaders and the changes in market-orientation. The phase of 'market intelligence' is considered a crucial one for distinguishing the market-oriented party from the sales- and product-oriented parties. Many of the above case studies suggest that new leaders have used market intelligence to uncover why the party has suffered electoral defeats, and then used this information to change party policies, personnel and image. But this may be ascribing too great a causal power to market intelligence. Do leaders really need to use marketing techniques to find out why their parties have suffered successive electoral defeats? Is it such a puzzle why the party is so unpopular? Did Tony Blair really need to use focus groups to find out that the UK Labour Party was seen as being dominated by trade unions or that Clause IV of the party's constitution, '*To secure for the workers by hand or by brain the full fruits of their industry . . .*', made the party appear outdated? Is it not more likely that the findings of market intelligence were used to justify and legitimate courses of action to which new leaders were already committed?

We still believe that structural and semi-structural factors are immensely important for understanding political parties and their behaviour, electoral behaviour and what orientation parties decide to follow. Nevertheless, one overall conclusion we have reached is that there exists significant barriers for parties to become market-oriented, and these barriers are very difficult to overcome in the absence of contextual factors, such as an electoral shock. The structural and semi-structural factors matter, but so do more flexible and time-bound factors related to particular countries, circumstances, electoral outcomes and party leaders.

New themes in political marketing practice

There is no irreversible, linear progression of party development. Parties shift from sales- to market-oriented, and back again. There is also no 'contagion' effect in the way that parties of the right imitated the mass party structures of the left, while the left parties imitated the catch-all features of the parties of the right (Duverger, 1964; Kirchheimer, 1966). Given that not all parties have vote-maximizing as their only or first priority, clearly not all aim to adopt a market-orientation in order to attract such votes, as Mortimore and Gill note in Chapter 17. It is the case that parties at least to some extent do imitate each other in terms of adopting more professional or modern campaigning techniques, but this is not the same as imitating party orientation. For example, in Germany the SPD innovations in campaigning at the 1998 election were copied by the FDP, CDU and (less enthusiastically) the Greens for the 2002 election – yet all the parties remained primarily sales-oriented.

As Lees-Marshment (2001) points out, a party that seeks to be market-oriented has to pay attention to a number of phases – beginning with market intelligence and concluding with delivery on policy promises. If a party only addresses some of these phases, it can have significant counter-productive consequences. For example, parties that assiduously consult target electorates, formulate policies in response to these targeted voters, win government office, but then fail to deliver on such promises, are likely to face a harsher electoral backlash than the sales-oriented party that fails to deliver. In the case of the sales-oriented party, there is less of a feeling of 'broken promises' amongst voters, and there is less of a risk of alienating party members, activists or core voters.

In addition to the delivery phase, attempts to be more market-oriented have also foundered at the product adjustment phase. Parties have tended to be just *marketing*-oriented rather than the more inclusive *market*-oriented (Ormrod, 2005). The former refers to the activities of the marketing department whereas the latter is a more encompassing term that refers to the mindset of the whole organization and its relationship with various stakeholders. This distinction is important. In a number of our case studies we noted that party members or core voters often blocked the willingness and ability of a party leadership to pursue a market-oriented approach. In other words, a party leadership can employ marketing professionals, conduct marketing exercises – focus groups and the like – but the market intelligence gathered may not be acted upon if members or external support groups are unwilling to respond positively.

Recently, leaders have been attempting to apply market-orientation comprehensively to both internal and external markets with careful adjustment. However a big issue for parties trying to be market-oriented is how to carry out product adjustment in practice. They want to be responsive but still credible, authentic and retain some principles so they can satisfy internal as well as external markets. There are some examples of major parties trying to adopt a market-oriented approach but in a more comprehensive manner than did, say Bill Clinton or Tony Blair, with more attention paid to product adjustment in response to both external *and* internal input. This makes the process of adopting a market-orientation strategy more complex, but potentially more successful in the long-term. However adopting a market-oriented strategy in full is difficult within a limited time-frame – for example, the three-year electoral cycle in New Zealand and Australia or even the four-year electoral cycle that is most common around the world.

Market-driven or market-driving?

It is evident from many of the country case studies that parties have adopted some political concepts (such as segmentation) and political marketing techniques (such as polling and focus groups). It is also the case that these concepts and techniques are used as a means to gather intelligence about the electoral market, and that some parties use this information to shape policies that will be more congruent with the perceived wishes of voters. Yet we further found that many parties did not maintain a market-orientation when in power – in particular they failed to fulfil expectations or deliver on promises. We believe this reflects what Henneberg (2006) calls a 'tactical populist' party, one that is customer-driven but with only short-term goals (usually the next election). Such parties do not seek to develop a long-term relationship with their voters. A true market-oriented party, however, seeks to balance *following* the market with *leading* the market as well: the party seeks to build a relationship with its voters in a way that policies can be developed that fulfil the latent needs of voters. In other words, parties may offer policies that voters have expressed no desire for but which parties believe will benefit voters in the long-term, and based on the trust and loyalty between a party and its voters, voters are willing to support the party nonetheless.

The problem with seeking to be market-driving and taking a long-term outlook is that there is little evidence that voters adopt a long-term perspective when making their voting choice and, as we have already seen, fewer and fewer voters are so committed to a party that they are willing to suspend judgement on performance much further than the next election. The media increasingly focuses on the horse race and frame politics as a strategic game rather than as a contest over ideas and issues (Strömbäck and Kaid, 2008). The role played by the media contributes to the focus on short-term outcomes of political activity. So, it is not surprising that parties opt for following, rather than leading. Yet this ensnares parties in a vicious circle, where over-promising leads to a failure to fully deliver, which further disillusions voters and further distances voters from building a stable relationship with a chosen party. Furthermore, when a party does try to lead rather than follow, this appears so idiosyncratic as to simply reinforce voter dissatisfaction (for example, Blair and the war in Iraq). People – and the media – might on the one hand say that they want stronger and more bold political leadership, while on the other hand simultaneously punishing political leaders that try to exercise precisely such a leadership and take a long-term approach to politics. Ever more adversarial media, focusing mostly on the 'here and now', do not make the task easier of striking a balance between long-term societal needs and short-term 'responsiveness' to voters' expressed wants.

By being perceived as too market-oriented, the parties might be criticized for being populist and not exercising political leadership; by being perceived as too sales-oriented, the parties might be criticized for only spinning and manipulating the media and the public; by being perceived as being too product-oriented, the parties might be criticized for being unresponsive. Clearly, for a political party it is not easy to find acceptance for whatever orientation they adopt. Underlying this discussion and these kinds of criticisms are, as highlighted by Temple (this volume), different notions of the essential nature and purpose of political parties, and different normative conceptions of the relationship between the parties, their members, the voters at large, the media, and democracy. Would it strengthen democracy if parties became more market-oriented, or would it weaken democracy? As Temple and others note there is no easy answer to this question, but the desirability of political marketing and market-orientation cannot be discussed in isolation from various normative assumptions and standpoints.

Related to this, it is not entirely clear what 'winning' means in politics. In the commercial world where marketing originated, winning usually means increasing market shares and profits. Any product or service that can achieve this is a good and strong product or service, as long as it is produced and sold within the bounds set by the regulatory and legal environment in which commercial businesses operate, and as long as the business practices do not lead to the kind of public criticism that might offend potential customers and tarnish the corporate brand. In politics the matter is more complicated. Of course all parties want to increase their vote share, but the major question is at what price this is achieved – if it is achieved at all. When setting out their strategies and adopting their orientation, parties do not know whether they will be successful or not. The party members and activists do not know either, and what is more, it might take years before they know. The question facing parties contemplating whether to adopt a sales- or a market-orientation is thus twofold. First, is becoming more market-oriented desirable even if it means downplaying the party's core values or historically adopted policy positions, or would sacrificing parts of the party's traditional policies amount to a defeat even if it would increase the vote share at the next election? Second, is becoming market-oriented likely to lead to electoral success, or might it on the contrary risk leading to an electoral backlash?

At present, the simple answer is that we do not know. While there are indications from some countries (for example, the UK) that parties that are more market-oriented are more likely to win an election (Lees-Marshment, 2001), this volume shows that this is not necessarily universally true. What is true with respect to commercial markets might not be true with respect to political markets, and despite the notion that marketing and management theory can be applied to politics, there continue to be some significant differences between commercial markets and political markets and between commercial firms and political parties.

This means that there is no quick fix for parties, their activists and members who contemplate what orientation to adopt. The question of what orientation to adopt cannot be discussed in isolation from the question of what the party, at the end of the day, is really for. Few would argue that a party that is small, never increases its vote share and does not influence government policy is successful. Yet it is not necessarily the case that a party is successful if it abandons its ideology, core values and principles, even if by doing so, it meets voters' wants and needs, and increases the share of votes received by the party.

The complexity of a market-orientation in practice

The book has shown that not only do systemic factors influence how political marketing is used globally, but there are other factors that act as barriers to parties achieving a market-orientation even if the leaders wish them to, and that a market-orientation is much more complex than the theory suggests. In chapter 17 Mortimore and Gill provided a practitioner's reflection on the market-oriented party concept. They caution against quick, over-simplistic criticisms of a market-orientation in politics where it is caricatured as being about slavishly following polls and abandoning all other considerations such as leadership judgement in favour of purely pragmatic short-term grubbing for votes. Not only does the Lees-Marshment (2001) model argue against such a simplification, Mortimore and Gill's experience analysing public opinion and advising with political parties suggests that where politicians consider the views of the public, they do so alongside other stakeholders (see Hughes and Dann, 2006; Ormrod, 2005) including party members, party figures, experts and think tanks. Thus, as Mortimore and Gill note, 'a truly market-oriented party will be monitoring all of these markets and trying to find the best way to reconcile them, not merely allowing some a veto and ignoring others altogether'.

Furthermore, when politicians consider how to change their product in response, they do not simply change all the party's policies to give voters what they want. The market is much more subtle and complex, and politicians still need to exercise judgement and leadership in how they respond to it. Thus whilst politicians can and should engage in market intelligence this need not entail abandoning ideology or reducing the role played by leadership.

Indeed, public opinion research can help politicians lead the market as well as respond to it, by ensuring they understand potential opposition to a proposed change in policy and helping them create effective communication to change opinions or behaviour. It also helps them understand that the political product is varied and not just about policies but the competency and skills of the leadership team.

With regard to questions over the methods used when collecting market intelligence, whilst acknowledging the potential for any method such as focus groups to be misused, Mortimore and Gill point out that 'politics remains an art' and a mix of qualitative and quantitative research is beneficial for political elites. Whilst group discussion may not be accepted as scientific, 'the things a party strategist needs to understand about the state of public opinion are not all numerically measurable'. It is important to understand that 'public opinion always has to be interpreted rather than being read raw'.

Mortimore and Gill's chapter therefore adds further insight into the complexity of market-oriented politics. It makes it clear that whilst the market-oriented party should not be caricatured as being about doing what voters want without consideration of leadership and ideology, in practice public opinion is utilized as one of many different sources of ideas. However achieving a more balanced, adjusted product requires careful interpretation and exercise of judgement and is therefore a complex activity. This may therefore help explain the diverse and varying patterns of party behaviour in terms of political marketing orientation that the country studies in this book discovered.

Democratic implications of market-oriented parties

The difficulty of discussing political marketing and democracy is that the process is still under development. Certain scholars may see the potential before it has been achieved in reality. Mortimore and Gill make a profound point that there remains the possibility that market-oriented political marketing can become more of a 'two-way communication between politicians and voters' if developed into a formal consultative mechanism. In this respect therefore it can be good democratic practice to consider market intelligence, and the practitioners comment that 'we believe that it is right for politicians to take public opinion into account, not only in their own interests of maximizing their chances of electoral success, but also in the interests of good government'.

More sceptical scholars highlight a range of deficiencies with how political marketing may work, or has worked, in practice (Savigny, 2008). There are a number of valid concerns and in Chapter 18, Temple provides an overview of them. The most significant point Temple discusses that has not been sufficiently considered previously is the media–political party relationship. As Temple rightly notes, the media can frame and shape the very demands market-oriented parties are supposed to respond to. Given that parties and governments manage the media they therefore influence the media who influence the voter, and thus they control voter demands anyway. In this case, it is harder to argue that market-oriented party strategies elevate the voter in the political process. This is also true of how voters judge delivery, a crucial factor in determining the influence of this stage of the market-oriented party model in re-election. The media not only shape communication of delivery but their negative focus tends to encourage a rejection of positive success stories. This is an area that needs further consideration for both the practical utility of political marketing as an electoral strategy and the broader democratic ramifications.

Even without the factor of the media, Temple argues that there is a lack of evidence that political marketing makes politicians more responsive to the public. The idea of the 'citizen consumer' needs further work both theoretically and empirically. That marketing is being used by such a range of parties in diverse countries with differing democratic development suggests a greater urgency to such discussion. Particularly with regard to the use of micro-targeting and segmentation, encouraging focus on just certain sections of the electorate, this could mean as Temple notes that 'the public sphere is less informed, inhibiting the ability of the polity to hold political elites to account, and decisions are no longer taken in the interests of society as a whole'. This is clearly an area that needs further research.

There is one final point. Temple also makes the observation that 'the main impact and importance of Lees-Marshment's work may well be the debate it has engendered about the role of political marketing in modern democracies'. Mortimore and Gill argued that the problems often cited with political marketing are not due to marketing or academic models, but democracy itself:

> an MOP is no more than the most efficient expression of the democratic will. If there is a danger here, it does not rest in the possibility that parties might become market-oriented but that the will of the voters might cause market-orientation to lead to wrong choices.

Consideration of the democratic implications of political marketing, raises questions about the nature of democracy itself in the twenty-first century, an issue of global concern to parties all around the world.

Final words

The book also showed the complexity of the market-oriented concept. As Lees-Marshment (2001) first argued, the concept of a market-oriented party is not just about following market demands. It involves using market intelligence as one factor among many; and the product response to demands may also be driven by ideological anchors, expert opinion and party members' input as opposed to the outputs of focus groups. Political marketing in practice as well as theory is not as black and white as has been assumed; it is not the case that parties either follow public concerns and therefore use marketing or ignore them and don't. As such, fresh questions and trends in practice have thus emerged for political marketing research with, for example, new market strategies emerging for understanding the market, balancing internal and external market demands, achieving and communicating delivery, maintaining a market-orientation in government, and understanding and incorporating the role of the media in political marketing research. Future comparative studies may also consider different aspects of marketing such as market-oriented communication, branding and positioning. Another significant development has been e-marketing, which has been used in the US not just to sell but to understand the needs of volunteers and create structures that enable greater participation as well as serving to increase campaign resources in terms of on-the-ground labour and funds (for a recent overview of the political marketing literature see Lees-Marshment 2009). If there is one prediction that can be made therefore, it is that further research will undoubtedly uncover yet more variance in behaviour and what factors shape global political party marketing.

References/further reading

Andrews, J. T. and Jackman, R. W. (2008) '"If Winning Isn't Everything, Why Do They Keep Score?" Consequences of Electoral Performance for Party Leaders', *British Journal of Political Science*, 38(4): 657–675.

Cook, T. E. (2005) *Governing with the News: The News Media as a Political Institution*, 2nd edn, Chicago: University of Chicago Press.

Duverger, M. (1964) *Political Parties: Their Organisation and Activity in the Modern State*, London: Methuen.

Esser, F. (2008) 'Dimensions of Political News Cultures: Sound Bite and Image Bite News in France, Germany, Great Britain, and the United States', *The International Journal of Press/Politics*, 13(4): 401–428.

Gibson, R. and Römmele, A. (2001) 'Changing Campaign Communications: A Party-Centred Theory of Professional Campaigning', *The Harvard International Journal of Press/Politics*, 6(4): 31–43.

Hallin, D. C. and Mancini, P. (2004) *Comparing Media Systems: Three Models of Media and Politics*, New York: Cambridge University Press.

Harmel, R. and Janda, K. (1994) 'An Integrated Theory of Party Goals and Party Change', *Journal of Theoretical Politics*, 6(3): 259–287.

Henneberg, S. (2006) 'Leading or Following? A Theoretical Analysis of Political Marketing Postures', *Journal of Political Marketing*, 5(3): 29–46.

Hillygus, D. S. and Shields, T. G. (2008) *The Persuadable Voter: Wedge Issues in Political Campaigns*, Princeton: Princeton University Press.

Hughes, A. and Dann, S. (2006) 'Political Marketing and Stakeholders', paper presented at the *Australia and New Zealand Marketing Academy Conference*, Queensland University of Technology, Brisbane, Queensland, 4–6 December.

Kirchheimer, O. (1966) 'The Transformation of the Western European Party Systems', in J. LaPalombara and M. Weiner (eds) *Political Parties and Political Development*, Princeton: Princeton University Press. [177–200]

Lees-Marshment, J. (2001) *Political Marketing and British Political Parties*, Manchester: Manchester University Press.

Lees-Marshment, J. (2009) *Political Marketing: Principles and Applications*, Abingdon, Oxon; New York: Routledge.

Ormrod, R. P. (2005) 'A Conceptual Model of Political Market Orientation', *Journal of Nonprofit and Public Sector Marketing*, 14(1/2): 47–64.

Savigny, H. (2008) *The Problem of Political Marketing*, London: Continuum.

Strömbäck, J. (2007) 'Political Marketing and Professionalized Campaigning: A Conceptual Analysis', *Journal of Political Marketing*, 6(2/3): 49–67.

Strömbäck, J. and Kaid, L. L. (eds) (2008) *The Handbook of Election News Coverage Around the World*, New York: Routledge.

Index